AN
ILLUSTRATED DICTIONARY
OF
BRITISH STEEL ENGRAVERS

An
Illustrated Dictionary
of
British Steel Engravers

Basil Hunnisett

Scolar Press

First published 1989 by
Scolar Press
Gower Publishing Company Limited
Gower House, Croft Road
Aldershot GU11 3HR
England

Gower Publishing Company
Old Post Road
Brookfield
Vermont 05036
U.S.A.

British Library Cataloguing in Publication Data

Hunnisett, Basil
An illustrated dictionary of British steel
engravers
1. British steel engravings. Engravers–
Biographies
I. Title
769.92′2

Library of Congress Cataloging-in-Publication Data

Hunnisett, Basil.
An Illustrated Dictionary of British Steel Engravers.
Bibliography: p.
1. Engravers–Great Britain–Biography–Dictionaries.
2. Engravers–Great Britain–Portraits–Dictionaries.
i. Title.
NE625.H86   198   769.92′2   (B)   88–4696.

ISBN 0–85967–740–0

Printed in Great Britain at the University Press, Cambridge

TO
ELIZABETH JANE
JONATHAN PIERS
and their families

Contents

List of Portraits

List of Plates

Notes on Sources

The prime source of biographical information on engravers of the nineteenth century is the *Art Union*, begun in 1839, and continued until 1912 as the *Art Journal* from 1849. This gave a good, if selective, news service for the art world, and its articles have provided the basis for most of the entries in later major biographical works, both of the nineteenth and twentieth centuries, and so information tends to be repeated in much the same form in each of them.

Many of the engravers included in this work have not appeared before in biographical works and many others have no information in English about them. Thieme and Becker and the 1976 edition of Benezit mention some of them, but apart from identifying the person and noticing his existence, no further information is given. Since the major contribution of any engraver working in steel was likely to have been in the field of book illustration, examples have been given in all cases, but no list is exhaustive. The aim has been to represent the engraver's work over the whole period during which he worked. One of the features of engravings in this period is the number of times they were used in a succession of books. For this reason, each example given may not be of the first time of the plate's use, and this is especially so where collections such as G. N. Wright's *Gallery of engravings* 1844–6 are concerned. The phrases 'engraved for' and 'done for' indicate first publication, as far as can be ascertained, and 'published in', 'was used for', 'issued in' and 'appeared in' indicate some doubt on this point.

The peculiar publication habits of men like Henry Fisher have also led to the use here of unorthodox dating methods, (eg. each time the plate is used, the date is changed in the publication line) especially as there is no guarantee that later editions of the same work have the same plates in them. Where the later edition has been seen, that has normally been quoted, and in the case of works like Scott's *Waverley Novels* no date has been assigned because so many issues appeared between the 1840s and 1870s bearing reprints of the same plates. Information on dates when engravers joined the Artists' Annuity Fund is derived from J. Pye's *Patronage of British Art*. The 1837 petition on the status of engravers in England was presented in February of that year to the King, and, of the forty-eight signatories, thirty-three were steel engravers.

List of Sources

A   *Annual biography and obituary.*

Ad   Adams, B. *London illustrated 1604–1851.* Library Association, 1983.

       Arnold's *Library of the fine arts*, Vol. 1 1831.

AJ   *Art Journal.* Virtue, 1849–1912.

AU   *Art Union.* Chapman and Hall, 1839–48.

       Beattie, William. Letters. Camden Public Libraries [unpublished].

B   Benezit, E. *Dictionnaire critique . . . des peintres . . .* Rev. ed. Paris, Librairie Grund, 1976, 8 vols.

Br   Bryan, M. *Bryan's dictionary of painters and engravers.* New ed. Bell, 1926–34. 5 vols.

C   Clayton, E. C. *English female artists.* Tinsley Bros, 1876. 2 vols.

D   Delaborde, H. *Engraving . . .* Cassell, 1886.

DAB   *Dictionary of American Biography.* New York, Scribners, 1928–58. 22 vols.

DNB   *Dictionary of National Biography . . . to 1900.* Smith, Elder & Co., 1885–1902. 66 vols.

       Dyson, A., *Pictures to print . . .* Farrand Press, 1984.

       Engen, R. *Dictionary of Victorian engravers . . .* Chadwyck-Healey, 1979.

F   Fincham, H. W. *The artists and engravers of British and American bookplates.* Kegan Paul, 1897.

Fi   Fielding, Mantle. *Dictionary of American Painters . . .* New York, J. F. Carr, 1965. (A reprint of the work originally published in 1926.)

       Ford, J. *Ackermann 1783–1983.* Ackermann, 1983.

       Ford, J. & J. *Images of Brighton.* St Helena Press, 1981.

G   *Gentleman's Magazine.*

       Graves, A. *A Dictionary of Artists . . . 1760–1880.* Bell, 1884.

       Guise, H. *Great Victorian engravings . . .* Astragal Books, 1980.

       Hauser, H. *Anischten vom Rhein . . .* Köln. Graven, 1963.

H   Hunnisett, B. *Steel-engraved book illustration in England.* Scolar Press, 1980.

Ho   Holloway, M. comp. *Steel engravings in nineteenth-century British topographical books; a bibliography.* Holland Press, 1977.

       Lister, R. *Prints and print making . . .* Methuen, 1984.

M   Mallet, D. T. *Index of artists . . .* New York, Bowker, 1935.

Ma   Mackenzie, D. *The Bank of England note.* Cambridge University Press, 1953.

       McKenzie, D. F. *Stationers' Company apprentices 1701–1800.* Oxford Bibliographical Society, 1978.

       Moir, D. G. *The early maps of Scotland.* Edinburgh, Royal Scottish Geographical Society, 1973.

       Phillips, J. F. C. *Shepherd's London.* Cassell, 1976.

P   Pye, J. *Patronage of British art.* Longman, 1845.

R   Redgrave, S. *A dictionary of artists of the English school . . .* New ed. Bell, 1878.

Ro   Roget, J. L. *A history of the Old Water Colour Society . . .* Longman, 1891. 2 vols.

Ross, A. *William Henry Bartlett*. University of Toronto Press, 1973

Royal Society of Artists, Birmingham. *Exhibition of engravings by Birmingham men*... Birmingham, Osborne, 1877.

Russell, R. *Guide to British topographical prints*. David & Charles, 1979.

S   Slater, J. H. *Engravings and their value*. 6th ed. Link House, 1929 (and earlier editions).

Sa   Sandby, W. *History of the Royal Academy of Arts*... Longman, 1862. 2 vols.

SocA   (Royal) Society of Arts. *Transactions*...*1800–39*

      (Royal) Society of Arts. *Journal*. 1858–66.

Sp   Spemann, A. *Masterpieces of landscape steel engraving*. Stuttgart, Spemann, 1952.

St   Stauffer, D. M. *American engravers upon copper and steel*. New York, Grolier Club, 1907. 2 vols. *Supplement* by M. S. Fielding. Philadelphia, 1917.

      Tallis, J. *John Tallis's London street views 1838–1840*. Nattali & Maurice, 1969.

T   Thieme, U. and Becker, F. *Allgemeines Lexikon der bildenden Kunstler*... Leipzig, Englemann & Seeman, 1907–50. 37 vols.

Ta   Taylor, W. B. Sarsfield. *The origin, progress and present condition of the fine arts*... Whittaker & Co, 1841. 2 vols.

W   Walford, E. *Men of the time*. Routledge, 1862.

      Willis, N. P. *Pencillings by the way*... Virtue, 1835.

YA   *Year's art*. Macmillan & Co, 1880–1949.

Where other general sources such as the *Athenaeum* and *Illustrated London News* have been used, these are acknowledged individually.

Prints by most of the steel engravers here may be seen in the Print Departments of the British Museum and Victoria and Albert Museum. Many provincial Art Galleries also have good collections, especially of topographical prints.

The books themselves, available in many large public libraries, are the main source. They were found in several collections, among which were the British Library (Reference Division), East Sussex County Libraries, Brighton Divisional Library, Reference Department, and West Sussex County Libraries, Worthing Divisional Library, Reference Department. Volumes from the author's own collection have also been drawn upon. Editions on microfiche of some works, especially the annuals and publishers' records, are also available.

The sources of the Plates are gratefully acknowledged as follows: British Library (Reference Division), Plate 4; East Sussex County Libraries, Brighton Divisional Library, Reference Department, Plates 3, 8, 9, 12, 13, 14, 19, 20, 25, 29, 32, 36, 37, 41, 48, 58, 62; West Sussex County Libraries, Worthing Reference Library, Plate 27.

The sources and acknowledgements for the portraits of engravers used in the Dictionary are as follows: E. P. Brandard, G. T. Doo, R. Graves, F. Holl, T. Landseer, T. A. Prior, J. Pye, J. H. Robinson, W. B. Scott, L. Stocks and F. W. Topham from the *Illustrated London News*, courtesy of East Sussex County Libraries; J. Carter from a drawing in possession of Mr. J. Cuthbert-Brown of Findon, Sussex; C. Heath from an unpublished volume entitled *One Hundred etchings by Mrs. Dawson Turner* 1822, courtesy of the Trustees of the British Museum; W. Miller from W. F. Miller's *Memorials of Hope Park* 1886 (frontispiece), courtesy of the Trustees of the National Library of Scotland; E. Scriven and C. Warren from J. Pye's *Patronage of British Art* 1845, courtesy of East Sussex County Libraries; J. Swan from T. Murdoch's *Early history of lithography in Glasgow* ... 1902, courtesy of the Mitchell Library, Glasgow; J. T. Willmore from an oil painting (artist and date unknown), courtesy of the Birmingham Art Gallery.

Definitions

ENGRAVERS have been grouped according to a very rough classification by the type of work they undertake. These are defined as follows:

ARCHITECTURAL ENGRAVER. He engraves buildings, interiors and exteriors, reproducing architectural drawings, plans, etc., as well as undertaking pictures of buildings which are primarily topographical in character.

FIGURE ENGRAVER. An engraver of the human figure, whether characters of plays, scenes from ordinary life (genre), etc.

HISTORICAL ENGRAVER. This term is used for the engraver of purely historical events, real or imaginary, the latter including imaginative treatments of historical events, quasi-historical approaches (e.g. 'When did you last see your father?') etc.

LANDSCAPE ENGRAVER. An engraver of scenes, which may include buildings as minor objects, primarily designed to give an impression of countryside, distant views of towns, harbours, etc. Includes sea- and sky-scapes.

PORTRAIT ENGRAVER. An engraver of portraits of actual, named people.

SCULPTURE ENGRAVER. An engraver of statuary, bas-reliefs, high reliefs, etc.

Preface

This work owes its origins to my *Dictionary of British steel engravers* (1980), which has been out of print for some time. Since, in the seven years which have elapsed, fresh information has come to light, some of it from descendants of the engravers listed, and since I have been able to inspect more volumes of plates, the opportunity to enlarge that work has now been taken. In addition, because the history of steel engraving is best studied in a series of illustrations taken from the whole range of publications in which they appeared, a plate section has been added. The new material forms a significant part of the present volume, and supplements that in my *Steel-engraved book illustration in England* (1980).

I am much indebted to a number of people for their kind help, information and assistance. Mr Roger A. Rowlandson Barltrop of Burgess Hill sorted out the Baker family for me; I met Mrs Winifred A. Walter of Wimborne, great granddaughter of Edward Paxman Brandard; and Mr J. L. Rayment of Ongar, great grand nephew of James Carter, was most helpful. The assistance given by Mr John Heath of Bath, great great great grandson of James Heath, concerning his family, was invaluable. Dr Arthur Chick of Brisbane, Australia, introduced me to Mr. John Heath, and also provided valuable information about early steel-engraved publications. Mr Laurence Worms of Ash Antiquarian Books, together with his colleagues Vanessa Harding and Deborah Hanks, has also given considerable and much valued assistance with specific books and engravers. Mr M. Gosney of Wickham Common was kind enough to inform me about his ancestor Walter Alfred Cox.

The support and encouragement afforded by my wife and family are gratefully acknowledged; without that support and encouragement, and the proof reading done by my son-in-law Adrian, this book would not have been completed.

B. H.
Hove 1988

Introduction

Printing plates of iron or steel developed in the sixteenth century as a by-product of the armoury trade. However, since steel's one great advantage over the more usual copper—the ability to produce a great number of prints—was not in demand at the time, the practice lapsed.

During the eighteenth century, Jean-Baptiste Grateloup (1735–1817), a French engraver of portrait miniatures, was reputed to have used steel for nine portraits. These were done by him between 1765 and 1771, possibly in an effort to refine an already microscopic technique. In England, Stephen Hoole, the plate maker, is thought to have produced hard steel plates in about 1793.

In 1802, John Thomas ('Rainy day') Smith engraved a picture of the ceiling of the Star Chamber on an old saw-blade, but was so discouraged by the breakage of gravers, and the difficulty of engraving the metal, that he gave it up.

The need to avoid the forgery of bank notes provided the incentive which encouraged the use of steel on both sides of the Atlantic during the first two decades of the nineteenth century; for steel allowed the production of thousands of notes from the same plates, all precisely the same. In England, Abraham Raimbach experimented for the Bank of England, and John Oldham solved many of the problems for the Bank of Ireland, but Jacob Perkins had already gone a long way to producing the most satisfactory system, which was called 'siderography'. This was developed from 1782 for the State of Massachusetts coinage, and then brought to England in 1819 in response to the prize offered for a solution to the counterfeiting problem.

Since 1817, the Society of Arts had also been discussing the matter, and a number of engravers had shown some interest in it, so by 1820 some members of the profession had some acquaintance with steel. Charles Heath was one of the most prominent of these, and, together with some members of his family, had gone into partnership with Perkins, whose steel blocks were used for the first steel-engraved book illustrations produced in England (see Plate 1).

Longman was the first publisher to realise the advantages of steel over the traditional copper. Many more good quality copies could be obtained from a single plate, thus eliminating expensive duplicate plates and repairs. In due course, a wider range of tone and a greater fineness of line were also achieved. Engravers were also encouraged to use steel by the scarcity and high price of copper, caused by the absorption of most of the metal industry's output by the Royal and Merchant navies for the underwater protection of their ships. W. H. Pyne in his *Wine and walnuts*, 1823–4, said of Thomas Rowlandson that he 'etched as much copper as would sheathe the British Navy'.

By 1825, Longman had used seventy plates in twenty-two works. But before the profession would fully accept the change of metal, the difficulties attendant upon case-hardening the steel, a necessary part of siderography, had to be overcome or avoided. The technical problems of producing a steel *plate* of normal thickness (as opposed to the *block* used by Perkins), and of optimum hardness (thus overcoming the problems of case-hardening by avoiding the need to use it) were solved by Charles Warren and his plate-maker, Richard Hughes. The first steel plates were used for the frontispiece and engraved title page of Philip Doddridge's *Rise and progress of religion in the soul*, published by the Rivington consortium in May 1822 (see Plate 4).

None of these developments occurred in isolation, however. The printing industry had increased the efficiency of its presses and introduced viable stereotyping, so that editions of up to 5,000 copies were not unusual, measured previously in hundreds. Bookbinding had become the concern of the publishers, who produced cloth-covered books from the 1820s. The mass-produced book was technically possible at a time when demand for illustrated books was on the increase, fed by the Ackermann production of hand coloured aquatints in editions of 1,000 copies, and the ordinary volumes illustrated with copper or wood engravings of no great merit. The use of steel brought the highest form of engraving to the masses at just the right time—to possess line-engraved pictures of impeccable workmanship was, to many, very desirable.

In a number of books, the pictures became the central focus of the work, and the text was provided in the forms of extended captions. The issue of the majority of such works in parts facilitated their purchase at a modest weekly or monthly outlay, or the subscriber could wait for the complete work to be issued in a specially designed, and often handsome, casing.

Changes in the bookselling trade led to the emergence of the publisher as a dominant force, controlling the selection of texts and topics, and the employment of artists and engravers. The shared publication of the first two decades of the century gave way to those produced by family firms such as Fisher, Virtue and Tallis, all of whom specialised in finely illustrated books.

In the early days of steel engraving, attention was often drawn to the fact of its use in a work by captions such as 'Engraved on steel by . . .'; but by 1830 its use was universal and the practice disappeared.

Books and Book Publishers
The first book in England to be illustrated with steel engravings was Thomas Campbell's poem *The pleasures of hope* 1821 (see Plate 1) (first published in 1799 and regularly reissued in the subsequent twenty years). The previous edition had been in 1818, when Charles Heath had engraved the same designs on copper. The content of the new, steel-engraved book plates only differed by the addition of 'Engraved on steel' before the engraver's name, and 'Perkins, Fairman & Heath, at the foot of the plate, the latter inscription referring to the firm which had provided the steel block. Three thousand copies were produced of the 1821 edition, at a total cost of £370, the greater part of which, £210, was for the cost of engraving. All copies were sold by November 1824, when another edition of 3,000 was printed, apparently from the same blocks. November 1826 saw yet another edition, of 4,500 copies, again from the same blocks, and in neither of these latter entries in the Longman ledgers was mention made of repair costs. This well illustrates the longevity of the steel blocks (or plates) (printing 10,500 copies) contrasted with the copper plates (3,000 copies exhausting at least one set of plates). The two sets of illustrations—one on steel, one on copper—are almost indistinguishable in appearance, but this is characteristic of the very early work on steel, where the main concern was the extra number of good copies steel could provide. By 1823, in, for example, Heath's title page vignettes to *The poetical works of Sir Walter Scott*, a better understanding of the tonal possibilities was being shown; possibilities developed still further in plates such as 'Cascades of Gavarnic' after Harding, engraved by Robert Wallis for *Forget me not* 1825. Some publications carried a mixture of plates, some on copper and some on steel; for example, the fourth edition of Peter Hawker's *Instruction to young sportsmen* 1825, printed in an edition of 1,000 copies, contained four plates on steel and six on copper.

The annuals, inaugurated by Rudolf Ackermann in 1822, fully exploited steel, averaging between 5,000 and 9,000 copies per edition, although *the Literary souvenir* in 1828 ran to as many as 12,500 copies, and in some years *Forget me not* reached 20,000.

The years 1829 and 1830 saw a phenomenal increase in the publication of steel-engraved works. By this time the engravers had come to terms with the new metal, exploring its possibilities and building up a list of books from which the newly expanded book buying public could choose. There was a spate of topographical works (these being the kind which would attract attention), building on publications that used copper plates such as the long-drawn-out series of 732 plates issued between 1818 and 1824 and 1824 and 1829 by John Preston Neale under the title of *Views of the seats of noblemen*.... The first series was published in six volumes by W. H. Reid, and the second in five volumes by Sherwood, Jones & Co.

Jones had joined the famous eighteenth-century bookselling firm begun by James Lackington at the Temple of the Muses in 1820. By the end of the decade it had introduced a publishing programme which included a partial reprint in three volumes of Neale's illustrations as *Jones' Views of the seats, mansions, castles, etc.* 1829–31. It is thought that these prints were done on steel and were re-engravings of the earlier designs. There is no doubt, however, that the illusrations in *Metropolitan improvements* by James Elmes, of which the first of forty-one parts appeared in 1827, *London and its environs* 1829–31 and *Modern Athens* 1829–31, both by Thomas Hosmer Shepherd, *Bath and Bristol* by John Britton 1829 and *Wales illustrated*... 1830 by Henry Gastineau, all published by Jones & Co., were executed on steel plates.

Henry Fisher, Son & Co. printed the text of *Modern Athens*, and, having seen the advantages of publishing in conjunction with printing, began, in 1829, its intensive programme of publishing and printing with W. H. Pyne's *Lancashire illustrated*..., issued in parts, 1829–31, followed by Britton and Brayley's *Devonshire and Cornwall illustrated* 1832, Elliot's *Views in India*..., issued in parts, 1831–3, and Thomas Rose's volumes on the northern counties — *Cumberland* 1832 etc. Thomas Allom was his chief artist in many of these volumes.

George Virtue, who had moved into 26 Ivy Lane in June 1823, produced popular and cheap illustrated books, and began his great series of steel-engraved books with works on the English counties; for example S. W. H. Ireland's *England's topographer* (commenced publication 1828) and Thomas Wright's *Picturesque beauties of Great Britain*...: *Essex* 1831–4. He commenced his European series with William Beattie's *Switzerland*, issued in parts, 1833–6 and *Waldenses* 1838, using William Henry Bartlett's skill as an artist. He later turned his attention to the Middle East (Julia Pardoe's *Beauties of the Bosphorus*, issued in parts, 1838–40), the New world (N. P. Willis's *American scenery* 1840 and *Canadian scenery* 1842), Scotland (Beattie's *Scotland illustrated* 1838) and Ireland (J. S. Coyne's *Scenery and antiquities of Ireland* 1840).

Although perhaps better known as the instigator of cheap reprints of standard works, Charles Tilt of Fleet Street sponsored a wide variety of volumes with steel engravings, beginning with Fisher's *Angler's souvenir* 1835. There followed Thomas Roscoe's *Wanderings and excursions in North Wales* 1836, and ...*in South Wales* 1836, *Views in the Tyrol* [1836], [B. and H.] *Winkles's*... *cathedral churches of England*... 1836–42, B. Winkles's *French cathedrals* 1837, Finden's *Tableaux*... from 1837, *The Oriental annual* from 1837, and Finden's *Gallery of beauty* 1841.

Robert Jennings was established as a publisher by 1812, and from 1825 published the later volumes of Robert Batty's topographical works. With Thomas Roscoe as author he started *The Landscape annual*, and its first volume, *Tourist in Switzerland and Italy*, came out in 1830. William Chaplin joined him as a partner for the second volume, *Tourist in Italy* in 1831. Charles Heath superintended the engravings until the 1833 volume, when, following a disagreement, Jennings himself assumed this role. The series ended in 1838. In 1832 Jennings issued Sir William Gell's *Pompeiana*..., which contained eighty-five plates.

A latecomer to publishing was John Tallis (1818–76), a bookseller who turned to canvassing publishing in about 1836. A canvassing publisher sold books in parts on the doorstep, thus reaching a public which never visited bookshops and was not in the habit of buying books. His publishing output was varied and culminated in works inspired by the Great Exhibition of 1851. Then, in order to relieve himself of sole responsibility for a printing and publishing operation after an unsuccessful partnership with his brother Frederick, he created, with Ephraim Tipton Brain, the London Printing and Publishing Company in December 1853. Brain was a printer who had been bought out by Tallis, and had become superintendent of the latter's printing works in 1849. He brought his stock of old engraved plates to be used in the new firm.

Illustrations to literary texts were among the first to be steel-engraved, and the practice of producing for such works separate sets of prints to be used with any suitable printed text became common. For example, Thomas Campbell's *Loves of the angels* 1823 was reprinted regularly, but Longman the publisher provided no illustrations. At the end of the published volume, an advertisement offered prints after Westall, engraved by Charles Heath, at a cost of five shillings. Four plates and an engraved title page could thus be added by the purchaser before his volume was bound to his own specifications. Editions of Scott, Byron and Shakespeare were similarly treated.

Among the most satisfactory editions, however, were those with steel-engraved vignettes printed directly onto the text page. Samuel Rogers' *Italy* 1830 and *Poems* 1834 were the earliest of this genre. Rogers, a banker and poet, commissioned these works, which attracted the favourable comments of critics such as John Ruskin and Philip G. Hamerton. (J. M. W. Turner drew for these two volumes and also for editions of Byron (1832–4), Scott (1834–6), Milton (1835) and Thomas Campbell (1837), the engravings from all of which were used many times subsequently.) The vignette form was used in Thomas Moore's *Lalla Rookh*, published by Longman in 1838, and Byron's *Childe Harold's pilgrimage* 1841, where sixty vignettes were engraved by Edward and William Finden after designs by a number of professional and amateur artists, including H. Warren and Thomas Creswick. Many editions of collected works, including those of Oliver Goldsmith (1837), George Crabbe (1847), Dryden (1859) and Eliza Cook (1869), appeared with a steel-engraved frontispiece and title page to each volume. That of William Cowper published by T. Nelson (1855) carried mauve impressions of steel plates, printed by lithography. There were a number of editions of the works of Robert Burns, with steel-engraved illustrations, many of Scottish origin, being printed and published in that country in about 1840, and editions of Bunyan's *Pilgrim's progress* with steel-engraved illustrations were popular throughout the British Isles from 1830.

The depiction of characters taken from the works of popular authors formed the basis of volumes such as *Finden's Byron beauties* 1836, *Heroines of Shakespeare* 1848 and Finden's *Beauties of Moore* 1846. Some Of the best steel engravings were those done after Gustave Doré to illustrate Arthurian scenes inspired by the literature, the most recent of which was Alfred Lord Tennyson's poetry: *The Story of Enid and Geraint* [1869] is one of several slim folio volumes containing such steel engravings published by Edward Moxon, Son & Co.

Historical works, in which traditionally illustrations were rarely if ever present, were subjected in respect of illustration to some of the greatest changes in this period. The majority of historical plates had had a topographical basis, showing places of interest (such as battlefields), buildings (especially castles or houses) with historical associations, and portraits of important people. The historical 'action' picture was much rarer, but the appearance of steel engravings after the works of Benjamin West, J. Opie and James Northcote, etc., redressed the balance. These appeared more frequently in works published in the second half of the century. The most frequently illustrated history was the one based upon that of David Hume, first published in 1754–62, taking the *History of England . . .* up to the end of James II's reign. An addition by Tobias George Smollett brought the text up to the end of George II's reign, first published 1762–5. These, together with further additions by various authors, made up a work which ran through over a dozen editions in the nineteenth century. One such was by Thomas Gaspey, published by John and Frederick Tallis [c. 1847], but the most popular one, by the Revd Thomas Smart Hughes, was issued in 1834–6, 1837 and (published by George Bell) 1854–5. The engravings to this last edition were 'entirely re-engraved for this edition, comprising a selection of historical illustrations from Bowyer's History of England, and from paintings . . .' (Robert Bowyer had illustrated the 1793–5 edition of Hume and Smollett.)

By 1830, the vogue for county histories was well under way, and occasionally steel was used, although the number of copies issued of each was not great. Among the earliest examples were two by Thomas Allen—*A new . . . history of the county of . . . York* 1828–31 and *The history of the county of Lincoln* [1830–1]. Tierney's *History . . . of Arundel* 1834 and E. Baines's *History of . . . Lancaster* 1836 were further examples, and the latter was a source book for illustrations to the same author's *History of the cotton manufacture in Great Britain* [1835] and G. N. Wright's *Lancashire* 1842.

The Revd Dr James Taylor of Glasgow produced a number of histories for Virtue and William Mackenzie, which included *The pictorial history of Scotland* 1852–9, with eighty plates, *The family history of England* [1870–5], with sixty engravings, and *The age we live in; a history of the nineteenth century* [1884].

The great historical events of the mid-nineteenth century—the Crimean War and the Indian Mutiny—brought the reissue of appropriate works, such as Julia Pardoe's *Beauties of the Bosphorus* [1854] and Robert Montgomery Martin's *Indian Empire* [c. 1857], which reprinted Elliot and White's plates. There were also specially written volumes, such as Henry Tyrrell's *History of the war with Russia* ... [1855–8], Charles Ball's *History of the Indian Mutiny* [c. 1858] and E. H. Nolan's *Illustrated history of the British Empire in India* [1858–60].

Periodicals

The long run of copies required by periodicals suited steel engraving, and should, on the face of it, have led to the medium's adoption by them. Indeed, one of the earliest uses of steel was in *The Methodist magazine* from 1821, followed by plates in *The Evangelical magazine*. In 1824, *The mirror of literature, amusement and instruction* carried two steel-engraved portrait frontispieces, and, in the same year, *The youth's instructor and guardian* had an engraved title page on steel by T. Brown.

But, because Periodicals by their nature tended to be more topical, cheaper, and tied to a closer time-scale in their production than books, steel engravings, which took some time to prepare and had to be printed separately from the text and then inserted into the part or volume (the practice of printing engravings and text on the same sheet of paper was just as time consuming and therefore expensive), were not readily used—the cheaper and more popular magazines continued to use wood engraving, which could be combined with, and printed at the same time as, the text. This was the process used by Charles Knight's *Penny magazine* 1833, *Punch* 1841, *The Illustrated London News* 1842 and *The Graphic* 1869. Where speed was not required, and good quality reproduction was important, steel engraving could provide a highly satisfactory alternative. This is shown most effectively in the numbers of *The Art Journal* from 1847 to 1890. It reproduced many original engravings of contemporary works taken from those shown in the London exhibition galleries, the collection of Robert Vernon and the Queen's collection. Its most revolutionary and controversial feature was sculpture engraving (1847–84), which was at that time a neglected branch of art. The gradual decline of steel engraving in the face of competition from etching and photogravure in the last two decades of the century led to the phasing out of steel engravings in *The Art Journal*, and the series ended with J. C. Armytage's plate of Keeley Halswelle's 'Non angli, sed angeli' (see Plate 62).

Engraving

Engravers were employed to translate artists' originals, frequently executed in colour, into black-and-white pictures, using all the nuances which could be achieved by fine lines exhibiting ranges of tone by thickness of ink printed on off-white semi-absorbent plate paper. The skill required to do this was based upon artistic abilities not very dissimilar to those which produced the originals; dissimilar only in that it did not require the qualities of originality and imagination which distinguish a Turner, Bartlett or Allom. Some engravers indeed possessed a sufficient degree of these latter qualities to enable them to exhibit paintings at the Royal Academy, the British Institution, etc., and F. W. Topham, for example, deserted engraving to become an important watercolour painter.

The first step in translating an original was to prepare an engraver's outline, which was best done in monochrome, although many were done in colour. Many eminent artists were not above engaging in this work, and since the outlines were usually of a size similar to the finished engraving, they could be traced directly for transfer to the plate. For larger pictures the preparation of a pencil sketch adjusted the size and translated colours and tones into black-and-white equivalents. The plate itself was made of polished steel and was coated with either a white wax or a resin based etching ground, upon which the tracing or reduction could be laid face downwards to produce a design in reverse. Pressure from a rolling press transferred the pencil graphite to the ground. The engraver was then able to expose the steel by cutting through the ground with an etching needle. This exposed metal was then subjected to the biting action of nitric acid, or other suitable menstruum, and when eaten away to a suitable depth the lines were 'stopped out' with varnish. The main features were thus etched, as can be seen in the foreground of many engravings, the lower half of a picture showing darker lines, freely drawn. After that, the engraving proper began. A sharpened steel-point set in a semi-round wooden handle (a burin) was used to strengthen etched lines, to give them a sharper edge. It was also used to create light areas of tone by engraving thin and shallow lines in the plate. A ruling machine was used for large areas, especially sky, to produce evenly spaced lines with a minimum of effort.

The ground was then removed from the plate, the steel surface of which was then very susceptible to atmospheric conditions, especially damp, from which it had to be protected by a special coating.

Printing was achieved by spreading ink over the heated plate, carefully wiping excess ink from the surface—leaving it clean and the ink in the etched and engraved lines—and bringing it into contact with a piece of damp plate paper. Pressure was applied by passing the plate and paper through a rolling press, after which the engraving was hung up to dry. The edge of the plate produced a characteristic 'plate mark', which the case of many book illustrations was trimmed off by the binder. In the early 1820s, some engravers were still printing their own plates, but as demand grew, specialist firms such as McQueen, Dixon and Ross and Fenner, Sears & Co. came to the fore.

The engravers

In 1761, Joseph Collyer published *The parents' and guardians directory...*, in which he detailed the attributes necessary for an engraver. A good eye, a steady hand, a lively imagination and a power of fertile invention were indispensible. Above all, an ability, developed early in life, to paint and draw and to discern the nuances of light and shade was necessary. Although the trade did not require great physical strength, a sound constitution was a great asset. Added to all this, nineteenth-century engravers were, it appears, very patient men, and their contemporaries found them to be kind, warm-hearted, conscientious, generous, admired, respected and very dedicated to their craft. It was a sedentary occupation, which perhaps accounts for the longevity of many of its practitioners. In a survey of 143 engravers for whom sufficient information exists, nearly 31% lived into their seventies, about 24% into their sixties, 17% into their eighties and 13% into their fifties. A surprising 4% reached their nineties, the eldest being James Charles Armytage, 95, Edward Hacker, 92, John Pye, 92, and S. V. Hunt and Edward James Portbury, both aged 90.

Only one engraver is said to have been seriously affected in health by his work (although J. C. Bentley, F. W. Fairholt and J. Thomson contracted pulmonary consumption (tuberculosis)). Arthur Willmore developed lung disease, reputed to have been caused by his stooping over plates. Overwork was another problem, occasionally exacerbated by the need to provide for a large family; Joseph Goodyear and John Talfourd Smyth had promising careers cut short due to this at the ages of 41 and 32 years respectively. Other afflictions were heart disease, paralysis and 'inflammation' (of what is not specified). J. C. Allen was described as eccentric, but only in two cases did the cares of this world overwhelm them sufficiently to result in suicide. Robert Staines, who was naturally delicate, and who survived three wives, finally succumbed to dysentry at the age of nearly 44. Failing sight in their sixties seriously affected Richard Hatfield and Charles Heath, but because of the close nature of the work, most engravers will have strained their eyes to a greater or lesser extent.

Three engravers' families came to Britain from Germany. W. B. Cooke's father was a burgomaster there, and became a wholesale confectioner here; Francis Engleheart's family came from Silesia (his son T. S. Engleheart returned to Germany in about 1840); and F. W. Fairholt's father emigrated from Prussia and became a tobacco manufacturer in London.

Family backgrounds were quite diverse, although by far the largest number had fathers who were engravers. Edward Paxman Brandard and Robert Brandard's father was Thomas Brandard, a Birmingham engraver; Letitia and Elizabeth Byrne were taught engraving by their father, William; Charles Heath was the son of James Heath, and Charles in his turn was father to Alfred Theodosius and

Frederick Augustus Heath (engraver of the penny black stamp); and the brothers Benjamin, Charles, Francis and William Holl were the sons of William Holl the elder. J. Hopwood, J. Jenkins, Thomas Landseer, John Henry Le Keux. C. G. Lewis, J. W. Lowry, Edward Radclyffe, William Bell Scott, H. S. Storer, Henry, Robert and William Wallis and R. Woodman were all second generation engravers. G. J. Corbould was the son of a portrait painter, A. R. Freebairn, of a landscape painter, F. J. Havell, of a drawing master; J. Hinchliff and Francis Engleheart were sons of sculptors, and Robert Graves was the son of a printseller. The metal trades were represented among the occupation of engravers' fathers by a button manufacturer (James Baylis Allen), wholesale pewter manufacturer (Henry and John Le Keux) and silver ware manufacturer (Arthur and James Tibbetts Willmore). James Stephenson, Alfred William Warren and Charles Warren were (or, in the case of the Warrens, may have been) the sons of boot and shoe makers, J. C. Allen of a Smithfield salesman, James Carter of a comb maker and Benjamin Eyles of a carpenter. J. C. Bentley's father was a lawyer, C. J. Smith's a surgeon, S. Davenport's a land surveyor and architect, B. P. Gibbon's and J. Thomson's were clergymen, and that of C. Fox was steward to Lord Stafford. A coal mine owner was father to Lumb Stocks and a cotton spinner to T. L. Grundy.

Engraving was inclined to be a solitary profession, carried on in a workshop, often located in residential accommodation. In London, Celina Fox (in *London Journal*, Vol. 2, No. 1, 1976, p. 3) identifies 'Fitzrovia' as the area, based on Fitzroy Square and spreading out to Gray's Inn Road to the east and Somers Town to the west, that contained the greatest concentration of engravers. There were a small number of ateliers, through which most of the important engravers, both English and Continental, passed, such as those run by Charles Heath, the Finden brothers and Willaim Holl. Where the engraver also printed his plates, larger premises were necessary to house a rolling press.

Once the heyday of steel engraving was over, after about 1845, a handful of engravers turned to wood engraving, in order to work in which there was very little need to adapt basic techniques, since only the surface material changed. In many cases, engravers used a variety of methods for different kinds of work, but it does seem that specialisation in one technique was the norm. In response to the relative decline, others worked abroad, in France (J. Outhwaite), Germany (A. H. Payne, H. and B. Winkles) and America (J. Rogers and C. Westwood), some became postage stamp engravers (W. Humphrys, C. H. Jeens) and yet others went over to lithography, which process was often undertaken in the same printing establishment as steel engraving (Virtue, Day & Son).

Line engravers were still being trained in the 1880s. For example, Walter Alfred Cox (1862–c. 1910) was apprenticed in 1879 to J. Ballin, the Danish line engraver working in London. Cox, left to his own devices when his master returned to Copenhagen in 1882 after three years of his apprenticeship, turned to etching, which was then gaining in popularity and respectability, due in some part to F. Seymour Haden and the Society of Painter-etchers. This, in turn, was superseded by photogravure, in which Cox took lessons at the Regent Polytechnic in about 1889, and he went on to produce many plates for most of the print and book publishers, including Virtue.

The Decline of Steel Engraving

Steel engraving declined in the face of a rapidly changing technology, which quickened and cheapened the production of book illustration. The main factor was the application of photography to the printing processes, resulting in the use of half-tone and line-block illustrations for books. For the best reproduction of tone, the old-fashioned mezzotint enjoyed a brief revival for short runs of prints, but a more serious contender was photogravure, which provided a good tone process with the added advantage of long runs from a single plate. Lithography was also gaining ground, especially in the area of colour printing, in which the wood engravers, under Edmund Evans, also shared. Steel engraving was too time consuming and expensive to compete in this situation. The new media were able to cut production times in a way that line engraving, by its very nature and method of printing, was unable to do. By the end of the century, steel engraving had all but disappeared, and survived only the production of certificates, stamps and bank notes.

A

Abreck (fl. 1834) Landscape engraver. 'Waterloo Bridge' after T. H. Shepherd appeared in *Tombleson's Thames* 1834. His name is possibly a mistake for 'Abresch' (q.v.).

Abresch, Franz (fl. 1832–41) Landscape engraver. 'The mosque at Schwetzingen' and 'Sargans' after Tombleson were published in Fearnside's *Tombleson's Upper Rhine* [c. 1835]. He was a pupil of Frommel, a celebrated German steel engraver. Most of his work was published in Germany. He was doubtless connected with Friedrich Abresch, with whom Henry Winkles (q.v.) was in partnership. B.

Acon, John (fl. 1832–46) Landscape engraver. 'Ferry near Oberried' after Tombleson appeared in Fearnside's *Picturesque beauties of the Rhine* [c. 1846]. B; T.

Acon, Robert (fl. 1818–50) Architectural engraver. Six plates after T. H. Shepherd were published between 16 June 1827 and 28 March 1829 in J. Elmes's *Metropolitan improvements* 1829, including 'London Ophthalmic Infirmary, Finsbury' and 'The Guild-hall', twelve engravings after Shepherd were done for Shepherd's *London and its environs* 1829–31, and Shepherd's *Modern Athens* 1829–31. Acon had engraved some plates for 'Excise Office, Drummond Place' for J. P. Neale's *Views of the seats of noblemen ...* 1818–24. He engraved 'West window of Tintern Abbey...' after H. Gastineau for the latter's *Wales illustrated ...* 1830, and 'Water Street' after G. & C. Pyne for W. H. Pyne's *Lancashire illustrated ...* 1831. 'Erith, Kent' after W. Tombleson was done for *Tombleson's Thames* 1834, and 'The Mansion House, London' and 'Apsley House...' after Shepherd came out in T. Dugdale's *England and Wales delineated* [1838–9].

Adcock, George Henry (fl. 1836–49) Figure engraver. 'John Philip Kemble, Esq.', a rather poor engraving after Sir Thomas Lawrence, was engraved for E. Baines's *History of ... Lancaster* 1836, and used again in G. N. Wright's *Lancashire* 1842. 'Kemble in the character of Hamlet' after Lawrence and 'John Hunter' after J. Reynolds appeared in G. N. Wright's *Gallery of engravings* 1844–6, and nine engravings after Old Masters came out in Fisher's *Historic illustrations of the Bible* [1840–3], seven of which were used again in J. Kitto's *Gallery of scripture engravings* 1846–9. He joined the Artists' Annuity Fund in 1831. B.

Adlard, Henry (fl. 1828–69) Landscape and figure engraver. A prolific engraver by whom over 200 plates are known, he was probably one of the London family of printers and engravers. The frontispiece and plates opposite pages 310, 320 and 370 of P. Hawker's *Instructions to young sportsmen*, 4th edition, 1825 were engraved on steel. Thirty-seven plates were executed, beginning in June 1828, for S. W. H. Ireland's *England's topographer* (commenced publication 1828) after G. Shepherd, H. Gastineau, T. Baynes, W. H. Bartlett and J. Fussell, including 'Westgate, Canterbury', 'Penshurst' and 'Malling Abbey, Kent'. For H. Gastineau's *Wales illustrated ...* 1830, he engraved twenty-two illustrations after the author's own designs. Three engravings after Cotes, Stroehling, and Baynes appeared in Huish's *Memoirs of George the Fourth* 1830–2. He did 'The Druid's stones, near Keswick' and 'Holme Hall...' for T. Rose's *Cumberland* 1832, 'Hayswater...' and 'Grisdale...' for Rose's *Westmor-land* 1832, all after T. Allom, and four plates after W. Hogarth for Hogarth's *Works* 1833. 'Remains of Maison Dieu' after G. Constable and 'St. Mary's Gate, Arundel', both vignettes printed on the page, appeared in M. A. Tierney's *History of Arundel* 1834, eighteen views after Bartlett, Baynes and Campion in Thomas Wright's *Picturesque beauties of Great Britain...: Essex* 1834, and 'Holker Hall, Lancashire' after G. Pickering in E. Baines's *History of ... Lancaster* 1836 (used again in G. N. Wright's *Lancashire* 1842). Two engravings after T. Allom were done for T. Noble and T. Rose's *Counties of Chester ...* 1836, six after W. H. Bartlett for W. Beattie's *Switzerland* 1836, including 'Bridge over the Rhine...' (a good example of his work), seven after Bartlett and Allom for J. Carne's *Syria* 1836–8, including title page vignettes for volumes 1 and 3 and six after the same artists for Beattie's *Scotland illustrated* 1838. 'Dalgarno & Glenvarlock' after J. Franklin was done for G. N. Wright's *Landscape-historical illustrations of Scotland* 1836–8, 'Turin and the plain of Piedmont' and 'La Chalpe and Brunichard' after Bartlett and 'Ruins of Fort Hirabouc' after Brockedon for W. Beattie's *Waldenses* 1838, 'Village of Khandoo...' after Allom (Plate 34) for G. F. White's *Views in India ...* 1838, four after Allom and W. L. Leitch for R. Walsh's *Constantinople* 1838–40 and a plate of the Acropolis at Athens after W. Purser for C. Wordsworth's *Greece* 1839. 'Batalha. East End' after Holland appeared in W. H. Harrison's *Tourist in Portugal* 1839 and six vignettes after Nixon, C. Landseer, Wright and Hart in W. Scott's *Lay of the last minstrel* 1839. Four engravings after W. H. Bartlett were published in J. Pardoe's *Beauties of the Bosphorus* 1840, including 'Column of Marcian', and eight in N. P. Willis's *American scenery* 1840, including 'The outlet of Niagara River'. Twelve plates, mainly after Allom, came out in E. W. Brayley's *Topographical history of Surrey* 1841–8 and five, including 'Timber depot near Quebec', all after Bartlett, in N. P. Willis's *Canadian scenery* 1842. 'Gravesend' was done for Beattie's *Ports, harbours ...* 1842, three for the same author's *Danube* 1844 and 'Luggela' and 'Pontoon bridge...' for J. S. Coyne's *Scenery and antiquities of Ireland* 1840. Six plates after Allom appeared in G. N. Wright's *China* 1843, 'Italia from a coin of Hadrian' after H. Corbould and 'Rocca d'Anfo' after G. Barnard in W. Brockedon's *Italy ... 1842–3*, 'Dormeilleuse, High Alps...' after Bartlett in Wright's *Gallery of engravings* 1844–6, 'Bethany' after Allom and 'Remains of the port of Tyre' after Bartlett in J. Kitto's *Gallery of scripture engravings* 1846–9, 'St. Alban's Abbey' after Allom and 'Rochester Castle' after G. F. Sargent in Beattie's *Castles and abbeys of England* 1845–51 and eleven engravings after C. Varley, A. E. Chalon, J. Childe and the author in P. Hawker's *Instructions to young sportsmen*, 9th edition, 1844. Eight plates of fish, meat and fowl appeared in E. Acton's *Modern cookery*, 5th edition, 1856 and seven vignettes after J. Marchant, including 'The old water mill' and 'The old arm chair' after T. Smart, in E. Cook's *Poetical works* 1869. 'Wilderness of sin' after Laborde and 'Jerusalem. From the Mount of Olives' after Fyfe were published in *The Self-interpreting Bible* 1864, and two vignettes after J. Marchant in Inglis's *Gleanings from the English poets ...* [c. 1865]. His portraits, such as Mrs Robinson from Huish and Peter Hawker, were not as successful as his landscapes. T.

Aikman, Alexander T. (fl. 1841–3) Figure and landscape engraver in Edinburgh. He engraved 'The charge to Peter...' and 'The Madonna of Sextus' after Raphael Sanzio and 'The farrier's family', a good plate after P. Wouvermans, for *Engravings after the best pictures of the Great Masters* 1841–3, as well as 'Inverlochy' after W. L. Leitch for Scott's *Waverley novels*.

Aikman, G. (fl. 1841–9) Architectural engraver in Edinburgh. He engraved 'High School of Edinburgh', 'St. Giles' cathedral', 'Heriot's hospital from the Grassmarket' after Storer, dated 1 July 1841, 'Royal Institution' after G. M. Kemp, 'Roslin Castle' after D. Mackenzie and plans of Edinburgh and Glasgow for *Black's picturesque tourist of Scotland* 1849.

Alais, William John (fl. 1845–84) Landscape engraver. He is known to have engraved several prints of Brighton and to have published locally. For the *Art Journal*, he did 'Lion hunt' after Vernet (1880), 'Highland group' after Landseer (1881) and 'The rivals' after Garland (1884). He collaborated with his father, Alfred Clarence Alais, to engrave 'Van Amburgh and the lions' after E. Landseer for the *Art Journal* 1879.

Albutt, W. E. (fl. 1836–63) Landscape and architectural engraver. Seven plates of cathedrals at York, Winchester, Lincoln and Chichester after R. Garland and Hablot Browne were done for *Winkles's ... Cathedral churches of England ...* 1836–42 and 'Chartres cathedral...' after Garland, dated 1 June 1836, for Winkles *French cathedrals* 1837. 'Naples from the Mole' after a photograph appeared in D. Costello's *Piedmont and Italy* [c. 1855] and two vignettes after J. C. Armytage (q.v.), 'Victoria hospital, Netley' and 'Old Basing Church', in B. Woodward's *General history of Hampshire* 1863.

Allen. 'Signing of the Magna Charta by King John ...', an outline engraving after Backler and Lonsdale, appeared in W. Beattie's *Castles and abbeys of England* 1845–51. There is no indication which Allen was responsible.

Allen, Daniel (fl. 1830–4) Figure engraver. His major work was done for S. Rogers' *Italy* 1830, for which he engraved seven vignettes after T. Stothard (including 'Morning banquet by the fountain side', a bride and groom, and a large urn as a tailpiece) and 'St. Mark's Place' after Titian. Two more vignettes were done for the same author's *Poems* 1834, i.e. a large bowl on a pedestal and an old man, the latter after Callot.

Allen, James Baylis (fl. 1803–76) Landscape and historical engraver. Born in Birmingham on 18 April 1803, the son of a button manufacturer, he was apprenticed to his elder brother, Josiah, a general engraver in Colmore-row, about 1818, working on labels, patterns, etc., and in 1821 went to J. V. Barber's school to improve his drawing. Three years later, in 1824, he entered the Findens' studio in London, after which he worked for Charles Heath (q.v.), Robert Wallis (q.v.) and the Bank of England, for which he engraved Britannia as a test piece. His early steel work appeared in S. W. H. Ireland's *England's topographer* (commenced publication 1828) (including 'Danejohn Hill, Canterbury' after G. Shepherd and 'King's Gate on the Isle of Thanet' after H. Gastineau), J. Elmes's *Metropolitan improvements* 1829 (two plates after T. H. Shepherd), T. H. Shepherd's *London and its environs* 1829–31 (six plates after the author) and the same author's *Modern Athens* 1829–31 (six plates after the author). Four views of Bath after T. H. Shepherd appeared in J. Britton's *Bath and Bristol* 1829. Four plates after Allom, Harwood and Pyne were done for W. H. Pyne's *Lancashire illustrated ...* 1831 and 'Pont y Glyn' and 'Pont Aberglaslyn' after H. Gastineau for the artist's *Wales illustrated ...* 1830. In volumes by T. Roscoe, he engraved three plates after S. Prout for *Tourist in Switzerland and Italy* 1830, three plates after Prout for *Tourist in Italy* 1831, five after J. D. Harding for *Tourist in Italy* 1833 (including 'Narni'), four after Harding

for *Tourist in France* 1834 and three after D. Roberts for *Tourist in Spain. Granada* 1835. Five plates after the author's drawings were done for Sir William Gell's *Pompeiana ...* 1832. In works by L. Ritchie, he did 'Swiss cottage, near Brieg' after C. Stanfield for *Travelling sketches in the north of Italy* 1832, 'St. Malo' after C. Stanfield for *Travelling sketches on the sea coasts of France* 1834 and 'St. Germains' after J. M. W. Turner for *Wanderings by the Seine* 1835, and two views of Windsor Castle after J. D. Harding appeared in *Windsor Castle* 1848. 'Fall of the Rhine' after J. M. W. Turner was done for *The Keepsake* 1833 and 'Evenings' after C. Dietricy for the 1849 volume. 'Austrian pilgrims' after Lewis was engraved for the *Literary souvenir* 1834. An excellent plate after C. Stanfield, 'Dartmouth', was engraved for *Stanfield's coast scenery* 1836, 'Venice – the Rialto' after Stanfield for *Finden's illustrations of the life and works of Lord Byron* 1833–4 and 'Beirout and Mount Lebanon' after W. H. Bartlett for J. Carne's *Syria* 1836–8. 'Theatre in the Palace of Versailles' after F. Mackenzie and 'Court of Louis XVth at play...' after C. Aubry (a good example) appeared in *Heath's Versailles* [c. 1836]. 'Val d'Ossola from the Simplon' and three other plates after W. H. Bartlett appeared in W. Beattie's *Switzerland* 1836, three after T. Allom in his *Scotland illustrated* 1838 and 'Inner Court of the mosque of Sultan Osman' after Allom in R. Walsh's *Constantinople* 1838–40. 'Mussooree...' after Turner and 'View at Simla' after Roberts were engraved for G. F. White's *Views in India ...* 1838, three plates, including 'Loch-Levin Castle' after Turner, for G. N. Wright's *Landscape-historical illustrations of Scotland* 1836–8 and 'Convent of the Serra, Oporto' and 'Villa Nova' after Holland for W. H. Harrison's *Tourist in Portugal* 1839. 'Palace at Tassisudon, Bootan' and 'State prison in Delhi' after W. Daniell were published in J. Caunter's *Lives of the Moghul emperors* 1837, two plates after Bartlett in J. Pardoe's *Beauties of the Bosphorus* 1840, seven plates after W. Brockedon and W. L. Leitch in Brockedon's *Italy ...* 1842–3 and four after Bartlett in J. S. Coyne's *Scenery and antiquities of Ireland* [1840]. 'Trent in the Tyrol' after A. W. Callcott was done for Finden's *Royal Gallery of British Art* 1838–49 and 'Frederickton...' after Bartlett for N. P. Willis's *Canadian scenery* 1842. Six engravings after T. Allom were done for G. N. Wright's *China* 1843, 'Bale' after G. Barret for Scott's *Waverley novels*, 'Etham, near Bethlehem' after Bartlett for H. Stebbing's *Christian in Palestine* [1847], 'A rustic fair' after Huskinson for *The Keepsake* 1846 and 'Tivoli' after Barber for *The Keepsake* 1848. 'The welcome', a vignette after G. Cattermole, appeared in Calabrella's *Evenings at Haddon Hall* 1845, 'Place de la Concorde à Paris' after Bonne in *The Keepsake* 1849 and 'York from the wall' and 'Sheffield' after H. Warren in T. Baines's *Yorkshire past and present* 1871–7. Three plates after Skinner Prout were engraved for Booth's *Australia* [1873–6]. He engraved eighteen plates for the *Art Journal*, although 'Naples' after W. L. Leitch from Brockedon's *Italy ...* 1842–3 was used again in the *Art Union* 1846. The series began in 1850; in 1863 it issued his 'Decline of Carthage' after Turner and in 1864, after the same artist, 'Temple of Jupiter...', both of which were used again, together with 'Death of Nelson' and 'Phryne going to the bath as Venus', in R. W. Wornum's *Turner Gallery* [c. 1878]. He had worked from 1830 on Turner's *Rivers of France* and *Coast scenery*. He was to have earned eighty guineas for 'Bullfight at Seville', issued in a volume of Jennings's *Landscape annual*, but the publisher, delighted at the result, wrote a cheque for one hundred guineas. He engraved the landscape for Joseph Goodyear's (q.v.) 'Greek fugitives' after C. L. Eastlake, and suggested the *Art Journal's Illustrated catalogue of* the Great Exhibition 1851 to the then editor, S. C. Hall. He joined the Artists' Annuity Fund in 1831. He died on 11 January 1876 at his residence in Camden Town after a long illness, leaving a son, Walter J. Allen, who was a wood engraver and member of the *Art Journal* staff. He was buried in Highgate cemetery, near his friend Goodyear. AJ; H; R.

Allen, James C. (fl. 1821–33) Architectural and landscape engraver in London. The son of a Smithfield salesman, he was apprenticed to William Bernard Cooke, for whom he worked many years after his indentures had ended. He engraved 'St. Mawes, Cornwall' after Turner for *Picturesque views on the southern coast of England* 1826, and in 1831 'Defeat of the Spanish Armada' after de Loutherberg was done for the *Gallery of Greenwich Hospital.* Twelve engravings of south coast sites after Bartlett, Cox and Gastineau were published in *Watering places* ... 1833, and four were used again in *Fashionable guide* ... [c. 1838]. He also engraved 'Portsmouth from Spithead' after C. Stanfield and 'Temple of Isis' after Cockburn. He was eccentric, and was affected by bad health with the result that he died in middle age. DNB; M; R; T.

Allen, R. (fl. 1842) Landscape and architectural engraver. He engraved four plates after F. F. Palmer, 'Monastery of St. Bernard, Charnwood Forest' after J. F. Lee and 'Geology of Charnwood' after J. B. Jukes for T. R. Potter's *History and antiquities of Charnwood Forest* 1842. Ho.

Allen, S. (fl. 1865) Figure engraver. Known for two vignettes after J. Marchant published in Robert Inglis's *Gleanings from the English poets* ... [c. 1865].

Anderson, R. (fl. 1870–8) Figure engraver. 'The enshrouding of Christ' after P. Delaroche and 'Mary and John at the sepulchre...' after Blockhorst (a good example of engraving) were issued in an edition of the *Holy Bible* edited by Murdoch [c. 1870]. Eight plates after Dyce, Herbert, Johnston and Williams were done for Thomas Archer's *Pictures and royal portraits* ... [c. 1878].

Annedouche, A. J. (fl. 1859–60) Figure and portrait engraver. 'Childhood' after J. B. Greuze (coarsely but effectively engraved) and 'The Lady Digby' after Van Dyck appeared in the *Art Journal* for 1859 and 1860 respectively.

Appleby, James (fl. 1820–45) Armorial engraver. J. Appleby of 9 New Cut, Lambeth, or 8 Thanet Place, Temple Bar, engraved four bookplates between 1820 and 1830. For J. Burke's *Heraldic illustrations* 1845, he engraved five plates, dated 1843, for volume 1, three, dated 1844, for volume 2 and two, dated 1845, for volume 3, all of various coats of arms. Fi.

Appleton, J. W. (fl. 1834–43) Landscape engraver. His early work included 'Gallery on the "Tete noire" near Trient' (1834), 'Interlacken, Canton Bern' (1835) and 'Lausanne (Canton Vaud)' (1 July 1834) after W. H. Bartlett, published in W. Beattie's *Switzerland* 1836, and 'Mount Dauphin and Champcellas, Val Durance' (1837) in Beattie's *Waldenses* 1838, also after Bartlett. 'Kursalee...' after C. Bentley was engraved for G. F. White's *Views in India* ... 1838 and 'Stirling Castle' (1836) after G. Campion for Beattie's *Scotland illustrated* 1838. 'Rye old harbour', 'Dover pier' and 'Worthbarrow Bay, Dorsetshire', all after C. Stanfield, appeared in *Stanfield's coast scenery* 1836, 'Damascus – distant view from the mountain side' (1837) and 'Port of Beirut' (1838) in volumes 2 and 3 of J. Carne's *Syria* 1836–8, a view

of Tripolitza after Holland from a sketch by Purser in C. Wordsworth's *Greece* 1839 and 'Brow on the Solway' after D. O. Hill in Wilson and Chambers's *Land of Burns* 1840. 'City of ancient Greece' (December 1840) after W. Linton, one of his largest, and perhaps his best plate, was engraved for Finden's *Royal Gallery of British Art* 1838–49. 'Port Glasgow' (1841) after Bartlett was published in Beattie's *Ports, harbours* ... 1842, 'The Waldensian College at La Tour' after W. Brockedon from a sketch by Mrs Gilly in Brockedon's *Italy* ... 1842–3 and 'Naples from the west' after J. Hakewill in *Casquet of literature,* volume 1, 1874. T.

Appold, J. L. (fl. 1870) Figure engraver. 'Virgin enthroned' after Da Murano appeared in the *Art Journal* 1870.

Archer, J. (fl. 1850) Map engraver. Pentonville, London. He engraved twenty-one maps in all, after his own designs, for T. Dugdale's *England and Wales delineated* [1838–9].

Archer, John Wykeham (1808–64) Landscape engraver. Born in Newcastle upon Tyne on 2 August 1808, he was apprenticed to John Scott, the animal engraver, in London. Scott's ill-health curtailed his indentures and he returned home to join an artistic circle which included George Richardson (q.v.). About 1827 he went to draw buildings in Edinburgh, but by May 1828 he was in London again, engraving 'St. Mary's Church, Wyndham Place' after T. H. Shepherd for J. Elmes's *Metropolitan improvements* 1829. In order to improve his steel engraving, he went to work for the Findens about 1830, which may account for the fact that there are few plates signed by him. The first plate done for his new masters, after A. W. Callcott, was so successful that they doubled his salary. He engraved 'Kooner Pass, Neilgherri Mountains' (1 October 1839) after Creswick for T. Bacon's *Oriental annual* 1840, etched 'Swallows in the banks of the River Mole' (1 April 1841) after Thompson and engraved 'Croydon church' (April 1842) after Allom for E. W. Brayley's *Topographical history of Surrey* 1841–8 and engraved 'St. Goar – Rhine' after Leitch for Wright's *Rhine, Italy and Greece* [1842]. He drew many of the designs for W. Beattie's *Castles and abbeys of England* 1845–51, for which he also engraved 'Arundel Castle' after T. Allom. As line-engraved commissions decreased (engraving animals for the *New Sporting Magazine* was some of the work to which he resorted), he turned to wood-engraving for *The Illustrated London News* etc. from 1842 onwards and to watercolour work, a collection of which was bought from the executors of William Twopenny of the Temple by the British Museum in 1874. J. W. Archer and George Lance married two sisters; the two men and Lance's wife died within months of each other, John being the second, dying on 25 May 1864. AJ; Br; DNB; R.

Archer, W. (fl. 1839–41) Historical engraver. 'British troops fording the Esla' and 'Charge of 7th Hussars at Orthez' after A. Cooper were published in Maxwell's *Life of ... the Duke of Wellington* 1839–41.

Armstrong, Cosmo (1781–1836) Landscape and historical engraver. Born in Birmingham in 1781, he was a pupil of Thomas Milton (c. 1745–1827), and was employed by him for five years. He became an engraver of some repute, but his work was uneven and was too eccentric to reach the front rank. He was a governor of the Society of Engravers (founded 1803). His first important work was done for Miller's edition of *Arabian nights* after Smirke (1802), followed by engravings for the series published by Cooke, Sharpe and Suttaby, the 1805 edition of Shakespeare, and Cadell's *Don Quixote* 1818.

His ventures in steel engraving included 'Broadstairs, Kent' after G. Shepherd in *England's topographer* by S. W. H. Ireland (commenced publication 1828) and 'Peter the Great shipwrecked' after P. F. Stroehling in *The Amulet* for 1828, and eight plates after W. Hogarth for Hogarth's *Works* 1833. B; DNB; R; T.

Armytage, James Charles (1802–97) Landscape, figure and historical engraver. He probably came out of his apprenticeship about 1823 at the time when steel engraving was being developed, and became one of the most prolific engravers of the time—nearly 200 of his plates have been positively identified. Much of his early work was done for the publisher Virtue, after W. H. Bartlett and in books by W. Beattie. The extent of his employment in the 1830s indicates a well-developed talent, first used in T. H. Shepherd's *London and its environs* 1829–31, in which 'St. Clement's Church', 'St. Bennet Fink' and 'Ironmonger's Hall, Fenchurch St.' were done after the author's designs. T. Wright's *Picturesque beauties of Great Britain...: Essex* 1834 contained fourteen engravings, dated between 1831 and 1833, after Bartlett and two after G. B. Campion. 'Confluence of the Seine and Marne' and 'Troyes' after J. M. W. Turner appeared in L. Ritchie's *Wanderings by the Seine* 1835, and 'Fall of the Rhine on the Roffla' (1 June 1834) and 'The castle of Lauffen' (1836) after W. H. Bartlett were engraved for W. Beattie's *Switzerland* 1836. For the same author's *Scotland illustrated* 1838, he engraved 'Loch Achray, Perthshire' (1835), 'Loch Leven...'(1836) and 'Strathpeffer mineral wells' (1836), all after T. Allom, and 'Lady Melville's Lake...' (1834) was engraved after the author's drawing for J. Ross's *Narrative of a second voyage ...* 1835. For Thomas Roscoe's *Tourist in France* 1834 he did 'Mont Ferrier' after J. D. Harding, and for the same author's *Tourist in Spain. Granada* 1835 he engraved 'Descent into the plain of Granada' after D. Roberts. 'St. Malo', 'Hamoaze, Plymouth' and 'Roque de Guet' were engraved for *Stanfield's coast scenery* 1836. 'View near Wandepore', 'Mausoleum of Toglokshah' and 'Boats on the Ganges', all dated 1 October 1836 and after W. Daniell, appeared in J. Caunter's *Lives of the Moghul emperors* 1837, and 'Constantinople from Cassim Pacha' after T. Allom was done for R. Walsh's *Constantinople* 1838–40. G. N. Wright's *Landscape-historical illustrations of Scotland* 1836–8 contained 'It's Auld Ailie hersell' after Turner. W. H. Harrison's *Tourist in Portugal* 1839 included 'The Bar of the Douro' after Holland, dated 28 October 1838. In 1839 he engraved 'Bridge at Norwich (Connecticut)', 'Natural bridge, Virginia' and 'Schuylkill waterworks (Philadelphia)' after W. H. Bartlett for N. P. Willis's *American scenery* 1840, and for the same author and after the same artist, he did ten plates for *Canadian scenery* 1842. For J. S. Coyne's *Scenery and antiquities of Ireland* [c. 1840], he did 'Abbey of Moyne' after W. H. Bartlett, and 'Tam O' Shanter' after J. Burnet appeared in R. Burns's *Complete works* [c. 1840]. In 1840 and 1841 he produced one of his longest series of plates, sixteen in all, for W. Beattie's *Ports, harbours ...* 1842, all after W. H. Bartlett, which contained two particularly interesting plates, namely, 'Conway Castle' and 'Blackpool sands', and in 1844, for the same author and after the same artist, he engraved thirteen plates for *The Danube*, which included 'Walls and bridge of Ulm', 'Bridge of Linz', 'Castle Thebon' and 'The Kazan Pass'. For *Friendship's Offering* 1844 he engraved two vignettes after 'J[ohn] R[uskin]', 'The coast of Genoa' and 'Le glacier des bois', and for S. C. Hall's *Gems of European art* 1846, he engraved ten plates, i.e. 'King Charles the first' and 'The children of Charles the first' after Van Dyke, 'Belisarius'

after F. Gerard, 'The Good Shepherd' and 'The fruit seller' after Murillo, 'The Magdalen' after Correggio, 'The Lady Dover' after Sir Thomas Lawrence (also issued in the *Art Union* 1847), 'Moses in Midian' and 'The finding of Moses' after Schopin and 'The captives in Babylon' after Bendemann. 'Modern Jerusalem' after Bartlett (Plate 43) was probably the largest steel line engraving ever done for a book (it measured 15⅜ by 9⅛ inches). It was published, together with six other plates by Armytage, in H. Stebbing's *Christian in Palestine* [1847], and was used again as the frontispiece to *Practical and devotional family Bible* of 1860. Nine plates after Sir David Wilkie were engraved for *Wilkie gallery* [1849] notably 'The rat hunters', 'The cottage toilet' and 'The parish beadle'. For what is considered by some to be John Ruskin's greatest work, *The Stones of Venice*, first published in 1851–3, Armytage engraved twelve plates after the author's designs, which included two good examples—'Wall-veil decoration. San Michele. Lucca' and 'The vine, free and in service'. The plate 'Mosaics of Olivetree and flowers' from volume 3 was printed in blue to give a special effect. His most celebrated series of engravings, however, was that done for volumes 3, 4 and 5 of J. Ruskin's *Modern painters* 1856–60. The majority of the twenty-seven plates were after the author's drawings, but five were after designs by J. M. W. Turner, namely, a vignette—'By the wayside'—, an outline engraving—'Richmond from the moors'— 'By the brookside', 'Clouds' and 'Lochs of Typhon'. 'Foreground leafage' and 'The Dryad's toil' are two of the best examples of the artistic use of machine ruling, and the vignette 'Aspen unidealized' is an excellent example of steel engraving, perhaps one of the best ever engraved. 'The Dryad's crown' was printed in greygreen ink, and represented a cluster of oak leaves (Plate 50). Ruskin declared himself greatly pleased with the fine quality of the plates. The Print Department of the Victoria and Albert Museum has a copy of 'Mountains partly concealed by clouds, with river in the foreground', an unpublished plate after J. Ruskin. 'Castle of Verrex' after W. Brockedon appeared in D. Costello's *Piedmont and Italy* [c. 1855] and 'Gov. Edward Winslow', which, although unsigned, is ascribed to J. T. Armytage in the list of illustrations, in W. H. Bartlett's *Pilgrim Fathers* 1853. E. H. Nolan's *Illustrated history of the British Empire in India* [1858–60] contained a vignette, 'Sacred temple and tank—Umritsar', after Carpenter. In *The Practical and devotional family Bible* of 1860 he engraved, after Bartlett 'Halt above the north end of the Dead Sea' and 'Baths and City of Tiberius'. For B. Woodward's *General history of Hampshire* 1863 Armytage drew a number of designs (engraved by other artists), as well as engraving five vignettes himself. Three were after his own designs, 'West Gate, Winchester' after W. H. Bartlett, and a very good example, 'Defeat of Adam de Gurdon', after E. H. Corbould. Four of his engravings after Turner appeared in R. W. Wornum's *Turner Gallery* [c. 1878], i.e. 'Dutch boats in a gale', 'Sun rising in a mist', 'Venice—the Bridge of Sighs' and the best of the series, 'Approach to Venice'. In 1872, *Works of Shakspere* [sic], *Imperial edition*, edited by Charles Knight, contained 'Prince Henry, Doins, and Falstaff' after W. Q. Orchardson, 'Troilus and Cressida' after V. W. Bromley, and 'The death of Caesar' and 'Cleopatra and Caesar' after J. L. Gérôme, all of which were subsequently reissued in the *Art Journal* in 1872, 1873, 1874 and 1877 respectively. Seventeen plates after Baines, Carr, Chevalier, Skinner Prout and some of his own designs were engraved for Booth's *Australia* [1873–6]. In all, forty-two of his engravings appeared in the *Art Journal* between 1847 and 1890, and his was the last steel engraving to be published by that periodical, i.e. 'Non angli sed angeli' after Keeley Halswelle (1890) (Plate 62). The figures were well done for 'Drawing the net at Haweswater' after J. Thompson (1870). 'The sonnet' after W. Mulready (1876) and 'Adoration' after A. Scheffer (1879) were coarsely engraved in the Continental style, and 'Death of the stag' and 'The beggar' (1876) after Sir Edwin Landseer were both outline engravings. The editor of the *Art Journal*, Marcus B. Huish, consulted Armytage as a veteran steel engraver about his editions of Turner's *Richmondshire* 1891 and *The Seine and the Loire* 1895, the introductions to both of which provide revealing comments on some of Turner's engravers, such as R. Brandard, W. Miller, J. Cousen, R. Wallis, T. Higham, J. T. Willmore and W. Radclyffe. With his long association with Virtue the publisher it seems probable that Armytage worked for them preparing and retouching plates for their extensive publication programmes. He died on 28 April 1897, aged ninety-five. AJ; B; H.

Artlett, Richard Austin (1807–73) Sculpture and portrait engraver. He was born on 9 November 1807, and was first apprenticed to Robert Cooper, finishing his studies under James Thomson (q.v.) His portraits, done mainly for the print publishers, included Lord Ashburton after T. Lawrence, Lord Lyndhurst after A. E. Chalon and Mrs. Gladstone after W. Say. He was best known for his engraving of sculpture plates, some of which were done after exemplars in the British Museum, and of which forty-five were done for the *Art Journal* between 1849 and 1873. Some of the drawings were done by F. R. Roffe (a member of the family which was also famous for sculpture engravings), e.g. 'Religion consoling Justice' (1856) and a bas-relief (1864). 'Jepthah's daughter' after Oesterley and 'The Marys at the sepulchre' after Carracci, both with ornamental borders, one of which was designed by Luke Limner, appeared in *The Self-interpreting Bible* 1864. One of his last plates was of the sculpture 'The siren and the drowned Leander' (1873). The only picture engraved by him for the *Art Journal* was 'The Countess' after T. Lawrence (1850). His book illustrations are rarer, e.g. 'Turkey' after F. Stone for *Finden's tableaux of ... national character* 1837 and the frontispiece of the Chandos portrait of Shakespeare for the Imperial edition of the Works 1872. He also engraved some scriptural subjects for Blackie & Son, Glasgow. He died on 1 September 1873. AJ; B; DNB; S.

Ashley, A. (fl. 1852) Landscape engraver. Known by 'Brighton Viaduct on the Hastings Branch' after Burrell, drawn and engraved for Clarke's *British Gazetteer* 1852.

Aspland, L. (fl. 1829) Architectural engraver. 'Speke Hall...' and 'Hale Hall...' after G. and C. Pyne, dated 1829, were first issued in W. H. Pyne's *Lancashire illustrated ...* 1831, and later in E. Baines's *History of... Lancaster* 1836 and in G. N. Wright and T. Allen's *Lancashire ...* [c. 1845].

Audinet, Philip (fl. 1827–31) Portrait and figure engraver. 'Henry 5th, his queen and family' was published in H. Walpole's *Anecdotes of painting* 1827, 'John Howard, Duke of Norfolk' and 'Sir William Burrell' after R. T. Bone in Cartwright's *Parochial topography of the Rape of Bramber* 1830 and eight plates in the Industry and Idleness series after W. Hogarth in *Hogarth moralized* 1831.

Austin, H. (fl. 1840–8) Figure engraver. 'The Marchioness of Douro' (1 October 1840) after J. Hayter, a stipple vignette, appeared in *Heath's Book of beauty* 1841, and for the 1847 volume he did 'Angiolina' after J. W. Wright (Plate 42). 'Virgilia' after A. Johnston was published in *Heroines of*

Shakespeare 1848. 'The Lady Emmeline' after W. Drummond, dated 1 October 1841, was engraved for *The Keepsake* 1842.

B

Bacon, Frederick (1803–87) Figure engraver. He was born in London and was H. Fuseli's pupil at the Royal Academy. He learned engraving under the Findens, to whom he became an assistant. He joined the Artists' Annuity Fund in 1829. His name appears on plates done for the *Literary souvenir* – 'Feramorz relating the story of the Peri' after I. I. Stephanoff, dated November 1828, (1829) and 'The secret' after J. P. Davis (1831) – and for *The Keepsake* – 'Isabella and Gertrude' after A. E. Chalon (1830), 'Chacun à son gout' after F. P. Stephanoff (1831), 'The champion' after Chalon and 'Dressing for the ball' after De Verria (1832), 'One peep was enough' after H. Richter (1833), 'Bertha' after H. Briggs (1834), 'Carolina' after F. P. Stephanoff and 'The widowed mother' after Miss L. Sharpe (1835) and 'The bashful lover' after A. Solomon (1855). For *Keepsake français* 1831 he engraved 'Le Chev^r de Lauzan' after E. Devéria. Two vignettes – 'The temptation on the pinnacle' after Turner and 'L'Allegra' after R. Westall – were done for Milton's *Poetical works* 1835. For S. C. Hall's *Book of gems* 1836, he did 'The fairies' dance' (a vignette) after E. T. Parris, and 'The garden' (a vignette) after the same artist appeared in the 1838 volume. 'The smuggler's intrusion' (1 January 1838) after D. Wilkie, 'Escape of Francesco Novello de Carrara' (1 April 1839) after C. L. Eastlake and 'Anne Page and Slender' (August 1840) after A. W. Callcott were published in Finden's *Royal Gallery of British Art* 1838–49, 'The departure of Iran' after E. Corbould in T. Moore's *Lalla Rookh* 1838, the vignette of 'Damon and Pythias' after Turner on the engraved title page of Fisher's *Drawing room scrap book* 1842, and 'The apotheosis of Prince Octavius' after B. West in S. C. Hall's *Gems of European art* 1846. 'The nymph of the waterfall' after D. Maclise came out in the *Art Union* 1848, and was used again in Mrs Hall's *Drawing room table book* 1849. 'Fall of Clarendon' after E. M. Ward and 'The penitent' after W. Etty appeared in the *Art Journal* 1849 and 'The parting' after P. F. Poole in the 1866 volume. 'Hagar and Ishmael' after F. Overbeck was done for *The Pictorial Bible* 1855, and 'The great Balas ruby' after S. A. Hart appeared in volume 3 of *Casquet of literature* 1874. He worked for the print publishers in the 1840s, taking four years over 'Prince Charles Edward' after Duncan (1845), and in 1848 and 1851 did two plates for the Art Union of London. 'The fisherman's drowned child' after Burton, probably for the Royal Irish Art Union 1845, brought him in 700 guineas, but was considered to be a poor affair, injurious to his reputation. He retired from engraving in 1869. He emigrated to California in 1882, invested in property, and died there in 1887. AJ; B; Br; S.

Bailey, (fl. 1831) Landscape engraver. 'Ashton-Hall, near Lancaster...' and 'Conishead-Priory, near Ulverston...', both after Harwood, appeared in W. H. Pyne's *Lancashire illustrated ...* 1831, and again in E. Baines's *History of...Lancaster* 1836. 'Conishead-Priory...' was also used in *The British Switzerland*, issued by The London Printing and Publishing Company in 1858.

Baker, James H. (1829–c. 1880) Portrait and sculpture engraver. Born at Beaconsfield, he was a pupil at the Royal Academy and studied engraving under H. T. Ryall (q.v.). His major work was the twenty-eight plates of sculpture done for the *Art Journal* between 1851 and 1872, including 'The lion in love' (Plate 45), in the 1855 volume. In the 1860s his portraits of Bright, Lord Hawke and Cobden for the printsellers attracted some attention. 'Conversion of St. Paul' and 'Christ in the garden' appeared in the Revd F. L. Pearce's *Altar at home* [c. 1860]. A portrait of Goldsmith after Sir Joshua Reynolds appeared in Forster's *Life of Goldsmith* 1871, and 'Juliet' came out in *The Royal Shakespeare* 1883–4. B; T.

Baker, Robert (1793–1858) Historical engraver. He was born on 31 July 1793 in Leeds, where his father Robert worked as a cloth dresser in the woollen industry. By 1819 he had married Susanna and moved to The Broadway, London (near Ludgate Hill), and a family tradition links him with Thomas Rowlandson, possibly as an aquatint engraver. By 1826 he had moved to 66 Goswell Road, where he lived for the rest of his life. He did the engraved title pages for the *Literary souvenir* of 1826 and 1827 after designs by H. Corbould, but his most noteworthy plate was 'Mary, Queen of Scots, going forth to execution' after J. Stephanoff, engraved for *Friendship's offering* 1831. He had three sons by his first wife, the second of whom died in infancy. The eldest, Robert Rowlandson (q.v.), and the third, Alonzo, both became engravers. Robert died, aged 57, of a 'prostatic disease'.

Baker, Robert Rowlandson (1819– after 1866) Ornamental and heraldic engraver. He was born in London, the eldest son of Robert (q.v.), and was baptized at St Ann, Blackfriars. His second name derived, according to tradition, from Thomas Rowlandson, and survives today as a family name in the person of Roger Arnold Rowlandson Barltrop. In 1843 Robert Rowlandson married a solicitor's daughter, Rosella H. Green, at St James's, Clerkenwell, and about 1850 they moved to Islington. They had three sons and five daughters, one of whom, Julia, died in infancy. Nothing more is known of Robert R. Baker after his eldest son's marriage in 1866. His best-known book work was seventeen engravings of coats of arms, dated 1844 and 1845, which appeared in J. Burke's *Heraldic illustrations* 1845, of which plate 22, the arms of Hugh Robert Hughes, is especially well done. In *The Self-interpreting Bible* 1864, he engraved the frame, drawn by Luke Limner, which surrounded the frontispiece, and it is probable that frames to other illustrations, although unsigned, were engraved by him.

Balding, H. C. (fl. 1869–84) Sculpture engraver. Twenty plates of sculptures and two of bas-reliefs appeared in the *Art Journal* from 1869 to 1884, commencing with 'Nymph of the Lurlei' after G. Herold.

Ball, H. S. (fl. 1846) Figure engraver. 'The Peri' after H. Warren was published February 1846 in *Beauties of Moore* 1846.

Banks, W., and Co. (or Son) (fl. 1855–90) This company was located in Edinburgh, and was responsible for engraving twenty-one plates in H. Martineau's *Complete guide to the English Lakes* 1855, six in W. K. Hunter's *History of the Priory of Coldingham* 1858, thirty-one in W. Banks's *Views of the English Lakes* [c. 1860] and twenty-five in *Scenery in the Western Highlands* [c. 1890]. Ho.

Barber, Thomas (fl. 1818–46) Landscape engraver. He engraved plates for *Excursions through Sussex* 1818–22 and J. P. Neale's *Views of the seats of noblemen...* 1818–24, going on to steel in May 1827 with 'Scene from the ascent to Mount Genevre', together with two other plates done in 1828 after W. Brockedon, for the artist's *Illustrations of the passes of the Alps* 1828–9. On 5 May 1827 was published 'Villa in the

Regent's Park', which, together with ten other plates after T. H. Shepherd, came out in J. Elmes's *Metropolitan improvements* 1829, and between 1829 and 1831, he did twelve after Shepherd for the latter's *London and its environs* 1829–31, and eleven for Shepherd's *Modern Athens* 1829–31. He did the engraved title page vignette 'The Menai Straits' (to volume 1) and twelve other plates after Henry Gastineau for the latter's *Wales illustrated...* 1830. 'Civita Castellana' after S. Prout came out in T. Roscoe's *Tourist in Italy* 1831 and 'View in Metz' and 'Port and Lake of Como' after Prout in the *Continental annual* 1832. He produced *Barber's picturesque illustrations of the Isle of Wight* [c. 1835], for which he drew thirteen and engraved fourteen of the plates. Of the latter five were after his own designs, the remainder by W. H. Bartlett, including 'Ryde', 'Town Hall, Newport' and 'Carisbrook Castle'. Six plates, probably after Thomas Allom, were done for *Views in the Tyrol* [1836], including 'Landseer' and 'Starrenberg'. Two plates of Chester after T. Allom came out in T. Noble and T. Rose's *Counties of Chester...* 1836, two engravings after Bartlett in J. Carne's *Syria* 1836–8 and four plates, dated 1836, after T. Allom in W. Beattie's *Scotland illustrated* 1838, including 'Jedburgh Abbey...' (a good plate), and 'Gate of entrance to the reception room of the Seraglio' after Allom was done for R. Walsh's *Constantinople* 1838–40. 'Temple of Juggernaut' after A. G. Vickers appeared in G. N. Wright's *Gallery of engravings* 1844–6, 'Oppenheim' and 'Freyburg' after Tombleson in Fearnside's *Tombleson's Upper Rhine* [c. 1835] and three plates after the same artist in Fearnside's *Picturesque beauties of the Rhine* [c. 1846].

Barenger, M. S. (fl. 1818–31) Landscape engraver. He contributed some plates to J. P. Neale's *Views of the seats of noblemen...* 1818–24. Six engravings on steel, dated December 1827 to February 1829, were done for J. Elmes's *Metropolitan improvements* 1829 (four signed 'M. Barrenger'), and three appeared in T. H. Shepherd's *London and its environs* 1829–31 (one signed 'M. S. Barenger'). He is possibly related to James Barenger (1780–1831), a nephew of the engraver William Woollett. B; DNB.

Barker, J. (fl. 1846) Landscape engraver. 'Mayence' after W. Tombleson appeared in Fearnside's *Picturesque beauties of the Rhine* [c. 1846].

Barlow, Thomas Oldham (1824–89) Basically a mezzotint engraver, he is known to have engraved a stipple and line portrait of David Roberts after J. W. Gordon for Ballantine's *Life of David Roberts* 1866. He was apprenticed to James Stephenson (q.v.). AJ; B; DNB.

Bauer, Job (fl. 1883–4) Figure engraver. 'The two Dromios' after Richter, 'Caesar and Calphurnia' after F. Dicksee and 'Volumnia and Coriolanus' after H. A. Bone were published in *The Royal Shakespeare* 1883–4.

Bauer, Tobias (1827–c. 1878) Historical engraver. He was born in Nuremberg and worked in London. He engraved 'Departure of the Pilgrim Fathers...' and 'The opening scene of the Great Civil War', both after C. W. Cope, and 'The Marquis of Montrose at the place of execution...' after E. M. Ward for T. Archer's *Pictures and royal portraits...* [c. 1878]. B.

Becker, Francis Paul (fl. 1837–61) Map and heraldic engraver. He engraved a 'facsimile of Goldsmith's handwriting' for volume 2 of Prior's *Life of Goldsmith* 1837 and a double page 'Map of Spain and Portugal' for Maxwell's *Life of... the Duke of Wellington* 1839–41. Between 1843 and 1845

he did fifty-four plates of coats of arms for J. Burke's *Heraldic illustrations* 1845, the best of which was that of Prince Albert's arms. In T. Moore's *Irish melodies*, illustrated by D. Maclise, 1848, he used a process identified in Stannard's *Art Exemplar* as 'omnigraphy', where the letters are punched into the metal plate, thus enabling text and illustrations to be printed together in intaglio. Contemporaries thought this to be a book calculated to 'elevate' British art. A map of the roads from Cork to Kilkenny was 'engraved by the omnigraph F. P. Becker & Co. Patentees', and appeared in S. C. and A. M. Hall's *Week at Killarney* 1858. A series of eight attractive vignettes after H. C. Selous were engraved for the *Book of Common Prayer* 1854.   AU.

Beckwith, Henry S. (fl. 1835–1900) Landscape and heraldic engraver. He was the brother-in-law of another engraver, Francis W. Topham (q.v.), who combined with him to provide the thirty-three vignette illustrations to P. Fisher's *Angler's souvenir* 1835. (Topham drew and Beckwith engraved.) 'Fisher' was the pseudonym of William Andrew Chatto, author of *A Treatise on wood-engraving*. Beckwith worked in New York from 1842–3. Five plates of coats of arms were done in 1843 for J. Burke's *Heraldic illustrations* 1845, and between 1848 and 1850 he contributed five plates to the *Art Journal*, four of which were after Sir Edwin Landseer. He contributed 'Phaedra and Hyppolytus' after P. Guérin to S. C. Hall's *Gems of European art* 1846.   B; Ro; St.

Beckwith, J. H. (fl. 1849) Ornamental engraver. He engraved a title page after W. H. Rogers to Mrs Hall's *Drawing room table book* 1849.

Beckwith, W. (fl. 1843) Heraldic engraver. Plate 28 of coats of arms, dated 1843, was done for J. Burke's *Heraldic illustrations* 1845.

Bedford, C. (fl. 1828–9) Landscape engraver. 'Ramsgate harbour...' and 'The barracks and town of Hythe' after G. Shepherd appeared in *England's topographer*, by S. W. H. Ireland, (commenced publication 1828).

Bell, Robert Charles (1806–72) Landscape, historical and portrait engraver. He was born in Edinburgh and apprenticed to the painter and engraver John Beugo (or Beugho) (1759–1841), friend of Burns. He attended classes at the Trustees' Academy under Sir William Allan. His first important commission was for a series of Scottish views for Joseph Swan of Glasgow, and in the 1840s he produced plates for the New Association for the Promotion of the Fine Arts in Scotland, the Art Union of Scotland and the National Art-union for Ireland. Ten plates were published in the *Art Journal* between 1850 and 1874, but his largest plate, 'Battle of Preston Pans' after Allan, was finished only just before his death, which occurred on 5 September 1872. He used copper extensively, even in the 1840s, when his three plates for *Engravings after the best pictures of the Great Masters* 1841–3 were engraved in this metal. Much of his book work was of single plates, mainly frontispieces, e.g., that of John Knox to McCrie's *Life of John Knox* 1840. Two plates were engraved for volume 3 of *Works of John Bunyan*, 1853. 'Glencoe, looking down the Pass' after T. B. Howard appeared in *Casquet of literature*, volume 3, 1874. Francis Croll (1827–54) (q.v.) finished his apprenticeship with him about 1846 and stayed a further two years.   AU; AJ.

Bellin, Samuel (c. 1799–1894) Architectural and figure engraver. Born in London, he worked mainly for the printsellers and the Art Unions, but in 1835 he engraved two plans of St Stephen's Chapel after R. W. Billings and J. R. Thompson for E. W. Brayley and J. Britton's *History of the ancient palace... at Westminster* 1836. He died in January 1894, at over ninety years of age.   AJ; S.

Benjamin, E. (fl. 1834–46) Landscape engraver. 'Mont Blanc from above Sallenche', dated 1 May 1834, and two other plates after W. H. Bartlett were engraved for W. Beattie's *Switzerland* 1836, two plates after Bartlett and C. Bentley for J. Carnes's *Syria* 1836–8, 'The ruins of Hierapolis...' after T. Allom and 'Pass and waterfall in the Balkan mountains' after F. Hervé for R. Walsh's *Constantinople* 1838–40, four plates after Bartlett for J. Pardoe's *Beauties of the Bosphorus* 1840 and another four after Bartlett for N. P. Willis's *American scenery* 1840. Eight engravings after Allom and one after Bartlett were done in 1836 and 1837 for Beattie's *Scotland illustrated* 1838, and 'Lismore Castle' after Bartlett appeared in J. S. Coyne's *Scenery and antiquities of Ireland* [c. 1840]. 'Entrance to the port of Dundee' and 'Radcliffe Church & basin, Bristol' after Bartlett came out in W. Beattie's *Ports, harbours...* 1842. For N. P. Willis's *Canadian scenery* 1842 the same artist provided drawings for five plates, including 'Portage des Chats', and two plates were done for W. Beattie's *Danube* 1844. 'The Kilns at King-tan' after Allom appeared in G. N. Wright's *China* 1843 and 'Mountain temples, Lake of Aboo' after H. Melville in G. N. Wright's *Gallery of engravings* 1844–6.

Bentley, C. (fl. 1832–50) Landscape engraver. 'Teignmouth Bridge...' and 'Sharpham...' after T. Allom were published in J. Britton and E. W. Brayley's *Devonshire and Cornwall illustrated* 1832, and 'St. Michael's Church, St. Alban's...' after C. Marshall was done for W. G. Fearnside and T. Harral's *History of London* [c. 1850].

Bentley, Joseph Clayton (1809–51) Landscape engraver. The fifth child of Greenwood Bentley, a well-known Bradford lawyer, he came from a long established Yorkshire family which had produced many eminent lawyers but no previous artist. Trained as a landscape painter, he was only mediocre, but it was an interest he followed in parallel with his engraving under Robert Brandard (q.v.). His progress as an engraver was such that his work immediately found its way into contemporary books. His first published plate was 'Feniscowles', dated 1832, after G. Pickering, done for E. Baines's *History of ... Lancaster* 1836, with 'Farnworth paper mills...' and 'Windleshaw Abbey...' after the same artist in volume 3. This was quickly followed by eight plates after T. Allom and one after H. Gastineau for T. Rose's *Cumberland* 1832, two after Allom for Rose's *Durham and Northumberland* 1832 and three engravings after Allom and one after J. Harwood for J. Britton and E. Brayley's *Devonshire and Cornwall illustrated* 1832. 'Burlington quay...' after Chambers and 'Warwick Castle' after G. Cattermole were issued in *Watering places...* 1833 and 'Approach to Antioch from Aleppo' after Bartlett in J. Carne's *Syria* 1836–8. 'Ramsgate' and 'Broadstairs' after C. Stanfield were done for *Stanfield's coast scenery* 1836. 'The palace called Beautiful' and 'Then said the shepherds...' after H. Melville appeared in J. Bunyan's *Pilgrim's progress* 1836. Five plates after Melville, Franklin and Topham were done for G. N. Wright's *Landscape-historical illustrations of Scotland* 1836–8. 'Crossing by a Sanga...' after Allom came out in G. F. White's *Views in India ...* 1838. 'St. Ambrogio, near Susa' after Bartlett was engraved for W. Beattie's *Waldenses* 1838. '[The deluge] The same day were all the fountains...' after Poussin, dated 1840, appeared in the first series of Fisher's *Historic illustrations of the Bible* [1840–3]. Seven engravings after Allom (including 'The great cemetery at Scutari' and 'The triple wall of

Constantinople'), 'Village in Rumelia...' after J. Salmon and 'Valley of the Suli' after W. L. Leitch appeared in R. Walsh's *Constantinople* 1838–40, 'The twa brigs, Ayr...' after Bartlett and 'Ravenscraig Castle' after Allom in W. Beattie's *Scotland illustrated* 1838 and three plates after Allom in G. N. Wright's *China* 1843. 'Dark tree...' after Allom was published in Fisher's *Drawing room scrap book* 1842. His work after W. H. Bartlett was extensive, and the important series of plates were those which appeared in J. Pardoe's *Beauties of the Bosphorus* 1840 (four plates), N. P. Willis's *American scenery* 1840 (six plates, including 'Village of Catskill'), *Canadian scenery* 1842 (seven plates), W. Beattie's *Ports, harbours*... 1842 (two plates, including 'Bath'), J. S. Coyne's *Scenery and antiquities of Ireland* [c. 1840] (eleven plates, including 'Glengariff Inn' and 'The Dargle'), W. Beattie's *Danube* 1844 (six plates), Beattie's *Castles and abbeys of England* 1845–51 (three vignettes and 'The ferry at Tintern'), H. Stebbing's *Christian in Palestine* [1847] (ten plates) and Bartlett's own books—*Walks about... Jerusalem* [1844] ('Pool of Hezekiah...' and 'Enclosure of the Temple, Jerusalem'), *Forty days in the desert* 1848 (four vignettes), *Nile boat* 1849 (five vignettes, including 'The Sphynx' and 'Luxor from the water') and *Footsteps of Our Lord* 1851 (two vignettes, 'The Rock of Corinth' and 'Tiberias'). A vignette and plate, unsigned, but after Bartlett, appeared in the latter's *Scripture sites and scenes*... 1849, and five vignettes were done for his *Gleanings... on the overland route* 1851. Six engravings after W. Purser, Copley Fielding, Capt. Irton, R. Brandard and F. Arundale were published in C. Wordsworth's *Greece* 1839. 'The fountain' after F. Zuccarelli, 'A sunny day' after A. Cuyp (used again in the *Art Journal* 1868), 'The market cart' after T. Gainsborough, 'The old woman's feast' after G. Douw and 'The alchemist' after A. van Ostade (used again in the *Art Journal* 1872) were engraved for S. C. Hall's *Gems of European art* 1846, for which publication he also made some water-colour copies. 'Ship in flames' and 'The cataract' were two good vignettes done for Calabrella's *Evenings at Haddon Hall* 1845, together with 'Ancient hall with soldiers carousing', all after G. Cattermole, and 'Barking Church, Essex' after C. Marshall came out in W. G. Fearnside and T. Harral's *History of London* [c. 1850]. His work for the *Art Journal* began in 1849 with plates for the 'Vernon Gallery', including 'Wooden bridge' after A. W. Callcott, 'Valley farm' after J. Constable and 'Way to church' after T. Creswick. Eight engravings appeared in all, ending with 'Sea shore in Holland' after Callcott (1852), which was probably his last plate. 'Lake Avernus' after R. Wilson (1851) is a very good example of his work. At least 200 plates by him are known, and it is remarkable that in nineteen years his output had been as great as that of any of his contemporaries, due principally to the speed at which he worked. This, combined with a high standard of achievement and an ability to meet deadlines, recommended him to the publishers for whom he worked, notably Fisher and Virtue. It was his industry which weakened him, however, and early signs of tuberculosis appeared in 1843–4. He moved to Sydenham in the hope that a change of air would effect a cure, but by the end of June 1851 the disease had a firm hold and he died at his residence, Perry Vale, on 9 October 1851. He left a widow and two children, but his membership of the Artists' Annuity Fund (he had been a member since 1839) alleviated their lot to some extent. AJ; Bradford Antiquary 1895, p. 65 *et seq.*; DNB.

Berthier (fl. 1870) Figure engraver. 'Christ teaching by the seaside' after C. F. Jalabert was issued in Murdoch's edition of the *Holy Bible* [c. 1870].

Bertrand, C. (fl. 1876–9) Landscape engraver. 'Virgil's House, Brindisi' after C. Werner was published in *Picturesque Europe* 1876–9.

Bibby, H. (fl. 1850–74) Landscape engraver. For Tallis's *Illustrated atlas* [1851] he drew the designs and engraved three vignettes on a map of Brighton. Five plates after Skinner Prout and one after N. Chevalier were engraved for Booth's *Australia* [1873–6]. He engraved 'Balaklava' after E. Doré and 'Geelong' after H. Winkles. 'Town Hall and Market Place, Liège' after his own design and 'The Town Hall Antwerp' after W. Jones appeared in a publication by John Tallis [c. 1850].

Billings, Robert William (1815–74) Painter, architect, sculptor and architectural engraver. Two plates of Westminster Hall and St Stephen's Chapel after his own designs were done for E. W. Brayley and J. Britton's *History of the ancient palace ... at Westminster* 1836, and about twenty plates were done for his *Architectural illustrations of Carlisle cathedral* 1840. He drew and engraved thirty-one plates for his *Architectural illustrations... of the Temple Church, London* [c. 1843].

Bingley, James (fl. 1831–4) Landscape engraver. Ten engravings after G. B. Campion and one after T. H. Williams were done for T. Moore's *History of Devonshire* 1831. For T. Wright's *Picturesque beauties of Great Britain...: Essex* 1834 he engraved a folding map of Essex (15½ by 14½ inches). Ho.

Bishop, J. (fl. 1835–59) Landscape engraver. 'High Cross near Bonn' and 'Village of Splugen...' after Tombleson appeared in Fearnside's *Picturesque beauties of the Rhine* [c. 1846], and R. Elliot's *Views in India...* 1835 contained 'The Cave of Karli' after G. Cattermole.

Bishop, T. (fl. 1834) Landscape engraver. Fearnside's *Tombleson's Thames* 1834 contained 'East Farleigh, Kent' after W. Tombleson.

Bittleston, W. (fl. 1870) Historical engraver. He is known by five engravings which appeared in the *Universal family Bible* [c. 1870], of which 'Mordecai honoured' was well engraved and 'The Pool of Bethesda, Jerusalem' was done after a photograph by permission of the Commandant of the Royal Engineers.

Black, I. (fl. 1846) Landscape engraver. Fearnside's *Picturesque beauties of the Rhine* [c. 1846] contained 'Town and castle of Werdenberg' after W. Tombleson.

Bond, H. W. (fl. 1827–49) Landscape and architectural engraver. He contributed five plates after T. H. Shepherd to J. Elmes's *Metropolitan improvements* 1829, four after Shepherd to Shepherd's *Modern Athens* 1829–31 and one after J. P. Neale to J. Britton's *Bath and Bristol* 1829. His most important series was of twenty-three engravings after H. Gastineau for the latter's *Wales illustrated...* 1830 of which 'Kidwelly Castle...' is a good example. Two views after Allom were engraved for books by T. Rose—'Birker Force...' for *Cumberland* 1832 and 'Barrow Hall...' for *Westmorland* 1832. 'Lahneck Castle' after Tombleson appeared in *Tombleson's Views of the Rhine* 1832 and 'Suspension Bridge, Gt. Marlow, Bucks' after the same artist in Fearnside's *Tombleson's Thames* 1834. 'Schaffhausen' after Tombleson appeared in Fearnside's *Picturesque beauties of the Rhine* [c. 1846], three plates after J. Fussell in *Continental tourist* [1838], and five plates signed 'H. Bond' after Shepherd in Dugdale's *England and Wales delineated* [c. 1838–9]. Br.

Bond, T. (fl. 1850) Landscape engraver. 'Chichester, Sussex' and 'Salisbury, Wiltshire' after T. H. Shepherd were published in T. Dugdale's *England and Wales delineated* [c. 1838–9].

Bond, William (fl. 1803–27) Architectural and portrait engraver. A William Bond was a governor of the Society of Engravers in 1803. Plates signed 'W. Bond' appeared in J. Elmes's *Metropolitan improvements* 1829, i.e., 'Chapel of ease, West Hackney' and 'St. John's, Hoxton' dated 22 September 1827, and three portrait engravings in H. Walpole's *Anecdotes of painting* 1827.   Br.

Bond, W. H. (fl. 1829–32) Architectural engraver. 'Serjeant's Inn Hall, Chancery Lane', and 'Staples Inn Hall, Holborn', both after T. H. Shepherd, appeared in Shepherd's *London and its environs* 1829–31, and 'St. Sidwell's Church Exeter' and 'St. David's Church Exeter', both after W. H. Bartlett, in Britton and Brayley's *Devonshire and Cornwall illustrated* 1832.

Bosher, S. (fl. 1835) Landscape engraver. 'Wootten Bridge' appeared in *Barber's picturesque illustrations of the Isle of Wight* [c. 1835].

Bourne, Herbert (fl. 1851–85) Figure and historical engraver. He is thought to have been born about 1820. Many of his engravings were translations of paintings by Old and Modern Masters, and his book work included an attractive vignette— 'Hindoo maidens floating lamps on the Ganges' after Armytage – and 'The most noble the Marquis of Hastings' after Shee in E. H. Nolan's *Illustrated history of the British Empire in India* [1858–60]. Of three plates done for the *Works of Shakspere* [*sic*], *Imperial edition* 1872, two appeared in 1873–4 in the *Art Journal*, for which most of his work was done—forty-one plates in all from 1851–1886—, his peak being reached with five plates published in the 1867 volume. Two of his most striking engravings were 'New shoes' after Frith (1866) and 'The last of England' by Madox Brown (1870). In 1861, Bourne finished an engraving for H. C. Shenton, who was going blind, and in 1872 he produced a version of Rothwell's 'The novitiate mendicants', which had been done in 1841 by Samuel Sangster for the Royal Irish Art Union. For a Catholic edition of the *Bible* published about 1870, he engraved four plates after Portaels and H. Vernet and two after Ary Scheffer, i.e., 'Ruth and Naomi' and 'The Maries at the sepulchre', both with a curved top, and for T. Archer's *Pictures and royal portraits* . . . [c. 1878], eleven plates were engraved after J. L. Williams, E. M. Ward, G. F. Watts, C. R. Leslie, etc. A very large print, 'Christ leaving the Praetorium', was engraved by him, the reduction of which, in sections, was done by photography. J. C. Bourne may also have been involved in the engraving of this plate.   AJ; B; T.

Bourne, J. (fl. 1836) Landscape engraver. 'Patan tomb at Toglokabad, Old Delhi' after W. Daniell, dated 1 October 1836, was published in J. Caunter's *Lives of the Moghul emperors* 1837. This could possibly be John Cooke Bourne, draughtsman, lithographer and engraver.   AU.

Bower, J. (fl. 1849–60) Landscape engraver, possibly in Edinburgh. Two vignettes of Kelso were done for Rutherford's *Border hand-book* 1849, and 'Plain Er-Rahah—Mt. Sinai' was issued in M'Farlane's edition of the *Bible* 1860.

Boys, T. (probably Thomas Shotter Boys) (fl. 1834–60) Landscape engraver. 'Jumma Musjid—Agra' was engraved for R. Elliot's *Views in India* . . . 1835, two plates of 'Arch masonry' for Ruskin's *Stones of Venice* 1851–3 and two plates after Turner for volume 4 of Ruskin's *Modern painters* 1856–60.

Bradley, Thomas (fl. 1849) Architectural engraver. 'The Forum at Rome' was the frontispiece to volume 2 of Clarke's *Pompeii* 1849. He tried out new graver handles for the Society of Arts in 1831.   SocA.

Bradshaw, G. (fl. 1836) Landscape engraver. 'The Needles' after C. Stanfield appeared in *Stanfield's coast scenery* 1836. He may be George Bradshaw (1801–53), the producer of railway timetables, who was trained as an engraver. (See *Dictionary of National Biography*.)

Bradshaw, Samuel (fl. 1832–80) Landscape engraver. He may be a brother of G. Bradshaw (q.v.). He joined the Artists' Annuity Fund in 1836. Among his early works were 'Dilston Hall . . .' and 'Prudhoe Castle, on the Tyne' after T. Allom for T. Rose's *Durham and Northumberland* 1832, and for the same author and artist he did four plates published in *Westmorland* 1832. 'Scene near Chillah Tarah Ghaut . . .', a vignette on the engraved title page after H. Melville from a sketch by Col. Barton, appeared in R. Elliot's *Views in India* . . . 1835, 'Borro Boedoor' after W. Purser in Fisher's *Drawing room scrap book* 1836, 'The new bridge, Chester' and three other plates after Allom in T. Noble and T. Rose's *Counties of Chester* . . . 1836, 'The gardens of Versailles' and 'The heights of Satory . . .' after W. Callow in *Heath's Versailles* [c. 1836] (used again in *Keepsake français* 1840), 'Convent of Mount Carmel' and three other plates after W. H. Bartlett and 'The monastery of Santa Saba' after Allom in J. Carne's *Syria* 1836–8 and 'The town of Dumfries . . .' after Bartlett in W. Beattie's *Scotland illustrated* 1838. 'Oporto from St. John's' after J. Holland was engraved for W. H. Harrison's *Tourist in Portugal* 1839. One of his best plates was 'Obelisk of Theodosius in the Atmeidan' after Allom, engraved for R. Walsh's *Constantinople* 1838–40. Four plates after Bartlett were done for J. Pardoe's *Beauties of the Bosphorus* 1840. 'View from Mount Washington' and 'Village of Little Falls (Mohawk River)' after Bartlett appeared in N. P. Willis's *American scenery* 1840, five plates after Bartlett in Willis's *Canadian scenery* 1842, including 'Working a canoe up a rapid', 'Gougaure Barra' and 'Castle Howard, Vale of Avoca' after Bartlett in J. S. Coyne's *Scenery and antiquities of Ireland* [c. 1840], two vignettes—'The Gap of Dunloe, Kerry' and 'Londonderry'—after T. Creswick in S. C. and A. M. Hall's *Ireland* 1841–3 and three plates after Bartlett in W. Beattie's *Ports, harbours* . . . 1842. His longest series of plates in one volume was the nine after Allom which appeared in G. N. Wright's *China* 1843, after which he did 'Tomb of the Virgin, Jerusalem' and 'Rachel's tomb near Bethlehem' after Bartlett for Bartlett's *Walks about* . . . *Jerusalem* [1844]. Further plates after Bartlett were done for works by Beattie, two for *The Danube* 1844 and one for *Castles and abbeys of England* 1845–51. 'The sylvan calm' after Claude Lorraine appeared in S. C. Hall's *Gems of European art* 1846, four plates after Bartlett in H. Stebbing's *Christian in Palestine* [1847], 'Alessandria', an unusually long picture (8⅜ by 4¼ inches), after S. Read and 'Venice' after J. B. Pyne in D. Costello's *Piedmont and Italy* [c. 1855], six plates in W. H. D. Adams's *History* . . . *of the Isle of Wight* 1858, including 'Osborne . . . as seen by the telescope . . .' (Plate 48), the engraved title page vignette—'The Island of Reichenau by the Lake of Constanz (Unter See)'—, 'Eglisau' and 'Bregenz' after Birket Foster in J. Mayhew's *Upper Rhine* 1860, 'Plain of Esdraelon from Jenin' after Bartlett in M'Farlane's edition of the *Bible* 1860, three vignettes—'View from St. Catherine's

Hall' after Bartlett and 'View of Twyford' and 'Selbourne (from the Hanger)' after J. C. Armytage—in B. Woodward's *General history of Hampshire* 1863 and 'Huddersfield' after H. Warren in T. Baines's *Yorkshire past and present* 1871–7. Eight plates after Carr, Chevalier and Skinner Prout were engraved for Booth's *Australia* [1873–6]. 'Hebron' after H. C. Selous and 'Salonika...' after H. G. Hine were in the *Imperial Family Bible* 1873, originally published in 1844, and 'Kynance Rocks, Cornwall' after J. Mogford (painted in 1874), 'Bamborough Castle' also after Mogford (on an engraved title page), 'St. Mary's porch, Oxford' after S. Read, 'Turnbury Castle' and 'Innspruck' [*sic*] after Birket Foster and 'Monte Pellegrino, Palermo' after H. Fenn appeared in *Picturesque Europe* 1876–9. He contributed five plates to the *Art Journal*, namely, 'Fisherman's cave' after E. W. Cooke (1854), 'Parting of Hero and Leander' (1861), 'Regulus leaving Carthage' (1863) and 'View of Orviello' (1864), all after Turner, and used again in Wornum's *Turner Gallery* [c. 1878], and 'Gurth the swineherd' after C. E. Johnson (1886). He exhibited a landscape at Suffolk Street in 1869. B.

Bragge, S. (fl. 1872) Portrait engraver. 'John Evelyn' after G. Kneller was used as the frontispiece to volume 1 of J. Evelyn's *Diary and correspondence* 1872.

Brain, John (fl. 1836–79) Historical engraver. He joined the Artists' Annuity Fund in 1839. In 1831 J. Brain of 49 Bartholomew Close, was given the Silver Isis medal of the Society of Arts for a copy in chalk of a head. He had Charles Henry Jeens as a pupil. Probably, his most attractive engraving was also among his first, namely, 'The peasant Child', a vignette after A. Cooper, which appeared with two other engravings in S. C. Hall's *Book of gems* 1836–8. For *Friendship's offering*, he engraved 'The fountain' after R. Westall (1839) and 'The sacrifice' after G. Cattermole (1844); for *Forget me not* 1846, 'Imogen' after Stephanoff; and for *The Keepsake*, 'The pearl hilted poignard' (1842) and 'The banquet' (1844) after Cattermole, 'The love letter' after Wright (1845), 'Marie' after Wood and 'The quarrel' after Stephanoff (1846). 'The ancient prude' after Jenkins appeared in G.. Wright's *Gallery of engravings* 1844–6. Two engravings after Weigall were done for N. P. Willis's *Pencillings by the way* 1845. 'The duel' after W. P. Frith, first issued in S. C. Hall's *Gems of European art* 1846 and later used for the *Works of Shakspere* [sic] *Imperial edition* 1872, was one of his more popular engravings. 'Philosophy. The school of Athens' was engraved as the frontispiece to Ogilvie's *Imperial dictionary* 1850. Forty outline engravings were done after M. Retzsch for Anna Swanwick's edition of Goethe's *Faust* 1879 (Plate 59). Twenty-six of Retzsch's designs had been engraved in outline by Henry Moses for an 1821 edition of the work. It is possible that he turned to engraving after having been a landscape painter. Benezit lists a John Brain who exhibited at the Royal Academy 1832–6. B; SocA.

Brandard, Edward Paxman (1819–1898) Landscape engraver. He was the third son of Thomas Brandard, engraver, of Birmingham, after whose death in 1830 Edward went to live with his elder brother, Robert (q.v.), in Islington. Robert taught Edward engraving, and since J. M. W. Turner was a frequent visitor to their home, a number of their engravings were done after the painter's pictures, and when Edward died it was said that he was the last of the steel engravers and the last to work under the personal superintendence of Turner. Edward was twenty-four when he engraved seven plates after T. Allom for G. N. Wright's *China* 1843, and this was

Edward Paxman Brandard

followed by a succession of books with illustrations engraved mainly after W. H. Bartlett. These included six plates for W. Beattie's *Danube* 1844, four for Bartlett's *Walks about... Jerusalem* [1844], five for Beattie's *Castles and abbeys of England* 1845–51, nine for H. Stebbing's *Christian in Palestine* [1847], eleven for Bartlett's *Scripture sites and scenes...* 1849, five for Bartlett's *Gleanings ... on the overland route* 1851, four for Bartlett's *Nile boat* 1849, ten for Bartlett's *Pictures from Sicily* 1853, nine for Bartlett's *Pilgrim Fathers* 1853, seven for Conybeare and Howson's *Life and epistles of St. Paul* 1854 and one for S. C. and A. M. Hall's *Week at Killarney* 1858. Many of these were vignette illustrations. 'The repose by the way' after P. F. Mola appeared in S. C. Hall's *Gems of European art* 1846, and he engraved thirteen plates for the *Art Journal* from 1853, the last one being 'Iona' after MacWhirter in 1887. Three plates were done for E. H. Nolan's *Illustrated history of the British Empire in India* [1858–60], one after Warren for Taylor's *Family history of England* [c. 1860], eight vignettes for B. Woodward's *General history of Hampshire* 1863 and two after Doré for *The Story of Enid and Geraint* [1869]. Sixteen plates after Brierly, Chevalier and Skinner Prout were engraved for Booth's *Australia* [1873–6]. His engravings after Turner—'Grand canal, Venice', 'Apollo and Daphne in the Vale of Tempe' and 'Venice from the Canal of the Guidecca'—should be mentioned. He exhibited at a number of London galleries from 1849 to 1885, including the Royal Academy and the Society of Painter-etchers. Some of his later engravings, in the 1860s and 1870s, were done after Birket Foster, e.g., 'Lauffenberg' in *Picturesque Europe* 1876–9. He was living at 2 Albion Grove, Barnsbury, in 1885, and died on 3 April 1898. It is thought that he had four daughters, the eldest of whom was Suzanna, who died in about 1882, leaving a daughter, Florence (1872–1946), to be looked after by the grandparents. Florence married a publisher's clerk in Natal in 1897 and received some pictures (and possibly engravings) as a wedding present, which, however, were stolen during the Boer War. Replacement gifts were destroyed in 1947 when a pantechnicon overturned and caught fire in an accident. About five pieces remain in the possession of Edward's great granddaughter, Mrs Winifred Anne Walter. AJ; B; Br; *Illus. Lond. News* 1898, p. 249; YA 1886.

Brandard, Robert (1805–62) Landscape engraver, etcher, oil and watercolour painter. The eldest son of Thomas Brandard, engraver, copper-plate printer, etc., of Barford

Street, Deretend, Birmingham, he obviously learned the rudiments of his craft from his father, and when in 1824, at the age of nineteen, he moved to London, it was to extend his experience under the roof of Edward Goodall. Robert remained with him for a year, and, probably through Goodall, met J. M. W. Turner, for whom both Robert and Edward Brandard were to work. Setting up on his own in about 1825 or 1826, one of his earliest bookplates was 'Love's jubilee' after T. Stothard, published in the *Literary souvenir* [1826], followed by 'Sans souci' after the same artist in the first volume of W. Pickering's *Bijou* 1828. He also engraved for *Friendship's offering* ('The bridge of Alva' after Purser (1833)), *The Keepsake*, *Landscape annual* and Heath's *Picturesque annual*. For the 1833 volume of the latter, L. Ritchie's *Travelling sketches on the Rhine*, he engraved four plates after C. Stanfield, including 'Ehrenbreitstein from Coblence'. After the same artist, he did 'Approach to St. Malo' for *Stanfield's coast scenery* 1836. Eight plates after W. Brockedon were engraved for Brockedon's *Illustrations of the passes of the Alps* 1828-9, in which the first plate, 'Scene from Little St Bernard', was issued in February 1827. He engraved three plates after Creswick for Ritchie's *Ireland...* 1837 and six after Brockedon, Stanfield and Bartlett for W. Beattie's *Waldenses* 1838. Five were done for J. Pardoe's *Beauties of the Bosphorus* 1840, six for J. S. Coyne's *Scenery and antiquities of Ireland...* [c. 1840], twelve for N. P. Willis's *American scenery* 1840, nine for Willis's *Canadian scenery* 1842 and nine for Beattie's *Ports, harbours...* 1842, all of which were after W. H. Bartlett. 'Genoa' after Brockedon was done with six other plates for Brockedon's *Italy...* 1842-3, a vignette after G. Cattermole—'Dismasted vessel in a storm'—for Calabrella's *Evenings at Haddon Hall* 1845 (with two other plates in the same volume), and 'Going to the ferry' after Wouvermans for S. C. Hall's *Gems of European art* 1846. 'Corinth from the Acrocorinthus—Greece' after Major Irton came out in J. Kitto's *Gallery of scripture engravings* 1846-9. Three plates after Bartlett were done for H. Stebbing's *Christian in Palestine* [1847] and seven plates after Stanfield and Collins for Scott's *Waverley novels*. Fifteen plates were issued in the *Art Journal* between 1851 and 1866, among which were the interesting plate 'The snowstorm' after Turner (1861), where Robert very successfully tackled the indeterminate tones of snow flurries (something which is very difficult to achieve in an engraving, but better done on steel than copper) and 'Rain, steam and speed', also after Turner (1860), and later published in R. Wornum's *Turner Gallery* [c. 1878]. One of his last plates, 'Whalers' after Turner, was thought by a comtemporary to be 'a gem on which his reputation may well rest', and the description in the *Art Journal* 1863 (p. 156) is one of the most lyrical given to an engraved plate. 'Crossing the brook' after Turner, engraved in the 1830s or 1840s but never published, was regarded by others as his *magnum opus*, which to some extent is confirmed by its exhibition, together with 'The snowstorm', at the International Exhibition of 1862. The published engraving was done by W. M. Richardson, and appeared in the *Art Journal* 1862 and Wornum's *Turner Gallery* [c. 1878].

He joined the Artists' Annuity Fund in 1827 and signed the 1837 petition to the King on the admission of engravers to the Royal Academy. In 1844, he appears to have been living at Eynsford in Kent, since it was from this address that he published, jointly with J. Hogarth, *Scraps of nature*, a series of seventeen etchings of the coast and weald of Kent, one of two such volumes he issued. Two examples of these etchings were published in the *Art Journal* 1875 (p. 340). He exhibited paintings at the British Institution and Royal Academy, from

the former of which, on 'varnishing day', the Earl of Ellesmere purchased 'The Forge', an oil painting. Besides his brother Edward, he had James Clayton Bentley (q.v.) as a pupil from 1832, and his brother-in-law, Mr Floyd of Highgate, Birmingham, was probably William Floyd (q.v.), also an engraver. Another brother, John (1812-63), worked in lithography, and is especially known in connection with the design of music title pages (he joined the Artists' Annuity Fund in 1839). Robert died at his residence in Camden Hill, Kensington, on 7 January 1862, aged fifty-seven.   AJ; DNB; R; S.

Brandard, W. (fl. 1835) Landscape engraver. 'Futtypore Sicri...' after W. Purser was engraved for R. Elliot's *Views in India...* 1835, and was used again in R. M. Martin's *Indian Empire* [c. 1857] and Ball's *History of the Indian Mutiny* [c. 1858].

Brannon.

Brannon, Alfred (fl. 1840-51) Landscape and architectural engraver. He produced ten plates, dated between 1840 and 1851, published in *Brannon's Graphic delineations of... the Isle of Wight* [c. 1857].

Brannon, George (fl. 1825-67) Landscape engraver, artist and publisher. An Irishman by birth, he adopted the Isle of Wight as his province and published a number of books on it over a period of years — from Southampton in the early days and Wootton Common in the later ones. With other members of his family, he produced *Brannon's Graphic delineations of... the Isle of Wight* [c. 1857], to which he contributed seven steel engravings.

Brannon, Philip (fl. 1839-57) Landscape engraver. He contributed thirteen engravings to *Brannon's Graphic delineations of... the Isle of Wight* [c. 1857], dated between 1839 and 1857. He was also the author of guides to Poole, Southampton and Corfe Castle.

Brett, Henry (fl. 1845) Figure engraver. 'The parting word' after W. Barclay appeared in G. N. Wright's *Gallery of engravings*, volume 3, 1846.

Brice, A. (fl. 1838) Landscape engraver. 'Schoenforst' after J. Fussell was published in *Continental tourist* [1838].

Brice, R. (fl. 1838) Landscape engraver. Seven plates after J. Fussell and G. S. Shepherd appeared in *Continental tourist* [1838], including views of Namur, Liège and Linz.

Brodie, J. (fl. 1860) Landscape engraver. 'Pool of Hezekiah' appeared in M'Farlane's edition of the *Bible* 1860.

Bromley, William (1769-1842) Mezzotint engraver, but he engraved in line the frontispiece 'Hon. Horace Walpole' after J. Reynolds for Walpole's *Anecdotes of painting* 1827.

Brown, Joseph (fl. 1836-59) Portrait and sculpture engraver. One plate, 'Greville' after Mayall from *The Greville Memoirs* 1896, is signed 'Joseph Brown; others are signed 'J. Brown'. A Joseph Brown, historical and portrait engraver, joined the Artists' Annuity Fund in 1839 and exhibited from 1857 to 1886 at the Royal Academy, indicating that around 1860 he deserted engraving for painting. J. Brown engraved the Granger Society prints in the early 1840s. He engraved 'Hinda' after Stephanoff for T. Moore's *Lalla Rookh* 1838, 'The rescue' after Browne for Finden's *Tableaux...* 1840, 'Gulnare' after E. Corbould for *Heath's Book of Beauty* 1847, 'Silvia' after Wright and 'Cleopatra' after K. Meadows for *Heroines of Shakespeare* 1848 and 'H.R.H. Prince Albert' as a frontispiece to volume 10, of the *Art Union* 1848. 'The Duke of York's column' after T. H. Shepherd appeared in Dugdale's

England and Wales delineated [c.1838–9], four portraits after Hayter in the first three volumes of *The Court album* 1852–4 and 'Sir H. Pottinger' in E. H. Nolan's *Illustrated history of the British Empire in India* [1858–60]. Five plates of sculptures were contributed to the *Art Journal* between 1853 and 1859. AU; B; P.

Brown, Thomas (fl. 1871–87) Historical engraver. 'The death of the Earl of Warwick' after J. C. Houston appeared in the *Works of Shakspere* [*sic*], *Imperial edition* 1872 and in the *Art Journal* 1873. Nine portraits and three historical plates were engraved for T. Archer's *Pictures and royal portraits...* [c.1878]. Fourteen of his plates appeared in the *Art Journal* between 1871 and 1887, including 'Our pets' after E. Castan (1871), 'Feast of cherries' after Birket Foster (1876), 'Venetian fruit seller' after L. Fildes (1881) and 'Christ in the house of his parents' after Millais (1883). Much of his work was done in the contemporary 'open' style, with lines further apart, but 'Taking home the bride' after J. D. Watson (1881) was done in the manner typical of steel engraving.

Buckle, D. (fl. 1832–50) Landscape engraver. He engraved 'Bywell Hall...' and 'Ayden Castle...' after T. Allom for T. Rose's *Durham and Northumberland* 1832, 'Buttermere Lake and village...' and 'Goldrill Beck and Ullswater...' after G. Pickering for T. Rose's *Cumberland* 1832, four plates after Allom for Noble and Rose's *Counties of Chester...* 1836, 'Mont Blanc from Chamouni' and 'Lake of Brientz...' (a good example) after Bartlett for W. Beattie's *Switzerland* 1836, 'Loch Linnhe...' after Allom for Beattie's *Scotland illustrated* 1838, 'View near Kursalee' after Purser for G. F. White's *Views in India...* 1838, 'Theberton House...' after Marchant for Dugdale's *England and Wales delineated* [c.1838–9] and 'New harbour at Rhodes' after Salmon for Wright's *Shores and islands of the Mediterranean* 1840.

Bull, S. (fl. 1833–46) Historical engraver. He contributed one plate to *The Works* of W. Hogarth 1833, 'The mourners' after T. Stothard to S. C. Hall's *Book of gems* 1838, 'The royal prisoner' after J. Nash to *Friendship's offering* 1839, five plates after J. M. Wright to the *Complete works* of Robert Burns [c.1842], 'The baron's vow' after G. Cattermole to *The Keepsake* 1843 and 'Strafford's farewell' and 'Col. Pride...', both after G. Cattermole, to R. Cattermole's *Great Civil War* 1846.

Burnet, John (1784–1868) Figure and landscape engraver. He did comparatively few plates for books and worked frequently in mezzotint. 'Reedham Mill' after J. Stark was published in J. W. Robbard's *Scenery of the rivers of Norfolk* 1834, and 'Three children of Charles I' after Van Dyck appeared in the *Art Journal* 1856. AJ 1850; Ho.

Bush, R. (fl. 1838) Landscape engraver. 'The Eschenheim Gate, Frankfurt' after G. S. Shepherd appeared in *Continental tourist* [1838].

Byrne, Elizabeth (fl. 1809–49) Landscape engraver and painter. Youngest daughter and a pupil of the engraver William Byrne, she was best known for her flower and fruit engravings. Four steel engravings after J. P. Neale, were done for *Jones's Views of the seats...* 1829–31. She exhibited in London between 1838 and 1849. B; R; T.

Byrne, Letitia (1779–1849) Landscape engraver and etcher. She was born on 24 November 1779, the third daughter of William Byrne and elder sister of Elizabeth. By the time she was twenty she was exhibiting landscape views at the Royal Academy, which continued until 1848. One of her few excursions into steel engraving was 'The Pentland Hills ...' for T. H. Shepherd's *Modern Athens* 1829–31. She died on 22 May 1849, and was buried in Kensal Green cemetery. Br; DNB; R.

C

Cahusac, R. F. (fl. 1832) Map engraver. 'Plan of the latest excavations at Pompeii 1826' was engraved for W. Gell's *Pompeiana ...* 1832.

Capon, W. (fl. 1860) Landscape engraver. Known from 'Speier' after Birket Foster in J. Mayhew's *Upper Rhine* 1860. It is just possible that the plate was done by W. H. Capone (q.v.), who is known to have signed one plate 'W. H. Capon'.

Capone, William Holmes (fl. 1832–47) Landscape engraver, who probably worked in London. He joined the Artists' Annuity Fund in 1837. He engraved 'Jarrow on the Tyne...' and 'Stanhope Castle...' after T. Allom for T. Rose's *Durham and Northumberland* 1832, six plates after W. H. Bartlett for J. Carne's *Syria* 1836–8, including 'Village of Eden' (used again in J. Kitto's *Gallery of scripture engravings* 1846–9), 'Anne of Geierstein...' after F. W. Topham for Wright's *Landscape-historical illustrations of Scotland* 1836–8, four plates, including Allom's 'Interior of a Turkish Caffinet', for R. Walsh's *Constantinople* 1838–40, 'Baoli...' for Bacon's *Oriental annual* 1840, 'Reggio...' after Brockedon for Brockedon's *Italy...* 1842–3 and seven plates after Allom for Wright's *China* 1843, including 'A street in Canton'. A vignette, 'Residence and tomb of Washington', after Brooke appeared in G. N. Wright's *Gallery of engravings* 1844–6. One plate, signed 'W. H. Capon', 'Bridge over the Guill...' after Bartlett, was published in W. Beattie's *Waldenses*. B.

Carse, A. (fl. 1832) Landscape engraver. Known for 'View on the river Exe, near Exeter' after Allom in Britton and Brayley's *Devonshire and Cornwall illustrated* 1832. B.

Carter, James (1798–1855) Landscape engraver. Born in Shoreditch, the eldest surviving son of James Carter, comb maker, he was apprenticed to Tyrrel, an architectural engraver, and in 1819 was awarded a silver medal by the Society of Arts for a drawing. After serving his time, about 1820, he taught himself landscape and figure engraving,

James Carter

which characterised most of his later work, although he found his architectural experience useful when translating Prout's work. Among his earliest steel plates were two after T. H. Shepherd, dated 16 August 1828, for J. Elmes's *Metropolitan improvements* 1829, followed on 28 October 1829 by 'Sion' after Prout in Roscoe's *Tourist in Switzerland and Italy* 1830. This latter plate was used in 1872 for a new edition of Evelyn's *Diary and correspondence*. He engraved 'Saint Mark's Place, Venice' after Prout for Roscoe's *Tourist in Italy* 1831, 'Mayence cathedral' after Tombleson for *Tombleson's views of the Rhine* 1832, 'Milan' after Stanfield for Ritchie's *Travelling sketches in the north of Italy* 1832, 'Church of St. Pierre at Caen' after Prout for the *Continental annual for 1832* 'Strasbourg' and 'Rotterdam' after Stanfield for Ritchie's *Travelling sketches on the Rhine* 1833, 'Vic' after Harding for Roscoe's *Tourist in France* 1834, 'Carding...' and 'Calico printing' after Allom for E. Baines's *History of... Lancaster* 1836, four plates for Fearnside's *Tombleson's Thames* 1834, 'Gate of Justice' after Roberts for Roscoe's *Tourist in Spain. Granada* 1835, 'Tarsus' after Bartlett for J. Carne's *Syria* 1836–8, 'St. Michael's Mount...' and 'Boulogne...' for *Stanfield's coast scenery* 1836, 'Carlisle Castle...' after Richardson and 'Festival of the popinjay' after Davis for G. N. Wright's *Landscape-historical illustrations of Scotland* 1836–8, 'The castle of Doune' after Allom for Beattie's *Scotland illustrated* 1838, six plates after Bartlett, including 'Interior of St. Sophia's' (Plate 35), for J. Pardoe's *Beauties of the Bosphorus* 1840, two plates after Holland for Harrison's *Tourist in Portugal* 1839, two plates after Bartlett for Coyne's *Scenery and antiquities of Ireland* [c. 1840], two plates after Bartlett for Willis's *Canadian scenery* 1842, five plates for Brockedon's *Italy...* 1842–3, 'Judith with the head of Holofernes' after Allori for Hall's *Gems of European art* 1846, 'Verona' after Prout and 'The portrait' after Chisholm for *Forget me not* 1846, 'St. Paul's Gate, Basle' after Tombleson for Fearnside's *Picturesque beauties of the Rhine* [c. 1846] and 'Interior of the house of a Christian family in Jerusalem' after Bartlett for Stebbing's *Christian in Palestine* [1847]. He was a natural choice to be one of the leading engravers of the rejuvenated *Art Journal*, and in 1848 he began work on F. Goodall's 'The Village Festival', which was issued in 1850. This was acclaimed as one of his best works to date even though it was regarded as 'an exact copy of the original', but in the 1853 *Art Journal* he excelled himself and produced E. M. Ward's 'The South-Sea Bubble', where 'every face is an exact facsimile of the original'. (*Art Journal* 1850, p. 29; 1853, p. 16.) Two other *Art Journal* plates are 'Hadrian's Villa' after Wilson (1850) and 'Anglers nook' after Nasmyth (1853).

In 1840 he was, like so many of his fellows, unsuccessful in a publishing venture, failing to get support for a work on Windsor Castle. Weale, the architectural publisher, put some work his way, and he did plates for Stuart's *Antiquities of Athens*, Chambers's *Civil Architecture*, Gwilt's edition of Vitruvius and *Charles Martel and the Moslems*. Ackermann also employed him to do three small plates for the Queen. He engraved his own design for 'Cromwell dictating to Milton the despatch on behalf of the Waldenses' and a portrait of Sir Marc Isambard Brunel after Samuel Drummond. His last plate was a large one of E. M. Ward's 'Benjamin West's First Essay in Art' and the anxiety created by it brought on the fatal attack of 'determination of blood to the head', from which he had long suffered. He died suddenly on 23 August 1855, leaving a wife, Sarah, and seven daughters totally destitute. The poor pay of engravers was given as the reason for his inability to save sufficient funds for them to live on, and by the end of the year a subscription had been raised to help the family. His eldest daughter, Elizabeth (who later married Louis Godfrey, engraver), and fourth daughter, Sophia, went to live with James's brother John, for whom they worked. John was a flourishing manufacturer of ivory goods in Fleur de lis Street, near Bishopsgate Station. James was the usual kind-hearted, generous and conscientious man met with among engravers and some of his financial problems were probably caused by the fact that most of his hard-working life had been spent in the atelier of a master engraver (one might guess at Heath or the Findens). AJ; DNB; R.

Castles, [C?] (fl. 1831–50) Architectural and landscape engraver. 'Shirley House' after J. Fletcher appeared in Allen's *History... of Surrey and Sussex*, volume 2, 1831 and 'Llandewi Cardiganshire' after Samnol (signed 'Castel') and 'Stratford Suffolk' after De Ville in Dugdale's *England and Wales delineated* [1838–9].

Cave, Henry (1780–1836) Painter, landscape and architectural engraver. He was born at York about 1780. He executed forty-one plates for *Antiquities of York...* and is known for 'North west view of York Minster, engraved on steel by H. Cave'. He exhibited at the Royal Academy and British Institution from 1814 to 1825, and died at York on 4 August 1836. B.

Challis, Ebenezer (fl. 1831–63) Architectural and landscape engraver, specialising in interiors. Among his earliest steel plates were those after T. Allom in Britton and Brayley's *Devonshire and Cornwall illustrated* 1832, of which 'Truro Church, Cornwall' is dated 1831 and signed 'Ebenezer Challis'. Most of his later work was signed 'E. Challis'. One of his most effective engravings was 'Durham' after Allom in T. Rose's *Durham and Northumberland* 1832. In the companion volume, *Cumberland* 1832, he engraved 'Mardale Head...', also after Allom. Two plates, dated 1833, appeared in volumes 3 and 4 of E. Baines's *History of... Lancaster* 1836 and a further plate appeared in volume 2, all three after T. Allom. 'Church of St. Nizier, Lyons' after J. D. Harding, dated 28 October 1833, appeared in T. Roscoe's *Tourist in France* 1834 and 'Hall of Judgment (Granada)' after D. Roberts, dated 28 October 1834, was issued in T. Roscoe's *Tourist in Spain. Granada* 1835. 'Excavated temple of Kylas...' and 'Cootab Minar...' after Prout were engraved for R. Elliot's *Views in India...* 1835. 'Glasgow Cathedral (Lanarkshire)' (1836) after Allom appeared in volume 2 of W. Beattie's *Scotland illustrated* 1838, and five plates were engraved for R. Walsh's *Constantinople* 1838–40, again all after Allom. He engraved 'Mausoleum of Don Emanuel...' after Holland for Harrison's *Tourist in Portugal* 1839, and 'Hindoo and Mahomedan buildings' after David Roberts as the frontispiece to Emma Roberts' *Hindostan...* 1848 (Plate 44). It was in 1838 that he engraved his first plate after W. H. Bartlett—'Interior of the Great Temple at Balbec' in J. Carne's *Syria* 1836–8—and began a long association with this artist, which included 'The Citadel of Quebec' in Willis's *Canadian scenery* 1842, six plates in Beattie's *Danube* 1844, nine in Stebbing's *Christian in Palestine* [1847] and plates in Bartlett's own books, such as three in *Walks about... Jerusalem* [1844], two vignettes in *Nile boat* 1849, four vignettes in *Pictures from Sicily* 1853 and four vignettes in *Jerusalem revisited* 1854. This marks the end of his original book work, but reissues of his plates occurred in the 1836, 1842 and 1844 volumes of Fisher's *Drawing room scrap book* and in Bibles of 1860 and 1877. In 1863 two plates after Bartlett—'Winchester cathedral' and 'Porchester Castle'—

were issued in Woodward's *General history of Hampshire*. He contributed six plates to the *Art Journal* between 1849 and 1861, three after D. Roberts, one each after S. Hart and G. Jones and the last after J. M. W. Turner, 'Arch of Titus, Rome', which was reissued in R. Wornum's *Turner Gallery* [c. 1878]. He also engraved an almost unbroken series of plates depicting buildings and interiors for the Cambridge University Almanack from 1832 to 1847, where large plates (about 16 by 10 inches) were engraved, probably on steel, for this annual publication. From 1833 to 1837 he engraved his own designs but from 1840 most of the drawings were by G. Dodgson. The plate for 1841, 'Clare Hall', was mis-signed 'Edwd. Challis'. He began to paint about 1846 and from this time until 1863 he is recorded as exhibiting at the Royal Academy and Suffolk Street. B; T.

Chapman, William (fl. 1842–73) Landscape engraver, said to have worked in York and afterwards in London. He is first known for 'Melrose Abbey', dated 1 September 1842, after W. H. Townsend in *Black's picturesque tourist of Scotland* 1849. Six plates were published in the *Art Journal* between 1868 and 1873. 'Carreg-Cennan Castle—Llandilo' after D. Cox and 'Entrance to Portsmouth Harbour' after Stanfield in the 1868 volume were poorly engraved but 'Stormy Sunset' after H. Dawson the following year showed some improvement. The 1870 volume included 'Norham Castle' after Turner and a circular engraving, 'On the Yorkshire coast', after J. B. Pyne. The final contribution, in 1873, was 'Scarborough' after Turner, which showed the latter-day Continental fondness for coarse engraving and cross-hatching, far removed from the careful approach of traditional steel engraving. He exhibited at the Royal Academy in 1866–9. B; T.

Chavanne, E. ('Chavane', 'Chavan' and 'Charan' are alternative spellings found on plates) (fl. 1833–51) Landscape and figure engraver. 'Hymen and Cupid' and an impression from a silver tankard designed and engraved by W. Hogarth appeared in the latter's *Works* 1833. 'Near Woking, Surrey' after Beattie was published in Dugdale's *England and Wales delineated* [1838–9], and seven plates of the interior of the Crystal Palace after Read, T. H. Shepherd and the engraver were done for *Remembrances of the Great Exhibition* [1851].

Chevalier, William (fl. 1833–51) Landscape and figure engraver. He first came into prominence with the eight plates, published between 1 March 1833 and 15 August 1834, which appeared in the two volumes of Allan Cunningham's *Cabinet gallery of pictures by the first masters* ... 1836. They included landscapes after Cuyp, Berghem, Hondekoeter and Both, 'A Dutch Village' after Ruysdael, 'The Young bull' after Potter and 'The trumpeter' after Terburg. 'Taking possession' after Sir John Ross was done for the artist's *Narrative of a second voyage* ... 1835, and for *Stanfield's coast scenery* 1836, he engraved 'Arched Rock...' (Plate 26), to be followed by two vignettes for Hall's *Book of gems* 1836 'Worship of the lyre' after J. Wood and 'L'Allegro and il penseroso' after M'Clise. He engraved plates for *The Keepsake*, notably 'The spirit of the Wye' after Stephanoff (1835), 'Count Rodolph's heir' after Leslie and 'The artist's love' after Stephanoff (1836) and 'The bride' after Parris (1837). He also did a version of Leonardo da Vinci's 'Last Supper' which appeared in Fisher's *Historic illustrations of the Bible*, 3rd series, 1842. By the 1840s he had turned to work for the printsellers after a difficult experience with a plate for the Art Union of London. In 1841 he was engaged to engrave 'The Saints' day' after J. P. Knight, to be ready for printing in March 1842, but

when in November of that year it was still unfinished, a public rebuke was printed in the *Art Union* 1842 (p. 262). Impressions were eventually ready by 9 May 1843 after Geo. Barclay had successfully electrotyped the plate. 'Boy with game' after Landseer was published by Boys in 1844 and 'Naomi and her two daughters-in-law' after O'Neil by Graves in 1847, and he also engraved 'The first ear ring' after Wilkie and 'The falconer's son' after E. Landseer. One of his last plates was 'Intemperance' after Stothard, which appeared in the *Art Journal* 1851. AU; T.

Clark, J. (fl. 1846) Architectural engraver. Known from 'Town Hall, Cologne' after W. Tombleson in Fearnside's *Picturesque beauties of the Rhine* [c. 1846].

Clark, Thomas (fl. 1832–51) Landscape and architectural engraver. 'The tower at Oberwesel' after Tombleson on the engraved title page of *Tombleson's views of the Rhine* by Fearnside was issued in 1832, and 'Basle' after Tombleson appeared in Fearnside's *Picturesque beauties of the Rhine* [c. 1846]. Thirteen plates after R. W. Billings, J. R. Thompson and T. Clark, dated between January and September 1835, were published in E. W. Brayley and J. Britton's *History of the ancient palace ... at Westminster* 1836, and at least one plate of Carlisle cathedral after Billings was done for the artist's *Architectural illustrations of Carlisle cathedral* 1840. 'Boston Church...', 'Grantham market place...', 'Castle of the Peverils in the Peak...' and 'Rutland Cavern, near Matlock...' after T. Allom were engraved for T. Noble and T. Rose's *Counties of Chester* ... 1836. Two interiors of the Crystal Palace were engraved for *Remembrances of the Great Exhibition* [1851]. A. T. Clark, of 42 Pratt Place, Camden Town, was awarded the Large Silver medal of the Society of Arts for an engraving of Chichester Cross in 1831. SocA.

Clayton, C. and P. (fl. 1862) A firm of publishers and engravers of 150 Fleet Street, London. 'Building for the International Exhibition of 1862, West front view' was a published vignette after T. Boys.

Cleghorn, John (fl. 1827–80) Architectural engraver. He appears to have begun work as an engraver, but as commissions became scarcer in the 1840s he turned to landscape painting and wood carving, exhibiting in London from about 1840 to 1880. His earliest steel engraving was done on four plates, dated between 7 July 1827 and 5 July 1828, for J. Elmes's *Metropolitan improvements* 1829, all after Thomas H. Shepherd, followed by two plates of the new churches at Margate and Ramsgate after G. Shepherd for S. W. H. Ireland's *England's topographer* (commenced publication 1828). Four plates, dated 1830, were engraved for Knight's *Paris* ... 1831, and plans of four cathedrals after his own designs were done for volume 1 of *Winkles's ... Cathedral churches of England* ..., by Moule, 1836. 'Interior of Roslyn Chapel' after Allom appeared in Beattie's *Scotland illustrated* 1838 and 'Hall at Branksome' after Nixon, dated 1835, in Scott's *Lay of the last minstrel* 1839. The last of his book work was views of two Cologne churches, one after Tombleson for Fearnside's *Picturesque beauties of the Rhine* [c. 1846]. A page of 'Episcopal seals' appeared in B. Woodward's *General history of Hampshire* 1863. He engraved ten bookplates between 1840 and 1860. What appears to have been a book from his collection was sold in 1978. This had his name and the date 1830 on the title page, and was Barraud's *New book of single cyphers*, all the plates of which were dated 1782. B; Fi; T.

Cleghorn, T. (fl. 1829–31) Architectural engraver. Known from 'Burlington House, Piccadilly' after Thomas H.

Shepherd in Shepherd's *London and its environs* 1829–31. It is just possible that the initial was mistaken by the writing engraver for 'J'.

Cochran, John (fl. 1821–65) Portrait engraver and miniaturist. He exhibited portraits at the Royal Academy and Suffolk Street 1821 and 1827, from which date he devoted most of his time to engraving. 'The favorite dove' after Miss M. Chalon appeared in the *Literary souvenir* [1826] and some plates in Whittaker's *La belle assemblée* 1827. 'Baboo' after Miss J. Drummond was done for R. Elliot's *Views in India ...* 1835 and thirty-six portraits for the second edition of Lodge's *Portraits ...* 1835. Some plates appeared in *The Methodist Magazine* and the *English annual*, and some were done for Jerdan's *National Portrait Gallery* 1830–4. Six portraits, dated between 1833 and 1836, appeared in Baines's *History of ... Lancaster* 1836, including a portrait of the author after Hargraves, 'Sir Robert Peel' after Lawrence and 'Henry Fisher' after H. Moses. This was followed by 'A Mahomedan at prayers' after W. Daniell, dated 1 October 1836, for Caunter's *Lives of the Moghul emperors* 1837, three vignette portraits for Wilson and Chambers's *Land of Burns* 1840, 'Akbar Shah, 2nd emperor of Delhi' for Bacon's *Oriental annual* 1840, 'Reverie' after W. Drummond as the frontispiece to *Forget me not* for 1846 and 'The young cavalier' after W. Salter for Hall's *Gems of European art* 1846. Twelve of his plates appeared in Wright's *Gallery of engravings* 1844–6, among them 'Victoria R at the age of 18' after Hayter, 'Culzean Castle, Ayrshire...' after W. Daniell and 'Rt. Hon. J. G. Lambton...' after Lawrence, the last two being signed 'J. Cochrane'. Other books which contain Cochran's engravings include Burke's *Gallery of distinguished females*, Locker's *Naval Commanders* and Pettigrew's *Medical portrait gallery* 1839. He joined the Artists' Annuity Fund in 1826. B; T.

Cook, Charles (fl. 1860–75) Portrait engraver. Nine portraits appeared in the *Imperial dictionary of universal biography* [c. 1861], including Mendelssohn after Leighton, Macaulay after a photograph and Raimondi after Raphael. Four plates, with ornamental borders by Luke Limner, were done for *The Self-interpreting Bible* 1864, and a portrait of John Knox appeared in the second edition of Chambers's *Biographical dictionary of eminent Scotsmen* 1875. T.

Cook, Conrad (fl. 1830–50) Portrait and figure engraver. 'The arrest' after Johannot, dated November 1830, appeared in the *Literary souvenir* 1832. T.

Cook, George (fl. 1854–60) Portrait and figure engraver. 'The crucifixion' and 'Praise ye the Lord' were engraved for the *Book of Common Prayer* 1854, and portraits of Alfred the Great after Warren, Bach after Sichlong and Bacon after Houbraken and 'Moses delivering the law' after Warren appeared in the *Imperial dictionary of universal biography* [c. 1861].

Cook, Henry (fl. 1813–47) Portrait and figure engraver. The earliest plate signed 'Henry Cook' is said to have appeared in *The Military Chronicle* 1 October 1813. Further plates seem to have been done for the *Lady's Monthly Magazine* 1819. He first used steel in the 1830s, when his earliest plate, 'James Brindley' after F. Parsons, dated 1832, appeared in Baines's *History of ... Lancaster* 1836. Several plates were engraved for Bell's *Court Magazine* 1833, among which may be noted that of Miss Maria Millicent Barton after Holmes in no. 16 for October 1833. 'Diana Vernon' after J. W. Wright, dated November 1834, graced the 1835 volume of the *Literary souvenir* and 'The Jew's harp' after D. Maclise, dated 1836,

came out in Ritchie's *Ireland ...* 1837. Two plates were done for Heath's *Book of beauty* 1835, of which 'Mrs. Knowlys' was an attractive picture. Further plates were done for *The Keepsake* for 1835, 1837 and 1838, three for *Friendship's offering* 1839 and five for Fisher's *Drawing room scrap book* 1842. A portrait, 'His Majesty Ernest Augustus, King of Hanover', after G. I. Saunders was published by Fisher in 1837 and was signed 'H. B. Cook'. Vignette portraits appeared in Maxwell's *Life of ... the Duke of Wellington* 1839–41 and Wilson and Chamber's *Land of Burns* 1840, the frontispiece to which was an engraving of a statue of Burns after J. Irvine. Saunders' *Political reformers* 1840 also carried some of his plates. In 1844 four portraits after Maclise appeared in Hall's *Sketches of Irish character*, and seven Biblical subjects after the Old Masters were engraved for a Bible, and were used again in the *Imperial Family Bible* 1873. Fourteen plates appeared in Wright's *Gallery of engravings* 1844–6, after J. Brown, W. Perring, J. Bostock, H. H. Pickersgill, jun., Sir W. C. Ross and H. Dawe. 'Love's inquest' in volume 1 is a vignette after J. Brown. Finally, the *Art Union* carried an engraving of a statue, 'Maternal love', by Baily in 1847, the engraver's reduction of which was done by H. Corbould. Plates are usually signed 'H. Cook' or 'H. R. Cook'. B; T.

Cook, J. W. (fl. 1827–55) Portrait engraver. 'Roubiliac' after Carpentiers, 'William Kent' after Aikman and eight medallion portraits of early masters after Lewis appeared in Walpole's *Anecdotes of painting* 1827. Engraved title pages and presentation plates after H. Corbould were done for *Friendship's offering* 1831, 1833, 1837 and 1839 (the 1833 volume also contained 'The Highland huntsman' after Hayes), 'Revd Matthew Henry' for *A new family Bible ...* [c. 1840], 'The lyrist' after Haines for *Wreath of friendship* [c. 1850] and 'Jacob's covenant with Laban' after Schnorr for *The Pictorial Bible* 1855.

Cooke, T. (fl. 1833) Figure engraver. 'Henry VIII and Anna Boleyne' after W. Hogarth appeared in Hogarth's *Works* 1833.

Cooke, William Bernard (1778–1855) Landscape engraver. The Cooke family originated in the free city of Frankfurt-am-Main, where the father was burgomaster. (When he came to London, he set up as a wholesale manufacturer of confectionery.) The two sons were both engravers, the elder of whom was William Bernard, apprenticed to William Angus (d. 12 October 1821, aged sixty-nine), and the younger was George, apprenticed at the age of fourteen to James Basire in 1795. In their early days, they collaborated to publish several volumes illustrated by their own line engravings on copper, notably *Views on the Thames* with seventy-five plates, *Southern coast of England*, the text by W. Combe and Mrs Hofland, with forty-eight views and thirty-two vignettes, begun in 1813 and completed 1826, and, with J. C. Allen, *Views on the River Rhone* with twenty-four engravings.

William undertook some publications on his own, notably *Cooke's Eastern and western coasts of England* with eighty plates and forty vignettes and T. L. Donaldson's *Pompeii* 1827, the ninety engravings in which took him eight years' hard work to complete. His book work in steel does not appear to have been extensive. It commenced with his *Gems of art* 1827. His best plates were the marine views done after W. C. Stanfield for *Stanfield's coast scenery* 1836, namely 'Stonehouse Bridge, Plymouth', 'Martello Tower', 'Dieppe' and 'Eddystone Light-house'. One plate after W. H. Bartlett, 'Baths of St. Gervais' (1835), was issued in Beattie's

Switzerland 1836, and nine plates of views in Rome after W. L. Leitch and Col. Cockburn appeared in Costello's *Piedmont and Italy* [c. 1855]. Three plates after W. L. Leitch were done for Adams's *History ... of the Isle of Wight* 1858, five views of Sussex after J. M. W. Turner were published by Virtue and Company in the *Art Journal* of 1865 and *Beauties of Claude Lorraine* contained twenty-four landscapes engraved on steel. He was also connected with Turner and Girtin's *River Scenery*, with text by Mrs Hofland and containing mezzotints on steel. Much of his work was done in conjunction with the publisher John Murray, at whose London offices a series of letters from about 1813 can be seen referring to his negotiations and projects. In 1822 Cooke held the first of three annual exhibitions of prints, drawings etc. at his publishing house at 9 Soho Square, at the second of which, in January 1823, the public at large was introduced, probably for the first time, to steel mezzotints by T. G. Lupton and C. Turner. (Copies of the catalogues are in the William Smith bequest at the Victoria and Albert Museum.) He was a trustee of the Artists' Annuity Fund, of which he was a founder member. There is no mention of his having married or having had a family. (His brother George was father to Edward William Cooke, R.A.) He died of heart disease at Camberwell on 2 August 1855, aged seventy-seven.   AJ; B; DNB; T.

Cooke, William John (1797–1865) Landscape engraver. Born in Dublin on 11 April 1797, his parents left Ireland for London in the following year. Apart from a reference in Benezit to his being educated by his Uncle George, there is no mention of a connection with the family of William Bernard Cooke, and only then if one assumes that George Cooke the engraver was the person in question. He was one of the first engravers to become interested in the possibilities of steel engraving, and on 21 December 1825, he submitted a paper to the Society of Arts on the etching of steel plates. In it, he gave detailed instructions on plate preparation, and illustrated a device comprising a stick inside a funnel, by means of which a controlled flow of acid could be directed upon skies and other tints needing a gradated etching. These processes were performed on tinted steel plates in the presence of the Committee of Polite Arts to their entire satisfaction, and to that of several engravers who were specially invited to witness them. For this, the Society awarded him the Gold Isis medal. (Society of Arts *Transactions*, vol. 44, 1826, pp. 48–52.) His address was given as 5 Seymour Street North, Clarendon Square, 'The cascade of Tivoli' after Henning was done for the *Literary souvenir* [1826] and five plates after Whittock appeared in Allen's *New ... history of the county of York* 1828–31. Two plates after Whittock were done for Allen's *History of ... Surrey and Sussex* 1829–31, the frontispiece to Rose's *Westmorland* 1832 after G. Pickering, a vignette of Newark Castle after Turner for Scott's *Poetical works* 1833, three after Purser, Boys and Prout for Elliot's *Views in India ...* 1835, two after Melville and Stanfield for White's *Views in India ...* 1838, and four plates appeared in Walsh's *Constantinople* 1838–40. Among his other works were engravings published in Beattie's *Switzerland* 1836 and Carne's *Syria* 1836–8 after W. H. Bartlett, 'Portsmouth harbour' after Stanfield in *Stanfield's coast scenery* 1836, five plates in Hall's *Book of Gems* 1836, of which 'Thames at Mortlake' was after Turner, two plates of Arundel Castle after C. B. Ottley in Tierney's *History of Arundel* 1834, 'Near Buxaduniar, Bootan' after W. Daniell in Caunter's *Lives of the Moghul emperors* 1837, 'Storming of Cuidad Rodrigo' after G. B. Campion in Maxwell's *Life of ... the Duke of Wellington* 1839–41 and 'Ephesus...' after Allom

in Kitto's *Gallery of scripture engravings* 1846–9. In 1840 he moved to Darmstadt, where he died in 1865. He joined the Artists' Annuity Fund in 1823.   B; Br; SocA.

Cooper, R. (fl. 1823–7) Portrait engraver. A portrait of Mrs Unwin after Devis, dated 30 December 1823, the frontispiece to volume 2 of Cowper's *Private correspondence* 1824, was possibly executed on steel, and for H. Walpole's *Anecdotes of painting* 1827 he did the portraits 'Sir Antonio More' and 'Isaac Oliver' after Seipse, 'Sir Nathaniel Bacon' after W. Bone and 'Nicholas Laniere' after Lievens.

Corbould, George James (1786–1846). Historical engraver. Born on 27 April 1786, the second son of Richard Corbould, a portrait painter, he entered the Royal Academy in 1801 his entry piece being a portrait of a lady. He was a pupil of James Heath, and in 1806 began his book illustration work in the works of Ossian and Dryden. He engraved a plate for Ottley's *Engravings of the ... Marquis of Stafford's ... pictures* 1818, and contributed to the edition of Gray's *Poetical works* published by Sharpe with a vignette after Richard Westall, 'Progress of poesy', dated 1 December 1820. He also worked on plates for the edition of Shakespeare illustrated by R. Smirke, 1821. Among the earliest engravings on steel were the four plates he did for *Forget me not* 1825, i.e. 'The dying soldier' after Thomas Uwins and 'The royal nuptials', 'Ademdai' and 'Sacontala' after Henry Corbould. He died on 5 November 1846.   R; T.

Corbould, R[ichard?]. (fl. 1831) Figure engraver. 'L'âne et les reliques' after Le Prince appeared in *Keepsake français* 1831.

Court, I. (fl. 1830–1) Landscape engraver. 'Sundorne Castle, Shropshire' and 'Apley Park, Shropshire' after I. Jones were engraved for West's *Picturesque views ... in Staffordshire and Shropshire ...* 1830–1.

Cousen, Charles (1813?–1889) Landscape engraver. Born in Bradford, the younger brother of John Cousen (q.v.), there is considerable confusion over his date of birth. Slater gives 1805 and Thieme and Becker 1819, but the *Bradford Antiquary* (vol. 2, p. 204) gives 1813, which, in the light of the fact that his earliest known book work is dated 1836, seems to be the most likely. Extensive searches undertaken in local parish and other records have failed to confirm this evidence. He was taught engraving by his brother, and Thieme and Becker indicate that he was a pupil of the Findens. Other sources do not mention this. The majority of his book work was done after W. H. Bartlett, very often as attractive vignettes, over a period of about thirty years. Examples are 'Junction of the Rhine and Tamina...' in W. Beattie's *Switzerland* 1836, three plates (with one by T. Allom) in the same author's *Scotland illustrated* 1838, two plates in Beattie's *Waldenses* 1838, eight in Willis's *American scenery* 1840, including 'Albany' (an outstanding plate), six in Coyne's *Scenery and antiquities of Ireland* [c. 1840] and 'Fort Beil-Gorod' in Pardoe's *Beauties of the Bosphorus* 1840. Plates after Bartlett also appeared in Willis's *Canadian scenery* 1842 (ten plates), in Beattie's *Danube* 1844 (five plates), in the same author's *Castles and abbeys of England* 1845–51 (three plates), and in Stebbing's *Christian in Palestine* [1847] (ten plates), and for the artist's own books, Cousen engraved four plates in *Walks about ... Jerusalem* [1844], four vignettes in *Forty days in the desert* 1848, five in *Nile boat* 1849, 'View from Mount Hor' in *Scripture sites ... and scenes ...* 1849, six plates in *Footsteps of Our Lord* 1851, four in *Gleanings ... on the overland route* 1851, five in *The Pilgrim Fathers* 1853, seven in

Pictures from Sicily 1853 and seven in *Jerusalem revisited* 1854. 'The cottage door' after T. Gainsborough' and 'Scene on the River Nile...' and 'Petra...' after Bartlett appeared in S.C. Hall's *Gems of European art* 1846 and 'A group of camels at Smyrna' and 'The hooka-badar' after Wilkie in the *Wilkie Gallery* [c.1849]. 'Mount Casius...' and 'Larneca' after Bartlett and 'Antioch of Pisidia' and 'Konieh ... after Laborde appeared in Conybeare and Howson's *Life and epistles of St. Paul* 1854, four plates after Bartlett, Vacher and Brockedon in Costello's *Piedmont and Italy* [c.1855], two vignettes in Nolan's *Illustrated history of the British Empire in India* [1858–60], three plates after Bartlett in M'Farlane's edition of the *Bible* 1860, two plates after Bartlett, and 'Norris Castle' and 'Black gang chine', vignettes after Cousen's designs, in B. Woodward's *General history of Hampshire* 1863. 'Annan from the bridge' after C. Stanfield was done for Scott's *Waverley novels*, 'Touchstone and Audrey' after J. Pettie and 'Ophelia' after A. Hughes appeared in the *Works of Shakspere* [sic] *Imperial edition* 1872 and five plates after Chevalier and Skinner Prout were engraved for Booth's *Australia* [1873–6]. Fifty-nine plates appeared in the *Art Journal* between 1850 and 1888, including 'Bacchus and Ariadne' after Turner (1860), 'Venice—the arrival' after E.W. Cooke (1868), 'Tintern Abbey—moonlight on the Wye' after B.W. Leader (1875) and 'Catching a mermaid' after J.C. Hook (1888). Those produced in the mid 1870s showed a move towards Continental practice, being more heavily etched, but in 1879 he returned to his former style, and considering that he was probably seventy-six when he engraved his last plate, his skill was remarkable. Four plates appeared in R.W. Wornum's *Turner Gallery* [c.1878], including 'Abingdon, Berkshire', 'The Loretto necklace' and 'The opening of Valhalla'. He must have worked for Virtue full time for the latter part of his life, since when he died in November 1889, the *Art Journal* obituary mourned the 'death at an advanced age of an old and valued member of the *Art Journal* staff'. In his younger days he painted a few pictures and exhibited in 1848 at the Society of British Artists. AJ; Br; H; S; T.

Cousen, John (1804–80) Landscape engraver. Born at Mira Shay, an estate near Tewit Hall and Bradford Moor, to the north-west of Bradford on 19 February 1804, he was apprenticed to the animal engraver John Scott (1774–1828) in London about 1818, but his master suffered a paralytic stroke in 1821 before John had finished his indentures. His time would have been up about 1825, by when his preference for landscape engraving was firmly established, and he soon took his place as one of 'Turner's engravers', notably in the *Rivers of France*. Thieme and Becker indicate that he was a pupil of the Findens, a statement unsupported by other sources. His earliest steel plate was probably 'Val d'Ossola (November 1828) after W. Brockedon for the latter's *Illustrations of the passes of the Alps* 1828–9, followed by two plates after J.D. Harding and two after C. Stanfield for *Finden's illustrations of the life and works of Lord Byron* 1833–4, 'Cologne' after C. Stanfield for L. Ritchie's *Travelling sketches on the Rhine* 1833 and 'Fécamp' (a good example) and 'View near Havre' after Stanfield for Ritchie's *Travelling sketches on the sea coasts of France* 1834. 'Approach to Thiers' and 'Château de Villeneuve' after J.D. Harding were published in T. Roscoe's *Tourist in France* 1834. 'Ronda' after D. Roberts was done for Roscoe's *Tourist in Spain*. *Granada* 1835 and 'Victory. Dismasted in a gale ...' (a good plate) (Plate 22) and 'Victory finally stopped by ice' after Sir John Ross for his *Narrative of a second voyage ...* 1835. 'The storm'

after Stanfield was engraved for *The Keepsake* 1834, and for the 1836 volume he did 'The raft', a vignette after Vickers. 'Château Gaillard' (an engraved title page vignette) and 'Bridge of Meulan' after J.M.W. Turner appeared in L. Ritchie's *Wanderings by the Seine* 1835. Five plates after W.H. Bartlett were engraved for Beattie's *Switzerland* 1836 and two after W. Daniell for J. Caunter's *Lives of the Moghul emperors* 1837. 'Djouni...' after Bartlett appeared in J. Carne's *Syria* 1836–8. Eight plates after Bartlett, Allom, G.B. Campion and H. McCulloch were engraved for Beattie's *Scotland illustrated* 1838 and 'Constantinople' after Allom and 'Joannina, the capital of Albania' after W.L. Leitch for R. Walsh's *Constantinople* 1838–40. Two plates were done after Turner for White's *Views in India ...* 1838, two for Beattie's *Waldenses* 1838, after Bartlett and Brockedon, and two after Holland for Harrison's *Tourist in Portugal* 1839. 'Falmouth from the mills' 'Falmouth' and 'Britany' (sic) after C. Stanfield were engraved for *Stanfield's coast scenery* 1836 and 'The village churchyard', a vignette, after T. Creswick for S.C. Hall's *Book of gems* 1836–8. Five plates after Bartlett appeared in J. Pardoe's *Beauties of the Bosphorus* 1840. Seven plates after Bartlett were engraved for N.P. Willis's *American scenery* 1840, eight after the same artist for J.S. Coyne's *Scenery and antiquities of Ireland* [c.1840], and 'Maryport pier' after Bartlett for Beattie's *Ports, harbours ...* 1842. 'The temptation on the mountain', a vignette after Turner, was engraved for Milton's *Poetical works* 1835 and eleven plates after Bartlett were done for Willis's *Canadian scenery* 1842, including the engraved title page vignettes. Nine engravings after W. Leitch, J.D. Harding and W. Brockedon appeared in the latter's *Italy ...* 1842–3. 'The birth-place of Burns' after T. Creswick was done for the *Complete works of Robert Burns* [c.1842], two vignettes of Pembroke Castle after Bartlett for Beattie's *Castles and abbeys of England* 1845–51, 'Castle of Durrenstein...' and three others after Bartlett for Beattie's *Danube* 1844 and 'Day after the wreck' after C. Stanfield, dated 1847, for Finden's *Royal Gallery of British art* 1838–49. Eight plates after Bartlett were done for Stebbing's *Christian in Palestine* [1847], and for Bartlett's own works he did 'Pool of Siloam' for *Walks about ... Jerusalem* [1844], three vignettes for *Forty days in the desert* 1848, two vignettes for *Nile boat* 1849, six vignettes for *Footsteps of Our Lord* 1851, three vignettes for *Gleanings ... on the overland route* 1851, four vignettes for *Pictures from Sicily* 1853 and five vignettes for *The Pilgrim fathers* 1853. 'The wayside fountain' after N. Bergham and 'The noonday rest' after A. Cuyp were engraved for S.C. Hall's *Gems of European art* 1846. The engraved title page, showing 'Manse and church of Cutts, birthplace of Wilkie' after D. Kennedy, and 'Group of figures entering Madrid' after Wilkie appeared in *Wilkie gallery* [c.1849], two vignettes—'The magic fountain' and 'The terrace garden' (a good plate)—after G. Cattermole in Calabrella's *Evenings at Haddon Hall* 1845, 'Taymouth' after D.O Hill in *Black's picturesque tourist of Scotland* 1849 and three engravings after Bartlett in Conybeare and Howson's *Life and epistles of St. Paul* 1854. Seven plates after Stanfield, J. Leitch, Roberts and Creswick were done for Scott's *Waverley novels*, and he did six plates for J. Ruskin's *Modern painters* 1856–60, including 'Dutch leafage' and 'Rending of leaves'. 'Ryde...' appeared in Adams's *History ... of the Isle of Wight* 1858, and two vignettes after Bartlett in B. Woodward's *General history of Hampshire* 1863. He engraved thirty-two plates which appeared in the *Art Journal* between 1849 and 1866, including 'Peace' after E. Landseer (1854) (in which Cousen did the animals and L. Stocks (q.v.) the figures) and 'Peace—the burial of Wilkie' (1860) and

'Petworth Park' (1863) after J.M.W. Turner. His last engraving in this series, 'Evening in the meadows' after F.R. Lee (in which the cattle were done by T.S. Cooper), signalled the end of his career as an engraver, due to ill health, caused by overwork. He is known to have engraved only three large plates, i.e. 'Mercury and Herse' after Turner and 'Towing the Victory into Gibraltar' and 'Morning after the wreck' after Stanfield. He exhibited at the Royal Academy in 1863 and 1864. He died in South Norwood on 26 December 1880, aged seventy-six. AJ; DNB; H; T.

Cousins, J. (fl. 1833–6) Landscape engraver. In Ritchie's *Travelling sketches on the Rhine* 1833, appeared 'Coblence, from Ehrenbreitstein' after Clarkson Stanfield. For *Finden's illustrations of the life and works of Lord Byron* 1833–4, he engraved 'The Acropolis, Athens' after Turner from a sketch by T. Allison and for Beattie's *Switzerland* 1836, 'Ouchy, Lake of Geneva' after W.H. Bartlett (1834), also issued in Costello's *Piedmont and Italy* [c. 1855], as 'Ouchy, the port of Lausanne'.

Cowan, T. (fl. 1870) Figure engraver. Eighteen subjects, including 'Jonah cast into the sea', which depicted a magnificent ship, were engraved for the *Universal Family Bible*, published in Southampton about 1870. The format was a uniform curved top inside a rectangular frame, and only in three cases was an artist named, viz., de la Roche, Fraser and Martin.

Cox, J. (fl. 1834–46) Landscape engraver. Two plates are known, both after William Tombleson. 'View near Battersea, Surry' (*sic*) appeared in W.G. Fearnside's *Tombleson's Thames* 1834 and 'Ruins of Stolzenfels' in Fearnside's *Picturesque beauties of the Rhine* [c. 1846].

Cox, T. (fl. 1846–50) Landscape and architectural engraver. 'Ruins of Godesberg' after William Tombleson was engraved for W.G. Fearnside's *Picturesque beauties of the Rhine* [c. 1846] and 'Gate House, Highgate, Middlesex' after J. Henshall appeared in Fearnside and Harral's *History of London* [c. 1850].

Crew, John J. (fl. 1858–80) Landscape, architectural and portrait engraver, one of the last of the steel engravers. Three vignettes after designs by Crew himself and M.A. Hayes were done for Nolan's *Illustrated history of the British Empire in India* [1858–60], two vignettes of Lymington ad Petersfield after J.C. Armytage for Woodward's *General history of Hampshire* 1863, seven plates after Armytage, Baines, Carr and photographs for Booth's *Australia* [1873–6], including a title page vignette to volume 1, seven plates for *Picturesque Europe* 1876–9 (five after L.J. Wood, one after Werner and 'Orta' after Birket Foster) and five for Archer's *Pictures and royal portraits* ... [c. 1878], including 'Nelson boarding the "San Josef"...' after George Jones (Plate 58). Frontispieces for two volumes of *Casquet of literature* 1874–80, comprising portraits from photographs of six literary personalities, were engraved with W. Roffe (q.v.).

Croll, Francis (1827–1854) Portrait and figure engraver in Edinburgh, where he was born. He was articled probably about 1841 to Thomas Dobbie (q.v.), whose lack of engraving commissions resulted in his pupil receiving better instruction in drawing than engraving. When Dobbie died about 1846, Croll finished his time with Robert Charles Bell, with whom he stayed for two years, becoming a competent engraver. He then attended Sir William Allan's classes at the Trustees' Academy, which gave him greater facility in portraiture, as a result of which he engraved a number of portraits for the Edinburgh publishers. In 1852 his engraving the 'Tired soldier' after F. Goodall was issued in the *Art Journal*, and after this he was employed as one of a team of engravers to provide plates from 'The Cottar's Saturday night' after J. Faed for the Scottish Association for the Encouragement of Art. While engraving one of these plates he had the first of his heart attacks, which rapidly took their toll, and on 12 February 1854 he died at the early age of twenty-seven. Contemporaries estimated that he had considerable promise as an engraver and would have risen to eminence in a short time. AJ.

Crostick, T. (fl. 1828) Architectural engraver. Known from 'Fonthill' after J.M.W. Turner (dated 1 October 1828 and done for *The Anniversary* 1829), of which the greater part was etched.

Cruse, A. (fl. 1829–38) Landscape and architectural engraver. Seven plates were done for Shepherd's *London and its environs* 1829–31 after Thomas H. Shepherd and four for the same author's *Modern Athens* 1829–31. Five plates after William Tombleson were engraved for *Tombleson's views of the Rhine* 1832 (three engravings) and *Tombleson's Upper Rhine* [c. 1835] (two plates). Views in Brussels and Liège after J. Fussell appeared in *Continental tourist* [1838].

Cuff, R.P. (fl. 1850–60) Landscape engraver. He engraved seventeen (possibly nineteen) plates for Ruskin's *Stones of Venice*, first published 1851–3, all after the author's own designs. Two plates were signed 'R.E. Cuff', probably in error. He also did sixteen plates for volumes 3, 4 and 5 of Ruskin's *Modern painters* 1856–60, most of which were after the author's drawings, which were specially executed studies of foliage, etc., to illustrate his text. Ruskin adapted Turner's 'Castle of Rauffen' for the last plate in volume 5, and 'Dryad's waywardness' was printed in violet, a rare example of printing steel engravings in a colour instead of the usual black.

Cuff, (fl. 1845) Landscape engraver. Known from 'Ancient carvings ...' after T. Allom in E.W. Brayley's *Topographical history of Surrey* 1841–8. An engraver Cuff engraved a bookplate in 1850. Fi.

Cutten, (fl. 1832) Landscape engraver. 'St. Clementius Place at Coblenz' after W. Tombleson appeared in *Tombleson's views of the Rhine* 1832.

D

Dale, Thomas (fl. 1827–8) Architectural engraver. Nine plates after Thomas H. Shepherd, dated between March 1827 and April 1828, appeared in Elmes's *Metropolitan improvements* 1829, and included engravings of 'Whittington's alms-houses, Highgate', 'College of the Church Missionary Society', 'Regent's Quadrant' (signed 'Thos. Dale') and 'Theatre Royal, Drury Lane'. A portrait of a Thomas Dale (1797–1870) appeared in the *Drawing room portrait gallery* 1860 (ser. 4:9), engraved by D.J. Pound after a photograph. This may be the same person.

Danforth, Moseley Isaac (1800–62) American engraver, primarily of banknotes. He was born on 11 December 1800 in Hartford, Connecticut. At the age of seventeen he learnt engraving from Asaph Willard of the Hartford Graphic Company. When he was twenty-one he set up on his own at New Haven (Conn.) and later, moving to New York, became a founder member of the National Academy of Design. In 1827 he arrived in London to study at the Royal Academy, and his reputation as a water-colourist was enhanced by copies of Titian and Veronese, which were much admired, as were his drawings of the Elgin marbles, Among his plates engraved for the *Literary souvenir* were the portrait of Sir Walter Scott after Leslie in the 1829 volume, which was said to have sold 14,000 copies, 'A portrait', also after Leslie, for the 1830 volume and the title page vignette and 'The deserted' after Newton for the 1835 volume. He also did 'Don Quixote', and for Sterne's *Tristram Shandy*, 'The sentry box' after Leslie, considered by some to be his best plate. After ten years in Britain he returned, in 1837, to the United States, where he married a widow and established in about 1850, a company to undertake banknote engraving, Danforth, Underwood & Co., which, in due course, merged with the American Bank Note Company, of which he was vice-president until his death on 19 January 1862. DAB; T.

Darnill, Thomas F. (fl. 1841) Landscape engraver. 'Sutton Place...' after Thompson and 'Lyne...' after Allom were engraved in 1841 for Brayley's *Topographical history of Surrey* 1841–8.

Davenport, Samuel (1783–1867) Portrait engraver. He was born on 10 December 1783 at Bedford but was moved in infancy to London, where his father worked as a land surveyor and architect. He was apprenticed as an engraver, from about 1797 to 1804, to Charles Warren, whom he followed in the same vein of book illustration. He later specialised in portrait engraving, particularly in outline, of which Redgrave's *Dictionary...* records that 700 were done for a single publication, possibly one of the serial works then popular. Probably because of his connection with Warren, he was one of the earliest to use steel, and much of his work was executed in this medium, notably for the annuals. Some of his steel engravings were done after designs by H. C. Shenton (one of Warren's later pupils and his son-in-law) and H. Corbould, the majority of which were published in the *Forget me not* and listed in the *Dictionary of National Biography*. A vignette, 'The Harper', after T. Stothard was done for Rogers' *Italy* 1830, 'Ascanius in the lap of Venus' after Wood for *Friendship's offering* 1831 (used again in *Casquet of literature*, series 2, volume 2, 1874, but entitled 'Flight of Venus with Ascanius'), 'The astrologer' after Clint for Fisher's *Drawing room scrap book* 1836 and four plates after Hogarth for Hogarth's *works* 1833. Ten plates signed 'Davenport' after Cruikshank appeared in the latter's *Eighty-two illustrations on steel* [c. 1870]. He was almost certainly the author of an article on book illustration which appeared in the *Journal of the Society of Arts* in January 1865, the section on steel and machine engraving appearing on pages 134 and 135. He was also the author of *Engraving*, a pamphlet published by Edward Stanford in his series 'British manufacturing industries', edited by G. Phillips Bevan, some parts of which were published in 1870s. He died on 15 July 1867. B; DNB; T.

Davey, William Turner (1818–c. 1882) Portrait engraver. 'Christ and the woman of Samaria' appeared in Fleetwood's *Life of Our Lord...* [c. 1855] and 'Richard the first...' after de Loutherbourg and 'The Earl of Sandwich...' after Smirke came out in *History of England...*, edited by T. Gaspey and based on the work by Hume and Smollett, [c. 1847]. He was a pupil of Charles Rolls (q.v.) and did some engraving for the printsellers, including 'Inkerman' after Mrs Butler for the Fine Art Society, 1882. He also painted portraits and genre subjects. B.

Davies, Benjamin Rees (fl. 1820–40) Map, writing and landscape engraver. He was employed by Longman to engrave the inscriptions to the plates for Britton's *Cathedrals* in 1824 at a cost of £2.7s.6d. and in the following decade his excellence in this kind of work was well illustrated in the steel engraving he did for the *English Bijou Almanac* of A. Schloss, which commenced publication in 1836. (I. Bain, *Albert Schloss's Bijou Almanacs ...* Nattali and Maurice, 1969.) In Britton and Brayley's *Devonshire and Cornwall illustrated* 1832, appeared a map of Cornwall (which included a vignette, 'The Cheeswring') and 'Bodinnoc Ferry, Fowey, Cornwall' after T. Allom. There are two plates in this work which are signed 'Davies', both after Allom, and another two, signed 'J. R. Davies' after Bartlett and Allom, which could be by Benjamin (plates by John Davies are usually signed 'J. [or John] Davies'). Large maps (21 by 15½ inches) of Manchester (1833) and Liverpool (1 June 1836) after his own designs were published in Baines's *History of ... Lancaster* 1836, and similar engravings, of Syria and Asia Minor, appeared in Carne's *Syria* 1836–8. His address was given as 16 George Street, Euston Square.

Davies, Cyrus (fl. 1836) Landscape engraver. Known by 'Castle of Granson (Lake of Neufchatel)' after W. H. Bartlett in Beattie's *Switzerland* 1836.

Davies, John (fl. 1830–50) Landscape and architectural engraver. He engraved six plates after Austin, Harwood and Pyne, including 'Entrance to the tunnel of the Liverpool & Manchester Rail-way...' and 'Birkenhead Ferry, opposite Liverpool' (Plate 9), for Pyne's *Lancashire illustrated...* 1831, and 'Destroying the chrysalides and reeling the cocoons' after Allom for Wright's *China* 1843. 'Carrick-a-rede...' after Baynes appeared in Wright's *Gallery of engravings* 1844–6 and two plates after Wray and Shepherd in Dugdale's *England and Wales delineated* [1838–9].

Davies, S. T. (fl. 1836–51) Landscape and architectural engraver. He engraved mainly after W. H. Bartlett, whose designs for 'The Col-de-Balme' and 'Castle of Falkenstein' appeared in Beattie's *Switzerland* 1836, 'Pomaret...' and 'Lake la Roche...' (with two other plates, after Brockedon) in Beattie's *Waldenses* 1838, 'Mount Washington...' and 'The Exchange and Girard's Bank (Philadelphia)' in Willis's *American scenery* 1840 and 'Llanthony Abbey' in Beattie's *Castles and abbeys of England* 1845–51.

Davis, J. (fl. 1836–40) Landscape engraver. Known by 'The gardens of Versailles' after W. Callow, which appeared in *Heath's Versailles* [c. 1836] and *Keepsake français* 1840. There could be a connection with J. Davies, but no corroborative evidence will be forthcoming.

Dawson, R. (fl. 1837–60) Landscape and architectural engraver. 'Djebel Sheich and Mount Herman' after W. H. Bartlett was engraved in 1837 for Carne's *Syria* 1836–8, and was used again in J. Kitto's *Gallery of scripture engravings* ten years later. Four plates after Brockedon were done for Beattie's *Waldenses* 1838, and in 1860 he engraved, after a photograph by J. Cramb, 'Mosque of Omar', which was used for M'Farlane's edition of the Bible. 'Bristol during the riots 1831' after an old print appeared in J. Taylor's *Age we live in* ... [c. 1885]. The *Dictionary of National Biography* identifies a Robert Dawson (1776–1860) as a topographical artist and cartographer, but no connection is made with engraving.

Dean, T. A. (fl. 1773–1840) Portrait engraver and miniature painter. He started life as a painter, exhibiting at the major London exhibitions between 1773 and 1825, but turned later to engraving, probably at the time when steel was first used. 'William Shakspeare' (*sic*) was engraved on steel in July 1823 to be used as the frontispiece to a one volume octavo edition of *The Plays...* (Plate 5). Plates were engraved for Northcote's *Life of Titian* 1830 and *The Methodist Magazine* 1830–40.

'Lady Jane Grey' appeared in *The Bijou* 1830, 'The last look' after Porter in *Friendship's offering* 1831, 'Lady Agnes Buller' after Chalon in the series of Female Nobility no. 82, published October 1831, 'Affection' after Davis and 'Female pirates' after Wood in *Friendship's offering* 1833, 'Marie Thérèse...' after Holmes in Fisher's *Drawing room scrap book* 1836 and a vignette, 'Rev. Sydney Smith' (October 1840), and 'A society of antiquaries' after Jenkins and a vignette, 'Prince Philippe, Count of Flanders', after Ross in Wright's *Gallery of engravings* 1844–6. A longer list of separate engravings is given in Thieme and Becker.   B; T.

Deeble, William (fl. 1814–50) Architectural engraver and painter. He exhibited two views of Canterbury Cathedral at the Royal Academy in 1814, and did some copper engravings for E. W. Brayley's *Delineations of the Isle of Thanet* 1817–18 and *Excursions through Sussex* 1818–22. In 1823, when living at 1 Seymour Place, Islington, he was awarded the Silver Isis medal by the Society of Arts for his method of taking casts of leaves and foliage. The bulk of his early steel engraved work was done after T. H. Shepherd: engraving commencing in September 1827, thirteen engravings appeared in J. Elmes's *Metropolitan improvements* 1829 (of which 'St. Paul's School' is a good example) and three in T. H. Shepherd's *London and its environs* 1829–31. Four plates were engraved for Gastineau's *Wales illustrated...* 1830 after designs by the author, one of which, 'Gateway and bridge, Ragland...', was used again in Woodward's *History of Wales* 1853. He contributed 'Canterbury Cathedral' after his own design and 'St. Paul's Cathedral' after Hablot Browne to Winkles's... *Cathedral churches of England...*, volume 1, 1836 and 'Castle wind, Mars work and Cathedral (Stirling)' after T. Allom (1836) and 'The Royal Institution, Edinburgh' after G. M. Kemp (1837) to W. Beattie's *Scotland illustrated* 1838. A vignette, 'The nave, Llanthony Abbey', after W. H. Bartlett was engraved for W. Beattie's *Castles and abbeys of England*, volume 2, 1851. He is also thought to be the illustrator of the Spanish book *Un amor y una expiacion, por el Conde de C. M.*, published in Paris in 1849.   B; SocA; T.

Desvachez, David Joseph (1822–1902) Belgian figure engraver. Born at Valenciennes, he was taught by Calametta and Picot and exhibited at the Paris Salon from 1849–1878, obtaining medals for his work in 1861 and 1874. He became known in this country by his eleven engravings in the *Art Journal* from 1857 to 1883, some of them after fashionable artists of the day, e.g., 'Barthram's dirge' (1863) after J. N. Paton and 'The sisters' (1883) after Laura Alma-Tadema. Two which appeared in the *Works of Shakspere [sic] Imperial edition* 1872, 'Prince Arthur and Hubert' after A. J. Pott and 'Imogen in the cave' after T. Graham, were also published in the *Art Journal* for 1873 and 1874 respectively. He died in Brussels in 1902.   B.

Dick, Thomas (fl. 1841–74) Scottish figure, portrait and landscape engraver, working in Edinburgh. His earliest important work appeared in *Engravings after the best pictures of the Great Masters* (all by Scottish engravers), published by R. Ackermann between 1841 and 1843, i.e., two copper plates—'Thomyris with the head of Cyrus' after Rubens and 'Paul preaching at Athens' after Raphael. A large plate, 'The benefactress', after W. Bonner was done for the print publisher Alex Hill in 1843. His steel book plates included 'Edinburgh Castle from Princes Street' after his own design, published in J. Browne's *History of the Highlands* [c. 1845], and 'The Storm' after P. Delaroche, in *Casquet of literature* 1874. A bookplate engraved by him is known, done in 1870.   B; Fi; T.

Dixon, Charles Thomas (fl. 1842–57) Landscape engraver. 'Cormayor, Valley of Aosta, Italy' after Cockburn was engraved for Wright's *Rhine, Italy and Greece* [1842]. A vignette, 'Trim, Meath', after H. Gastineau was engraved for S. C. and A. M. Hall's *Ireland*, volume 2, 1843, and in the same year one plate appeared in each of the four volumes of G. N. Wright's *China*, all after T. Allom. Two designs had been worked up from sketches by R. Varnham and Captain Stoddart, R. N., and 'The Fountain-court in Consequa's House, Canton' in volume 2 had been taken from a drawing in the possession of Sir G. Staunton. Soon after this, he appears to have turned to landscape and genre painting, exhibiting at the major London exhibitions between 1846 and 1857. Three of his paintings can be seen in Sheffield Art Gallery.   B; T.

Dixon, Thomas (fl. 1832–38) Landscape and architectural engraver. He engraved four plates after Allom for Britton and Brayley's *Devonshire and Cornwall illustrated* 1832 (including 'Interior of St Andrew's Church, Plymouth' and 'Castle Hill, near South Molton, Devon'), six plates after Austin, Pyne and Harwood for Pyne's *Lancashire illustrated...* 1831, two views of Newcastle upon Tyne for Rose's *Durham and Northumberland* 1832, and 'Warrington market place, Lancashire', which was used for Baines's *History of... Lancaster* 1836 and Wright's *Lancashire* 1842. Three plates after Bartlett appeared in Carne's *Syria* 1836–8, of which 'Sepulchre at Seleucia' was largely etched.

Dobbie, Thomas (fl. 1840–6) Architectural engraver, working in Edinburgh. 'The house of John Knox' was engraved in 1840 after his own design for the engraved title page of T. McCrie's *Life of John Knox*, 2nd edition, 1840, and 'Edinburgh Old Town from Princes Street' drawn by T. M. Richardson jun., on 1 July 1841, appeared in the edition of *Black's picturesque tourist of Scotland* 1849. Francis Croll (q.v.) was articled to him, but since important engraving commissions did not come his way, the pupil was taught more drawing than engraving. Owing to his master's death, Croll finished his articles with R. C. Bell: from this it is inferred that Dobbie died in about 1846.

Done (or Dore), W. M. (fl. 1845–50) Architectural engraver. Four plates appeared in T. Dugdale's *England and Wales delineated* [c. 1838–9], of which 'Hampton Court Palace', 'Castle Howard' and 'The Wesleyan Theological College, Richmond' were after T. H. Shepherd and 'The Ruins of Farnham Castle' was after A. W. Wray. The two last-named are signed 'W. M. Dore'.

Doo, George Thomas, R.A., F.R.S. (1800–86) Figure and portrait engraver. Born on 6 January 1800 at Christ Church, Surrey, he studied under Charles Heath, his first published engraving being 'The Duke of York' after Sir T. Lawrence (1824). In 1825 he visited the engraving schools in Paris, and on his return, set up a life and antique academy in the Savoy. It was probably in the early 1830s that he took as an assistant pupil Thomas Leeming Grundy (q.v.), who remained with him for some time. In 1831 he was one of the engravers who tried out improved graver handles, recommending them to the Society of Arts. In 1836 he became Historical Engraver in Ordinary to King William IV, an appointment renewed in 1842 by Queen Victoria. His busiest time for engraving was in the 1840s, when he worked in the main for the print publishers and the Art Unions. C. L. Eastlake's 'Pilgrims coming in sight of Rome' was published by F. G. Moon in 1842, and between 1843 and 1845 he was engaged upon 'The convalescent from Waterloo' after W. Mulready for the Art

George Thomas Doo

Union of London, with an estimated demand for 30,000 copies. When it had been distributed it was 'disappointing.... The combination of great painter and great engraver had failed to produce a satisfactory print'. (A.U. 1848. p. 132.)

His work for book illustration and on steel was, therefore, slight. In January 1841 a portrait of Cuvier, the naturalist, after H.W. Pickersgill was advertised by the engraver as suitable for binding into folio or quarto copies of Cuvier's works. Some plates appeared in Jones's *National gallery*. His most celebrated work in this field was 'The Combat' after W. Etty, dated 1 June 1849, engraved for Finden's *Royal Gallery of British Art*, and as late as 1870 his frontispiece, 'Alexander Pope', graced volume 6 of the ten-volume edition of Pope's works. This was in a period when he had given up much of his engraving for oil painting, in which medium he had executed many portraits which were exhibited at the Royal Academy from 1853 onwards. In October 1856 he was elected as an Associate Engraver of the Royal Academy when two vacancies were the subject of elections. The first one went to J. H. Robinson, who gained seventeen votes to Doo's five, but against J. T. Willmore, he obtained seventeen votes to two. The following year, 1857, saw him contesting for full honours, and although he lost the first ballot, he obtained the Chairman's casting vote when he and Robinson had obtained fourteen votes each.

In 1861 he became President of the Artists' Annuity Fund, which he had joined in 1825, and was the chairman of Class 40, engraving and etching, for the 1862 International Exhibition in Paris. 'The Raising of Lazarus' after S. del Piombo, issued by Colnaghi in 1865, had taken him eight years to engrave, and created a stir when published under the auspices of several patrons who associated themselves together for the purpose of encouraging the art of historical line engraving in England, then in a bad way. Contemporaries regarded it as his finest engraving. In 1867 his 'St. Augustine and Monica' after Ary Scheffer was on show at the Paris International Exhibition of that year, and early in the year he resigned from the Royal Academy, for what reason is not disclosed. In 1841 he was living at 29 St Peter's Square, Hammersmith, but moved later to Stanmore, and it was at Sutton that he died on 13 November 1886, aged eighty-six.

He had lectured on painting at South Kensington, and was an honorary or corresponding member of Fine Art Institutions in Amsterdam, Parma and Pennsylvania. He married James Heath's daughter. AJ; B; Br; DNB; S; Sa; Soc A; T.

Douglas, William (fl. 1838–43) Landscape, architectural and historical engraver, working in Edinburgh. Two plates— 'Arch in Lincluden Abbey' after D. O. Hill and 'Grey Street' after T. M. Richardson and N. Castle—appeared in T. F. Dibdin's *Bibliographical ... tour in the northern counties of England* 1838 and 'The sacrifice at Lystra' after Raphael Sanzio and 'Coronation of Mary de Medicis, Queen of France, 1610' after Rubens were contributed to *Engravings after the best pictures of the Great Masters* 1841–3, both probably engraved on copper. B.

Dower, John Crane (c. 1790–1847) Map engraver and printer of 6 Cumming Place, Pentonville. He drew and engraved maps of Northern and Southern Greece (signed 'J. Dower') for C. Wordsworth's *Greece* 1839. He established his business in 1820, and in his will, proved April 1847, left it to his two sons, John James (1825–c. 1888) and Frederick James (1829–1887). (From information supplied by Mr Nigel Russell of Tring.)

Drury, J. (fl. 1832) Landscape engraver. Known by 'St. Goar and ruins of Fort Rheinfels' after W. Tombleson, which appeared in *Tombleson's views of the Rhine*, edited by W. G. Fearnside, 1832, and *Continental tourist* [1838].

Duncan, Andrew (1795–?) Portrait and figure engraver, working most of his life in London. An early portrait was of John Donne in Walker's *Effigies Poeticae* 1824. He joined the Artists' Annuity Fund in 1827 and was one of the signatories to the 1837 Petition. He tried out some improved graver handles for the Society of Arts in 1831, and contributed illustrations to some British Museum publications, such as the *Description of the Ancient Marbles in the British Museum* 1835. Four of his plates, dated 1832 to 1834, appeared in A. Cunningham's *Cabinet gallery of pictures by the first masters ...* 1836, viz. 'Christ in the sepulchre' after Guercino (which was very heavily etched), 'Holy Family' after Baroccio, 'The vigilant mistress' after A. Maas and 'The Mountebank' after J. Steen. 'The Last Supper. From the painting by West in the National Gallery' appeared in Fleetwood's *Life of Our Lord ...* [c. 1855] and 'Guy Mannering' after C. R. Leslie appeared, as a frontispiece, in the centennial edition of Scott's novels, 1871. B; SocA; T.

Dyer, R. H. (fl. 1832) Sculpture and portrait engraver. He contributed illustrations to T. K. Harvey's *Illustrations of Modern Sculpture* 1832, which were probably those reprinted in the *Art Union* of 1847 and 1848, when three plates, drawn by H. Corbould, were included, viz., of 'Resignation' by F. Chantrey, 'Venus' by Canova and 'Arethusa' by Carew. B; T.

E

Eagleton, W. (fl. 1835) Figure engraver. 'The carrier pigeon' after D. Maclise was published in *Heath's Book of beauty* 1835. It is possible that the writing engraver mistook the name—'Egleton' is more likely.

Easton, John (fl. 1878) Historical engraver. 'The first preaching of Christianity in Britain' after Cope appeared in Archer's *Pictures and royal portraits ...* [c. 1878].

Easton, R. (fl. 1837) Figure engraver. 'The letter from home' after H. Richter was published in *Friendship's offering* 1837.

Edwards, (fl. 1877) Figure engraver. Known from 'Jacob in the house of Laban' after Schopin, an engraving with a curved top from a Bible of 1877 printed at the Oxford University Press.

Edwards, J. C. (fl. 1821–35) Figure and portrait engraver and painter. He exhibited 'Little girl' at the Royal Academy in 1821 and 'Cupid taught by the Graces' after W. Hilton in 1824. He did some illustrations after R. Smirke for Shakespeare's *Works* 1829, and then a number of plates for the annuals followed. 'May Talbot' after Cooper was done for *The Gem* 1829. For the *Literary souvenir* he did 'Cupid taught by the graces' after Hilton (1829), 'Oberon and Titania' after Howard (1830) and 'Trojan fugitives' after Jones (1831), and for *The Keepsake* 'Juliet' after Miss L. Sharpe (1831) (a very good example of his work on steel), 'Caroline Dammeral' after Wright (1832), 'Rosina' after Boxall (1833), 'The widowed bride' after Eliza Sharpe (1834), 'Gipsey children' after Miss L. Sharpe (1835), and 'The last look' after Parris and 'The escape of Finella' after Chalon (1836). A portrait of Czar Peter appeared in *A Memoir of the Life of Peter the Great* 1832. He also tried out some improved graver handles for the Society of Arts in 1831. Robert Staines and Richard Hatfield (qqv.) were his pupils. B; SocA; T.

Edwards, W. (fl. 1845) Figure and portrait engraver. Known as the engraver of six plates for *Beauties of Moore* 1846, notably, three after W. Frith ('Black and blue eyes', 'Exile' and 'The pensive thought'). 'The Hamlet's pride' after H. Room also deserves a mention. A W. Edwards of Percival Street, Clerkenwell, received the Gold Isis medal for a portrait in oil in 1819 from the Society of Arts. It is possible that both of these can be identified with W. J. Edwards (q.v.). It is less likely that W. Edwards is William Camden Edwards (q.v.).

Edwards, William Camden (1777–1855) Portrait and figure engraver. He was born in Monmouthshire in 1777 and probably trained there as an engraver. Early in the nineteenth century, when about twenty-four years old, he went to work for the publisher Brightly at Bungay in Suffolk. There he worked on archaeological publications, editions of the Bible, and Bunyan's *Pilgrim's Progress*. His master died probably about 1808, when Edwards transferred to Childs, another local publisher, and it was here that he met Charles Fox (q.v.), who persuaded his father to allow him to become Edwards's pupil. Edwards worked hard, turning out many portraits of important people, notably Flaxman, Fuseli, Hogarth and Reynolds, and a complete series of his engravings and etchings was collected by Dawson Turner, the sale catalogue of whose collection lists the majority of them. Among his steel plates were the frontispiece to volume 1 (dated 30 December 1823) of W. Cowper's *Private correspondence* 1824, portraits of Hilliard, Flatman and Strange, which appeared in Walpole's *Anecdotes of painting* 1827, three portraits of Milton in his *Poetical works* 1841 and the frontispiece of Matthew Henry's *Exposition of the Old and New Testaments* 1844, 'engraved in steel by W. C. Edwards'. He settled in Bungay and died there on 22 August 1855, being buried in the cemetery of Holy Trinity Church. AJ; B; DNB; T.

Edwards, W. J. (fl. 1840–63) Portrait engraver. He may be the W. Joseph Edwards noticed by Benezit. His earliest steel plate was 'Sultan Abdul Medschid Chan' in J. Pardoe's *Beauties of the Bosphorus* 1840. 'A portrait' after Chalon was engraved for *The Keepske* 1841. Plates appeared in *Heath's Book of beauty* for 1843 and 1845, and for *The Keepsake* of 1847, he engraved 'The Debardeur's first love' after Lecount. 'Katherine' after A. Egg appeared in the *Heroines of Shakespeare* 1848, and for the *Wilkie gallery* [c. 1849] he did 'An Arab sheik' and 'Three Greek sisters at Therapia', in the latter of which the faces were very well engraved. 'The Lady Manners' after J. Hayter was published in *The Court Album* 1852, and 'P. Fawcett, the comedian' after Sir Thomas Lawrence appeared in the *Art Journal* for 1854. Two round engravings of—'General Garibaldi', and 'Pope Pius IX' (after a photograph)—were used in Costello's *Piedmont and Italy* [c. 1855], five portraits appeared in Nolan's *Illustrated history of the British Empire in India* [1858–60] and 'William of Wykeham' was issued in Woodward's *General history of Hampshire* 1863. He also worked for the print publishers, and exhibited an engraving at the Royal Academy in 1858. B; T.

Egleton, William Henry (fl. 1833–60) Portrait and figure engraver. Among his earlier works were some illustrations for Scott's *Waverley Novels* 1833, followed by plates for the annuals from 1836. Finden's *Tableaux ...* of 1837 contained 'Persia' after J. Browne, and 'Georgia' after T. Uwins (Plate 30), both signed 'H. Egleton'. 'Anne, Duchess of Monmouth' after Kneller, signed 'W. Eggleton', appeared in Scott's *Lay of the last minstrel* 1839 and 'The Lady Fanny Cowper' after Chalon in Heath's *Book of beauty* 1839. Ten Biblical pictures appeared in Fisher's *Historic illustrations of the Bible* [1840–3], five of which were used again in Kitto's *Gallery of scripture engravings* 1846–9. *Heath's Book of beauty* 1841 had 'Her Majesty the Queen in her nuptial dress' after W. Drummond as a frontispiece, together with a plate, 'Mrs. Edward Ellice', after A. E. Chalon, both dated 1 October 1840. From 1838 he engraved for *Finden's Portraits of the female aristocracy*. Finden's *Gallery of beauty* 1841 contained four portraits after J. Hayter and an edition of the Bible first issued 'Christ giving sight to the blind' after Henry Richter and 'Paul preaching at Ephesus' after Le Seceur, while G. N. Wright's *Gallery of engravings* 1844–6 carried 'Good night' after Edward Corbould. 'Aline' after Hayter was engraved for *The Keepsake* 1844, 'The heiress' after the same artist for the 1845 volume and 'Lady Georgiana Codrington ...' after E. Corbould for that of 1849. 'Leila', 'Zuleika' and 'Olimpia', all after J. W. Wright, were engraved for *Heath's Book of beauty* 1846, and 'The garden flower' (October 1845) after J. Wright, 'The lute' (December 1845) after A. Egg and 'The casket' (January 1846) after W. Maddon were among the excellent illustrations to *Beauties of Moore* 1846. *The Keepsake* for 1847 had 'Adelaide' after W. P. Frith as its frontispiece, and in *Heroines of Shakespeare* 1848, 'Portia', 'Lady Anne', 'Mrs. Page', 'Constance' and 'Lady Percy' were engraved after J. W. Wright, and 'Julia' and 'Maria' after A. Egg. 'Annunciation to the Virgin' after Murillo was the frontispiece to the *Book of Common Prayer* 1854. Some plates were done for *The Court Album* 1852–7, and one of his later engravings was of a sculpture, 'Maidenhood', by C. Hancock for the *Art Journal* 1859. He joined the Artists' Annuity Fund in 1834, and began to work for the print publishers in the 1840s. His larger plates included 'Coronation oath' after Hayter and 'The glorious company of the Apostles' (both before 1851), 'The evening star' after Richard (1858) and 'Latimer preaching at St. Paul's Cross' (1860). B; R; S; T.

Eke, James (fl. 1827–31) Landscape engraver. When living at 46 Clarendon Square, Somers Town, he was awarded the

Silver Isis medal for an engraving on steel of a cotton machine by the Society of Arts in 1827. 'View from the parapet of the public rooms, Teignmouth' after T. H. Williams was engraved for T. Moore's *History of Devonshire* 1831.   Ho; SocA.

Ellis, T. H. (fl. 1860) Landscape and figure engraver. Twelve Biblical pictures were engraved for the Revd F. L. Pearce's *Altar at home* [c. 1860] after Dolci, Coypel, Stothard, Potter and others. A vignette of 'Westminster Abbey' after T. H. Shepherd appeared on the engraved title page of Dryden's *Poetical works* 1859.

Emslie, John (1813–75) Map and heraldic engraver. He was born on 12 July 1813. He became a pupil of Thomas Harwood, was married when he was about twenty-six and had a son, John Phillip Emslie (1839–85). In 1843 and 1844 he was engaged on thirty-nine plates for volumes 1 and 2 of Burke's *Heraldic illustrations* 1845, and engraved fourteen more for volume 3, all of which were coats of arms assigned to various families. Three plates of clouds etc., were engraved for J. Ruskin's *Modern painters* 1856–60 after the author's drawings, and he engraved two bookplates about 1850. He was a Fellow of the Royal Geographical Society. He died on 8 June 1875. A collection of 197 of his engravings etc. was given to the British Museum in 1913.   B; Fi; T.

Engleheart, Francis (1775–1849) Figure and portrait engraver. A member of a large family of artists who settled in England at Kew from Silesia in the reign of George II. Engravers and miniature painters were among his relatives, who were originally from a noble family. His father Thomas was a sculptor from Egham. Francis was primarily a book illustrator, learning his craft under Joseph Collyer, and developing his skills under James Heath. Some of his early important work was done after designs by T. Stothard, and for Heath he did plates of the Canterbury pilgrims. In 1808 he published 'General Fairfax' after Bower. Some of his more successful work was done after the designs of R. Cook (notably 'The Castle' from Scott's *Lady of the Lake*) and R. Smirke, after whom Engleheart engraved nearly thirty plates for *Don Quixote* by Cervantes, 1818. For the *Literary souvenir* he engraved 'My own fire side' after Mulready for the 1826 volume, 'Lord Byron' after West (1827), 'Psyche borne by the Zephyrs...' after Wood (1828) and 'The supper by the fountain' after Stothard (1832). He also contributed to *The Gem*. Of some interest were 'Pastor of the Lac de Joux' after J. M. Wright, which was engraved for *The Amulet* 1827, and 'Garden of Boccacio' after T. Stothard, the engraved title page 'Dorathea' (*sic*) after F. P. Stephanoff, 'Flora' after Miss L. Sharpe and 'Sappho' after Howard, which appeared in *The Keepsake* for 1829, 1830, 1833 and 1834 respectively. 'Her most excellent Majesty Queen Adelaide' after Mrs Green appeared in *Wreath of friendship*. A vignette of a lute player after Parmagiano was engraved for S. Rogers' *Poems* 1834, 'The visionary' after H. Liverseege appeared in G. N. Wright's *Gallery of engravings* 1844–6, and a very well engraved subject in an oval, 'The Meeting with the shepherds' after T. Stothard, was used for editions of Bunyan's *Pilgrim's Progress*, the tenth edition of which came out in 1854. He also engraved some plates for *Description of the Ancient Marbles in the British Museum* 1835. His most important and last production was published when he was seventy-one, namely, 'Serena rescued by the Red-Cross knight' after W. Hilton, which appeared in the *Art Union* for 1846 and S. C. Hall's *Gems of European art* 1846. 'Katherine and Bianca' after Stephanoff appeared in *Casquet of literature*, volume 2, 1874. He was employed by Sir David Wilkie to

engrave 'Duncan Gray' and 'The only daughter', published by F. G. Moon. He joined the Artists' Annuity Fund in 1822, was a signatory to the 1837 petition and exhibited at the Society of British Artists. He died after a few hours' illness on 15 February 1849, aged about seventy-four. His son, Timothy Stansfield Engleheart (q.v.), was also an engraver.   AJ; Br; DNB; R; Ro; S.

Engleheart, John H. (fl. 1830–41) Landscape, architectural and historical engraver. 'Cardiff Castle' after H. Gastineau was engraved for volume 2 of the latter's *Wales illustrated...* 1830, 'Ambleside...' and 'Windermere...' after Pickering for Rose's *Westmorland* 1832 and 'Colonel Maxwell's last charge at Assye' after A. Cooper for W. H. Maxwell's *Life of ... the Duke of Wellington* 1839–41.

Engleheart, Timothy Stansfield (1803–79) Portrait and landscape engraver. He was the son of Francis Engleheart (q.v.), whose pupil he probably was. He engraved for the annuals, notably, *Forget me not, The Casket* and the *Literary souvenir*, for the 1835 volume of which he engraved 'Austrian peasants on a pilgrimage' after G. R. Lewis. With his father, he engraved some of the plates for *Description of the Ancient Marbles in the British Museum* 1835. Two plates were done for Hogarth's *Works* 1833 and 'The Black Linn of Linklater' after Chisholm was engraved for Wright's *Landscape-historical illustrations of Scotland* 1836–8. Portraits of Miss Anderson after Lawrence, Thomas Clarkson after Hazlitt and Dorothy Jordan after Morland are known. About 1840 he left for Germany, and was known to have engraved 'Ecce Homo' after G. Reni, executed at Darmstadt in 1840.   B; Br; DNB; T.

Ensom, William (1796–1832) Portrait engraver. When living at Swinton Street, Grays Inn Lane, he gained a silver medal from the Society of Arts in 1815 and 1816 for pen-and-ink drawings, one of which was a portrait of William Blake. Eight plates were engraved for J. P. Neale's *Views of the seats of noblemen...* 1818–24, and between 1825 and 1831 he exhibited six engravings at the Suffolk Street Gallery. In *The Amulet* of 1827 he engraved 'Sir Arthur Woodgate' after F. P. Stephanoff, and for *The Amulet* of 1828 his plate of 'Queen Elizabeth, Essex and Shakespeare' was done after T. Stothard. For *The Bijou* of 1829–30, he engraved portraits of George IV and Lady Wallscourt after Sir Thomas Lawrence (thought to be some of Ensom's best work); for the *Literary souvenir*, 'A conversation' after Stothard (1828), 'Allegra' after Chalon and 'The Marchioness of Salisbury' after Lawrence (1832) and 'The oriental love-letter' after Destouches (1834); and for *Friendship's offering* 1833, 'The morning walk' after Pastorini. He also engraved portraits of the Marquis of Salisbury, Mrs Arbuthnot and Master Lambton, and some Biblical plates, which included 'Christ blessing the bread' after C. Dolci, 'Christ appearing to Mary Magdalene' after Titian and 'St. John in the wilderness' after C. Cignani. He was also a painter in watercolours, exhibiting at the Suffolk Street Gallery. He was a friend of R. P. Bonington. Ensom died at Wandsworth on 13 February 1832, aged about thirty-six. His collection of engravings and drawings was auctioned on 12 December 1832.   B; Br; DNB; SocA; T.

Eyles, Benjamin (fl. 181847–54) Portrait engraver. For *Heath's Book of beauty* 1847, he engraved 'Astarte' after G. Steel and 'Haidée' after E. Corbould, followed by eleven plates for *Heroines of Shakespeare* 1848, six after J. W. Wright, two after A. Egg, two after K. Meadows and one after A. Johnston, the subjects represented including Anne Bullen,

Celia, Desdemona, Cordelia, Joan of Arc and Titania. He engraved a number of plates for *The Keepsake* between 1850 and 1857; one appeared in the 1852 volume, two in each of the volumes for 1850 and 1851, three in each of those for 1853–1856 and four in the 1857 volume. Many plates had the fashionable curved tops. Among the most interesting were 'My partner' after Naish (1854) and 'Mrs. Kingston James' (with a striking use of tone) and the oval picture of 'Lady Otway', both after Buckner and in the 1853 volume. Each of the first three volumes of *The Court Album* 1852–4 contained an engraving after J. Hayter, viz. 'Miss Lethbridge', 'Miss Baillie' and 'Lady Elizabeth Hay', the last two being vignetts. T.

F

Fairholt, Frederick William (1813–66) Figure engraver. His father emigrated from Prussia with the name 'Fahrholz', which was anglicised to 'Fairholt' when he had settled in London, where he went into business as a tobacco manufacturer. Frederick was the last survivor of sixteen children and the name died out with him, a bachelor. He was self-educated. At the age of eighteen, when living at 8 Denmark Street, Soho, he won the Silver Isis medal of the Society of Arts for a copy in watercolour of a landscape (Soc. Arts *Trans.* 1831), and in the same year contributed two papers to Hone's *Year Book* 1831. During the next few years he designed and engraved on wood for Charles Knight's publications, including the *Penny Magazine*, and from 1839 until his death contributed articles on diverse subjects to the *Art Union* and *Art Journal*. His engravings on metal were largely of coins for the Numismatic Society, of which he was a council member, and Hawkins's *History of our silver coinage*, and so adept at these was he that he could etch directly onto the metal without previous sketching. For Wright's *Caricature history* 1848, he engraved twelve plates after Hogarth, Gillray, Rowlandson and Sayer, and he also contributed to several series of Shakespeare illustrations, as well as to some antiquarian works, such as C. Roach Smith's *History of Richborough*, Faussett's *Inventorium Sepulchrale* and Londesborough's *Miscellanea Graphica*. With the last-named author and, later, with his son, he visited France and Egypt, but it would seem that foreign travel induced ill-health, and for the last year of his life he struggled against the ravages of tuberculosis and asthma. He died on 3 April 1866 and was buried in Brompton Cemetery. In 1844 he was elected a Fellow of the Society of Antiquaries, to whom he left part of his library (the remainder went to the British Museum and Shakespeare's house library and museum, or was sold, mostly for the benefit of the Royal Literary Fund). AJ; Br; SocA; T.

Faithorn, E. (fl. 1832) Landscape engraver, 'House of the tragic poet' was published in Sir W. Gell's *Pompeiana* 1832.

Faithorn, W. (fl. 1829–31) Landscape and architectural engraver. Known for four plates after J. P. Neale, published in *Jones's Views of the seats ...* 1829.

Fenn, C. (fl. 1850–77) Architectural engraver. His early work was done after T. H. Shepherd, after whom three plates, 'The Monument, London', 'The Nelson Column ...' and 'The birthplace of the first Sir R. Peel, Blackburn, Lancs', appeared as either frontispieces or engraved title pages to three divisions of T. Dugdale's *Engand and Wales delineated* [c. 1838–9]. His further work appeared in two books by T. Baines: in *Lancashire and Cheshire, past and present* 1867, 'Town Hall, Preston' after Scott, 'Exchange Buildings,

Liverpool' after Wyatt and 'Manchester New Town Hall' after Waterhouse appeared; and in *Yorkshire past and present* 1871–7, 'Town Hall, Leeds' after the architect Brodrick (Plate 56), 'New Exchange, Bradford' after the architects Lockwood and Manson, 'Town Hall, Halifax' and 'Estate buildings, Huddersfield' were published.

Fenner, Sears & Co. (1830–c. 1836) Architectural and landscape engravers. Rest Fenner (fl. 1812–33) established an engraving and printing business in 1817. Robert Sears (fl. 1831–9) joined him in 1830, when a new building was erected. They employed engravers such as H. Beckwith (q.v.), T. Engleheart (q.v.), W. Tombleson (q.v.) and F. W. Topham (q.v.). Plates from their establishment include three pages of autographs in the *Literary souvenir* 1825, 'Ham House, Surrey', 'Chichester Cathedral', 'Lewes Castle' and 'Hastings', all after N. Whittock and 'engraved and printed by Fenner, Sears and Co', in T. Allen's *History ... of Surrey and Sussex* 1829–31, twelve after Whittock in Allen's *New ... history of the county of ... York ...* 1828–31, two views of St. James's cemetery, Liverpool after Baynes in Pyne's *Lancashire illustrated ...* 1831, thirty-four engravings, mainly after the author, in Sir William Gell's *Pompeiana ...* 1832 (including 'Facsimile of the head of Achilles' (Plate 14)–a striking vignette–and 'Theseus and Ariadne'), 'Mont Blanc...' after Brockedon in *Wreath of friendship* and 'Pile of Fouldrey Castle' after G. Pickering in E. Baines's *History of ... Lancaster* 1836, reissued in G. N. Wright's *Lancashire* 1842 and the same author's *Gallery of engravings* 1844–6. 'Barrière de l'Etoile', 'Barrière St. Martin', 'Pont de la Revolution' and 'Barrière de Passy', signed 'R. Fenner' or 'Rest Fenner & Co.', were done for *Paris*, published by C. Knight, 1831. Rest Fenner engraved an ex-libris in 1820, and nine others are signed 'Fenner, Paternoster Row'. Fi; Ro vol. 2, p. 317–18.

Fernell, H. (fl. 1833–45) Figure engraver. 'Rakes progress, 8' and 'Industry and idleness 9' were published in Hogarth's *Works* 1833, a vignette, 'The destroying angel', after Harlow appeared in *Friendship's offering* 1844 and 'Richard Brinsley Sheridan' after Reynolds was the frontispiece to Sheridan's *Dramatic works* published by Bohn, [c. 1845].

Field, T. (fl. 18436) Landscape engraver. 'Eldfield' after Tombleson was published in H. G. Fearnside's *Picturesque beauties of the Rhine* [c. 1846].

Fife, James (fl. 1830) Landscape and architectural engraver. Seven plates, all after William Westall, were published in T. Moule's *Great Britain illustrated ...* 1830. They were 'Salisbury Crags near Edinburgh', 'Rochester Castle from the bridge', 'Hastings', 'Canterbury, gate of St. Augustine's', 'Holyrood House, Edinburgh', 'New Bridge, Lancaster' and 'Whitby from the south'. Ho.

Fincke, Hans (1800–49) Architectural engraver. Born in Berlin, he studied under Buchhorn and came to London to work with the Findens. He established a school of steel engraving in Berlin. His name appears as engraver on a variant of 'Black Friars Bridge' after T. Shepherd published in Fearnside's *Tombleson's Thames* 1834, other copies of which were signed 'C. Finke'. T.

Finden, Edward Francis (1791–1857) Landscape and portrait engraver. Born on 30 April 1791, he was the younger brother of William Finden (q.v.), and about 1806 he joined his brother as pupil to James Mitan (1776–1822). The brothers appear to have worked together for most of their lives, and in many cases it is impossible to separate their activities. When this is so, they are treated in the article on

William. In 1810, at the age of nineteen, Edward, then living at John Street, Fitzroy Square, was awarded the small Silver Palette for an outline drawing of the Laacoon by the Society of Arts. His early work is represented by the engraved title page to volume 2 of J. Milton's *Paradise Lost*, published by J. Sharpe in 1817, and a plate, dated 1 July 1817, in Ottley's *Engravings of the ... Marquis of Stafford's ... pictures* 1818. He went on to engrave the plates for J. Franklin's *Narrative of a journey to the shores of the Polar Sea* 1823, R. Lyall's *Character of the Russians* 1823 and other works, and one of his earliest excursions into steel came with the thirty-five plates to which he put his name which appeared in R. Batty's *Welsh scenery* 1825. Like Heath, the Findens set up an atelier, and it is difficult to believe the industry implied by the number of plates signed with their names; Edward could only have supervised or possibly put the finishing touches to many of his plates. The engravings in *Welsh scenery*, all after the author, are dated between January and August 1825, and included 'Chepstow from the cliff opposite the Tower', 'Hay', 'Cader Idris', 'Waterfall at Aber' and 'Wrexham'. He probably had more to do with the three engravings done for the *Literary souvenir* 1825, i.e. 'Kirkstall Abbey' (a poor vignette after C. Cope) and 'France—Lyons' and 'Spain—fortress of Saguntum' after W. Brockedon, while in the 1826 volume, appeared 'Bolton Abbey, Wharfedale' after J. M. W. Turner, in the 1827 volume three plates, including 'Alexander and Diogenes' after Martin, and in the 1831 volume 'The maiden astronomer' after Boxall. For *The Amulet* of 1826, he did 'The vicar's maid' after W. H. Brooke, 'Enduring affection' after R. Westall, 'Lambeth Palace' after L. Stephens and 'Mount of Olives from Jerusalem' after T. C. Croker. For the 1827 volume, he did 'The shipwrecked' after H. Corbould, and for the 1831 volume, 'The Florentine' after H. W. Pickersgill.

Ten plates after the author and his wife appeared in R. Heber's *Narrative of a journey ...* 1828 and included 'Jangheera', 'Nundedevi' and 'View in the Deccan' and his name appears on fifty plates after the author for W. Brockedon's *Illustration of the passes of the Alps* 1828–9, engraved between February 1827 and November 1829. Twenty-one of them were vignettes, the workmanship being of a very high standard never surpassed by Edward himself. Plates included 'Briancon', 'Tell's chapel...', 'Vale of Meyeringen' and 'Lago Maggiore'. 'The oriental love-letter' after H. W. Pickersgill was done for *The Bijou* 1828, and 'The little gleaner' after W. Beechey for *The Anniversary* 1829. 'The maid of Rajast'han after Col. James Tod was engraved for *Friendship's offering* 1831, and twelve plates after the author were done for H. D. Acland's *Illustrations of the Vaudois* 1831, all of which were well engraved with good tone variations. The longest series of plates under his name was that of seventy-nine for what became *Finden's illustrations of the life and works of Lord Byron* 1833–4, for which he and his brother took the sole risks, becoming thus their first publishing venture. The principal artists involved were C. Stanfield, J. M. W. Turner, D. Roberts, T. Creswick and J. D. Harding, and the series included 'Gibraltar', 'Malta', 'The tomb of Cecilia Metella', 'Cephalonia' and 'Negropont' after Turner, 'Ithaca', 'Santa Maura' and 'Corfu' after Stanfield and 'Chamouni', 'The Castle of Chillon' and 'Geneva' after J. D. Harding. In a number of these cases, however, the artist had worked up a sketch taken on the spot by another person. He produced frontispieces and engraved title page vignettes for each of the eight volumes of Crabbe's *Poetical works* 1834–8, mostly after Stanfield, and for Cowper's *Life and works* 1835–6, mostly after Harding, and 'Mosque of Mustapha Khan—Bejapore' after Purser for Elliot's *Views in India ...* 1835.

Four plates after J. Ross appeared in Ross's *Narrative of a second voyage* ... 1835 and 'Brading harbour', 'Powderham Park, Exmouth' and 'Boulogne old pier' after C. Stanfield were done for *Stanfield's coast scenery* 1836. 'Thomas Stanley' after Holbein appeared in E. Lodge's *Portraits ...*, 2nd edition, 1835 (plate dated 1 September 1831), 'The Phoenix Tower, Chester Walls' (a vignette) in T. Noble and T. Rose's *Counties of Chester ...* 1836 and eight plates in S. C. Hall's *Book of gems* 1836, including a vignette, 'Flight into Egypt', after J. Martin, an octagonal picture, 'Chaplet of flowers', after G. Patten and 'The disconsolate' after G. S. Newton. 'View of Lichfield...' after C. Stanfield was published in *Graphic illustrations of Samuel Johnson ...* 1837. 'Pericles bursting into tears...' after H. Corbould was done for volume 3 of Thirwell's *History of Greece* 1837, five plates after Turner, Harding, Roberts and Prout for Horne's *Biblical keepsake* 1837, four plates of 'Poland', 'Arabia', 'Portugal' and 'Africa' for *Finden's tableaux of ... national character* 1837, four engraved title page vignettes after T. Creswick for each of the volumes of O. Goldsmith's *Miscellaneous works* 1837 and the frontispiece 'Goldsmith's monument' after Nollekens for Prior's *Life of Goldsmith* 1837. Vignettes after Balmer, Stanfield and Creswick appeared as engraved title pages to four major works in an edition of Byron's works 1837, 'Bally-burgh Ness' after Turner and 'The tower of Wolf's Crag' after Melville in Wright's *Landscape-historical illustrations of Scotland* 1836–8, 'Bridge at Bhurkote' after Melville in White's *Views in India ...* 1838 and 'Foudai' and 'St. Joire' after Brockedon in Beattie's *Waldenses* 1838. 'The beggar's opera' after G. S. Newton, dated 1 January 1838, 'Happy as a king' after W. Collins, 1 May 1839, 'Othello relating his adventures' after D. Cowper, 10 April 1842, and 'The harvest waggon' after T. Gainsborough, 28 November 1843, were done for the Findens' ill-fated *Royal Gallery of British Art* 1838–49. 'The narrows from Staten Island' after W. H. Bartlett was done for N. P. Willis's *American scenery* 1840, 'Her Most Gracious Majesty Victoria' after R. J. Lane, fairies on the engraved title page after Marchant, 'Lady Wilhelmina Stanhope' after A. E. Chalon and 'Lady Ashby' after J. Hayter for *Finden's Gallery of beauty* 1841 and twenty-six plates for W. Beattie's *Ports, harbours ...* 1842. The latter was a work originally suggested to the Findens in 1836 by George Balmer and forty-eight plates were published by Tilt, but insufficient copies were sold to cover production costs, so the publisher was only too glad to hand the venture over to George Virtue, who extended it and issued this version. Included in both versions was 'Brighton' after Thomas Creswick, which features the newly built (1835) sea wall (Plate 28). He did twenty-nine vignettes printed on the text pages for Byron's *Childe Harold's pilgrimage*, first published in this form in 1842. Many of the sketches were by amateurs, e.g. Capt. Ireton, Lieut. Allen and R. Ford, worked up by T. Creswick, H. Warren, J. B. Aylmer and G. Howse. The vignettes included 'Delphi', 'Seville', 'The wolf of the Capitol' and 'View from Monte Albano'. 'The bachelor uncle' after D. Wilkie appeared in G. N. Wright's *Gallery of engravings* 1844–6, twenty plates in *Beauties of Moore* 1846, including 'Indian maid' after Elmore, 'Young Kitty' after J. Wright, 'Laughing eyes' after W. P. Frith, 'Ninetta' after A. Egg and 'Young Jessica' after E. M. Ward. 'Umpires of the combat' after F. Stone and 'The look-out' after A. Chisholm were done for *Friendship's offering* 1844 and twenty-two plates after Roberts, Stanfield, Barret, Daniell, Prout, Cattermole, Fielding, Newton and others for Scott's *Waverley novels*. 'Ships of war at Spithead'—a vignette first published as 'Men of war ...' in Beattie's *Ports, harbours ...*—after E. W. Cooke and

'Entrance to Portsmouth Harbour'—also a vignette—after W. J. Cook were used in B. Woodward's ... *General history of Hampshire* 1863. It was said that Edward was the man of business, superintending staff, finishing their plates and directing the issue of publications, but in the series of letters to Murray the burden seemed to be equally shared, and although they had a number of pupils only Richard Hatfield (q.v.) is expressly assigned to Edward. He joined the Artists' Annuity Fund in 1818. He was a kind, warm-hearted man. He died on 9 February 1857 after a painful bodily affliction had affected him for five or six years.   AJ; DNB; H; SocA; T.

Finden, George C. (fl. 1848–83) Figure and historical engraver. Although a positive relationship has not so far been established, this engraver is very likely to have been a son of either Edward or William, and in the absence of any signed work before about 1848, he is likely to have worked in the Finden atelier for the early part of his working life. His earliest signed plate was 'The cherry-seller' after W. Collins, which first appeared in the *Art Union* 1848, and was republished in Mrs Hall's *Drawing room table book* 1849. R. Ackerman published 'Wellington as Chancellor of Oxford University (1852). The *Art Journal* for 1853 carried 'A mythological battle' after T. Stothard, which was coarsely engraved in a fashion which spread from the Continent at about this time. For *The Story of Enid and Geraint* [1869], he engraved 'Geraint slays Earl Doorm' after Gustave Doré. Eight further plates were issued in the *Art Journal* between 1872 and 1883 (indicating perhaps that he worked more or less permanently for Virtue, the publisher), of which 'Shrine in Russia' after A. Yvon (1873) was coarsely engraved, 'Returning home' after T. Gerard (1878) and 'Pampered menials' after J. E. Hodgson (1879) were largely etched and 'The empty saddle' after S. E. Waller (1881) had some return to delicate engraving, especially in the foreground. 'The Cooper's family' after E. Frère came out in the *Art Journal* for 1875, and in the same year 'Lady Romney' after J. Reynolds was published. 'The condemnation of Anne Boleyn' after R. Smirke was issued in H. Tyrrell's *Royal history of England* 1877, and 'Joan of Arc and Charles' after H. C. Selous appeared in volume 1 of *The Royal Shakespeare*, with an introduction by F. G. Furnivall, 1883–4.   B; T.

Finden, William (1787–1852) Landscape and portrait engraver. He was the elder of the two brothers, and about the turn of the century was apprenticed to James Mitan (1776–1822), coming out of his time about 1808. He modelled his early work on the style of James Heath, and engraved many plates for the booksellers. His first important work was the fifteen plates engraved between 1810 and 1817 for Ottley's *Engravings of the ... Marquis of Stafford's ... pictures* 1818, one of which, 'Rent day feast' after Teniers, won him a gold medal from the Society of Arts in 1813. In 1814 he did the forty-five engravings after those of W. Hollar for the new edition of Sir William Dugdale's *History of St. Paul's Cathedral* 1818, and further work came out in T. F. Dibdin's *Aedes Althorpianae* 1822 and Walker's *Effigies poeticae* 1824.

The brothers were well into their thirties, with William close to forty, when they embarked upon the great series of steel engravings for which they are so well known. Their success was mainly due to their joint efforts, which enabled them to share in the running of the business, allowed them to take a number of pupils and assistants and, less successfully, encouraged them to go into publishing on their own account. They worked at their studio at 18 and 19 Southampton Place, Euston Square, aided at various times by J. B. Allen, J. W. Archer, F. Bacon, C. Rolls and L. Stocks as assistants, and S.

Hollyer, T. Phillibrowne, G. Price (all three of whom emigrated to America), S. Rawle (probably the younger, b. 1801), S. Sangster and J. H. P. Stubbs as pupils, with Robert Staines as both pupil and assistant. It is said that the brothers Charles and John Cousen were also pupils and that the German Hans Fincke (1800–59) also studied under them.

It is difficult to ascertain exactly the amount of work William put into the plates carrying his name, although he was reckoned to be the better engraver of the two brothers, and probably contributed more in this way than Edward. Among his early steel plates was 'The rivals' after C. R. Leslie, engraved for *the Literary souvenir* 1826, followed by two plates after H. Howard for *The Amulet*, i.e. 'The cottage girl' for the 1827 volume and 'The gipsey girl' for that of 1828. For the 1831 volume he contributed the frontispiece 'Countess Gower and her child' after T. Lawrence. 'Peter Oliver' after Van Dyck and 'Rysbrach' after J. Vanderbank appeared in H. Walpole's *Anecdote of painting* 1827, 'Chaucer in the arbour' (a mainly etched vignette) after W. Mulready, 'Joy of childhood' after T. Lawrence, 'The agony' after G. Jones and 'The funeral' after D. Wilkie in *The Bijou* 1828, 'The gored huntsman' after A. Cooper and 'The rivals; or, love in a mist' after R. Smirke in *The Keepsake* 1828 and 'Lucy and her bird' after J. M. Wright in *The Keepsake* 1829. 'The blackberry boy' after W. Hamilton was done for *The Anniversary* 1829, five vignettes after T. Stothard for S. Rogers' *Italy* 1830 and 'Poesie' after Carlo Dolci for *Friendship's offering* 1831. 'The new custom house, Liverpool' after T. Allom (used again in G. N. Wright's *Lancashire* 1842 and his *Gallery of engravings* 1844–6) and 'Lancaster' after J. Henderson appeared in E. Baines's *History of ... Lancaster* 1836, and twenty-six plates were done for *Finden's illustrations of the life and works of Lord Byron* 1833–4 after Stanfield, Turner, Stone, Prout, etc., of which 'The Hague' after T. S. Cooper was a good example. This last-named book was the first publishing venture in which the brothers took the financial risks, although the names of Murray and Tilt appeared on the title pages. William's name appeared on thirty-three plates, all (except five) vignettes, and all (except the one after Flaxman) after T. Stothard, in S. Rogers' *Poems* 1834. It should be noted that he engraved no plate after Turner in this volume: his work after this painter does not appear to have been rated very highly. Between July 1830 and November 1835 he engraved eleven portraits for E. Lodge's *Portraits ... 1835*. Frontispieces and engraved title page vignettes after J. D. Harding were done for several of the eight volumes of Cowper's *Life and works* 1835–6, 'Palace of the seven stories—Beejapore' after Purser for Elliot's *Views in India ... 1835*, 'Cols. Mannering, Hazlewood and the smugglers' after Turner for Wright's *Landscape-historical illustrations of Scotland* 1836–8 and 'Junction of a tributary stream with the Orontes' and 'Adana...' after W. H. Bartlett for J. Carne's *Syria* 1836–8. 'The semaphore, Portsmouth', 'Calais' and 'St. Pierre Port, Guernsey' after C. Stanfield were engraved for *Stanfield's coast scenery* 1836 and 'Thomas Campbells'—a vignette after a bust by E. H. Baily—as the frontispiece for T. Campbell's *Poetical works* 1837. Twelve plates after Harding, Roberts, Stanfield, Brockedon and the Hon. Capt. Fitzmaurice appeared in Horne's *Biblical keepsake* 1837, 'Albania' after F. Stone and 'Greece' after F. P. Stephanoff in *Finden's tableaux of ... national character* 1837, 'The Ganges entering the plains near Hurdwar' after Purser in White's *Views in India ... 1838* and 'Interior of a Highlander's house' after E. Landseer, dated 1 May 1839, and 'Returning from market' after A. W. Callcott, dated December 1840, in Finden's *Royal Gallery of British art* 1838–49. This last-named book was their *magnum opus*, but publication difficulties led to financial problems for them. William engraved twenty-three plates for the series suggested in 1836 by George Balmer, which, after a disastrous first publication by Tilt as *Views of ports and harbours . . .*, resulted in Virtue's production of W. Beattie's *Ports, harbours . . .* 1842: Balmer, Harding, Cooke and Creswick were the artists after whom he engraved his plates and examples include 'Entrance to the port of Berwick' (Plate 27) 'Cullercoats', 'Blyth', 'Tintagel Castle' and 'Dover, Kent'. 'Wilton House' after R. Wilson appeared on the engraved title page of T. Moore's *Poetical Works* 1843. Thirty-one plates appeared in Byron's *Childe Harold's pilgrimage* 1842, all vignettes with the exception of the frontispiece, which was 'Lord Byron in his Albanian dress', painted by T. Phillips, the original of which is still in possession of John Murray, the publisher. The engravings were done after H. Warren, C. R. Cockerell, G. Howse, T. Creswick and J. B. Aylmer, assisted by Capt. Ireton, Lieut. Allen, etc., and included 'Cadiz', 'Temple of Jupiter', 'Ali Pacha at Tepaleen', 'Ouchy–Lausanne' (a good engraving) and 'Fountain of Egeria'. The frontispiece 'The bride of Lammermoor' after E. Landseer was done for Scott's *Waverley novels*, 'The naughty boy', also after Landseer, appeared in Mrs Hall's *Drawing room table book* 1849 and 'Velletri' after Brockedon appeared in Costello's *Piedmont and Italy* [c. 1855].

The brothers had devoted most of their lives to book illustration, and only William had produced any large plates. Besides his early portrait of George IV in 1829, he turned increasingly to the print publishers in the 1840s, probably in an effort to relieve their (the Findens) financial difficulties. 'The naughty boy' after Landseer came out in 1843, 'The girl with the fish', also after Landseer, in 1844 and 'The Highlander's return' after Wilkie in 1845. Between 1848 and 1850 he was engaged upon 'Irish courtship' after F. Goodall for the Royal Irish Art Union and 'The Crucifixion' after W. Hilton for the Art Union of London, which was to be his last plate. He also found time to take part in various outside activities, and he was President of the Artists' Annuity Fund from 1834 to 1836, which he joined as a founder member in 1810. On 20 March 1845 he was elected to the Council of the Institute of Fine Arts, and just a week before he died he was named, with seven or eight of his colleagues, as a signatory of a petition to the Queen outlining the claims of engravers to full honours in the Royal Academy. Returning one evening from a meeting of engravers (probably the Chalcographic Society), he caught a cold, and, weakened by the pressure of work over the past few years, suffered a series of heart attacks expiring on 20 September 1852, in his sixty-fifth year. He was buried in Highgate cemetery.

He was a widower at his death, and it is possible that an Adam Edward Finden (1824–46), who died on 13 October 1846, aged twenty-two, was a son or nephew of his. He was part of a three-man deputation to Sir Thomas Lawrence in 1827 to explore the possibility of approaching the Government for approval of a project to engrave pictures in the National Gallery. This resulted in the establishment of the 'Associated Engravers' under John Pye's managership, and one of Finden's contributions was to be the engraving of Wilkie's 'Village festival'. Delays producing it held up the first number in 1830–1, and were the first indication of the breakdown of the project. It was still not delivered by March 1838, by which time his own publication programme was well advanced and he was too busy to attend to it

AJ; Br; DNB; *Encyc. Brit.* 11th ed. 1910; H; *Illus. Lond. News* 9 October 1852, p. 299; Letters in the possession of John Murray, publisher; Celina Fox, *London Journal*, vol. 2, No. 1, 1976, pp. 10–14.

Findlay, Alexander (fl. 1840) Map engraver. A map of the Mediterranean was engraved for G. N. Wright's *Shores and islands of the Mediterranean* 1840.

Finke, C. (fl. 1834) Architectural engraver. Known by 'Black Friars Bridge' after T. Shepherd, which was published in Fearnside's *Tombleson's Thames* 1834. A variant of this plate is known signed 'H. Finke' (q.v.).

Fisher, J. (fl. 1829–34) Landscape engraver. His first known plate is 'Market place, Kingston' (1829) after N. Whittock, published in T. Allen's *History . . . of the counties of Surrey and Sussex* 1829–31, followed by 'Mont Ferrand' (28 October 1833) after J. D. Harding, in T. Roscoe's *Tourist in France* 1834 and 'Tower of Comáres (28 October 1834) after D. Roberts, in T. Roscoe's *Tourist in Spain. Granada* 1835. The two last-named volumes appeared as the annual volumes of *The Landscape annual*, published by Jennings.

Fisher, Samuel (fl. 1830–55). He was born about 1802, probably in Birmingham, where he attended J. V. Barber's Great Charles Street Academy to learn drawing. He was a pupil of William Radclyffe (q.v.), from whom he learned the art of engraving, and, in common with most of the other engravers trained in Birmingham, moved to London in his late twenties to join the band of prolific engravers then working there. Seven plates after Gastineau were engraved for the latter's *Wales illustrated . . .* 1830 and 'On the Grand Canal, Venice' after Prout was published in T. Roscoe's *Tourist in Italy* 1831 (*Landscape annual* 1831), and four plates dated 1831 after T. Allom were issued in J. Britton and E. W. Brayley's *Devonshire and Cornwall illustrated* 1832. 'Pompeii. Gate of Isis' was engraved after T. Scandrett for Sir William Gell's *Pompeiana . . .* 1832. 'Verona' after C. Stanfield came out in L. Ritchie's *Travelling sketches in the north of Italy* 1832 and the engraved title page of the *Continental annual* 1832 carried 'Roman column at Igel near Treves' after S. Prout, with 'ornament by F. W. Topham' providing a decorative frame. 'Vietri' and 'Genoa', both dated 28 October 1832 and after J. D. Harding, appeared in T. Roscoe's *Tourist in Italy* 1833 and after the same artist he contributed 'Licenza . . .' to *Finden's illustrations of the life and works of Lord Byron* 1833–4. He contributed 'Sea view of St. Malo' after C. Stanfield to L. Ritchie's *Travelling sketches on the sea coast of France* 1834 and he did 'Saint Denis' and 'Bridge of St. Cloud from Sèvres' after J. M. W. Turner for L. Ritchie's *Wandering by the Seine* 1835.

For Sir John Ross's *Narrative of a second voyage . . .* 1835, he engraved 'Tilson's Islands' (1834) after the author's drawing, and for *Heath's Versailles* [c. 1836], he engraved three plates after W. Callow, two of which were republished in *Keepsake français* 1840. For White's *Views in India . . .* 1838, he engraved a vignette—'Runjeet Singh's encampment . . .'—after the author's design; for Wright's *Landscape-historical illustrations of Scotland* 1836–8; and for Bacon's *Oriental annual* 1840, 'The Pass of Leny' after Melville and two plates after W. Warren. In 1836, he began his work for the great topographical works published by Virtue and Fisher (after designs by T. Allom. W. H. Bartlett, and T. Creswick). After Bartlett, three plates were engraved for W. Beattie's *Switzerland* 1836, among which was 'Mer de Glace (Chamouni)', two plates, dated 1837, for J. Carne's *Syria* 1836–8, two plates, dated 1837, for W. Beattie's *Scotland illustrated* 1838, two plates for Beattie's *Waldenses* 1838, 'Court of the Mosque of Sultan Achmet' for Pardoe's *Beauties of the Bosphorus* 1840, 'View of Baltimore' for Willis's *American scenery* 1840 and 'Sidon and Mount Lebanon from the sea' for Stebbing's

Christian in Palestine [1847]. After T. Allom, he engraved four plates, dated 1836 and 1837, for W. Beattie's *Scotland illustrated* 1838, two, dated 1838, for J. Carne's *Syria*, five plates each for R. Walsh's *Constantinople* 1838–40 and G. N. Wright's *China* 1843 and three appeared in J. Kitto's *Gallery of scripture engravings* 1846–9. After T. Creswick, he did Irish vignettes—two for L. Ritchie's *Ireland* 1837 and six for S. C. and A. M. Hall's *Ireland* 1841–3. For *Barber's picturesque illustrations of the Isle of Wight* [c. 1835], he engraved one plate and for *Friendship's offering* 1844, he did two vignettes—'The well of St. Keyne' after E. C. Wood and 'The Maiden's tower, Constantinople' after G. L. Manwaring, a subject he had already engraved after T. Allom for R. Walsh's *Constantinople* 1838–40. For Finden's *Royal Gallery of British Art* 1838–49, he engraved 'Lucky escape' (20 June 1842) after W. F. Witherington, and a very good vignette—'The ruined abbey' after G. Cattermole—was published in Calabrella's *Evenings at Haddon Hall* 1845. He died some time before 1877, in which year fourteen of his works were exhibited (priced from 12/6d to £4 19s. 0d.) at the Exibition of engravings by Birmingham men held by the Royal Society of Artists, Birmingham; six were after Turner, three each after Roberts and Stanfield and one each after Prout and Witherington. B; T.

Flemming (or Fleming), T. (fl. 1841–74) Landscape and architectural engraver. Six plates after Allom were published in Brayley's *Topographical history of Surrey* 1841–8, and include 'Asgil House...' (signed 'T. Fleming'), 'Chessington Church' and 'View of Leith Hill'. 'Desolation of Ninevah' after H. Warren appeared in *The Self-interpreting Bible* 1864, and 'University of Glasgow, inner court' after S. Bough (with rounded upper corners) was engraved as the title page centre piece to volume 2 of Chambers's *Biographical dictionary of eminent Scotsmen*, 2nd edition, 1875.

Flowers, (fl. 1850) Landscape engraver. 'Hawthornden', a vignette, was published by T. & W. McDowall of 14 North Bridge, Edinburgh.

Floyd, William (fl. 1832–59) Landscape and architectural engraver. It may be possible to identify him with Robert Brandard's brother-in-law, who lived in Highgate, Birmingham, who probably trained in that city, and who was alive in 1877, according to the introduction of the *Exhibition of engravings by Birmingham men* 1877 (pp. 8, 37). The books with which he was connected indicate that he was well known to London publishers, and it is possible that if he did not actually work in the metropolis, then he visited it frequently to acquire commissions. His earliest work on steel was 'Babicombe [sic] Bay' (a vignette on a map, signed 'Floyd') after T. Allom, engraved for J. Britton and E. W. Brayley's *Devonshire and Cornwall illustrated* 1832, followed by the frontispiece 'Cathedral Tower, Antwerp' after S. Prout (signed 'Wm. Floyd') to the *Continental annual* 1832. 'Corby Castle'...' and two other plates were engraved after Allom for Rose's *Cumberland*, 'Stockton on Tees' and 'Wynyard...' for Rose's *Durham and Northumberland* and 'Upper Reach, Ullswater' for Rose's *Westmorland*, all published in 1832. Two contributions after Stanfield to *Heath's Picturesque annual* were 'Bingen' in Ritchie's *Travelling sketches on the Rhine* 1833 and 'Harbour of St. Malo' in Ritchie's *Travelling sketches on the sea coasts of France* 1834. Three Chinese views were done after Prout, Purser and Copley Fielding for Elliot's *Views in India ...* 1835. Four plates were done for Baines's *History of ... Lancaster* 1836, and *Stanfield's coast scenery* 1836 contained 'Porchester Castle' and 'Boulogne upper harbour'

(both signed 'W. Floyde'); these latter two were exhibited at the Birmingham exhibition of 1877. '"Christian got up to the gate"' and 'The land of Beulah' after Melville were issued in Bunyan's *Pilgrim's progress* 1836. Four plates after Bartlett, Allom and Salmon were published in Carne's *Syria* 1836–8 and reissued in Kitto's *Gallery of scripture engravings* 1846–9. 'Village of Koghera...' after Allom and 'Valley of the Dhoon...' after Turner were engraved for White's *Views in India ...* 1838 and two plates after Arnauld and Allom for Wright's *Landscape-historical illustrations of Scotland* 1836–8. A plate of ruins of an ancient temple at Corinth after W. Purser appeared in C. Wordsworth's *Greece* 1839. Six plates after T. Allom (with one after W. L. Leitch) were engraved for R. Walsh's *Constantinople* 1838–40, and included 'Mosque of Mahmoud II at Tophana', which is a very good example of his work, and 'The Valley of Guuik Suey, the sweet waters of Asia', both of which were in the Birmingham exhibition of 1877, and two plates, after Melville and Rembrandt, appeared in Fisher's *Historic illustrations of the Bible* [1840–3]. The most sustained series of plates (nine) was done for G. N. Wright's *China* 1843, all after T. Allom, of which 'Ships Imogene and Andromache...', drawn from a sketch on the spot by Lieut. White, Royal Marines, is unusual, inasmuch as about two-thirds of the plate was engraved, not etched. Two engravings represented him in Wright's *Gallery of engravings* 1844–6, and 'Hampton, Middlesex' after Marshall appeared in Fearnside and Harral's *History of London* [c. 1850]. 'The sea-port' after Claude Lorraine was issued in the *Art Journal* for 1859. Ten of his engravings after Allom, Stanfield, Cotman and Turner were on show at the 1877 Birmingham exhibition, including the 'Fish market' after Turner. Floyd joined the Artists' Annuity Fund in 1836. B; T.

Forrest, William (1805–89) Landscape and architectural engraver. He was one of the Scottish school of engravers in Edinburgh, and may, at a later date, have moved to London to work. His best series of plates was the ten done after D. O. Hill for Wilson and Chambers's *Land of Burns* 1840, and included 'Alloway kirk', 'Mill Monach on the Coil' and 'Lincluden'. He contributed three plates to *Engravings after the best pictures of the Great Masters* 1841–3 (all done by Edinburgh engravers), namely, 'Landscape with cattle, evening' and 'Landscape with goats', both after Claude Lorraine and 'Landscape, forest scenery' (dated 1 May 1843) after A. Waterloo, which was largely etched. Unlike some of the other plates in the volume, these three appear to have been done on steel. J. Browne's *History of the Highlands* [c. 1845] contained three Scottish scenes, two after J. C. Brown and one after J. W. McLea, seven views after G. S. Keith's daguerrotypes were done for A. Keith's *Evidence of the truth of the Christian religion ...* 36th edition, 1848, and for *Black's picturesque tourist of Scotland* 1849, he engraved five plates (two after G. Cattermole), dated between 1842 and 1847 (for the 17th edition, 1865, he contributed an extra plate, 'Dunkeld' after D. O. Hill). 'Woodstock' after Creswick appeared in Scott's *Poetical works* 1853, four views in *The Self-interpreting Bible* 1864 and a vignette after Stanley in Inglis's *Gleanings from the English poets ...* [c. 1865]. 'Richmond' after H. Warren appeared in T. Baines's *Yorkshire past and present* 1871–7, and eight Biblical scenes after S. Bough, W. L. Leitch, J. Martin and E. Walton were issued in the *Imperial Family Bible* 1873. Five plates after Chevalier and Skinner Prout were done for Booth's *Australia* [1873–6]. Eleven plates appeared in Scott's *Waverley Novels*, four after C. Stanfield, two after W. L. Leitch and one each after T. Allom, J. C. Brown, T. Creswick, H. McCulloch and A. Nasmyth. The only plate of his to appear in the *Art Journal* was 'Mallee scrub, Victoria' after N. Chevalier, which was a plate originally used for Booth's *Australia* [1873–6]. Volume 1 of the second edition of R. Chambers's *Biographical dictionary of eminent Scotsmen* 1875 carried a representation of the University of Edinburgh after S. Bough (which was largely etched, and had rounded upper corners) on its engraved title page.   B; T.

Fothergill, J. (fl. 1820–30) Architectural engraver. Known by 'St. James Street, Dover ...' after G. Shepherd and 'St. Mary's Church, Chartham' after W. Deeble (q.v.) (both dated 1829), which appeared in S. W. H. Ireland's *England's topographer* (commenced publication 1828). He is also known to have engraved five bookplates between 1820 and 1830.   Fi.

Fox, Augustus (fl. 1828–74) Figure engraver. Four small headpieces after T. Stothard, i.e. 'The warriors', 'A village festival', 'Poets involation' and 'Humble lovers', and 'Dreams of the youthful Shakespeare' after R. Westall appeared in *The Bijou*. 'The Hunterian Museum, Glasgow' was engraved for Shepherd's *Modern Athens* 1829–31. G. N. Wright's *China* 1843 contained five plates after T. Allom, including 'Canton. Barge-men fighting quails' and 'An itinerant barber', and for Scott's *Waverley novels* he engraved two frontispieces, i.e. 'Redgauntlet' after D. O. Hill and 'Woodstock' after G. Inskipp. 'The bag piper' after Wilkie was issued in *Casquet of literature* 1874. E. R. Whitfield (q.v.) was his pupil.   B; T.

Fox, Charles (1796–1849) Figure, landscape and portrait engraver. He was born on 17 March 1796 at Cossey, near Norwich, where his father was steward to Lord Stafford. His early interests were agriculture and floriculture, the latter of which, involving him in judging for the Horticultural Society and illustrating *The Florist*, was to be lifelong. He was instructed in drawing by Charles Hodgson of Norwich. When visited by W. C. Edwards (q.v.), the decision was made for Fox to become an engraver, and in due time he went to London to finish his education in the studio of John Burnet. The latter was at this time engaged upon his principal works after Wilkie, in which enterprise Fox joined, later going on to engrave several plates after the same artist for Cadell's edition of Scott's novels and, in 1847, the large plate of the 'First Council of the Queen', also after Wilkie. Among his engraved portraits are 'Bishop J. Milner' after G. A. Keman (1822) and that of James Hogg in Hogg's *Altrive tales* 1832. (He also did some excellent watercolour portraits, chiefly of his friends.) 'A Cauchaise girl' after Newton was engraved for *Literary souvenir* 1833. He engraved the illustrations for J. Stark's *Scenery of the rivers of Norfolk* 1834, and in G. N. Wright's *Gallery of engravings* 1844–6 appeared 'The Ionian captive' after H. W. Pickersgill. When Graves published 'The attack' after Hunt in a mixed style in 1845, the reviewer observed: 'We more than doubt, however, the policy of multiplying such subjects by the hands of such engravers as Mr. Fox.' Also in 1845, it was reported that he was to receive 'the enormous sum' of 1100 guineas for engraving 'Fight interrupted' after W. Mulready for the Royal Irish Art Union, but he was still working on the plate when he died of what appears to have been a heart attack on 28 February 1849 while visiting a friend at Leyton in Essex. Sources disagree as to his age: the *Art Journal* obituary (1849, p. 105) gives it as fifty-three next birthday, making the year of birth 1796; but Redgrave, followed by the *Dictionary of National Biography*, gives 'in his 55th year'–the former has been followed. He engraved

portraits of his two masters, of W. C. Edwards (a small copper engraving) and of J. Burnet after S. P. Denning. His own portrait was drawn and engraved by W. Carpenter for publication in *The Florist*.   AJ; DNB; R; T.

Fox, M. (fl. 1828) Architectural engraver. Known by 'New Treasury, Whitehall' and 'Italian Opera House, Haymarket', both after T. H. Shepherd and dated 23 October 1828, engraved for J. Elmes's *Metropolitan improvements* 1829.

Fraenkel, F. (fl. 1878) Historical engraver. 'Queen Elizabeth knighting Drake...' after Gilbert, 'The escape of Lord Nithsdale from the Tower...' after Osborn and 'Queen Victoria's first council...' after Wilkie were published in Archer's *Pictures and royal portraits...* [c. 1878].

Francis, Edward (fl. 1829–30) Landscape and architectural engraver. A series of forty-one plates, all after W. Westall, was engraved by him for T. Moule's *Great Britain illustrated ...* 1830, of which 'The Pavilion, Brighton', 'Chester from Barrelwell Hill' and 'Pentilly Castle on the Tamar' (dated 1829) are examples.   Ho.

Franklin, J. (fl. 1840) Historical engraver. He 'designed and etched' the combined frontispiece and engraved title page depicting the ten commandments for Fisher's *Historic illustrations of the Bible* [1840–3].

Freebairn, Alfred Robert (1794–1846) Landscape engraver. Probably of Scottish descent, he seems to have been the son of Robert Freebairn (d. 1808), a landscape painter, for whom he published posthumously *Outlines of Lancashire scenery from an unpublished sketchbook of the late R. Freebairn, designed as studies for the use of schools and beginners, and etched by the younger Freebairn* 1815. He became a student at the Royal Academy. Much of his steel engraved work was done for the annuals and popular books of the day. 'Venice' after S. Prout appeared in *The Keepsake* 1830, 'Entrance to Ivrea, Val d'Aosta' after J. D. Harding in T. Roscoe's *Tourist in Italy* 1833, 'Pont du Château' after J. D. Harding in T. Roscoe's *Tourist in France* 1834 and 'The Vermilion tower' after D. Roberts in T. Roscoe's *Tourist in Spain. Granada* 1835, the last-named three books being volumes of *The Landscape annual*, published by Robert Jennings. 'St. Michael's Mount, Normandy from the West' was engraved for *Stanfield's coast scenery* 1836 and 'Echo and Narcissus' after G. Arnold for S. C. Hall's *Book of Gems* 1836, and for the 1838 volume of the same book he did 'The gipsey' after R. Westmacott, drawn by H. Corbould, and two vignettes—'The way-side inn' after W. Mulready and 'Windsor, evening' after R. B. Pyne. A plate of the monument to George Evelyn at Wotton Church after his own design was done for volume 5 of Brayley's *Topographical history of Surrey* 1841–8.

Most of his engraving in the early 1840s appears to have been done in conjunction with John Bates' improved version of the anaglyptograph. This device was first used in France in 1817, and consists of a tracing point which is used to run over a relief surface such as a coin, medal, bas-relief, etc. and which is connected to an etching needle, thus scratching the resist on a steel or copper plate. A full description of the process appears in the *Art Union* 1846 (p. 14), and a representation of a medal, 'Science trimming the lamp of life', accompanied the article. By far his most celebrated example, however, was his engraving of J. Flaxman's 'Shield of Achilles'. The shield was first produced in bronze, selling at 3,000 guineas, or silver gilt, at 4,000 guineas, and the engraver had, at his own expense, issued a portfolio of eight engravings at two guineas, one plate from which was reproduced in the *Art Union* 1846. The plates were done on steel. Other examples of engravings in this mode included 'A salver of the 16th century' by Jean Goujon, a bookplate for Thomas Willement, 'Sarpedon borne off by Death and Sleep' after a sculpture by M. R. Watson (of which only fifty copies were printed, for private circulation — the plate was withdrawn from the sale of the sculptor's effects in 1848) and 'Part of the west frieze of the Parthenon', published in the *Art Journal* 1849, with the east frieze being reproduced in the same periodical in 1866. He joined the Artists' Annuity Fund in 1823, and in 1846 was living at 23 Mornington-place, Hampstead Road. While his father died when he was fourteen, his mother died in August 1846, and a few days later, on 21 August, he also died, suddenly, aged about fifty-two. He was buried in Highgate cemetery, and in 1847 a move was made to erect a monument over his grave, the sculptor C. H. Smith offering his services at the bare cost of materials and labour.   AU; DNB; R.

Freeman, Samuel (1773?–1857) Portrait and historical engraver. He is thought to have been a pupil of F. Bartolozzi, and he worked extensively in the stipple manner, especially in his early days. A. Tuer, in *Bartolozzi and his works* 1881, lists Bartolozzi's pupils and those of them who practised stipple, but although it is extensive Freeman is not mentioned. One of his earliest portraits was of D. Garrick after Reynolds, published in the *Monthly Mirror* 1807. In 1809 he was involved in the relief of Thomas Tagg, the etcher, and the beginnings of the Artists' Annuity Fund. For T. F. Dibdin's *Northern gallery*, he engraved portraits and illustrations, and for Tresham's *British gallery* 1815, he engraved Raphael's 'Virgin with diadem'. Other plates were done for Jones's *National gallery* and Fisher's *National portrait gallery*, and for H. Walpole's *Anecdotes of painting* 1827, he engraved 'Marriage of Henry VI and Margaret of Anjou'. A portrait of L. E. Landon after J. Wright was done for *New Monthly Magazine*, the original drawing for which is in the British Museum Department of Prints. Among his earliest works on steel was the vignette 'Statue of Achilles in Hyde Park', dated 7 July 1827, after T. H. Shepherd, engraved for J. Elmes's *Metropolitan improvements* 1829. He did the illustrations for Kotzebue's *New voyages round the world* 1830, and for a series of classical texts published by Jones in 1830–1, he engraved frontispieces of authors after antique busts, e.g. Livy, Tacitus and Xenophon. From 1829 to 1835 he engraved eleven plates for E. Lodge's *Portraits...*, 2nd edition, 1835, after artists such as Holbein, Lely and Kneller, notably, 'Edward Seymour, Duke of Somerset', 'Thomas Cromwell, Earl of Essex' and 'Thomas Radclyffe, Earl of Sussex', which was signed 'W. Freeman'. A vignette portrait of Lady Byron 'engraved on steel' was presented with the *Court Journal* 5 January 1833. Another long series of plates (fifteen) was done for Chambers's *Biographical dictionary of eminent Scotsmen* 1835, and for the 2nd edition (1875), five plates were removed and fifteen more added, of which one of the most interesting was the circular picture of Sir Robert Strange from the print engraved by Sir Robert himself. E. Baines's *History of ... Lancaster* 1836 contains two portraits, dated 1831 and 1832, of John of Gaunt and William Roscoe, the first of which, after George Vertue, undoubtedly provided the inspiration for the engraved title page of G. N. Wright's *Lancashire* 1842, where 'John of Gaunt of Castile and Leon, Duke of Lancaster' was 'painted by G. Vertue from an ancient glass window, in the Library of All Souls College, Oxon.' Four plates, after Northcote, Opie, Rembrandt and Rubens, were engraved for

Fisher's *Historic illustrations of the Bible* [1840–3]. G. N. Wright's *Gallery of engravings* 1844–6 contained 'Rt. Hon. W. Lamb, Baron Melbourne' after Lawrence, and 'Transfiguration' after Raffaele and 'Last Supper' after da Vinci appeared in the *Imperial Family Bible*, first published in 1844. What must have been some of his last plates, done when he was over seventy, were a series of eight engravings for J. Browne's *History of the Highlands* [c. 1845] after Kneller, Lawrence, Reynolds, Van Dyck and others, of which 'James, Earl of Derwentwater' and 'John Moore' should be noted. Twenty-eight, mainly royal, portraits, many after Vertue, were published in the eighteen volumes of Hume and Smollett's *History of England...* 1854–5. A vignette, 'Henrietta, Mademoiselle Sontag', after Grevedon appeared in *Casquet of literature* 1874. He died on 27 February 1857, aged about eighty-four.   DNB; R; T.

French, William (1815?–1898) Architectural and historical engraver. Two interiors of Amien's Cathedral, dated 1836, were done for B. Winkles's *French cathedrals* 1837, the one of the south aisle being after Hablot Browne. Two views of Norwich Cathedral appeared in *Winkles's ... Cathedral churches of England...* 1836–42, and in the *Art Journal* of 1882 his engraving 'Cromwell at Marston Moor' after E. Crofts was issued. His main work was the reproduction of contemporary paintings. He died at East Grinstead on 8 January 1898.   B; T.

Frost, (fl. 1832) Landscape engraver. 'Bingen' after W. Tombleson was engraved for *Tombleson's views of the Rhine* 1832.

Fry, William Thomas (1789–1843) Portrait and figure engraver. He was one of the earliest engravers to experiment with steel plates, first with those produced by J. Perkins from early in 1820, and then, more satisfactorily, with those made by C. Warren. With these latter plates Fry engraved the stipple portrait of the Revd William Naylor, dated February 1822, for *The Methodist Magazine*, and this was followed by further portraits on steel for the *Evangelical Magazine* 1823–4. He engraved frontispieces for *The London stage*, four volumes, 1824–7, and in *Forget me not* 1825, engraved two of the first steel plates to be used in an annual, namely, 'Lovers' tomb' after R. Westall and 'Madonna of St. Sixtus' after Raphael, both signed 'W. F. Fry'. He exhibited some of his engravings at Suffolk Street between 1824 and 1830. Between 1829 and 1835 he engraved eight portraits for E. Lodge's *Portraits...*, 2nd edition, 1835, after Holbein, Kneller and others, notably, 'King Henry the Eighth', 'Queen Elizabeth' and 'Sir Isaac Newton'. He contributed four plates to Fisher's *National Portrait Gallery* and eleven to Jones's *National Gallery*. 'The honors paid Raphael after his death' after Bergeret appeared in *Wreath of friendship*. Portraits after J. Jackson included those of Robert Hills, the animal painter, and John Scott, the animal engraver. Plates signed 'W. T. Fry' continued to be used in publications long after his death: for example, the *Art Union* of 1848 contained an engraving of a sculpture, 'Mercury and Pandora', by J. Flaxman, and the *Art Journal* of 1866 of another sculpture, 'The falconer', by J. E. Carew, both drawn by H. Corbould (d. 1844). *The Imperial dictionary of universal biography* [c. 1861] carried portraits of Halley and Turgot, and *The Royal Shakespeare* 1883–4 had a stipple engraved frontispiece vignette of Shakespeare to volume 2 after a 'Monumental bust'. Although he worked mainly in stipple, he is also known to have done some lithographs.   B; Br; DNB; R; S.

G

Garner, J. (fl. 1829–33) Architectural engraver. 'King's Bench Prison' and 'Sadler's Wells theatre' after T. H. Shepherd were published in the artist's *London and its environs* 1829–31. 'Marriage à la mode—contract' after W. Hogarth appeared in Hogarth's *Works* 1833. J. Garner could have been Thomas's father.

Garner, Thomas (1789–1868) Figure and landscape engraver. He was the son of a Birmingham engraver, possibly the J. Garner listed above, and was reputed to have had a natural bent for his father's profession. It is likely that he was apprenticed to his father, but he also attended Samuel Lines's classes, and, when he was in his late twenties, went to study at the Royal Academy schools (c. 1817). In the 1820s he joined Charles Heath's studio, and under the cloak of anonymity it placed around most of its engravers, did a number of plates for the annuals in which his master was then deeply involved. After a spell of hard work there, he returned to Birmingham, where the rest of his life was spent and the rest of his work done. From time to time he worked as William Radclyffe's assistant, and so it is not surprising that his own name appears on comparatively few plates. He was forty when his longest series of plates was published, in S. W. H. Ireland's *England's topographer* (commenced publication 1828), nine being after G. Shepherd (for example, 'Ashford Kent, market day' and 'Leeds Castle, Kent'), two after T. M. Baynes ('Dock yard, Sheerness' and 'Upnor Castle, near Chatham') and one after H. Gastineau, after a sketch by Deeble (q.v.) ('St. Stephen's Church, Hackington'). 'Copped Hall...' and 'Church End, Dunmow...' after Bartlett were engraved for Wright's *Picturesque beauties of Great Britain...: Essex* 1831–4. 'Viola' after H. Corbould was engraved for *Friendship's offering* 1833. 'A Mahomedan Fakeer' after W. Daniell, from an original by S. Davis, dated 1 October 1836, was engraved for J. H. Caunter's *Lives of the Moghul emperors* 1837. (It is interesting to note that, although by well-known engravers, most of the plates in this volume were badly engraved, probably due to the haste on the part of the publisher, Charles Tilt, to get a new venture started.) The first of his plates for an art periodical, 'The mountaineer' after P. F. Poole, copies of which were also used in Mrs Hall's *Drawing room table book* 1849, appeared in the *Art Union* 1848. In volumes of the *Art Journal* for 1854, 1856, 1858 and 1859 appeared 'A Greek vintage' after T. Stothard, 'L'Allegro' after W. E. Frost (thought to be his best work), 'Il Penseroso' after J. C. Horsley and 'Princess Charlotte' after Lawrence. He was well over seventy when what was probably his last plate, 'Chastity' after W. E. Frost, was issued in the *Art Journal* 1866. All but the Lawrence were on show at the 1877 Exhibition of Engravings by Birmingham men, as were seventeen others, which included portraits of Sarah Bache, James Kempson and the Revd Dr Candlish, 'Kenilworth Castle' after W. Green, 'The musicians' and 'John the Baptist' after Salvator Rosa, 'At the spring' after his own drawing and 'The Pet'. He engraved many portraits of local people, and he also did a small series of W. Hogarth's 'The Rake's progress'. As a founder member of the Birmingham Society of Arts, he devoted much time to its affairs, serving on the Hanging Committee for many years, and acting as director of the Life Academy until he was forced to give up because of failing health. He was also an accomplished violinist. When he died on 14 July 1868 in his seventy-ninth year, the school of Birmingham engravers resident in the city became extinct. AJ.

Gellatly, John (1803–59) Landscape engraver. Born at Forfar, he worked as an engraver, plate printer and litho printer in Edinburgh. In 1851 he employed twelve men and eight apprentices. He died on 26 April 1859. Vignettes of 'Stirling Castle' after A. S. Mason and 'Loch Long' after J. Ferguson were published by J. Menzies of Princes Street, Edinburgh.

Gibbon, Benjamin Phelps (1802–51) Portrait and animal engraver. He was the son of the Revd B. Gibbon, vicar of Penally, Pembrokeshire, who must have died when Benjamin was young, since he was educated at the Clergy Orphan School. He was then apprenticed to Edward Scriven, whose portrait (q.v.) he engraved for J. Pye's *Patronage of British Art* 1845, and when out of his indentures, about 1824, he went to work for J. H. Robinson (q.v.) in order to perfect his line engraving (Scriven worked largely in stipple). Both these influences are reflected in his work, which was done mainly for the print publishers, much of it being after Edwin Landseer. After this artist was done one of his few bookplates, 'The travelled monkey', dated 1 October 1828, which appeared in *The Anniversary* 1829. After the same artist he engraved 'The twa dogs' (14 January 1828), 'Jack in office' (1834), 'Shepherd's grave' and 'Shepherd's chief mourner' published by F. G. Moon (1844), 'Scotch terrier' published by M'Lean (1844) and 'Highlander's home', also published by M'Lean (1847). Some of his portraits appeared in H. Walpole's *Anecdotes of painting* 1827, and he exhibited at Suffolk Street in 1828. Other plates included 'Wolves attacking deer' after F. Gauermann (1834), for which E. Webb engraved the landscape, 'Arthur, Duke of Wellington' after J. Simpson (1839) and 'The boy with many friends' after Webster, which was half finished at his death, and was completed by Peter Lightfoot (q.v.). He is also credited with the engraving of W. Mulready's 'Wolf and the lamb' by S. Redgrave in his *Dictionary of artists...* 1875 (a statement followed by the *Dictionary of National Biography*), but in all the statements about the plate (which was sold about 1828 to provide a profit of over £1,000 for the Artists' Annuity Fund) J. H. Robinson (q.v.) is given as the engraver, at a fee of £840 (J. Pye's *Patronage...* 1845). The truth is probably somewhere in between: as Robinson's assistant, Gibbon may have engraved much of the plate, which, however, carried the master's name. He was of a delicate constitution and had been working so hard on his last plate that when he was attacked by English cholera, he succumbed, dying at his residence in Albany Street, Regent's Park, on 28 July 1851, aged about forty-nine. Although unmarried he looked after several orphans of relatives. (Thomas Dodd, MSS. vol. 8 f. 39.) (BM. Add MS. 33401.) AJ; B: Br; DNB; R; S; T.

Gibbs (fl. 1874) Figure engraver. 'Maiden meditation' after G. S. Newton was published in *Casquet of literature* 1874.

Gibbs, M. (fl. 1839) Figure engraver. 'The escape' after J. Browne was engraved for Finden's *Tableaux...* for 1840.

Gibbs, W. (fl. 1845) Figure engraver. 'The sunflower', dated 1 December 1845, after A. Derby appeared in *Beauties of Moore* 1846. It is more than likely that these three entries are for the same person, but the engravers' names are quite distinct on the plates inspected.

Giles, James (fl. 1840) Landscape engraver. Four plates after D. O. Hill were engraved for Wilson and Chambers's *Land of Burns* 1840. These were 'The braes of Ballochmyle', 'Scene on the Lugar', 'Coilsfield' and 'Friar's-Carse'. For

N. P. Willis's *American scenery* 1840, he engraved 'Fairmount Gardens . . . (Philadelphia)', dated 1839, after W. H. Bartlett. It is possible that this engraver can be identified with James Giles, landscape painter, who was born in Glasgow on 4 January 1801, and died in Aberdeen on 6 October 1870. AJ; B.

Gladwin, George (fl. 1821–54) Architectural and landscape engraver. 'Pompeii, Court of the Thermae' was engraved for Gell's *Pompeiana . . .* 1832 after the author's design. A plan of 'Parliamentary and other offices . . . Westminster' and 'Section of St. Stephen's Chapel and Crypt . . .' after R. W. Billings were engraved for E. W. Brayley and J. Britton's *History of the ancient palace . . . at Westminster* 1836. Three plans were engraved for Billings's *Architectural illustrations of Carlisle cathedral* 1840 after the author. Some plates, including 'Oil-mill', were engraved for C. Tomlinson's *Cyclopaedia of useful arts* 1854. Many of the technical plates in the *Transactions of the Society of Arts* were also engraved by him during this period. T.

Godden, J. (fl. 1841) Landscape engraver. 'Scene in Benevento' after C. Bentley was engraved for G. N. Wright's *Shores and islands of the Mediterranean* 1840.

Godfrey, John (c. 1817–1889) Landscape and architectural engraver. He was about twenty-five when his first important book work appeared—two vignettes, 'Achill, Mayo' after W. Evans and 'Errive, Mayo and Galway' after W. J. Fairholt, in volume 3 of S. C. and A. M. Hall's *Ireland* 1843. 'Ferrara' after S. Prout was engraved for W. Brockedon's *Italy . . .* 1842–3, followed by plates for two of W. Beattie's works, namely, *The Danube* 1844, which contained 'The Balkans from near Widden' after W. H. Bartlett, and *Castles and abbeys of England* 1845–51, which had 'Hall of Eltham Palace, A.D. 1365' (very delicately engraved) and 'Waltham Abbey', both after G. F. Sargent. *Forget me not* 1846 contained 'Bivouac' after J. H. van der Laar, and a vignette of 'Alton (from the North West)' after J. C. Armytage (q.v.) appeared in B. Woodward's *General history of Hampshire* 1863. Six plates after W. L. Leitch were published in Adams's *History . . . of the Isle of Wight* 1858, a vignette of the 'Mohammedan festival of the Mohurrum' in Nolan's *Illustrated history of the British Empire in India* [1858–60], two plates after Warren in Taylor's *Family history of England* [c. 1860] and two plates after Gustave Doré in *The Story of Enid and Geraint* [1869]. Five plates after Baines, Chevalier and Skinner Prout were engraved for Booth's *Australia* [1873–6]. For T. Baines's *Yorkshire past and present* 1871–7, he did 'Ripon Minster' for volume 1 and 'Bradford' after H. Warren for volume 3, and the frontispiece for volume 2 was 'York Minster' from a photograph by William Monkhouse of York. His best-known series of plates, however, was the eight which were done for *Picturesque Europe* 1876–9, published by Cassell. These were 'The Terrace, Haddon Hall' after J. Chase, 'Balmoral Castle' after W. Leitch, 'On the Lynn' after S. Cook, 'The Holstein gate, Lubeck' after C. Werner, 'The Bridge of Salamanca' after H. Fenn, 'The Bosphorus, Constantinople' after J. D. Woodward and 'The Bass Rock' and 'Verona', both after Birket Foster and probably his best plates. 'City of Durham' and 'Holyhead breakwater . . .' after Andrews appeared in Anderson's *English landscapes and views . . .* 1883. His last book plate was the engraved title page vignette 'The Globe theatre, 1613' after P. Skelton, published in *The Royal Shakespeare* 1883–4. Eleven plates were published in the *Art Journal* between 1852 and 1885. Of these 'The farm-yard' after T. S. Cooper (1852), 'The Council of

war at Courtray' after J. Haghe (a very fine piece of engraving) (1854), 'Milking time' after P. Potter (1856), 'The negro page' after A. Cuyp (1858), 'Defence of Latham House' after G. D. Leslie (1870) and 'The homely meal, Brittany' after F. Goodall (1876) need particular mention. His last plate, done when he was about sixty-seven, was 'Courtship of William II of Orange' after D. Wilkie's nephew, D. W. Wynfield, and was finished with the aid of his son Louis for publication in the *Art Journal* 1885. Godfrey did some work for the print publishers, notably Colnaghi. He died in April 1889, aged about seventy-two. AJ; B; T.

Godfrey, Louis (fl. 1880) Figure engraver. Son of John Godfrey (q.v.). He engraved 'Last bit of scandal' after Yeames for the *Art Journal* 1887. He married Elizabeth Alice, eldest daughter of James Carter, the engraver (q.v.).

Goldberg, Georg (1830–94) Figure engraver and pastel painter. Born at Nuremberg on 12 May 1830, he became a pupil of J. L. Raab in 1856. He engraved after the Old Masters and contemporary artists. Several engraved portraits were exhibited at the Ice Palace, Munich, in 1883. 'Dead Christ supported by Cherubs' after Giorgione, a plate coarsely engraved after the Continental fashion, appeared in the *Art Journal* for 1873. For *The Royal Shakespeare* 1883–4, he contributed seven plates—'Macbeth and Lady Macbeth' after V. W. Bromley, 'Hector Andromache and Cassandra' after Cipriani, 'Antony and Cleopatra', 'Constance, Arthur and Salisbury' and 'Othello and Desdemona' after F. Dicksee, 'Penance of the Duchess of Gloucester' after C. Green and 'Timon of Athens' after J. McL. Ralston. He died on 25 July 1894 in Munich. B; T.

Goodall, Edward (1795–1870) Landscape and figure engraver. He was born in Leeds on 17 September 1795, and from the age of sixteen concentrated on engraving and painting to the extent that he was self-taught. Until 1822 he painted mainly, and at the age of twenty-seven, by which time he was married with two sons, exhibited a landscape in oils at the Royal Academy. This attracted the attention of J. M. W. Turner, who made one of his more extravagant offers, to allow Goodall to engrave as many plates from his paintings as he would undertake. The immediate result was the production of three copper plates for *Picturesque views on the southern coast of England* 1826, which marked the beginning of a close association between the two men; nearly all his book illustrations were after Turner. About 1824, Robert Brandard (q.v.) came as a pupil for a year, and Thomas Leeming Grundy (q.v.) was his assistant for some considerable time. John Outhwaite was also his pupil. His first use of steel came with 'Richmond Hill', drawn expressly for the *Literary souvenir* 1826 by Turner, and he then did 'The return of a victorious armament to a Greek city' after Linton for the 1828 volume, 'Cleopatra embarking on the Cydnus' after Danby for the 1829 volume, 'Jacob's dream' after Allston for that of 1830, 'Ghent' after Nash for that of 1831 and 'Oberwesel on the Rhine' after Roberts for that of 1832. 'Florence' after Turner appeared in *The Keepsake* 1828. 'Morning' after W. Linton, 'The author of Waverley in his study' after W. Allan and 'Evening—twilight' after G. Barret were published in *The Anniversary* 1829, and sixteen plates, many of them vignettes, after Turner, T. Stothard and Col. Batty were published in S. Rogers' *Italy* 1830, the subjects including Lake of Geneva, Florence and the pilgrim. 'The mountain torrent' after Purser, a good example of his work, was engraved for *Friendship's offering* 1831, and for the 1837 volume, he did 'Gouri descending to the Lake of Oodipoor', also after Purser.

'Florence from the Chiesa el Monte' after Turner was published in *The Amulet* 1831, 'Isola Bella'—a vignette—and 'The Dogana, Venice' after C. Stanfield in L. Ritchie's *Travelling sketches in the north of Italy* 1832, and 'Trevi' after Harding in Roscoe's *Tourist in Italy* 1833. 'Carlisle', 'Caerlaverock Castle' and the vignettes 'Staffa', 'Johnny Armstrong's Tower' and 'Smallholm Tower' were engraved after Turner for Scott's *Poetical works* 1833–4, and twenty-seven plates were done, all except one after Turner, for Rogers' *Poems* 1834, including 'Desert storm', 'St. Julienne's well' and 'Columbus setting sail'. 'Luque' (a vignette) and 'The Alhambra from the Albaycir' after Roberts were engraved for Roscoe's *Tourist in Spain. Granada* 1835. Three vignettes after Turner—'The fall of the rebel angels', 'The expulsion from paradise' and 'Ludlow Castle...'—were done for Milton's *Poetical works* 1835 and 'Tiger Island' and 'El Wuish—Red Sea' after Stanfield for Elliot's *Views in India...* 1835. 'Howth lighthouse from the Needles' after Petrie appeared in Fisher's *Drawing room scrap book* 1835 and in the 1836 volume came 'Bombay harbour—fishing boats in the monsoon' after Stanfield. The engraved title page vignette 'Tréport' was done for *Stanfield's coast scenery* 1836 and 'Windsor Castle by moonlight' after Hofland for S. C. Hall's *Book of gems* 1836. A title page vignette after Turner was done for Bunyan's *Pilgrim's progress* 1836, and for another edition of this work, he engraved four oval pictures after Stothard. Thirteen vignettes after Turner were engraved for Campbell's *Poetical works* 1837, 'Rocks at Colgong on the Ganges' and 'Snowy ranges, from Tyne or Marma' after Turner for White's *Views in India...* 1838, 'The mosque of Sultan Achmet' after Allom for Walsh's *Constantinople* 1838–40, the engraved title page vignette 'Porto de Moz' and 'Coimbra' after Holland for Harrison's *Tourist in Portugal* 1839 and 'Stirling from the old palace' after D. O. Hill for Wilson and Chambers's *Land of Burns* 1840. 'Plain and bay of Sorrento...' after Harding, together with others engraved by Goodall, appeared in Wright's *Gallery of engravings* 1844–6 and 'The ferry' after F. R. Lee, dated 1847, in Finden's *Royal Gallery of British Art* 1838–49.

Sixteen plates were published in the *Art Journal* between 1854 and 1869, including eight after his son Frederick—e.g. 'Raising the maypole' (1854), 'The swing' (1862) and his last plate, 'The School of Sooltan Hassan' (1869)—, three after Turner—'Dido building Carthage' (1860), 'Caligula's Palace and bridge' (1861) and 'Ulysses deriding Polyphemus' (1863)—, 'Evening in Italy' after T. M. Richardson and 'Bridge of Toledo' after D. Roberts (1855). In the 1840s he devoted more time to larger plates for the print publishers and the Art Unions, but in this sphere he was less successful. 'Castello d'Ischia' after Stanfield (1845) and 'The Irish piper' after F. Goodall (1848) were done for the Art Union of London and 'St. Paul's cathedral...' after D. Roberts for the Royal Birmingham and Midland Counties Art Union in 1844. In 1820 he joined the Artists' Annuity Fund. He tried out new graver handles for the Society of Arts in 1831 and was elected to the Council of the Institute of Fine Arts in 1845. His authority on Turner's works was such that in 1864, together with John Pye, he was called upon to testify in a lawsuit as to the authenticity of a painting claimed to be by the artist, which both declared not to be by him. He died at his home in Hampstead Road after a short illness on 11 April 1870, aged nearly seventy-five.   AJ; DNB; H; W, p. 327.

Goode, T. (fl. 1831) Landscape engraver. Known by 'Kenmount' and 'Barjarg Tower', dated 1831 after J. P. Neale.

Goodeve, C. (fl. 1879) Architectural and figure engraver. 'Gateway of the Cathedral, Coire' after Samuel Hodson, painted in 1876, was engraved for *Picturesque Europe*, 1876–9 published by Cassell, and 'A Moorish chief' after J. E. Millais, coarsely engraved in the Continental fashion, was issued in the *Art Journal* 1879.

Goodman, H. (fl. 1832) Landscape engraver. 'Cologne and Deuz' after W. Tombleson was published in *Tombleson's views of the Rhine* 1832.

Goodman, J. (fl. 1838) Architectural engraver. 'Ruins of Essex Castle, Alderney' after J. Shepherd appeared in R. Mudie's *Hampshire* 1838.

Goodman, T. (fl. 1841–6) Landscape and historical engraver. A vignette, 'Carlingford, Louth', after H. Gastineau was published in S. C. and A. M. Hall's *Ireland* 1841–3, and 'Soldiers selling church plunder' after G. Cattermole was engraved for R. Cattermole's *Great Civil War* 1846.

Goodyear, Joseph (1797–1839) Figure engraver. One of the Birmingham school, he was born in November 1797, and was apprenticed first to John Tye of Water Street, Birmingham, a 'bright' engraver, working on silverware (e.g., spoons and teapots), and later to Josiah Allen of Colmore Row, for whom he engraved bill heads, bottle labels, etc. He took drawing lessons from J. V. Barber and Samuel Lines, becoming the fellow pupil of Thomas Creswick and J. T. Willmore, with whom Joseph combined to organise the presentation of a cup on behalf of his pupils to Barber in 1836. From 1822 to 1825 he worked for Charles Heath and through him obtained a great deal of work in the annuals and other illustrated books of the day. He was much sought after in this connection, primarily because of his punctuality, but also because of his obvious talent, and much of the best work done for the publishers bears his name. Among his earliest plates was 'Music's mishap' (done before October 1827) after J. M. Wright, published in *The Keepsake* 1828, and in succeeding volumes of this annual appeared 'The tapestried chamber' after F. P. Stephanoff (1829), 'Costandi' after the same artist (1830), 'The faithful servant' after A. Cooper (1830), 'The unlooked-for return' after Miss L. Sharpe (1833), 'Beatrice' after Miss F. Corbeaux and 'Love is the best physician' after Destouches (1834), 'Lord Surry (sic) and the fair Geraldine' after G. Cattermole (1835), 'The bribe' after Cattermole (1836), 'Lalla' after Mrs Seyfforth (1837), 'The tableau' after Herbert (1839) and 'The fate of Ribiero' after E. Corbould (1840). The *Literary souvenir* 1829 contained 'The departure of Mary Queen of Scots from France' after Leahy, from which two figures were omitted with the artist's permission, and for the 1830 volume he did 'The discovery' after F. P. Stephanoff, and for that of 1835 he did 'The vintage' after Stothard and one other engraving. 'The rejected' after F. P. Stephanoff was engraved for *Friendship's offering* 1831 and 'Unveiling' after Richter for the 1833 volume. For Scott's *Waverley novels* he engraved 'Kenilworth' after Leslie and 'The surgeon's daughter' after Stone, and for Wright's *Landscape-historical illustrations of Scotland* 1836–8 he did '"One foot nearer..."' after G. Cruikshank. He exhibited two engravings at the Suffolk Street Exhibition of 1830. M. Edgworth's *Moral tales* 1832 contained some of his work. In 1835, Joseph Andrews, one of America's best line engravers came to be taught by Goodyear. Two vignettes after G. Cattermole, 'Arming a young knight' and 'Knight's death', were engraved about 1836, later appearing in Calabrella's *Evenings at Haddon Hall* 1845. 'The poet's dream' after R. Westall was published in

Casquet of literature 1874. His last, largest and most important plate was 'Greek fugitives', dated 1 January 1838, after C. L. Eastlake, which was published in Finden's *Royal Gallery of British Art* 1838–49. He seems to have been exhausted by this effort and is said to have produced nothing after it. He contracted a lingering illness about the same time, and died on 1 October 1839, aged forty-one. He was buried in Highgate cemetery, where his friends erected a monument to him bearing a medallion portrait by Peter Hollins, a friend, and Vice-President of the Birmingham Society of Artists. Universally admired and respected, he had looked after his father for many years, and on his death, his meagre property and the charge of their parent devolved upon his brother. Nineteen of his engravings were shown at the 1877 Exhibition of engravings by Birmingham men, five of which are mentioned above. The remainder included 'Alice' after C. R. Leslie (1829), 'The Indian queen' after T. Stothard (1830), 'Helen MacGregor and Baillie Nicol Jarvie' after H. Corbould (1831), 'The musical painter' after A. E. Chalon (1832), 'Scene from Count Robert of Paris' after J. West (1833), 'Punch' after T. Uwins (1835) and 'Dorothea' after J. G. Middleton (1837).   AU; DNB; St; T.

Gough, J. (fl. 1829–31) Architectural engraver. Four plates were engraved for T. H. Shepherd's *London and its environs* 1829–31, namely, 'City of London lying-in hospital', 'Lunatic hospital, St. Lukes' (dated 1831), 'St. Catherine Cree, Leadenhall Street' and 'St. Mildred, Poultry', all after T. H. Shepherd.

Graham, A. W. (fl. 1832–69) Landscape engraver. Born in England, where he was a pupil of Henry Meyer (1783–1847), he engraved 'Windermere Lake, from Low Wood Inn' and 'Blea Tarn, Westmorland' after T. Allom, published in T. Rose's *Westmorland* 1832. Later, in 1832, he was in the United States. American views were engraved for *New York Mirror*. He worked for the annuals, and is known to have been in Philadelphia from 1838 to 1840 and 1844 to 1845. The last mention of him was of his being in New York in 1869.   B; St; T.

Graves, Robert (1798–1873) Portrait and figure engraver. Born on 7 November 1798 in St Pancras into a famous family of Yorkshire origin which had dealt in prints since his grandfather Robert became a printseller at Catherine Street, the Strand, about 1773. He was the eldest son, and his father, also Robert and like the grandfather a printseller, was reputed to be the best connoisseur of rare prints in his day, so his interest in engraving was not surprising. At an early age he attended a life school at Ship-yard, Temple Bar, and in 1812 he was apprenticed to John Romney (q.v.), the line engraver, earning himself at the same time many commissions for his excellent pen-and-ink facsimiles of rare engravings from collectors who could not obtain the originals. In this he followed his grandfather, who had the same ability. The majority of his book work, estimated at over 200 plates, was done before his election to the Royal Academy, after which time he followed more fashionable lines, most of his plates being issued by his brother, Henry Graves, the eminent print publisher of Pall Mall. It is likely, too, that his relations with other, especially book, engravers would have been strained by his election as Associate Engraver of the Royal Academy, then regarded almost as an insult to the profession instead of an honour.

Among his early work for books was a series of plates for Caulfield's *Remarkable persons from the Revolution in 1688 to*

Robert Graves

the end of the reign of George II, vignettes for Dove's *English classics* and some portraits for J. P. Neale's *History and Antiquities of the Abbey Church of ... Westminster* 1818–23. Plates engraved on steel for the annuals appeared in *The Amulet, Forget me not* and *Iris*); 'Viscountess Belgrave' after Lawrence was done for the *Literary souvenir* 1830 and 'J^e Veuve' after Rochard for *Keepsake français* 1831. He also did two oval engravings after T. Stothard for J. Bunyan's *Pilgrim's progress* 1854, namely, 'Christiana saluted by Secret' and 'The interpreter committing the pilgrims to the care of Great-heart'. For Scott's *Waverley novels* he engraved 'Old mortality' after D. Wilkie, 'Ivanhoe' after W. Boxall, 'The betrothed' after E. Landseer and 'St. Ronan's well' and 'Anne of Geierstein' after W. Mulready. A vignette, 'Paradise lost', after R. Westall was engraved for Milton's *Poetical works* 1835, and Burnet's *History of the Reformation* 1838 carried some portraits engraved by him. At the first exhibition of the Society of British Artists (in 1824), he exhibited for the first time with a medallion portrait of Sir Mark Masterman Sykes, the frontispiece to the sale catalogue of the latter's print collection. When James Fittler died in 1836, Robert was elected as an Associate Engraver with very little opposition, presenting as his diploma work an engraving of Thomas Phillips's portrait of Byron, owned by John Murray, and subsequently engraved by William Finden as the frontispiece to Byron's *Childe Harold's pilgrimage* 1842. Most of his important engravings were exhibited at the Royal Academy from this time until his death, e.g. 'The Abbotsford family' after D. Wilkie in 1837. His connection with Scottish artists brought him at least two commissions from the Association for promoting the Fine Arts in Scotland, i.e., 'The examination of Shakespeare...' (1839) and 'The castaway' (1840), both after G. Harvey, but his best plate is considered to be 'The Highland Whisky-still' after E. Landseer (1842). He contributed eight plates to the *Art Journal* between 1850 and 1872, commencing with 'Greek Girl' after C. L. Eastlake (1850), followed by three plates of Royal princesses after F. Winterhalter (1857), J. S. Copley (1860) and T. Lawrence (1855) and 'Origin of the harp' after D. Maclise, a most unusual oval picture (1862). In 1866 he began a series of portraits after Gainsborough and Lawrence, published by Henry Graves, the last of which, 'Lady Bowater', was unfinished at his death and was completed by James Stephenson (q.v.). His last completed work was a portrait of Dickens after W. P. Frith for the 2nd volume of J. Forster's *Life of Charles Dickens* 1871–4.

Robert married Miss L. M. Percy in 1832, and by her had two sons, Robert Edmund, who worked in the British Museum library from 1854, and Frederick Percy, a landscape artist. His only pupil (from 1836) was John Richardson Jackson (1819–77), who turned to mezzotint and engraved a portrait of his master. He died at his home, 20 Grove Terrace, Highgate Road, on 28 February 1873, and was buried in the family vault in Highgate cemetery on 6 March.   AJ; DNB; *Illus. Lond. News* 62:247 1873; Sa.

Greatbach, George (fl. 1846–80) Figure and landscape engraver. He was possibly a brother of William (q.v.). Some of his early work in steel was published in S. C. Hall's *Gems of European art* 1846, and included 'The money changers' after Q. Matsys, 'Joseph presenting his father to Pharoah' after F. Bol and 'Duncan Gray' after D. Wilkie. The last-named plate was used again in *Wilkie gallery* [c. 1849], for which he also engraved 'The pedlar'. 'Moses restoring the tables of the law', 'The triumph of Mordecai' and 'Christ blessing the children', all with ornamental borders by Luke Limner engraved by R. R. Baker (q.v.), appeared in *The Self-interpreting Bible* 1864. In 1852 he engraved the first of a series of ten plates for the *Art Journal*, which went on until 1875, most of the originals of which had been exhibited at the Royal Academy. They included 'Raffle for the watch' after W. Bird (1852), 'First day of the oysters' after G. Smith (1863), 'Breakfast table' after T. Webster (1866), 'The claim for shelter' after Rebecca Soloman (1869) and 'Shylock after the trial' after J. Gilbert (1873), which was rather coarsely engraved in the then fashionable Continental style. This last-named plate had already appeared in the *Works of Shakspere* [*sic*], Imperial edition 1872. For *Picturesque Europe* 1876–9, he engraved one of his few landscapes, 'Fishing boats on the lagoon, Venice' after H. Fenn. Some of his last work was done for *The Royal Shakespeare* 1883–4, his engravings portraying various characters (such as 'Viola and Olivia', 'Imogen and Posthumous' and 'Cardinal Wolsey') after H. C. Selous (three plates) and M. E. Edwards, C. Green and A. Hopkins (one plate each). He also executed portraits, particularly of comedians.   B; T.

Greatbach, Joseph (fl. 1877–82) Figure engraver. Four plates were published in the *Art Journal*, i.e., 'Volumnia reproaching Brutus and Sicinius' after J. D. Linton (1877), with the etching done by J. (probably James) Stephenson (q.v.), 'A reverie' after F. A. Delobbe (1880) (in conjunction with the famous German engraver Professor F. Knolle of Brunswick, who had himself contributed four other plates to the *Art Journal* 1860–71), 'Feeding time' after A. Paoletti (1880), which was very well engraved, 'The guests' after Baron Leys (1881) and 'Student in disgrace' after J. B. Burgess (1882). He may have been a son of George or William.

Greatbach, William (1802–c. 1885) Portrait and figure engraver. One of his earliest commissions, undertaken towards the end of his apprenticeship, or even the first one when out of it, was for some of the portraits in James' *Naval history* 1822, followed by plates for Shakespeare's *Works* after R. Smirke. The majority of his work was on steel, especially for the annuals, such as 'The Earl of Strafford' after Van

Dyke for *The Amulet* 1828, and for the 1831 volume of the same title, 'Cromwell at Marston Moor' after A. Cooper. For the *Literary souvenir* he did the engraved title page with John Lewis after John Wood's design and 'The ruby of the Philippine Isles' after A. E. Chalon (1828), 'The young novice' after Northcote (1829), 'The narrative' after Stothard and 'The lady and the wasp' after Chalon (1831), 'The tarantella' after Montvoisin (1832), 'The Chevalier Bayard confering [*sic*] knighthood on Francis I' after Fragonard (1833) and 'Hawking' after Cattermole (1834). 'Love me, love my dog', dated 1 October 1828, after J. Hoppner was signed 'W. Greatbach' and appeared in *The Anniversary* 1829, and for S. C. Hall's *Book of gems* 1836 he did seven engravings—a vignette, 'Cupid mourning over a broken lute', after J. Hayter, 'Cave of despair' after C. R. Eastlake, a vignette, 'Pleasure banquet', after S. Hart, 'Psyche' after W. Beechey, 'Happy age' after J. Reynolds, a vignette, 'Birth of Venus', after T. Stothard and 'Hawking', a vignette after R. B. Davis. For Scott's *Waverley Novels* he engraved the frontispiece 'Count Robert of Paris' after W. Boxall, and his contribution to Finden's *Royal Gallery of British Art* 1838–49 was 'First day of oysters' after A. Fraser, dated July 1841. 'The family of George Villiers . . .' and three plates depicting King Charles I and his family appeared in Keith's *Evidence of the truth of the Christian religion . . .*, 36th edition, 1848. Seven plates appeared in S. C. Hall's *Gems of European art* 1846, and included 'The Roman children' after W. Salter and 'The Vicar of Wakefield' after G. S. Newton, together with five after Sir David Wilkie. These included 'The village festival', 'Blind man's buff' (also in the *Art Journal* 1860, with 'The penny wedding'), 'Reading the will' and 'The Rent day' (Plate 49) (all after popular pictures of the time), which were used again in the *Wilkie gallery* [c. 1849]. This volume contained twenty-six of Greatbach's engravings after Wilkie, and also included 'The rabbit on the wall', which was reissued in the *Art Journal* of 1877, and 'The broken china jar', originally engraved by C. Warren for P. Coxe's *Social day* 1823. From 1849 he engraved regularly for the *Art Journal*, and thirty of his plates were published there. Some were reprints of his earlier published work, and others, e.g. 'Judgment of Wouter van Twiller' after G. H. Boughton, were painted expressly for engraving in the *Art Journal*. Most were of genre subjects by contemporary painters. His last plate to be published was 'Last voyage of Henry Hudson' after Hon. J. Collier (1887).

He engraved plates for A. A. Watts's *Lyrics of the heart* 1851 and T. Chatterton's *Poems* 1865. He did some work for the print publishers, e.g. a portrait of the Duke of Wellington after W. Salter (1844), 'Christening of the Prince of Wales' after J. Hayter (1847) and his principal plate, 'Banquet of Waterloo' after W. Salter. In 1847, he engraved an experimental plate on copper, 'The children in the wood' after W. Westall and J. H. Benwell, and a number of electrotypes were taken from it in order to spread the plate wear. The results are explained in detail in the *Art Union* 1847 (p. 62). He exhibited several engravings at the Royal Academy in 1859 and was an honorary member of the Academy of St Petersburg. He joined the Artists' Annuity Fund in 1827 and was a signatory to the 1837 petition. He had Charles Henry Jeens (q.v.) as a pupil in the mid-1840s, and in Jeens' obituary notice in the *Art Journal* 1879, Greatbach is described as 'one of our oldest living engravers', then being about seventy-seven.   AJ; B; S.

Greig, John (fl. 1800–40) Landscape and architectural engraver. He appears to have been born in the late eighteenth century and who was a trained engraver by 1800, in which year he published 'Stanislaus Auguste of Poland', followed by 'St. Matthew' (1803). He worked in London from 1803 until about 1812 with James Sargant Storer to produce topographical and antiquarian works, their first joint venture being *Cowper, illustrated by a series of views* 1803. Later works included plates for D. Hughson's *Walks through London* 1817, J. Hakewill's *Scenes of Windsor* 1820, *Excursions through Sussex* 1818–22 and F. W. R. Stockdale's *Excursions through Cornwall* 1824. The bulk of his steel engraved work was done for T. H. Shepherd, whose *London and its environs* 1829–31 contained six engravings after the author's drawings of the Guild halls, e.g. Fishmonger's Hall. *The Cottage girl . . .* [c. 1860] contained 'The Clifton Arms' after his own design, and in T. Dugdale's *England and Wales delineated* [1838–9] appeared the engraved title page 'Warkworth Hermitage, Northumberland' after Clennell and 'Peveril's Castle, The Peak, Derbyshire' after his own drawing. He was also a lithographer, which may account for the diminishing amount of his line engraved work done from the 1830s onwards. B; T.

Griffith, W. (fl. 1836) Architectural engraver. 'Winchester Cathedral; with transept' after R. Garland appeared in *Winkles's . . . Cathedral churches of England . . .* 1836–42. It is just possible that he can be identified with William Pettitt Griffith (1815–84), architect and archaeologist (see DNB and Thieme and Becker).

Griffiths, Henry (?–1849) Landscape and architectural engraver. He worked almost exclusively after W. H. Bartlett for the topographical books of the 1830s and 1840s, commencing with 'Brig, with the ascent of the Simplon' (used again in D. Costello's *Piedmont and Italy* [c. 1855] and 'Lucerne', both dated 1835 and after W. H. Bartlett, for W. Beattie's *Switzerland* 1836. A vignette, 'The wreck', after Turner was engraved for *The Keepsake* 1836. 'Church of the Holy Sepulchre, Jerusalem' after T. Allom, dated 1838, appeared in volume 3 of J. Carne's *Syria* 1836–8 and in J. Kitto's *Gallery of scripture engravings* 1846–9 (with the date altered to 1846), and a vignette, 'Custom House, Dublin', after T. Creswick was used in L. Ritchie's *Ireland . . .* 1837 and in S. C. and A. M. Hall's *Ireland* 1841–3. He engraved the family register pages after a design by E. Walker for *A New family Bible* [c. 1840]. Twelve plates were done for W. Beattie's *Scotland illustrated* 1838, five dated 1836, six 1837, and one 1838. Three—'Edinburgh from the castle ramparts', 'The Calton Hill' and 'Mausoleum of Burns'—were after W. H. Bartlett and the remainder after T. Allom, which included an excellent engraving, 'The new church and abbey, Dunfermline', and one with surprisingly poor execution of figures, 'St. Andrews from the pier'. 'The post of the Vaudois . . .' and 'The Valley of the Prajelas . . .' were done after Bartlett for Beattie's *Waldenses* 1838. For J. Pardoe's *Beauties of the Bosphorus* 1840, he engraved ten plates, all after Bartlett, among which the engraved title page 'Scene on the Barbyses, in the Valley of Sweet Waters', 'A scene in the Tchartchi' and 'Fountain and market at Tophanne' deserve mention. Six plates for N. P. Willis's *American scenery* 1840, also after Bartlett, included three good examples, all from volume 2, namely, 'View on the Susquehanna at Liverpool', 'View of Northumberland (on the Susquehanna)' and 'Colonnade of Congress Hall' (Plate 37), all dated 1839. Further plates after Bartlett included a vignette for the engraved title page— 'Dangan Castle'–, 'Ballina' and 'Ancient cross, Clonmacnoise' for J. Coyne's *Scenery and antiquities of Ireland* [c. 1840], 'Stonehaven' (1840) and 'Yarmouth, with Nelson's Monument' (1841) for W. Beattie's *Ports, harbours . . .* 1842, five

plates, including 'Canoe building at Papper's Island . . .', for Willis's *Canadian scenery* 1842, 'Village of Gladova' for Beattie's *Danube* 1844 and 'Pool at Hebron' for Stebbing's *Christian in Palestine* [1847]. Three plates after Allom were done for Brayley's *Topographical history of Surrey* 1841–8. A vignette, 'The Royal visit', after G. Cattermole appeared in Calabrella's *Evenings at Haddon Hall* 1845. He also did a portrait of General R. H. Sale, who died in 1845. He exhibited two genre paintings at the Society of British Artists Exhibition in 1835. B.

Griffiths, J. C. (fl. 1838) Architectural engraver. 'Willesden Church, Middlesex' after Wood was published in T. Dugdale's *England and Wales delineated* [1838–9].

Grundy, Thomas Leeming (1808–41) Landscape and figure engraver. Thought to be the third son of John Grundy, cotton spinner, and Elizabeth Leeming, he was born at Bolton, Lancashire, on 6 January 1808. He was apprenticed about 1822 to a busy writing engraver in Manchester, but wanting something more ambitious, he went to London about 1829, where he worked for the annuals, exhibiting considerable talent. Plates after C. Stanfield and 'The Orphan' after H. Liverseege are the most notable. He became assistant pupil to G. T. Doo (q.v.) in the early 1830s, staying with him for some time, and then worked for E. Goodall, after which he started up on his own. This probably accounts for the dearth of plates positively ascribed to him, among which may be noted 'Irvine', 'Dumfries; Market place' and 'Annan' after D. O. Hill for Wilson and Chambers's *Land of Burns* 1840, and probably (since they are signed simply 'Grundy') 'Lake of Como' after Stanfield in *The Keepsake* 1837 and 'The supper at Gaius' house', an oval engraving after T. Stothard, in J. Bunyan's *Pilgrim's progress* 1854. Among his best works were etched portraits of the Duke of Wellington and Lord Durham, the former of which was finished by T. G. Lupton, and he also engraved portraits of clergymen, as well as a large plate, 'Lancashire witch', after Bradley in line, stipple and mezzotint. An engraver of great promise, he had to refuse many large works because of failing health, and after being 'attacked with inflammation' he died on 10 March 1841, aged thirty-three, at his home in Brecknock Terrace, Camden Town, leaving a widow and child. He was buried in Old St Pancras churchyard. His two elder brothers were John Clowes Grundy (1806–67), printseller and art patron, and Robert Hindmarsh Grundy of Liverpool, who together had a hand in starting the Printsellers' Association, London, in 1847. AU; DNB.

H

Hacker, Edward (1813–1905) Animal and figure engraver. Two plates of racehorses—'Coronation' and 'Chuznee'—after J. F. Herring are signed, probably erroneously, 'F. Hacker' and were published in J. W. Carleton's *Sporting sketch-book* 1842. 'The scanty meal' after J. F. Herring was issued in the *Art Journal* 1850, and in the 1856 volume appeared 'The Troopers' after A. Cuyp. His second son, Arthur (1858–1919), was a well-known painter. DNB; T.

Haig, Henry (fl. 1841–3) Figure engraver in Edinburgh. He engraved on steel 'Flowers of the forest' after A. Sommerville for the Art Union of Scotland, and on copper, 'The taking down from the Cross' and 'The conversion of St. Paul' after

P. P. Rubens for *Engravings after the best pictures of the Great Masters* 1843. T.

Hall (fl. 1846) Architectural engraver. 'Convent of Nonnenworth and ruins of Rolandseck' appeared in *Continental tourist* [1838] and in Fearnside's *Picturesque beauties of the Rhine* [c. 1846]. There is no clear evidence to ascribe it to either C. Hall (q.v.) or H. B. Hall (q.v.).

Hall, C. (fl. 1834) Architectural engraver. 'Westminster bridge' after W. Tombleson was published in *Tombleson's Thames* 1834.

Hall, George R. (fl. 1851) Sculpture engraver. 'The Bavaria' after a drawing by F. R. Roffe of a sculpture was engraved for the *Art Journal* 1851. He was a brother of Henry Bryan Hall (q.v.), and emigrated to New York in 1854.

Hall, H. (fl. 1843–5) Animal and portrait engraver. 'A portrait' after Chalon was engraved for *The Keepsake* 1844, and 'Stricken deer', dated August 1845, after A. Elmore was published in *Beauties of Moore* 1846. There may be a connection with a person known variously as Harvey, Harry or Henry Hall, a painter of animals, who died in April 1882. A bookplate was engraved by H. Hall in 1820. Fi; T; YA 1883.

Hall, Henry Bryan (1808–84) Portrait and figure engraver. Born in London on 11 March 1808, he was apprenticed to Benjamin Smith, one of Boydell's engravers, in 1822. Later, he helped Henry Meyer on plates after Lawrence, and at the end of his apprenticeship (about 1830) he went to work for H. T. Ryall. He joined the Artists' Annuity Fund in 1838. His work appeared in Ryall's *Eminent Conservative Statesmen* 1836–8, and from 1838 to 1842, he helped H. T. Ryall to engrave the seventy portraits in the 'Coronation of Queen Victoria' after J. Hayter. His book work on steel includes two vignette portraits—'William Smellie' after G. Watson and 'Francis Grose' after N. Dance—for Wilson and Chambers's *Land of Burns* 1840, nine plates after various artists for Fisher's *Historic illustrations of the Bible* 1840–3, 'Viscountess Folkestone' after J. Hayter for Finden's *Gallery of beauty* 1841 and 'The Wanderer' (sailing ship) after O. W. Brierley and 'Flying Childers' (racehorse and jockey) for J. W. Carleton's *Sporting sketch-book* 1842. He married and taught himself portrait painting, becoming also a miniature painter on ivory, before emigrating to New York in 1850. He was joined there by his brother George (q.v.) in 1854. There was no shortage of commissions for portrait engraving, and he taught his three sons, Henry Bryan (junior) (who returned to London for a year in 1858), Alfred Bryan and Charles Bryan, and his daughter, Alice, as engravers. After the Civil War, father and three sons formed a company, H. B. Hall & Sons, to engrave and publish portraits, and among the best plates issued were a series of twelve of Washington. He etched his own portrait (1872). He was a collector of prints and watercolours, his collection being sold in 1885 after his death in Morrisania, New York, on 25 April 1884 of a paralytic stroke. B; DAB; St; T.

Hall, Sidney (fl. 1818–24) Map engraver. He was probably the earliest engraver to use steel plates for maps: three engravings were certainly done on Jacob Perkins's plates, dated 1821, for the Revd J. Goldsmith's *Geography; illustrated on a popular plan...* new edition 1824 (Plate 3). Keith's *Geography* 1826 also carried steel engraved plates by Hall.

Hamilton, G. (fl. 1835) Landscape engraver. 'Assar Mahal—Beejapore' and 'Ruins south of Old Delhi' after T. Boys were engraved for Elliot's *Views in India...* 1835.

Harland, T. W. (fl. 1844) Portrait engraver. 'Her Most gracious Majesty Queen Victoria' was engraved as the frontispiece to the 1844 edition of Beattie's *Ports, harbours...*

Harraden, F. (fl. 1838) Architectural engraver. Two plates each after T. H. Abraham and T. W. Richardson appeared in T. F. Dibdin's *Bibliographical ... tour in the northern counties of England* 1838. He was possibly a relation of Richard Bankes Harraden (1778–1862), aquatinter. Ho; T.

Harris, T. (fl. 1834–46) Architectural engraver. 'Datchet bridge, Bucks.' after W. Tombleson appeared in *Tombleson's Thames* 1834, and 'St. Martin's Church, Cologne' after Tomblesons [sic], and signed 'R. Harris', was published in H. G. Fearnside's *Picturesque beauties of the Rhine* [c. 1846]. (See also Hart, T.)

Hart, Robert (fl. 1833–40) Portrait and figure engraver. 'Martin Folkes' was engraved for Hogarth's *Works* 1833, 'Italian peasant' after Pickersgill for the *Literary souvenir* 1835, 'The coquet' after Stone for S. C. Hall's *Book of gems* 1836 and 'The entombment of Christ' after Northcote for *A New family Bible* [c. 1840]. Six portraits after Drouais, Lely, Raffaele Morghen and Ramsay were published in the *Imperial dictionary of universal biography* [c. 1861]. He also engraved 'Petrarch from a print by Raffaele Morghen after a picture by Tofanelli'.

Hart, T. (fl. 1846) Architectural engraver. 'Ruins of Sonneck' after Tomblesons [sic] appeared in H. G. Fearnside's *Picturesque beauties of the Rhine* [c. 1846]. Although the engraver's name is quite clear, it is possible that R. or T. Harris may have been intended.

Hartley, J. (fl. 1835) Landscape engraver. 'Lake of Lausanne above Pandex', dated 1835, after W. H. Bartlett ('The effect by T. Creswick' is in the centre lower border of the picture) appeared in volume 2 of W. Beattie's *Switzerland* 1836, and later in D. Costello's *Piedmont and Italy* [c. 1855].

Harwood, John and Frederick (fl. 1840–55) Landscape engravers. Among their early works were three series, totalling 150 views, published as *Harwood's scenery of Great Britain* [1842]. A number of plates signed 'J. & F. Harwood' are known, some of which seem to form part of a series, e.g., 'Victoria Fountain, etc., Brighton No. 702 July 1st 1846'. Thirty-five plates by them appeared in Roscoe's *Summer tour in the Isle of Wight* 1843, and in 1853 *Harwood's illustrations of the Channel Islands* was issued. Two plates appeared in Martineau's *Complete guide to the English Lakes* 1855. Their address was given as 26 Fenchurch Street. Ho.

Hatelie, (fl. 1835) Architectural engraver. 'Convent of Pfefferberg, C^tn St. Gallen' after Tombleson appeared in W. G. Fearnside's *Tombleson's Upper Rhine* [c. 1835].

Hatfield, Richard (1809–67) Figure engraver. He studied under J. C. Edwards and Edward Finden, and probably worked for the latter for most of his life, which would account for the lack of plates with his name attached to them. 'Shakespeare in his room at Stratford' after J. Boaden appeared in S. C. Hall's *Book of gems* 1836, a good plate, 'The agreeable surprise', after Richter was engraved for *Friendship's offering* 1839 and 'Lear and Cordelia', dated August 1840, after G. S. Newton and 'Reduced gentleman's daughter', dated 10 April 1842, after R. Redgrave were published in Finden's *Royal Gallery of British art* 1838–49. Failing sight compelled him to retire from engraving some time before his death in London in 1867. It is possible that this retirement took place soon after Edward Finden's death in 1857, since employment opportunities for ailing line engravers were scarce at that time. Br.

Havell, Frederick James (1801–40) Landscape and architectural engraver. He was the son of Luke Havell, drawing master at Reading, who had six sons in all, one of whom, John, also an engraver, died insane in February 1841 after taking up photography with excessive enthusiasm. Frederick occasionally collaborated with his elder brother, William (1782–1857), but he is the only one of the family to have made his mark upon steel engraving. Seven plates, dated between August 1827 and August 1828, were engraved after T. H. Shepherd for J. Elmes's *Metropolitan improvements* 1829, including 'St. Paul's Church, Balls Pond' (signed 'J. F. Havell') and 'Trinity Church, Cloudesley Sq.' (signed 'J. F. Havel'). Two views of 'Market Street ... Manchester' after Harwood, dated 1829, were engraved for Pyne's *Lancashire illustrated...* 1831. For J. Britton and E. W. Brayley's *Devonshire and Cornwall illustrated* 1832 he did 'Tregothnan House, Cornwall', 'Truro Cornwall', 'The public reading rooms ... Teignmouth', 'Dartmouth' and 'Buckfastleigh Abbey, Devonshire' (the last three signed 'F. J. Havill') after T. Allom. Four plates, mainly after the author's designs, were engraved for Gell's *Pompeiana...* 1832. 'The middle bridge in the Via Mala' and 'Wasserburg, Lake Constance' after W. Tombleson appeared in Fearnside's *Tombleson's Upper Rhine* [c. 1835]. Landscapes after R. Wilson, P. P. Rubens and P. J. Loutherberg, with 'A farmyard' after Teniers and a country public house after P. Nasmyth engraved between November 1832 and January 1834, came out in A. Cunningham's *Cabinet gallery of pictures by the first masters...* 1836, and 'Adalia' and 'Cemetery and walls of Antioch...' after W. H. Bartlett in J. Carne's *Syria* 1836–8. Ten plates after T. Allom appeared in T. Noble and T. Rose's *Counties of Chester...* 1836, including 'Hardwick Hall, Derbyshire', 'Lincoln from the Castle' and 'West front of Eaton Hall, Cheshire', which last was used again in G. N. Wright's *Gallery of engravings* 1844–6. 'Baluk Hana, and method of fishing for the red mullet...' after Allom was published in R. Walsh's *Constantinople* 1838–40, 'The silver cascade, in the notch of the White Mountains' after T. Doughty in N. P. Willis's *American scenery* 1840 and 'Hurdwar–the gate of Hari, or Vishnoo' after J. D. Harding in R. Martin's *Indian Empire* [c. 1857]. He also worked in mezzotint. The Havell pedigree is given in the *Print Collector's Quarterly* October 1916. AU; B; Br; DNB; T.

Hawkesworth, John (fl. 1819–48) Architectural engraver. 'St. Stephen's chapel' (an outline engraving) and 'Westminster Hall, south end' (an ordinary plate, signed 'Hawkesworth' and dated 1 August 1835) after R. W. Billings and 'Chantry chapels and cloister' after J. W. Thompson were published in E. W. Brayley and J. Britton's *History of the ancient palace ... at Westminster* 1836. He was also responsible for some of the engravings in *Spirit of the public journals* 1825 and Nicholl's *Literary illustrations* 1848. T.

Hay, Frederick Rudolph (1784–?) Landscape and architectural engraver. He engraved 'Luganer See' after J. Hakewill (1819) and was responsible for twenty-eight plates in J. P. Neale's *Views of the seats of noblemen...* 1818–24. Six plates after Austin, Harwood and Pyne were engraved for Pyne's *Lancashire illustrated* 1831 ... and 'Entrance to Beaumaris Castle' for Gastineau's *Wales illustrated...* 1830, the latter being used again in Woodward's *History of Wales* 1853. B; T.

Healds, (fl. 1840) Figure engraver. 'Children at Summerfield Cottage' after Mattocks appeared in *The Cottage girl...* [c. 1860].

Heath, Alfred Theodosius (1812–96) Figure engraver and Engraver and Miniaturist to the Queen: he taught the Queen and Prince Albert the rudiments of engraving and miniature painting. He was the second son and third child of Charles Theodosius Heath (q.v.), 'The orphan of Palestine' after J. W. Wright was engraved for *The Keepsake* 1837, 'The elopement' after E. Corbould for the 1841 volume, 'The surprise', also after Corbould, for that of 1842 and 'Sir Eglamour's Ladye love' after Corbould for that of 1843. He engraved twenty-nine plates for volumes of the same annual from 1845 to 1857, with plates in every volume. A picture of Joseph being sold to the Ishmaelite merchants after Zucchi was engraved for Fisher's *Historic illustrations of the Bible* [1840–3], and 'The marriage of St. Catherine' after Correggio appeared in S. C. Hall's *Gems of European art* 1846. 'Way-worn traveller' after Sir Augustus Callcott, a very dark engraving, was done for the *Art Journal* 1853. He married Caroline Philpott, but appears to have had no issue.

Heath, Charles Theodosius (1785–1848) Landscape and figure engraver. His father was James Heath, Royal Academician and Historical Engraver to the King. James married Eliza Thomas in 1777, and by her he had only a son, George (1779–1852). His other six children were born to him by Miss Mary Phillipson, of whom Charles was the only son and second child. The family originally came from Nottingham, where his great grandfather Joseph was a bookseller and writing master. His grandfather George was a bookbinder.

Charles Theodosius Heath

He was taught engraving by his father and although some good work had been done by him, he received his first important commission in 1811 and was soon inundated with so much work that he took on assistants and pupils to form an atelier. Such was his character, however, that he always wanted to have his name on plates with which he was connected even if his work on them was slight, so it is difficult to distinguish his from other men's work. Thomas Wallis, the father of Robert Wallis (q.v.), was the first of his assistants, followed by Richard Rhodes and Edward John Roberts (q.v.). His first pupil was James Henry Watt (q.v.), followed by R. J. Lane and George T. Doo (q.v.). J. Goodyear and J. T. Willmore (qq.v.) worked with him for three years, and J. B. Allen (q.v.) also had a spell with him. W. H. Mote and B. Eyles seem also to have been connected with him. He was one of the earliest engravers to use steel for book illustration, most of his early work being done on Jacob Perkins's patent hardened steel plates, used for siderographic printing, and a later writer, Marcus B. Huish, editor of the *Art Journal*, described his engravings as 'manufactured' plates because of his production-line techniques. He also 'superintended' many publications, being, in effect, their art editor, and his name is particularly associated with the annuals. What follows is a selection of engraved work carrying his name to give some indication of its variety. Four plates, dated 1820, were engraved for T. Campbell's *Pleasures of hope* 1821, all after R. Westall and all illustrating scenes from the poem, e.g., 'Or lisps with holy look his ev'ning prayer' on the engraved title page (Plate 1). These are generally regarded as the first published book illustrations engraved on steel. Five plates were done for *Forget me not* 1825, comprising a dedication page engraved by Perkins and Heath, 'The parting charge', 'The pilgrims in grey' and 'The tournament' after R. Westall and 'The rational lunatic' after T. Uwins. 'The decision of the flower' after T. M. Wright, 'Italy—bay of Naples' after C. Fielding and 'Ishmael and Miriam' (a vignette) after J. M. Wright appeared in the *Literary souvenir* 1825, 'The forsaken' after G. S. Newton, specially painted for the work, and 'Windsor Castle' after P. de Wint came out in the 1826 volume of that annual, and 'Girl in a Florentine costume...' after Howard was done for the 1827 volume. 'The Hebrew mother' and 'The murmurer instructed' after R. Westall and 'Infatuation' after R. Corbould were engraved for *The Amulet* 1826, and for the 1827 volume he engraved 'May-day in the village' after H. Corbould.

When he started his own annual, *The Keepsake*, in 1827 it was to have been expected that he would do many of the engravings himself, and ten out of the eighteen plates in the first volume (1828) had his name on them as engraver, e.g., 'Selina' after Lawrence, 'The peasant girl' after Constable and 'The enchanted stream' after Stothard. The 1829 volume also carried ten engravings by him, including 'The country girl' after Holmes, 'Adelinda' after Chalon and 'Mrs. Peel' (wife of the reformer Robert Peel) after Sir Thomas Lawrence (Plate 10). By the 1830 volume his contribution had fallen to six, including 'The prophet of St Paul's' after Chalon (upon which four different engravers worked, each doing their own speciality, e.g. flesh, drapery, etc. (Plate 15)). In 1831 it was back to eight, including 'Haidee' after Eastlake, and in 1832, down to four. Fourteen plates appeared in the volumes from 1834 to 1836 and seventeen in those from 1842 to 1848. The 1848 volume contained what is thought to be his last plate, namely, 'The last moment' after H. Warren. He engraved 'Petrarch's house at Arqua' and 'Bologna' after S. Prout for T. Roscoe's *Tourist in Switzerland and Italy* 1830, both dated 29 October 1829, but when he severed his connection with the publisher Robert Jennings, he transferred his work to his own series, *Heath's Picturesque annual*, for the 1832 volume of which he did 'Mazorbo' and 'Innsbruck' after C. Stanfield (the volume, by L. Ritchie, was entitled *Travelling sketches in the north of Italy*). 'The Drachenfells' and 'Near Bonn' after the same artist appeared in Ritchie's *Travelling sketches on the Rhine* 1833. 'The Abbot' after A. E. Chalon was done for Scott's *Waverley novels*. 'One morn a Peri at the gate...' after K. Meadows (Plate 33) appeared in Moore's *Lalla Rookh* 1838 and 'Queen Henrietta interceding for the King' after G. Cattermole in R. Cattermole's *Great Civil War* 1846. Of his large plates, 'Europa' after W. Hilton was finished early in 1841 after seven years' work. He had his financial troubles, becoming bankrupt in 1821, and in May 1826 he had to sell stock engravings in order to raise money. In June 1839 he sold drawings by modern artists and in April 1840 sold more stock

engravings, accumulated since 1826. He married Elizabeth Petch about 1808, and they had four girls and four boys, one of each sex dying in infancy. His sons Frederick Augustus and Alfred Theodosius (qqv.) became engravers, and his daughter Fanny Jemima married Edward Henry Corbould, whose designs, together with those of his father Henry, were extensively engraved by Charles. In 1838-9 he received a diamond snuff-box from Louis Philippe, King of France, in return for an edition of *Picturesque views in England* after Turner. By 1847 he was nearly blind, and he died on 18 November 1848, in his sixty-second year. In its obituary, the *Art Union* wrote that 'he has probably created as much work for his professional brethren as any living man'.   AU; AJ; B; DNB; H; R.

Heath, Frederick Augustus (1810–78) Portrait, figure and historical engraver. Son of Charles Heath, he was probably trained in his father's atelier, working for him for some years. Among his early independent commissions was the engraving of Queen Victoria's head after a design by Henry Corbould for the first postage stamp, in 1839, followed by a plate, 'Neapolitan wedding', after T. Uwins for the Art Union of London, begun in 1845 and finished towards the end of 1847. Among his early steel bookplates was 'The love quarrel' after 'Eliza Sharp[e]' for *The Keepsake* 1835, and for later volumes he did 'Lady Jemima [Heatherfield]' after Stone and 'Teresina' after Poole for that of 1842, 'The surprise' after Stephanoff for that of 1844 and twenty-five plates for nine volumes up to 1857. 'The King on his journey to the Scots' after G. Cattermole (signed 'Frederick T. Heath') was done for R. Cattermole's *Great Civil War* 1846 and 'Her Majesty the Queen' after E. Corbould for L. Ritchie's *Windsor Castle* 1848. The *Art Union* 1848 carried one of his plates, 'There sleeps Titania' (a semi-circular picture with an outline engraving of an archway) after R. Huskisson, which was used again in the *Works of Shakspere* [*sic*], Imperial edition 1872, together with 'The scene in the temple garden' after J. Pettie. From 1864 to 1879, thirteen plates appeared in the *Art Journal*, coinciding very nearly with exhibitions of his work at the Royal Academy (1863–74), and included 'Alice Lisle' (1864) and 'James II receiving news of the landing of Prince of Orange' (1861) after E. M. Ward, 'Going home' after T. Faed (1868), 'Choosing the wedding gown' after W. Mulready (1869), 'News from the war' (largely etched) after G. D. Leslie (1877) and his last plate, 'Queen of the vineyard' after P. Seignac (very coarsely engraved) (1879). He married a Mrs Matilda Inwood, but appears to have had no children.   B.

Heath, J. P. (fl. 1836-7) Landscape and architectural engraver, mainly after Bartlett and Callow. 'The Petit Trianon' after W. Callow was first used in *Heath's Versailles* [c. 1836], and again in *Keepsake français* 1840. 'Castle near Pambouk' and 'Sidon on the approach from Beirout', both after W. H. Bartlett and dated 1837, were published in J. Carne's *Syria* 1836-8, and the latter appeared again (re-dated 1847) in J. Kitto's *Gallery of scripture engravings* 1846-9. There appears to have been a John Palethorpe Heath who was a very distant cousin of Charles, but nothing further is known of him. The fact that few plates are ascribed to him, and that one of his plates appears in one of Charles Heath's publications may indicate membership of the latter's atelier.

Heath, Percy (fl. 1832-50) Landscape and architectural engraver. A relationship with Charles Heath has not been established. 'St. Nicholas's, or Drakes Island...' and 'The Lary bridge...' after T. Allom and 'Sidmouth from the cliffs' and 'The York hotel and library, Sidmouth' after W. H.

Bartlett were done for J. Britton and E. W. Brayley's *Devonshire and Cornwall illustrated* 1832, followed by 'Grand Canal, Venice' after Canaletto, dated 1 July 1833, for A. Cunningham's *Cabinet gallery of pictures by the first masters...* 1836 and 'Blue coat school, Liverpool' after T. Allom, dated 1834, for E. Baines's *History of ... Lancaster* 1836. 'Shuhur–Jeypore' after Purser was engraved for Elliot's *Views in India...* 1835. 'Tortosa from the island of Ruad' after W. H. Bartlett, dated 1838, is a good example of a steel engraving and appeared in J. Carne's *Syria* 1836–8, and again (re-dated 1847) in J. Kitto's *Gallery of scripture engravings* 1846–9. He also produced an improved version of a ruling machine for engravers, which was described in the *Transactions of the Society of Arts,* volume 51, 1837.

Heawood, Thomas (fl. 1850–79) Very little is known of this engraver, whose name is sometimes given as 'Headwood'. He appears to have spent much of his time in Germany, where he worked for A. H. Payne (q.v.) in Leipzig, engraving plates after C. Arnold, E. Linnig, C. A. Ruthart and Payne himself. The longest series of his plates to appear in England was published in *Picturesque Europe* 1876–9, published by Cassell, and included 'The tomb of the Howards–Arundel church' after S. Reed, 'Falls of the Hespte' after J. B. Smith, 'Edinburgh from Calton Hill' after Birket Foster, 'On the Dart, near Totnes' after E. M. Wimperis, 'Torre de las Infantas, Alhambra' after C. Werner, 'The Romsdalhorn from Aak' after J. D. Woodward, 'The leaning tower, Saragossa' and 'The Cathedral, Bruges' after E. George and 'Ruins of the Brunnenburg near Meran, South Tyrol' after E. T. Compton, the painting of which is dated August 1876. B; T.

Hennings, H. A. (fl. 1838–9) Architectural engraver. Other artists by this name are of German descent and this engraver may have been working in Germany, for he is known by only one engraving, viz., a vignette, 'Tintern Abbey', for the engraved title page of volume 2 of T. Dugdale's *England and Wales delineated* [1838–9].

Henshall, J. (fl. 1827–50) Architectural and landscape engraver. 'The Holme, Regent's Park' and 'Ulster Terrace, Regent's Park', both dated 15 September 1827, and four other London views, all after T. H. Shepherd, were engraved for J. Elmes's *Metropolitan improvements* 1829. These were followed by five plates of similar subjects after the same artist for T. H. Shepherd's *London and its environs* 1829–31 and 'The Quay at Ramsgate' and 'Gravesend', both dated 1832 and after J. Fussell, for S. W. H. Ireland's *England's topographer* (commenced publication 1828). Six engravings were done for Shepherd's *Modern Athens* 1829–31. He contributed several plates to the *Landscape annual,* e.g., 'The Rialto at Venice' (largely etched) after S. Prout to T. Roscoe's *Tour in Switzerland and Italy* 1830 and 'Convent of the Vallanbrosa', dated 28 October 1832, after J. D. Harding to the same author's *Tour in Italy* 1833, and a large map of the Isle of Wight was engraved for Roscoe's *Summer tour in the Isle of Wight* 1843. 'Irwell-Street Methodist chapel, Salford' after Harwood was engraved for Pyne's *Lancashire illustrated...* 1831, and four plates after the author appeared in Sir William Gell's *Pompeiana...* 1832. 'Tuileries, front of the Place du Carousel' and 'Church of St. Roch 28 July 1830' appeared in C. Knight's *Paris* 1831, and 'Restoration of Pompeii' after the author's drawing appeared as the frontispiece to volume 1 of W. Clarke's *Pompeii* 1849. His longest series–eight plates of subjects around London–was done for T. Harral's *Select illustrated topography of thirty miles round London* [c.1850], and included 'The Tottenham Mills, Middlesex' and four

other plates after C. Marshall, 'Dorking church...' after J. C. Allen, 'Ingatestone, Essex' after J. Meadows and 'Gravesend, from the Terrace Pier'–an oval vignette–after T. C. Dibdin, and he drew 'Gate House, Highgate', which was engraved by T. Cox.

Henshall, W. (fl. 1830–50) Architectural and landscape engraver. He was probably a brother of J. Henshall (q.v.), whose engravings also appear in the two works containing plates by this engraver. 'Carpenters' Hall, London Wall' (1830) and 'Fleet Street' (1831) after the author were done for T. H. Shepherd's *London and its environs* 1829–31. 'London' (a vignette), 'St. Alban's Abbey, Hertfordshire', 'Rochester Castle, Kent', 'Hornsey Church, Middlesex' and 'Walton Bridge, Surrey', all after C. Marshall, were published in T. Harral's *Select illustrated topography of thirty miles round London* [c. 1850].

Hewett, W. (fl. 1830) Portrait engraver. 'Scottish highland costume' after J. J. Jenkins was published by Longman.

Hicks, Robert (fl. 1820–36) Portrait engraver. He probably worked for both book and print publishers. Portraits from his hand are known from 1820 to 1836, and he contributed to Jerdan's *National Portrait Gallery* 1835. A representation of 'Antique helmet of bronze found at Rochester', originally engraved by J. Basire, was engraved in 1831 for E. Baines's *History of ... Lancaster* 1836. G. N. Wright's *Gallery of engravings* 1844–6 contained 'The African prince' (mainly stipple) after H. Meyer, 'Samuel Drew, MA' after J. Moore and 'Charles Grey, Earl Grey', a vignette stipple after T. Phillips. The latter print was first published in 1831. B; T.

Higham, Thomas (1796–1844) Architectural, landscape and figure engraver. He was possessed of considerable talent, and his ability as an architectural engraver was first exploited soon after the end of his apprenticeship in J. P. Neale's *Views of the seats of noblemen...* 1818–24, for which he did a number of plates. For G. N. Wright's *Historical guide to Dublin* 1821, he engraved 'The Castle [Dublin]', and 'St. Patrick's cathedral' (dated August 1821) after G. Petrie, and he drew and engraved many of the illustrations for *Excursions through Sussex* 1818–22. He exhibited engravings at the Society of British Artists in 1820 and 1833, and also exhibited at the Royal Academy, between 1824 and 1830. 'Egglestone Abbey, near Barnard Castle' after J. M. W. Turner was engraved for Whitaker's *History of Richmondshire* 1823 and appeared again in the *Art Journal* for 1875 and in *Turner's Richmondshire* 1891, edited by M. B. Huish. Among his early steel engravings were 'Suspension bridge over Thames at Hammersmith' and 'New London Bridge', both dated 16 August 1828, after T. H. Shepherd for J. Elmes's *Metropolitan improvements* 1829, four engravings after the author for T. H. Shepherd's *London and its environs* 1829–31, and two for the same author's *Modern Athens* 1829–31. He occasionally worked for the Findens. In 1830 he was probably the designer of a bookplate engraved by Byfield, and in 1831 tried out improved graver handles for their inventor. In the succeeding years he engraved only one or two designs for any one work, so they are scattered among a number of volumes. 'Venice', dated 28 October 1830, after S. Prout was published in T. Roscoe's *Tourist in Italy* 1831, 'The harbour, Holyhead' and 'South Stack light house...' in Gastineau's *Wales illustrated...* 1830, 'The Duke's Dock, & warehouses, Liverpool' after Harwood in Pyne's *Lancashire illustrated...* 1831, 'View of the court of the piscina' in Gell's *Pompeiana...* 1832 and 'Entrance to Aosta' and 'Mole' after Harding in Roscoe's *Tourist in Italy* 1833, and 'Interior of church at Polignac', dated 28 October 1833, and 'The old bridge on the Saone, Lyons', also after Harding, were engraved for Roscoe's *Tourist in France* 1834 and 'Casa del Carbou, Granada' and 'Court of the Lions', both dated 28 October 1834, after D. Roberts for Roscoe's *Tourist in Spain. Granada* 1835. These works by Roscoe were all volumes of the *Landscape annual*. He did four small plates for C. Knight's *Paris* ... 1831, to *Finden's illustrations of the life and works of Lord Byron* 1833-4, he contributed 'Castle of Ferrara' after S. Prout, 'Pisa' and 'Yanina, Palace of Ali Pacha' after J. D. Harding and 'Temple of Theseus (Athens)' after W. Page and 'The Grèves' appeared in *Stanfield's coast scenery* 1836. 'Ruins about the Taj Mahal—Agra' afer Austin, 'Jerdair—a hill village—Curwall' after Cox and 'Tomb of Ibrahim Padshah, Bejapore' were engraved for Elliot's *Views in India* ... 1835. E. Baines's *History of* ... *Lancaster* 1836 contained five of Higham's plates, including 'Hall i' th' Wood, near Bolton', first issued in Baines's *History of the cotton manufacture in Great Britain* [1835] and used again in G. N. Wright's *Lancashire* 1842, as well as in his *Gallery of engravings* 1844-6. L. Ritchie's *Wanderings by the Seine* 1835 contains the well-engraved 'Boulevards, Paris' after J. M. W. Turner, 'Marriage of Marie Antoinette' after F. J. Collignon was used in both *Heath's Versailles*, [c. 1836] and *Keepsake français* 1840 and 'Bridge at Old Delhi' and 'The north gate, Old Delhi' (dated 1 October 1836) after W. Daniell were published in J. Caunter's *Lives of the Moghul emperors* 1837. 'Scene on the River Orontes, near Suddeah' (1836) after W. H. Bartlett was issued in J. Carne's *Syria* 1836-8, and 'A street in Smyrnia' (a good plate) after T. Allom was first published in R. Walsh's *Constantinople* 1838-40 and reissued in J. Kitto's *Gallery of scripture engravings* 1846-9. 'Part of the Ghaut, at Hurdwar' after Turner appeared in White's *Views in India* ... 1838 and 'Edinburgh. March of the Highlanders', also after Turner, in Wright's *Landscape-historical illustrations of Scotland* 1836-8. 'Bern (Canton Bern)' 1835 after W. H. Bartlett was engraved for W. Beattie's *Switzerland* 1836, and for the same author's *Scotland illustrated* 1838, he did 'Inverary Castle' (1836) after T. Allom. A further series of plates after W. H. Bartlett included 'Fountain and square of St. Sophia' and 'Court of the Mosque of Bajazet' for J. Pardoe's *Beauties of the Bosphorus* 1840, three engravings for J. Coyne's *Scenery and antiquities of Ireland* [c. 1840], including 'The Custom House, Dublin' (Plate 38), and 'Abbey of Arbroath', 'Aberdeen' (both dated 1840) and 'Canning Dock and Custom House, Liverpool' (1841) for W. Beattie's *Ports, harbours* ... 1842. The title page vignette 'Lincluden, The poet's dream' and 'Dumfries' after D. O. Hill were engraved for Wilson and Chambers's *Land of Burns* 1840, and among his last works were five plates, three after the author's own designs, to Brockedon's *Italy* ... 1842-3. Eight plates, including 'Tombs of the Kings of Golconda' after Purser, appeared in Wright's *Gallery of engravings* 1844-6 and a vignette, 'The monk', after G. Cattermole in Calabrella's *Evenings at Haddon Hall* 1845.

J. C. Armytage, in conversation with Marcus B. Huish about 1894, is reported to have said that Higham was exceptionally good at architectural subjects, and that his 'Rouen Cathedral' must be considered one of the plates of the century. (*The Seine and the Loire* ... 1895, Introduction.) Higham was auditor of the Artists' Annuity Fund, which he joined in 1820, and he also signed the 1837 petition. DNB; SocA.

Hill (fl. 1838) Landscape engraver. 'Keonigstein' [*sic*] (a rather poor plate, largely etched) after Fussell was published in *Continental tourist* [1838].

Hill, H. (fl. 1841-3) Landscape engraver. 'Comme Dhuve, the Black Valley, Kerry' was a vignette after T. Creswick published in S. C. and A. M. Hall's *Ireland* 1841-3.

Hill, R. (fl. 1841-3) Landscape engraver. 'Turk [or Torc] Mountain, from Dinis Island, Kerry', a vignette after T. Creswick, was issued in S. C. and A. M. Hall's *Ireland* 1841-3. It is possible that H. Hill and R. Hill are the same person, but which initial is correct is not clear.

Hill, W. (fl. 1833-50) Landscape engraver. An engraver of this name of 3 Colemere Row, Birmingham, was awarded the Silver Isis medal of the Society of Arts in 1825 for an engraving of a landscape. His first published book plate was 'Frankfurt' after Clarkson Stanfield for L. Ritchie's *Travelling sketches on the Rhine* 1833, followed by two plates for *Literary souvenir* 1835, and 'Halt of a caravan in the desert', dated 1837, after W. H. Bartlett for J. Carne's *Syria* 1836-8, reissued, dated 1846, in J. Kitto's *Gallery of scripture engravings* 1846-9. 'Lake Leman ...' (1836), 'The Fall of Schaffhausen ...' (1836) (a peculiar indeterminate plate) and 'Castle of Spiez ...' (1 July 1834), all after W. H. Bartlett, appeared in W. Beattie's *Switzerland* 1836, and for the same author's *Scotland illustrated* 1838, he engraved 'The eastern pass of Glencoe' (1836) after T. Allom. 'Salbertrann' after Bartlett and 'La Traverse, Val Prajelas' and 'The mountains of the Vaudois ...' after Brockedon were engraved for Beattie's *Waldenses* 1838.

Hilliard, F. (fl. 1836-38) Architectural engraver. 'Rochester Cathedral; view of the crypt' after Hablot Browne was published in *Winkles's* ... *Cathedral churches of England* ..., volume 1, 1836, and 'Cathedral, Aix la Chapelle' after Fussell appeared in *Continental tourist* [1838].

Hinchliff, John James (c. 1805-75). Landscape, architectural and portrait engraver. At least ten of his plates have been signed 'J. [or J.J.] Hinchliffe'. Born about 1805, he was the son of John Ely Hinchliff (1777-1867), a sculptor, whose works appeared at the Royal Academy in the mid-1840s. John James decided to become an engraver early in life and among his artist acquaintances numbered John Landseer, the engraver. Soon after the end of his apprenticeship, he engraved 'Barracks at Woolwich' (1829) after W. H. Bartlett and 'Woolwich, Kent' (1829) after H. Gastineau for S. W. H. Ireland's *England's topographer* (commenced publication 1828), two engravings after T. H. Shepherd for J. Elmes's *Metropolitan improvements* 1829 and eight plates after Shepherd for the artist's *London and its environs* 1829-31. For T. H. Shepherd's *Modern Athens* 1829-31, he did one view and for J. Britton and E. W. Brayley's *Devonshire and Cornwall illustrated* 1832, two views after T. Allom. Ten plates after H. Gastineau were done for the latter's *Wales illustrated* ... 1830, and for Noble and Rose's *Counties of Chester* ... 1836, he engraved two plates after T. Allom. 'Coming home' after E. Barrett, 'Evening' after R. Reinagle and a very effective 'Hagar in the desert' after J. Robson were engraved for S. C. Hall's *Book of gems* 1838. 'Yenikeuij on the Bosphorus' after W. H. Bartlett was done for J. Pardoe's *Beauties of the Bosphorus* 1840, and two more after the same artist, Bartlett, 'Montrose' (1840) and 'Bridge to the South Stack Lighthouse' (1841) appeared in W. Beattie's *Ports, harbours* ... 1842. Six vignettes after Creswick, A. Nicholls, H. Gastineau and W. Evans were published in S. C. and A. M. Hall's *Ireland* 1841-3, and three more appeared in T. Rose's *Summer tour in the Isle of Wight* 1843, where the engraver's name was given in the lower part of the design, not on a separate line, as was usual. 'Tewkesbury Abbey' and

'Netley Abbey' after G. F. Sargent were engraved for W. Beattie's *Castles and abbeys of England* 1845–51, and for the same author's *Danube* 1844 he did 'Castle of Wissegraad' and 'Sarbling and Kirschan' after W. H. Bartlett. He engraved frontispieces for a number of books, e.g., portraits of Mohammed after Duflos for Ockley's *History of the Saracens* 1847 and Benvenuto Cellini after Vasari for Cellini's *Memoirs* 1847. For *The Book and its story* by 'L. N. R.', he engraved the frontispiece 'The first reading of the Bible in the Crypt at Old St. Paul's' after G. Harvey, and for the 1872 edition of J. Evelyn's *Diary and correspondance*, portraits of Sir Thomas Browne, Louis XIV, Jeremy Taylor, Marguerite de Valois and Mazarin were provided. He worked for many years as an engraver on Admiralty charts at the Hydrographic Office, and for H. Bohn, the publisher, provided a number of illustrations taken from originals in the British Museum. Genial, vivacious, a nature lover, a good conversationalist and well read, he had a great number of acquaintances. After his retirement from engraving, he lived for several years at Clifton, Bristol, later moving to Walton-by-Clevedon, Somerset, where he died on 16 December 1875, aged about seventy, after a short illness.   AJ; B.

Hinchliff, W. (fl. 1832) Architectural engraver. 'Walmer Castle, Kent' (9 January 1832) after G. Shepherd was issued in a reprint of S. W. H. Ireland's *England's topographer* (commenced publication 1828), a work to which J. J. Hinchliff also contributed.

Hinshelwood, Robert (1812–?) Landscape and architectural engraver. He was born in 1812 in Edinburgh, where he became a pupil of James and John Johnstone, engravers (qq.v.). He was educated at the Trustees' Academy under Sir William Allan, and went to the United States in 1835, when he was twenty-three and just out of his indentures. He worked for the Continental Bank Note Company in New York, and assisted James Smillie, the eminent American steel engraver. Hinshelwood (and J. A. Rolph (q.v.)) executed preliminary etchings for many of Smillie's engravings, collaborated in engraving the landscape areas of certain plates, e.g., 'The capture of Major André' after A. B. Durand (1845), and did the drapery (Rolph the etching) for 'Capuchin monk' after Ver Bryck. (F. Weitenkampf, *The Evolution of steel engraving in America* in *The Book Buyer*, series 3, vol. 23, 1901, pp. 23–5.) Smillie had abandoned landscape engraving by 1861 to concentrate on bank note work and it seems likely that Hinshelwood had returned to England by the 1870s; for four plates by him were issued in *Picturesque Europe* 1876–9, published by Cassell, namely, 'The Bent Cliff (west coast of Ireland)' and 'Rocks at Ross (near Kilkee, Ireland)' after H. Fenn, 'Chepstow Castle' after E. M. Wimperis and 'Tomb of Louis de Breze, Rouen Cathedral' after S. J. Hodson. He was almost certainly the engraver of 'Echo Lake, New Hampshire' after J. F. Cropsey, which appeared in the *Art Journal* 1876, although the engraving is signed 'P. Hinshelwood', and the accompanying letterpress substitutes the initial 'F'.   St; T.

Holl, Benjamin (1808–84) Portrait and figure engraver. Although he was baptized 'Henry Benjamin', only one plate is known signed 'H. B. Holl'; the remainder are signed simply 'B. Holl'. He was the second of the four sons of William Holl the elder (c. 1771–1838), an eminent portrait engraver, and was born on 11 March 1808. Taught by his father, his first independently published plate was the frontispiece 'William [IV]' after A. Wivell (1832) for R. Huish's *Memoirs of George the fourth* 1830–2. He did some plates for H. Jerdan's *National Portrait Gallery* 1830–34 and for Mrs Jamieson's *Beauties of the Court of Charles II* 1833. 'A Turkish letter-writer at Constantinople' after T. Allom is the one signed 'H. B. Holl' it appeared in volume 2 of R. Walsh's *Constantinople* 1838–40 and then in G. N. Wright's *Gallery of engravings* 1844–6. N. P. Willis's *American scenery* 1840 contained as a frontispiece the portrait of W. H. Bartlett after H. Room, and Finden's *Tableaux* 1840 had 'The Warning' after J. Browne. 'The alarm' after K. Meadows appeared in *The Keepsake* 1841, the frontispiece of T. Arnold after T. Phillips, dated May 1841, was done for A. P. Stanley's *Life of Arnold* 1846, and in *Heroines of Shakespeare* 1848 there appeared 'Viola' after A. Egg, dated 2 November 1846. Three plates of sculpture were engraved for the *Art Journal*, i.e., 'Prometheus' by Manning and 'Sleeping nymph' by Baily, both after Pistrucci (1847), and 'Narcissus' by Bacon (1848). Portraits of John Knox and Swift were issued in the *Imperial dictionary of universal biography* [c. 1861]. He exhibited at the Society of British Artists, Suffolk Street, in 1828–9. He died at Marisiana, in the United States in June 1884, aged seventy-six.   DNB; T.

Holl, Charles (c. 1810–82) Portrait and figure engraver. Born between 1808 and 1814, he was the third son of William Holl the elder (1771–1838), by whom he was taught. 'The agony' after Dolci, ' "Have mercy upon me, O God" ' after Guido and 'Captive Israelites' after Bendemann were published in the *Book of Common Prayer* 1854, 'Sir William Petty' after Closterman in Woodward's *General history of Hampshire* 1863 and 'Rebekah at the well' after Du Bourg (with an ornamental border by Luke Limner) in *The Self-interpreting Bible* 1864. 'George Augustus Elliot' after Reynolds, 'Rev. Andrew Thomson' after Watson and 'Sir David Brewster' were published in Chambers's *Biographical dictionary of eminent Scotsmen*, 2nd edition, 1875. 'A Bacchante' after Romney was engraved for the *Art Journal* 1854. The lack of plates signed by him is due to the fact that he worked in his brother William's studio for about thirty years. He died in 1882, aged about seventy.   DNB; T.

Holl, Francis (1815–84) Portrait and figure engraver. He was born on 23 March 1815 at Bayham Street, Camden Town, the fourth son of William Holl the elder (c. 1771–1838) and Mary Ravenscroft, his wife. Taught by his father, he worked for the print publishers as well as for book publishers, and frequently collaborated on plates with his elder brother William (q.v.), as with the four plates after J. Hayter for Finden's *Gallery of beauty* 1841 (which, since they are usually signed 'W. and F. Holl' are dealt with as if they were by the former). He was a fashionable engraver, working for twenty-five years on engravings of the Queen's Pictures, as well as receiving from Her Majesty commissions to execute private plates of herself and other members of the Royal Family. Only two of these were published, namely, one of the Prince Consort, done in the year of his death, which Holl was allowed to publish for his personal benefit, and one of Princess Alice. Seven plates were engraved for Fisher's *Historic illustrations of the Bible* [1840–3], and he did the frontispiece 'Charles 1st' and the portrait 'O. Cromwell', both after Van Dyke, for R. Cattermole's *Great Civil War* 1846. One of the most beautiful plates ever produced in steel was 'Holy eyes', dated June 1845, after J. G. Middleton, done for *Beauties of Moore* 1846. W. P. Frith was supposed to have painted the picture for this plate, but for some reason did not (see W. P. Frith, *My autobiography*, 3rd edition, vol. 2, 1887, pp. 199–207, and B. Hunnisett, *Steel-engraved book illustration in England*, 1980, p. 132). He engraved 'Mrs. Ford' after E. Corbould for *Heroines of Shakespeare* 1848 and the

Francis Holl

frontispiece 'Sir David Wilkie, R.A.' after T. Phillips for *Wilkie gallery* [c. 1849]. Seven plates appeared in the *Book of Common Prayer* 1854 and 'The agony...' after Dolci in *The Self-interpreting Bible* 1864. A vignette of the poetess Eliza Cook from a photograph by John Watkins was issued in her *Poetical works* 1869, five plates, together with nine joint plates with William, appeared in the *Imperial Family Bible* 1873 (first published in 1844) after Barroccio, A. Coypel, S. A. Hart, C. Begas and H. Lejeune, and 'John Hunter' was engraved for Chambers's *Biographical dictionary of eminent Scotsmen*, 2nd edition, 1875. In *Casquet of literature* 1874 was issued 'Three beauties' after Grevedon (a vignette inside a frame). 'Lord John Russell' after a photograph by Mayall (signed 'Holl') was probably by Francis Holl, and was done for James Taylor's *Age we live in ...* [c. 1885] (Plate 61). In F. Bacon's *Works* 1889–90, the frontispiece to volume 1 was 'Sir Francis Bacon' after an old print, and to volume 6, a vignette, 'Francis Bacon when a boy' after A. Hughes. He also illustrated Sir Theodore Martin's *Life of His Royal Highness the Prince Consort* 1875–80. 5 vols. Among his larger plates are 'The spinning wheel' after F. W. Topham, published by Lloyd Bros. in 1848, 'The coming of age in the olden time', 'The railway station' and 'Sherry sir?', all after W. P. Frith, 'The stocking loom' after A. Elmore and 'Christian graces' and 'Il penseroso and l'allegro' after G. E. Hicks, the latter published 1870.

He exhibited seventeen engravings at the Royal Academy between 1856 and 1879, and in 1874 his name was put forward for election as an Associate Engraver, but the attempt was unsuccessful, and he was only elected on 16 January 1883, almost exactly a year before his death. (His eldest son, Francis Montague (Frank) (1845–88), a painter, had been elected an Associate in 1878 and R.A. before 1883.) He contributed seven engravings to the *Art Journal* between 1862 and 1882, e.g., 'Lad and lassie' after E. Landseer (1877), a pair of oval engravings after J. S. Mann—'The country blossom' (1879) and 'City belle' (1880) (which last was beautifully engraved)—and his last plate, 'A siesta' after C. E. Perugini. His speciality was in portraits after G. Richmond. He was well known as an amateur actor, being a member of 'The Histrionics', who played in St James's Theatre. His portrayal of Mungo in *The Padlock* in 1842 was remarked

upon, and in the performances (held by an amateur company composed of eminent artists like Cruikshank, Tenniel, and Topham and led by Dickens) in 1846 and 1848 in aid of the Artists' Benevolent Fund, his characterisations of General Tarragon, Dr Ollaped and Dr Pangloss were first class. He also sang well and played the 'cello. On 23 September 1841 he married Alicia Margaret, daughter of Robert Dixon, a veteran of Trafalgar, and had two sons and two daughters. For many years they lived at 30 Gloucester Road, Regent's Park, but about 1879 he retired to Elm House, Milford, Surrey, where he died of peritonitis on 14 January 1884. He was buried in Highgate Cemetery five days later. Portraits by his son were exhibited at the Royal Academy in 1868 (in chalk), and in 1884 and 1889 (in oil). AJ; B; DNB; *Illus. Lond. News* 1883, p. 470; S; T.

Holl, William (1807–71) Portrait and figure engraver. Born at Plaistow, Essex, in February 1807, he was the eldest son of William Holl the elder (c. 1771–1838), who taught him engraving, mainly in stipple at first, but later in line on steel. In this connection, William the elder was a pioneer in stipple on steel with plates such as the portrait of the Revd John Roadhouse, (April 1821) and of the Revd R. Waddy (March 1823), both done for *The Methodist Magazine*. Since William the younger would not have been out of his apprenticeship until about 1827, it is reasonably safe to assume that plates before this date carried his father's name, and so his earliest independent work began when he was twenty-two with a series of twenty-one portraits for E. Lodge's *Portraits...*, 2nd edition, 1835. These began in May 1829 with 'Thomas Cranmer' and ended in November 1835 with 'Horatio, first Lord Walpole' after Vanloo. Holbein, Gerard, Van Dyke, Lely, Kneller, Mytens, Hoare Cotes and Copley were other artists represented in this series. For R. Huish's *Memoirs of George the Fourth* 1830–2, he engraved the frontispiece to volume 1 'George [IV]' after A. Wivell, 'William Pitt' after W. Owen and 'Charles James Fox'. Some plates were engraved for H. Jerdan's *National portrait gallery* 1830–4. He engraved 'Humphrey Chetham' (1831) and 'Bishop Oldham' (1835), both of which appeared in Baines's *History of ... Lancaster* 1836 and again in Wright's *Lancashire* 1842. The former volume also contained 'Sir Ashton Lever' after Shelley (1835) and 'Thomas Stanley' (1836). A portrait of Bunyan after Derby was engraved for the *Pilgrim's progress* 1836, and a stipple portrait of 'Mrs. [Frances] Trollope' (1835) after Miss L. Adams appeared in Fisher's *Drawing room scrap book* 1836. Ten of his plates were issued in Wright's *Gallery of engravings* 1844–6, including 'Rather queer' after W. Hunt and 'Raphael Sanzio' after Sanzio himself. 'Kaled' after J. W. Wright appeared in *Heath's Book of beauty* 1847, and 'Margaret' after the same artist was engraved for *Heroines of Shakespeare* 1848. His scripture engravings appeared in Fisher's *Historic illustrations of the Bible* [1840–3], which contained fourteen after artists such as Rembrandt, B. West and J. Northcote (whose '[Death of Sisera] "Jael smote the nail"' is striking), and the *Imperial Family Bible* 1873 (first published by Blackie, 1844), which had eight plates by William, of which 'Ruth and Naomi' after H. Lejeune is remarkable, and nine engravings done jointly with Francis, of which the round picture after Raphael 'Unto us a child is born' is notable. In 1847 two prints were issued by Lloyd Bros., namely, 'Irish mother' after R. W. Scanlan and 'Maid of Athens' after E. Landseer, of which the latter, as a stipple engraving, was thought to be 'a good example of the ability of Mr. W. Holl'. Three portraits of the Earls of Essex, dated 1852, appeared in Devereux's *Lives and letters... 1853*, 'The novice of St. Clair' after Absolon in *The Keepsake* 1855 and 'Ancilla Domini' (an outline engraving) and 'Hesperid Aigle' were done for Ruskin's *Modern painters* 1856–60. His later book work included nineteen portraits for the *Imperial dictionary of universal biography* [c. 1861], of which 'Beethoven' after Kloeber is a good example. Three portraits after photographs by Reylander and Mayall were issued in Taylor's *Family history of England* [c. 1860], four portraits after photographs in Baines's *Yorkshire past and present* 1871–7 and eight portraits in Chambers's *Biographical dictionary of eminent Scotsmen*, 2nd edition, 1875. A portrait of J. M. W. Turner was used as the frontispiece to Wornum's *Turner Gallery* [c. 1878] (first issued in the *Art Journal* 1865), and a portrait of George Grote as the frontispiece to volume 1 of Grote's *History of Greece* 1887–8. He contributed two plates to the *Art Journal* 1860 and a vignette of E. M. Ward after G. Richmond to the volume for 1879. In the 1860s he was engaged on portraits of the Royal Family; in 1863 those of the Prince and Princess of Wales after photographs by Mayall were issued by J. Mitchell, and were engraved in the ten days between 14 March and 24 March, being the 'most creditable examples of the art, combining great softness with richness of tone'. The same publisher issued 'by command' 'The Queen—1864' after A. Graefle, and in 1866 'The Queen and grandson'. From 1860 to 1871 Holl exhibited twenty-two works at the Royal Academy. His work for the Art Union of London began in 1851 with 'An old English merrymaking' after Frith, which was said to have been the first large plate to be done in the 'chalk' style. Two further plates after the same artist were 'The village pastor' and 'The gleaner and his wife', and just before his death he completed 'Rebekah' after F. Goodall for the Art Union of London.

He was a signatory to the 1837 petition, and secretary of the Erechtheum Club, St James' Square, from about 1853. In a letter to the publisher John Murray from 36 Ampthill Square dated 21 December 1861, he acknowledges receipt of a miniature of the Earl of Shaftesbury which he hopes to engrave in three to four months. He draws attention to several spots of what he takes to be mildew on the portrait and ends 'I think it well to mention this circumstance lest it might be imagined the fault was mine'. He died after a long and painful illness on 30 January 1871, aged almost sixty-four. For the previous thirty years he had been assisted by his brother Charles (q.v.) and F. Angelo Roberts (q.v.), who were, at his expressed wish, to finish all outstanding plates, which probably included 'Francesca da Rimini' after Gustave Doré, published in 1872. There is in the Library of the Royal Society of Arts a stipple-engraved portrait of a bald-headed painter with a palette seated before an easel, head turned to the right. 'W. Holl' is stipple-engraved in large letters beneath the portrait, which could be either a portrait of himself or an unfinished plate—no artist is given. AJ; B; DNB; T.

Hollis, George (1793–1842) Landscape and portrait engraver. Born at Oxford in 1793, he came to London in about 1807 to be apprenticed to George Cooke. Consequently his name was employed mainly on topographical works, his name first appearing in 1818, on six views of Chudleigh after H. F. De Cort. Further plates appeared in E. Dodwell's *Tour through Greece* 1819, Ormerod's *History of Cheshire* 1819, J. Hakewill's *Tour in Italy* 1820 (which contained Italian views after Turner), J. Stanhope's *Olympia* 1824, R. C. Hoare's *History of Wiltshire* 1824 and Warner's *Glastonbury Abbey*. He engraved a series of views of Oxford colleges and halls, some after his own designs, and in 1837 finished a large plate after Turner,

probably 'St. Mark's Square, Venice', which was exhibited at the Royal Academy in 1838. Some engravings after G. and T. Hollis were done for Cumberland's *British theatre* 1834, and among his works on steel were some line engravings for *The Oriental annual* 1834. 'Borwick Hall, Lancashire' after G. Pickering, dated 1835, was published in E. Baines's *History of ... Lancaster* 1836, and in 1839 he, with his son Thomas (1818–43), began work on *Monumental effigies of Great Britain* 1840–2, but died at Walworth on 2 January 1842 before it was completed, aged forty-nine. (His son died of consumption on 4 October 1843, aged twenty-five.) Some of his plates were published posthumously in Tallis's *Drawing room table book* 1851. B; DNB; R; T.

Hollis, J. (fl. 1833–46) Portrait and figure engraver. For volume 3 of *Finden's illustrations of the life and works of Lord Byron* 1833–4 he engraved a portrait of M. G. ('Monk') Lewis after G. H. Harlowe, and for T. Moore's *Lallah Rookh* he did 'Lalla Rookh' after K. Meadows and 'Zelica' after E. Corbould. For Finden's *Tableaux* 1840, he produced 'The death of Luath' after J. Browne, and 'The penitent and his penance' after McIain, dated 1846, came out in *Forget me not* 1846.

Hone, T. (fl. 1846) Landscape engraver, possibly connected with the Irish painter and engraver Nathaniel Hone (1718–84) and his son Horace (1756–1825). 'Oberwesel' after Tombleson appeared in H. G. Fearnside's *Picturesque beauties of the Rhine* [c. 1846].

Hood, W. (fl. 1832) Landscape engraver. 'Convent of Laach' after W. Tombleson appeared in Fearnside's *Tombleson's views of the Rhine* 1832. He is possibly connected with Thomas Hood (1799–1845), poet and humourist, who was taught engraving by Le Keux.

Hopwood, James (1795–?) Portrait engraver. Born in Yorkshire, he was the son and pupil of James Hopwood (1752–1819), and brother of William Hopwood (1784–1853), both of whom were engravers. He worked chiefly in stipple, and for *Finden's illustrations of the life and works of Lord Byron* 1833–4, he engraved 'Sir John Cam Hobhouse' after A. Wivell. He designed and engraved a number of other book illustrations, including some for the annuals, but in 1828 he began a series of French portraits, which were published in Paris, where eventually he went to continue his work. Among his popular portraits there were those of King Louis-Philippe and Queen Amelia Mary. Ferdinand Gaillard the well-known French engraver was Hopwood's pupil. His last work was done about 1855. Br; DNB; R; T.

Hords, R. (fl. 1831) Landscape engraver. Known from two plates after Austin in G. N. Wright's *Ireland illustrated* 1831, namely, 'Jenkinstown Castle, Co. Kilkenny' and 'Castle Howel, Co. Kilkenny'. Ho.

Horsburgh, John (1791–1869) Landscape and portrait engraver. Born at Prestonpans, near Edinburgh, on 16 November 1791, he early in life lost his father. He studied drawing at the Trustees' Academy, and in 1805 was apprenticed to Robert Scott, landscape engraver, for whom he worked several years after his indentures had expired. Among his fellow pupils were John Burnet and James Stewart. 'Whitstable' after J. M. W. Turner appeared in *Picturesque views on the southern coast of England* 1826, and in the same year he was elected a founder member (Associate Engraver) of the Royal Scottish Academy, but withdrew after the first meeting, being one of nine who were alarmed at the magnitude of the undertaking, and was never re-elected. His earliest steel plate was 'Ponte Sesto, Rome' after S. Prout, dated 28 October 1829, for T. Roscoe's *Tourist in Switzerland and Italy* 1830, and in the same year he engraved the portrait of Walter Scott by J. W. Gordon, used as the frontispiece to Scott's *Waverley novels*. For the same work he produced thirteen other plates, which included 'On the coast of Galloway' and 'Cathedral of Glasgow' after C. Stanfield and 'Convent of St. Saba...' after D. Roberts. He engraved title page vignettes after H. Corbould for *The Amethyst* 1832, 1833 and 1834. 'Ashestiel', 'Mayburgh' and 'Bemerside Tower' after Turner were vignettes engraved for Scott's *Poetical works* 1833–4, and 'Turnberry Castle' after D. O. Hill appeared in Wilson and Chambers's *Land of Burns* 1840. The *Imperial Family Bible* 1844 contained 'Belshazzar's feast' after Martin, and 'The blessing' after Bonnar was published in *Casquet of literature*, 2nd series, volume 1, 1874. A second, coarsely engraved portrait of Scott, after Lawrence, was published in the *Art Journal* 1858. His other works included 'Mackay the actor, as Baillie Nichol Jarvie' after Sir William Allan, Taylor's disputed portrait of Burns, engraved for the Royal Scottish Association, 'Prince Charles reading a dispatch' after W. Simson for the Glasgow Art Union and 'Italian shepherds' after McInnes.

About the time he was sixty, in the early 1850s, he retired from engraving. From about 1832, he had worked, unpaid, as a minister in the Scottish Baptist Church, in which capacity he was much respected, and his pastoral addresses, prefaced by a short memoir, were published in 1869. He died at 16 Buccleuch Place, Edinburgh, on 24 September 1869, aged nearly seventy-eight.   AJ; Br; DNB; R; T.

How, J. (fl. 1832–46) Landscape and architectural engraver. All his known plates are after W. Tombleson, the earliest of which, signed 'Howe', and entitled 'Oberlanstein [market cross]', appeared in Fearnside's *Tombleson's views of the Rhine* 1832. 'Hampton Court Bridge', 'Southwark Bridge' and 'Aylesford, Kent' (signed 'G. How') were published in Fearnside's *Tombleson's Thames* 1834, and 'Bonn Cathedral' (signed 'J. Howe') and 'Constance' appeared in Fearnside's *Picturesque beauties of the Rhine* [c. 1846]. 'Convent of Reichenau', 'Castle of Friedrichshafen' and 'Roman tower at Marsoil at Chur' were issued in Fearnside's *Tombleson's Upper Rhine* [c. 1835].

Howard, T. (fl. 1832–46) Landscape and architectural engraver. All his known plates are after W. Tombleson, the earliest of which is 'Fountain at Mayence' (signed 'Howard') in Fearnside's *Tombleson's views of the Rhine* 1832. 'Wallingford, Berks.' was done for Fearnside's *Tombleson's Thames* 1834, and 'Interior Bonn Cathedral' (signed 'J. Howard') appeared in Fearnside's *Picturesque beauties of the Rhine* [c. 1846].

Howison, William (1798–1850) Portrait, figure and landscape engraver. Born in Edinburgh, he was educated at George Heriot's Hospital, and was apprenticed in due course to Andrew Wilson, an engraver. In the early years of his career he worked on small plates, and in comparative obscurity, but through the offices of D. O. Hill, he received his first important commission, to engrave 'The Curlers' after Sir George Harvey, sometime President of the Royal Scottish Academy. This plate led to his election in 1838 as an associate of the Academy, the only time such an honour was conferred upon an engraver. Further plates after Harvey were 'Covenanters' communion' (1846) and 'A Skule Skailin', both of which, together with his plate after Sir William Allan's 'The Polish exiles', further enhanced his reputation. His steel book plates included the vignette portraits 'Allan Ramsay' and 'Hector

Boece' for Chambers's *Biographical dictionary of eminent Scotsmen* 1835, with three more added to the 2nd edition (1875). 'Scene on the Doun, near its source' after D. O. Hill was engraved for Wilson and Chambers's *Land of Burns* 1840, and 'The lovesick maid' after Mieris and 'The cobbler of Duddington' after Fraser appeared in *Casquet of literature* 1874. At the time of his death he was working on an engraving of J. Faed's 'First letter from the emigrants' for subscribers to the Association for the promotion of the Fine Arts in Scotland. He died at 8 Frederick Street, Edinburgh, on 20 December 1850, aged fifty-two, and was buried in Greyfriars Churchyard.   AJ; B; DNB; R.

Hughes, W. (fl. 1840–51) Map engraver. Much of his work was done for the publisher Virtue, and was drawn by himself. For Willis's *American scenery* 1840, he engraved a map of 'The north eastern part of the US', for Coyne's *Scenery and antiquities of Ireland* [c. 1840], a map of 'Ireland' and for Beattie's *Danube* 1844, two maps 'The Danube' and 'The Black Sea and surrounding countries'. In works by W. H. Bartlett he produced an outline engraving (after the author) of 'Gradual formation of Jerusalem' for *Walks about ... Jerusalem* [1844], maps of Egypt and the Plain of Thebes for *Nile boat* 1849, four plates for *Scripture sites and scenes...* 1849, two for *Gleanings ... on the overland route* 1851, a 'Map to illustrate travels of Our Lord' for *Footsteps of Our Lord* 1851 and a map for *Pictures from Sicily* 1853. A map of Palestine with a vignette, 'Enclosure of the temple', was engraved for Stebbing's *Christian in Palestine* [1847]. A map of India with five vignettes was done for Nolan's *Illustrated history of the British Empire in India* [1858–60]. In 1840 his address was given as Aldine Chambers, Paternoster Row, but by 1847 he had moved to 6 Brook Street, Holborn.

Hulland, W. (fl. 1853–60) Figure engraver. 'Ruth Summerfield & Percy Clifton', 'Miss Clifton and Tracy', 'The smugglers at home' and 'Charlotte Monckton' were published in *The Cottage-girl...* [c. 1860]. 'The Negro' after Simpson appeared in the *Art Journal* 1853, and 'Christ crowned with thorns' after Van Dyck was also engraved by him.

Humphrys, William (1794–1865) Figure and portrait engraver. Born in Dublin, he went in early life to America, where he worked at bank note engraving in Philadelphia under George Murray, who was a pupil of Anker Smith. A trade card from this period describes him as 'W. Humphrys, Engraver of history, landscapes, etc., Philadelphia'. He returned to England in about 1822 or 1823, well versed in engraving on steel at a time when its popularity was just beginning here, especially for the annuals, and his earliest plate was 'Mother and child' after W. Brockedon for the *Literary souvenir* 1825. In 1826 he was awarded the Gold Isis medal by the Society of Arts for his work on etching fluids for steel plates, notably the first recipe to omit nitric acid. 'The kiss' and 'Blondel and Richard Coeur de Lion' after J. M. Wright appeared in the *Literary souvenir* 1826, 'Cupid and Psyche' after W. E. West in the volume for 1827, 'The thief discovered' after Chalon in that for 1828, and for *The Bijou* 1828, he engraved a vignette of a cupid in a wreath after T. Stothard for the engraved title page and the frontispiece 'Child and flowers' and 'The boy and dog', both after Lawrence. He received £40 for a vignette, 'The nun' (signed 'Humphrys'), after T. Stothard for S. Rogers' *Italy* 1830. 'Adelaide' after Leslie was engraved for *Friendship's offering* 1831, 'Curiosité' after Roqueplan for *Keepsake français* 1831 and 'Il Biglietto d'amore...' after Davis for *Wreath of*

Friendship. In the next decade, he began to work for the print publishers, and his most successful prints included 'Sancho and the duchess' after C. R. Leslie, 'Master Lambton' after Lawrence, 'Spanish peasant boy' after Murillo and 'Magdalen' after Correggio (1839). This last was one of his last line engravings of this kind, and was published 'on his account', but although it was successful artistically, it was a financial failure (*Art Union* 1839, p. 157) which was doubtless a factor in encouraging him to turn to mezzotinting, as did many other line engravers. One of his earliest mezzotint attempts was 'Master Lock' in the *Works of Thomas Lawrence* 1839, and by 1841, with the publication by H. Graves of 'Milton Hunt' after F. Grant, he was 'rapidly maintaining his right to a foremost rank among British engravers in mezzotinto—a less arduous but more profitable branch of the profession' (*Art Union*, 1841, p. 190). He returned to America in 1843 and there contributed illustrations to editions of Bryant, Longfellow and other poets, and to the annuals, for example, in 1844, *The Gift* published an illustration of an incident in the early days of Washington. In 1845, he engraved a portrait of General Isaac Putnam for the *National Portrait Gallery*, and later returned to London, where he became known as 'the American engraver'. He engraved 'Egeria' after Correggio for the Royal Irish Art Union in 1846, and for Finden's *Royal Gallery of British Art* 1838–49, he engraved 'The coquette' after Sir Joshua Reynolds in 1849. His later engraved work was connected with postage stamps, his most celebrated designs being that done in July 1855 for the first New Zealand stamps, together with his head of George Washington for United States postage stamps. This was virtually the end of his career as an engraver, and he became an accountant to the musical firm of Novello. Late in 1864 he suffered a paralytic stroke, and in the hope of recovering his health he accepted Arthur Novello's invitation to convalesce at the Villa Novello in Genoa. He died there on 21 January 1865, aged seventy-one. Br; DNB; R; St; T.

Hunt, Samuel Valentine (1803–1893) Landscape engraver. Born at Norwich on 14 February 1803, he was originally trained as a taxidermist and taught himself engraving. He exhibited at the British Institution between 1826 and 1828, and did a portrait of the landscape painter J. Stennard after G. Clint (1831). In 1834 he emigrated to America, where he worked for publishers in New York and Cincinnatti. One of his few steel engravings to be published in this country was 'The Ghetto, Rome' after L. Haghe in *Picturesque Europe* 1876–9. He died at Bay Ridge, Long Island, New York, in 1893, aged ninety. B; St; T.

Hunt, T. W. (fl. 1840–84) Portrait, figure and sculpture engraver. He engraved some stipple portraits for *The Methodist Magazine*, but his book work in steel began with the portrait 'Robert Burns' after Nasmyth for the *Complete works of Robert Burns* [c. 1840]. 'The daughter of Admiral Walker' and 'The senorita and her nurse', both after Sir David Wilkie, appeared in *Wilkie gallery* [c. 1849]. He engraved three portraits for Nolan's *Illustrated history of the British Empire in India* [1858–60] and 'John baptizing...' after Poussin (with an ornamental border by Luke Limner) for *The Self-interpreting Bible* 1864. He engraved ten plates for the *Art Journal*, commencing with a sculpture of Queen Victoria after J. Gibson in 1849, followed by 'Reflection' (a girl's head) after Rippingille (1851), Sir Joshua Reynolds' self portrait and 'Morton, the dramatist' after Sir Martin Shee (1854) and ending with a series of six sculptures in 1861, 1870, 1875, 1877, 1880 and 1884. B; T.

Hunter, James (fl. 1848) Figure engraver. 'The golden age', a round engraving after Edward Magnus was first issued in the *Art Union* 1848, and was reprinted in Mrs A. M. Hall's *Drawing room table book* 1849.

J

Jackman, W. (fl. 1840) Portrait and figure engraver. 'A man's a man for a' that' after J. M. Wright appeared in the *Complete works of Robert Burns* [c. 1840]. He is probably the W. G. Jackman who emigrated to America about 1841 to work for publishers in New York. B; St.

Jackson, J. (fl. 1832–5) Landscape and architectural engraver after W. Tombleson. 'Biberich, seat of the Duke of Nassau' was published in Fearnside's *Tombleson's views of the Rhine* 1832 and 'Arbon, Lake Constance' in the same author's *Tombleson's Upper Rhine* [c. 1835].

Jackson, T. (fl. 1832–46) Landscape engraver after W. Tombleson. 'Boppart' was issued in Fearnside's *Tombleson's views of the Rhine* 1832 and 'Coblenz and Ehrenbreitstein' in Fearnside's *Picturesque beauties of the Rhine* [c. 1846].

Jarman, G. (fl. 1853) Landscape engraver. Six Liverpool views were engraved for Brooke's *Liverpool as it was during the last quarter of the eighteenth century...* 1853. Ho.

Jeavons, Thomas (c. 1800–67) Landscape and architectural engraver. The earliest work to bear his name, dated 1 September 1822, is 'Sutton Hall, Derbyshire', one of thirteen engravings done by him, probably on copper, for volume 1 of J. P. Neale's *Views of the seats of noblemen...* 1818–24. Plates by him appeared in all the important topographical books in the 1830s and 1840s, commencing with seven engravings after W. Brockedon for the artist's *Illustrations of the passes of the Alps* 1828–9, which included 'Scene in the valley of the Reuss' (November 1827), 'Lecco' (May 1828) and 'Tende' (August 1829). By October 1829 he had completed two plates after S. Prout—'View of Vincenza' and 'Place Salone Padua'—for T. Roscoe's *Tourist in Switzerland and Italy* 1830, and after the same artist and for the same author, he engraved 'Temples of the Vesta and Fortuna Virilis Rome' (dated 28 October 1830) for *Tourist in Italy* 1831. 'The destruction of Babel' after 'H. E. S[e]lous' was engraved for the *Literary souvenir* 1831, and in the three volumes by T. Rose published in 1832, he engraved two plates after Pickering for *Cumberland*, two after Allom for *Durham and Northumberland* and three after Allom and two after Gastineau for *Westmorland*. For Roscoe's *Tourist in Italy* 1833 he engraved 'Convent of La Santa Trinita' and 'Castel Madama' after J. D. Harding, both dated 28 October 1832. L. Ritchie's *Travelling sketches in the north of Italy* 1832 contained 'Dome d'Ossola' and 'Landech' after C. Stanfield, *Travelling sketches on the sea coasts of France* 1834 had 'Distant view of St. Michel', also after Stanfield, and *Wanderings by the Seine* 1835 contained 'Hotel de Ville and Pont d'Arcole' after J. M. W. Turner. 'Strawberry Hill ... Twickenham' after W. Tombleson was issued in Fearnside's *Tombleson's Thames* 1834, and in Baines's *History of ... Lancaster* 1836 there was issued 'Stonyhurst College', dated 1831, after Copley Fielding, which was used again in G. N. Wright's *Lancashire* 1842. 'Chinese Pagodah...' after Copley Fielding and 'Bejapore' after Prout were engraved for Elliot's *Views in India...* 1835. About 1836 he began his connection with Virtue, the publisher: for 'The Jungfrau (Bernese Oberland)' (dated 1 August 1834) and 'Airolo' (dated 1835), both after W. H.

Bartlett, were issued in W. Beattie's *Switzerland* 1836, followed by 'Approach to Caipha, Bay of Acre' (dated 1837) and 'Antioch from the west' (mis-signed 'J. Jeavons') after the same artist for J. Carne's *Syria* 1836-8. One of his best book plates is 'Loch Lomond from the road above Inversnaid Mill' after T. Allom, dated 1836, in W. Beattie's *Scotland illustrated* 1838. 'Viu and the Monte Mole...' after Brockedon was engraved for Beattie's *Waldenses* 1838. 'Pass in the Balkan mountains' after C. Bentley and F. Herve was engraved for R. Walsh's *Constantinople* 1838-40, three Scottish scenes after D. O Hill, including 'Ellisland' (Plate 39), appeared in Wilson and Chambers's *Land of Burns* 1840, 'The Ghugun Mahal, Penkonda' was done for Bacon's *Oriental annual* 1840, a vignette, 'The Boyne obelisk, Louth', after A. Nicholl appeared in S. C. and A. M. Hall's *Ireland* 1841-3, three Italian scenes, two after Brockedon and one after Stanfield, were done for W. Brockedon's *Italy...* 1842-3, and 'The peaceable kingdom' after J. Martin was done for the *Imperial Family Bible* 1844. His only contribution to the *Art Journal* was in 1849, when his 'Dutch boats in a calm' after E. W. Cooke (probably his largest plate) appeared. He is also known to have engraved a series of vignettes exemplified by views of Brighton published by W. Grant, a newsagent, of 5 Castle Square, Brighton, after G. Atwick, F. Forde, R. H. Nibbs and G. Ruff, used also to head notepaper, as in the case of 'Fish market on the beach, Brighton (from the sea)'. The 'West view of the city of Chichester' after G. F. Robson was published by John Britton on 1 November 1826. In 1829 he joined the Artists' Annuity Fund, and in 1831 he tried out some new graver handles for the Society of Arts. On page 31 of the *Art Journal* of 1865 he was reported dead, but on page 62 there was published a very quick disclaimer saying that he was still in 'the land of the living'. He had retired to Welshpool in the 1860s, and therefore the *Art Journal*, having lost touch with him, assumed the worst. He died on 26 November 1867 after a few weeks' illness. AJ; B; DNB; SocA; T.

Jeens, Charles Henry (1827-1879) Portrait and figure engraver. Born at Uley, Gloucestershire, the son of Henry and Matilda Jeens, on 19 October 1827, he was a pupil engraver in the early 1840s under John Brain, and later studied under William Greatbach, acquiring a reputation as the miniaturist of engravers, a follower of Bartolozzi (H. Delaborde, *Engraving; its origin...* 1886, p. 314). This view is supported by his early work, which was done for postage stamps, engraving stock dies of Queen Victoria's head, and the vignettes of the early pictorial Newfoundland stamps, issued in the 1860s. He was employed by the *Art Journal* as an engraver, and contributed seventeen of his own plates between 1854 and 1879, which included 'Summer gift' after G. Lance (1854), 'Walk at Kew' after Gainsborough (1856), 'The duenna' after G. S. Newton (1861), 'The birdcage: a scene from Boccaccio' after J. M. W. Turner (1862 and also used in Wornum's *Turner Gallery* [c. 1878]), 'Drift-wreck from the Armada' after P. R. Morris (1870) and 'Leaving home' after F. Holl (1879), which was coarsely engraved in the Continental fashion then prevalent. His book work largely comprised frontispieces such as those to Edwards' *Life of Sir Walter Raleigh* 1868 (a portrait of Raleigh) and Forster's *Life of Oliver Goldsmith* (an engraving of a statue of Goldsmith). 'The Battle of Meeonee' and 'The Battle of Moodkee' (both vignettes) after Armitage and Hayes respectively appeared in Nolan's *Illustrated History of the British Empire in India* [1858-60]. About 1860 he did some miniature stipple engravings, such as the gem medallions of Plato and Socrates, for the

'Golden Treasury' series published by Macmillan which added to his reputation. For Murdoch's edition of the *Holy Bible* c. 1870, he engraved 'Rebekah and Eliezer' after H. Vernet and for *The Royal Shakespeare* 1883-4, 'Armado and Jacquenetta' after J. Holmes. 'Head of a girl' after da Vinci was engraved as a frontispiece to W. H. Pater's *Studies in the history of the Renaissance*, and 'The Queen and Prince Consort fording the Poll Tarff' after C. Haag appeared in Queen Victoria's *Journal of our life in the Highlands* 1868. His extensive series of portraits included those of William Blake, Allan Ramsay and Charles Young and a series of 'Scientific Worthies' for *Nature* (comments upon this aspect of his work appeared in P. G. Hamerton's *Graphic arts* 1882, p. 362). In 1863 he began his association with the Art Union of London when he was asked to finish the plate 'A labour of love' after F. R. Dicksee, begun by H. C. Shenton but not completed by him, because of his failing sight. In 1877 he engraved 'Joseph and Mary' after E. Armitage, and began work on 'Stolen by gipsies—the rescue' after J. B. Burgess (finished after his death by Lumb Stocks for issue to subscribers in 1883). There is a letter in the possession of Thomas Ross and Son, dated October 1871, concerning some financial arrangements with McQueen about the printing of his plates, and a volume of proofs of his vignettes is in the Department of Prints and Drawings, British Museum. AJ; B; Br; D; DNB; T.

Jenkins, Joseph John (1811-85) Portrait and figure engraver. He was the son and pupil of the engraver D. Jenkins, who in turn was a pupil of William Holl the elder. Born in London in 1811, he was equally at home designing plates and engraving them, and both activities went hand in hand. He is thought to have first exhibited in 1825 at the age of fourteen, and between then and 1881 he exhibited works at all the major London exhibitions. By 1846 he seems to have abandoned engraving altogether because of delicate health, and thereafter devoted his time to watercolour painting. His earliest steel book plate was a portrait, 'Sir Richard Arkwright', after J. Wright, dated 1833. This was published in Baines's *History of the cotton manufacture in Great Britain* [1835] and, together with 'John Bradford', in Baines's *History of... Lancaster* 1836 (which also contained 'Cardinal Allen', dated 1835), and again in G. N. Wright's *Lancashire* 1842. For R. Walsh's *Constantinople* 1838-40 he engraved 'The Sultana in her state Arrhuba', 'The Medak, or eastern story-teller' and 'The favourite Odalique', all after T. Allom. The last two were issued again in G. N. Wright's *Gallery of engravings* 1844-6, together with 'T. Campbell' after D. McClise, an oval engraving 'To Agnes...' after J. Wood and 'The devotee' after his own design. He engraved seven plates for Fisher's *Historic illustrations of the Bible* [1840-3], five of which were used again in Kitto's *Gallery of scripture engravings* 1846-9, and 'The poor widow's two mites' after Leloir (with an ornamental border by Luke Limner) was issued in *The Self-interpreting Bible* 1864. His designs for the annuals were published in *The Keepsake* 1835 and 1838, *Forget me not* 1838 and 1840, *Heath's Book of beauty* 1838 and Fisher's *Drawing room scrap book* 1838, 1839, 1840, 1850 and 1851, and were executed by a number of engravers, including W. H. Mote, H. Rolls and P. Lightfoot. He also did portraits for *The Methodist Magazine*. In the early 1840s he went to Wales, Scotland and Belgium to gather sketching material, but nothing impressed him greatly until he went to Brittany in 1846. About 1852 he began to collect materials for a history of watercolour painting in England, but which gradually became more suitable for a history of the Old Water Colour Society, of which he became Secretary from 1854 to 1864. These materials were eventually used by J. L. Roget and published in 1891. He died, unmarried, on 9 March 1885 at 67 Hamilton Terrace, St John's Wood, aged seventy-four. His books and prints were sold on 2 July 1885 and his drawings on 1 March 1886. His brother, Henry Bateman Jenkins, was awarded the Silver Isis medal by the Society of Arts in 1830 for an engraving of a portrait.   B; Br; DNB; Ro; SocA; T; YA 1886.

Johnston, W. & A. K. (fl. 1855) Map engravers of Edinburgh, 'Map of countries mentioned in the Bible' and 'Canaan as divided by Joshua...' appeared in *The Pictorial Bible...*, new edition, 1855.

Johnstone, James (fl. 1829–80) Architectural and figure engraver, working in Edinburgh. 'East side of St. Andrew's Square' was engraved for Shepherd's *Modern Athens* 1829–31. 'The Valentine' after W. Bonner was issued in the 1874 edition of *Casquet of literature*, and in the volumes issued about 1880 of the same work, 'Melrose Abbey (restored)' and 'The Calton Hill, Edinburgh' after G. M. Kemp, architect, 'Bothwell Castle, River Clyde' after Kidd and 'Rotterdam. Church of St. Lawrence' after D. Roberts appeared, the latter being signed 'J. and J. Johnstone, Edinburgh'.

Johnstone, John (fl. 1835) Portrait engraver. 'Sir John Leslie...' (a stipple portrait) appeared in Chambers's *Biographical dictionary of eminent Scotsmen* 1835, signed 'Jno. Johnstone'. He is probably the other half of the J. and J. Johnstone mentioned above.

Jones, E. (fl. 1835) Architectural engraver. 'Stairs and passage from St. Stephen's Chapel to cloister' after R. W. Billings, dated 1 August 1835, was published in Brayley and Britton's *History of the ancient palace ... at Westminster* 1836.

Jones, J. (fl. 1835) Architectural engraver. 'St. Lawrence Church' after H. Winkles was published in *Barber's picturesque illustrations of the Isle of Wight* [c. 1835].

Jones, T. (fl. 1832–46) Landscape engraver after W. Tombleson. 'Ruins of Ehrenfels' was issued in Fearnside's *Tombleson's views of the Rhine* 1832 and 'Baths Langen—Schwalbach' in Fearnside's *Picturesque beauties of the Rhine* [c. 1846].

Jordan, E. (fl. 1833) Figure engraver. One plate after W. Hogarth appeared in Hogarth's *Works* 1833.

Jorden, Henry (fl. 1829–53) Landscape and architectural engraver. His earliest steel engraved work was 'St. Katherine's docks from the basin' after T. H. Shepherd for Shepherd's *London and its environs* 1829–31. Three plates for G. and C. Pyne of Liverpool scenes, including 'Lyceum newsroom and Library, Bold Street', were engraved for W. H. Pyne's *Lancashire illustrated...* 1831 and four pictures after the author for Gastineau's *Wales illustrated...* 1830. 'Colonnade of St. Peter's, Rome', dated 28 October 1830, after S. Prout was published in T. Roscoe's *Tourist in Italy* 1831, and was signed 'H. Jordan'. For L. Ritchie's *Travelling sketches in the north of Italy* 1832 he engraved 'Constance' after C. Stanfield and for J. Carne's *Syria* 1836–8 he did 'Damascus from above Salahych' and 'Mount Casius, from the sea' after W. H. Bartlett, and after the same artist he did 'The Ponte Alto (Simplon)', 'The Pays de Vaud from above Lausanne' and the 'Castle of Lausanne' for W. Beattie's *Switzerland* 1836. This last plate was issued again later in D. Costello's

Piedmont and Italy [c. 1855]. 'The head of Loch Lomond, looking south' after T. Allom, dated 1836, was engraved for Beattie's *Scotland illustrated* 1838, 'Crossing the River Tonse by a Jhoola' after Purser was engraved for White's *Views in India...* 1838 and 'Canton' after Melville was published in Wright's *Gallery of engravings* 1844–6. About 1836 he emigrated to the United States and worked for the American engraver Alfred Jones (1819–1900), eventually setting up as a member of the engraving firm of Jorden and Halpin. Whether he was related to a Professor Jorden (1800–83), President of the Academy of Arts at St Petersburg, who worked as an engraver in London and achieved a reputation by his plate of Raphael's 'Transfiguration', is an open question.   St; T.

Joubert de la Ferté, Jean Ferdinand (1810–83) Portrait, figure and landscape engraver. Born in Paris on 15 September 1810 into a family ruined by the Revolution, he entered the École des beaux-arts there on 31 March 1829 to study under the engraver Henriquel Dupont. He very soon began to engrave for book illustration and did the portraits for Thiers's *History of the Revolution*. He exhibited in the Paris Salon of 1840, and soon afterwards came to England, where he married an English lady, and was naturalised. Among his earliest engravings to be published in England was 'Penseroso', after Winterhalter, issued by Gambart in 1845, and in the *Art Union* 1848 the first of ten plates published in the *Art Journal* appeared, 'Salvator' after D. Maclise. This was followed by 'Age of innocence' after Reynolds (1850), 'Queen Henrietta Maria' after Van Dyck (1857), two oval pictures—'Simplicity' after J. B. Greuze (1860) and 'Cupid and Psyche' after W. Etty (1863)—, 'Gipsy Queen' after P. F. Poole (1865), 'Infant Jesus and St. John the Baptist' after Rubens (1875) and 'Messenger of good tidings' after F. W. W. Topham (1884). Soon after his arrival in England the demand for stamp engravers caught his attention, and he engraved the dies of many postage and other stamps for a number of nations. He was associated as chief engraver with the printers De la Rue until 1865, and before 1854 he had engraved the heads for English fiscal stamps, and in 1855 the head for the first Indian issue. In order to circumvent the patent held by Jacob Perkins on the siderographic process, he introduced 'en épargné', a French method of producing a relief, instead of an intaglio steel block, which gave a very similar appearance to an engraved print. In the 1850s he collaborated with Henri Garnier in Paris on the process of 'acierage' or 'steel-facing', which he brought to England, patented in March 1858 and developed here (see B. Hunnisett, *Steel-engraved book illustration in England* 1980, chapter 10). He exhibited at the Royal Academy between 1855 and 1881, and continued to exhibit also in Paris, where he obtained third class medals in 1859 and 1863. Some of his best engravings were done after E. J. Poynter, such as 'Feeding the sacred ibis...' and 'Faithful unto death', done, respectively, for the *Art Journal* for 1874 and (published posthumously) 1886, 'Atalanta's race', a plate which took him four years to engrave, published by the Fine Art Society in 1881, and ten book illustrations for J. Keats's *Endymion*, published by Moxon in 1872. Two further steel engravings—'In the Borghese Gardens' after G. G. Kilburne and 'Town Hall, Halberstadt' after C. Werner—were done for *Picturesque Europe* 1876–9. Other plates of this period were a portrait of Mrs Theodore Martin after Lehmann, published by Holloway in 1875, and 'Nina' after J. B. Greuze, published by Mrs Noseda in 1877. He spent much time and money in working out a process of permanent photographic printing, and also did some work in mezzotint. He died at Mentone on 17 November 1883. AJ; B; H; S; SocA; T.

56

K

Kearnon, T. (fl. 1834) Architectural engraver. Four plates after B. Ferrey were contributed to E. W. Brayley's *Antiquities of the Priory of Christ-church*... 1834. One is signed T. Kearman'. Two outline engravings—'View of the front facing Trumpington St. of the Fitzwilliam Museum...' after Basevi and 'New Houses of Parliament' after Barry (both dated 21 May 1836)—done for subscribers to the *Athenaeum* were each signed 'Kearnan'. B; Ho; T.

Kelley, T. J. (fl. 1840–64) Portrait and architectural engraver. 'Burns's Cottage' after D. O. Hill and 'John Syme', a vignette (signed 'J. T. Kelley'), appeared in Wilson and Chambers's *Land of Burns* 1840. Five engravings (with ornamental borders by Luke Limner) were done for *The Self-interpreting Bible* 1864.

Kelsall, W. H. (fl. 1830–38) Landscape and architectural engraver. 'The interior of St. John's Market, Liverpool' was done for Pyne's *Lancashire illustrated*... 1831, and was used again in Baines's *History of ... Lancaster* 1836. 'Marsden Rocks, coast of Durham' and 'Tyne from South Shields, Durham' were engraved for Rose's *Durham and Northumberland* 1832 and two views from Langdale Pikes, one looking south-east and the other towards Bowfell, for the same author's *Westmorland* 1832. All five were after designs by Allom. 'Pompeii. Cell of the Temple of Augustus' after the author was engraved for Gell's *Pompeiana*... 1832 and 'Skeleton group in the Rameswur, Caves of Ellora' after G. Cattermole for Elliot's *Views in India*... 1835. 'The Great Khan at Damascus' (1836) and 'General view of Balbec and Anti-Libanus' (1837) were engraved after Bartlett for Carne's *Syria* 1836–8.

Kennion, Edward (fl. 1830–4) Landscape and architectural engraver. He was probably one of the sons of Edward Kennion (1744–1809), engraver and painter. For H. Gastineau's *Wales illustrated*... 1830, he engraved 'Solva, Pembrokeshire' and 'Dinas Pembrokeshire', both after the author's designs, and he did a plate after B. Ferrey for E. W. Brayley's *Antiquities of the Priory of Christ-church*... 1834. B; Br; DNB.

Kernot, James Harfield (fl. 1828–58) Landscape engraver. 'Ventimiglia' (July 1828) after W. Brockedon was engraved for the artist's *Illustrations of the passes of the Alps* 1828–9 and 'Castle of Angero' (28 October 1829) after S. Prout (mainly etched) for T. Roscoe's *Tourist in Switzerland and Italy* 1830. 'Dogana ... Venice' after Prout appeared in Roscoe's *Tourist in Italy* 1831. 'Pompeii. Street of the Mercuries' after the author's design was done for Gell's *Pompeiana*... 1832 and 'View in Ghent' after S. Prout for the *Continental annual* 1832. 'Ventimiglia, coast of Genoa' (28 October 1832) after J. D. Harding appeared in Roscoe's *Tourist in Italy* 1833, 'Brussels' after C. Stanfield in L. Ritchie's *Travelling sketches on the Rhine* 1833 and 'The town of Pont du Chateau' and 'Pont Benéze and Villeneuve from Avignon' (both dated 28 October 1833) in Roscoe's *Tourist in France* 1834. 'Entrance to the Cave of Elephanta' after Purser and 'Jumma Musjid—Manloo' after Austin were engraved for Elliot's *Views in India*... 1835, two plates after Melville for Bunyan's *Pilgrim's progress* 1836 and three after Melville and one after Turner for Wright's *Landscape-historical views of Scotland* 1836–8. For Baines's *History of ... Lancaster* 1836, he engraved 'Smithills-Hall' (1831) after Copley Fielding, 'Silverston and Cartmel sands' (1833) after T. Allom and 'Bigland Hall, Lancashire'

(1835), 'Walton-le-dale, Lancs.' (1834), 'Houghton Tower' (1832) and 'Sankey viaduct...' (1831) after G. Pickering. The last two were used again in G. N. Wright's *Lancashire* 1842. 'A brisk gale' after W. Vandervelde (dated 1 January 1833), 'The watermill' after J. Ruysdael and 'The glade cottage' (dated 1 October 1833) after J. Crome appeared in A. Cunningham's *Cabinet gallery of pictures by the first masters*... 1836. 'Christian's monument...' and 'Graham's valley' (both dated 1834) were engraved for Sir John Ross's *Narrative of a second voyage*... 1835, 'Palace of the Genéralife from the Alhambra' after D. Roberts, for Roscoe's *Tourist in Spain. Granada* 1835 and 'The shipwrecked' after S. Prout (signed 'E. Kernot') for S. C. Hall's *Book of gems* 1838. For W. Beattie's *Switzerland* 1836 he engraved a plate after W. H. Bartlett entitled 'Hospice, Grand St. Bernard (Vallois)', and two plates after the same artist appeared in J. Carne's *Syria* 1836–8, namely, 'Pass in a cedar forest about Barouk' and 'Ruins of Soli, or Pompeiopolis—Asia Minor'. He did 'The sound of Kerrera' after T. Allom for W. Beattie's *Scotland illustrated* 1838, 'View near the source of the Jumna' and 'Gungootree, the sacred source of the Ganges' after Allom for White's *Views in India*... 1838 and twenty-two plates, mainly after Allom, for Brayley's *Topographical history of Surrey* 1841–8. For S. C. and A. M. Hall's *Ireland* 1841–3, he engraved a vignette after T. Creswick—'The Abbey of the Holy Cross, Tipperary'—, for *The Imperial Family Bible*, first published in 1844, he engraved 'Damascus' after W. Telbin, for Henry's *Exposition of the Old and New Testaments*... 1844, he did the engraved title page to volume 2, depicting 'Aaron's tomb, Mount Hor' after L. de Laborde and for *Forget me not* 1846, he did 'The silent avowal' after A. Colin. In G. N. Wright's *Gallery of engravings* 1844–6, there was included 'The Church of Vasili Blagennoi, Moscow' after A. G. Vickers, and 'The well of St. Lawrence...' (a vignette) and 'Scratchell's Bay...', both after Walton, were engraved for Adams's *History ... of the Isle of Wight* 1858. He engraved 'Fisherman's return' after E. Le Poittevin for the *Art Union* 1848 and 'Waiting for the boats' after Sir Augustus Callcott for the *Art Journal* 1849. Other plates by him included 'Jacob and Laban' and 'Jacob's dream' after Murillo, and 'Bank of England ... 1799' after Marlow, published in February 1844 in aid of the Bank's Widows' Fund. He joined the Artists' Annuity Fund in 1830, and was a relation of William Kernot Shenton, son of H. C. Shenton (q.v.). B; T.

Kershaw & Son. (fl. 1845–60) A London firm of print publishers who produced a numbered series of steel engraved views, such as those of Brighton, which included 'Sussex County hospital...' (no. 662) and 'The Public Dispensary...' (no. 665), both done about 1850.

King, Thomas (1781–1845) Portrait, architectural and landscape engraver, and antiquary. Although not born in Sussex, he spent the latter part of his life in Chichester, where he lived in East Street, lodging with a Lydia Humphrey, some ten years his senior. Many of his engraved plates were of local interest, such as the six plates done for volume 2 of Tierney's *History of Arundel* 1834, which included two outline engravings—'Collegiate chapel in Arundel Church' and a vignette, 'Tomb of William Fitzalan'—, two plates of effigies and two vignette portraits, of Thomas Fitzalan and John Fitzalan, printed onto the text page. Similar plates of tombs and brasses, with a plan of Cissbury, appeared in Cartwright's *Parochial topography ... of Sussex* 1830. B; *Chichester papers* no. 29, 1961–2.

Knight, C. (fl. 1855) Sculpture engraver. 'Love reviving life' after a sculpture by Finelli was engraved for the *Art Journal* 1855.

Knight, J. (fl. 1844) Figure engraver. 'The rajah's daughter' after F. P. Stephanoff appeared in volume 1 of G. N. Wright's *Gallery of engravings* 1844–6.

Knight, T. W. (fl. 1846–75) Portrait, figure and sculpture engraver. 'The cottage maid' after E. M. Ward, dated February 1846, was engraved for *Beauties of Moore* 1846, and for *Wilkie gallery* [c. 1849], he did 'Scene at Toledo', reissued as 'The confessional' in the *Art Journal* 1866. 'Miss Buckley' after J. Hayter (signed 'T. Knight') was engraved for *The Court album* 1852, and a circular engraving, 'Prince Napoleon', appeared in D. Costello's *Piedmont and Italy* [c. 1855]. 'Warren Hastings' after Reynolds and 'The Right Honble. Lord Metcalfe' were done for Nolan's *Illustrated history of the British Empire in India* [1858–60] and 'The return of the ark', a circular engraving after Domenichino (with an ornamental border by Luke Limner), for *The Self-interpreting Bible* 1864. 'Rt. Rev. Benjamin Hoadley', 'Rev. Isaac Watts' and 'Rev. Thomas Warton, poet laureate', portraits after Sir Joshua Reynolds, appeared in B. Woodward's *General history of Hampshire* 1863, 'Carrying away into captivity' after G. Jager was issued in the *Imperial Family Bible*, first published in 1844, and 'Maj. Gen. Sir Thomas Munro' after Sir M. L. Shee, 'Sir Henry Raeburn...' (after a self-portrait) and 'James Stewart' were published in Chambers's *Biographical dictionary of eminent Scotsmen*, 2nd edition, 1875. He also contributed four sculpture plates to the *Art Journal* in 1850, 1856, and 1861, the first being 'Grief' by J. H. Foley (the 1856 plate was signed 'T. M. Knight'). B; T.

Krausse, Alfred (1829–94) Landscape and portrait engraver. Born on 12 February 1829 at Rössnitz, he was a pupil of Henry Winkles at Leipzig. He engraved two plates after Harry Fenn for *Picturesque Europe* 1876–9, namely, 'Ventimiglia on the Cornice Road' and 'Capri'. Three royal portraits after J. L. Williams appeared in Archer's *Pictures and royal portraits...* [c. 1878]. He also engraved portraits of eminent Germans. He died on 20 August 1894 at Leipzig. B; T.

L

Lacey, H. (fl. 1830–51) Landscape engraver. 'Caernarvon', 'Caernarvon Castle', 'Snowdon from Capel Curig' and 'Fall of the Ogwen, in Nant Frangon' after H. Gastineau were engraved for volume 1 of the latter's *Wales illustrated...* 1830. He also drew and engraved forty-nine border illustrations to maps done by John Rapkin for *Tallis's Illustrated plan of London* 1851, at a cost of 200 guineas.

Lacey, Samuel (fl. 1818–46) Landscape and architectural engraver. A prolific book plate engraver, of whose works over a hundred have been identified as being done on steel. Some of his early work was done for J. P. Neale's *Views of the seats of noblemen...* 1818–24, and he engraved nine views for T. H. Shepherd's *Modern Athens* 1829–31. Six views after Shepherd were published in J. Elmes's *Metropolitan improvements* 1829 dated between 31 January and 15 November 1828 (one of which, 'NE side of Belgrave Square, Pimlico', was signed 'S. Lacy'), and eight views, also after Shepherd, were done for the latter's *London and its environs* 1829–31, dated between 14 November 1829 and 1831, and included 'Cornhill and Lombard St,...' and 'St. Sepulchre's, Skinner St.'. Twenty-

eight scenes were done for Gastineau's *Wales illustrated...* 1830 after the author's designs, and between 1829 and 1835 he was engaged on thirteen plates of scenes in Kent after T. M. Baynes, H. Gastineau and G. Shepherd for S. W. H. Ireland's *England's topographer* (commenced publication 1828), including 'Christ's Church Gate, Canterbury', 'Hever Castle, Kent' and 'Knowle Park ... Kent'. Nineteen plates after Allom were engraved for the three volumes by T. Rose published in 1832: five appeared in *Cumberland*, eleven in *Durham and Northumberland*, including 'High Force of the Tees...' and 'Bamborough Castle...' and four in *Westmorland*, including 'Brougham Castle...'. He did comparatively little work for the annuals, some of the few exceptions being 'Bruges' after C. Stanfield for L. Ritchie's *Travelling sketches on the Rhine* 1833 and the engraved title page of a head on a medal by W. Wyon for *The Keepsake* 1833. 'Seat of Duke of Buckingham, Richmond' and 'Chelsea Hospital, Middlesex' were engraved after Tombleson for Fearnside's *Tombleson's Thames* 1834, six plates after Bartlett and Baynes for Wright's *Picturesque beauties of Great Britain...*: *Essex* 1831–4, 'Pulo Penang' after Austin and 'Ruins—Old Delhi' after Prout for Elliot's *Views in India...* 1835, 'Clithero, Lancashire...' after Pickering for Baines's *History of ... Lancaster* 1836 (used again in Wright's *Lancashire* 1842), 'Glacier of Bossons (Vale of Chamouni)' after Bartlett for Beattie's *Switzerland* 1836 and eight plates, mainly after Allom, for *Views in the Tyrol* [1836]. Two views of Antioch after Bartlett were used in Carne's *Syria* 1836–8, 'The Almeidan or Hippodrome...' and 'Gurzel-Lissar...' after Allom in Walsh's *Constantinople* 1838–40, 'The Valley of Maglan from Comblou', 'Migève—Savoy' and 'Bonneval, Valley of the Arc', all after Brockedon, and 'The approach to Briançon from Mont Genèvre' after Bartlett in Beattie's *Waldenses* 1838 and 'Snowy range from Landour' after Melville in White's *Views in India...* 1838. 'State Street Boston' (one of his best plates), 'The Park and City Hall, New York' and 'Saw-mill at Centre Harbour', all after Bartlett, were engraved for Willis's *American scenery* 1840. 'Montmorency Waterfall and cone, near Quebec' after W. Purser and Col. Cockburn and 'Stolzenfels, an ancient robber fortress on the Rhine' after Bartlett appeared in G. N. Wright's *Gallery of engravings* 1844–6, and more plates after Tombleson appeared in Fearnside's *Picturesque beauties of the Rhine* [c. 1846], two in Fearnside's *Tombleson's Upper Rhine* [c. 1835], including 'Isle of Meinau, Lake Constance'. He joined the Artists' Annuity Fund in 1823. P.

Lacey, W. (fl. 1834–46) Landscape engraver, after W. Tombleson. 'Oxford', 'Old Windsor Locks' and 'Sunbury Locks' (all with unusual outline frames) appeared in Fearnside's *Tombleson's Thames* 1834. 'Convent of Laach', 'Baden-Baden', 'Rheineck, Ctn. St. Gallen', 'Source of the back Rhine from the Rheinfeld glacier' (these last two signed 'W. Lacy') and 'Frankfort A/M.' were published in Fearnside's *Picturesque beauties of the Rhine* [c. 1846], and from Fearnside's *Tombleson's Upper Rhine* [c. 1835] came 'Heidelberg', 'Ruins of Badenweiler' and 'The middle Rhine in the Valley of Curlim'.

Lambert, J. F. (fl. 1829–32) Landscape and architectural engraver. 'Interior of Croydon Palace, Surrey' and 'Land gate, Rye, Sussex' after N. Whittock were published in T. Allen's *History ... of Surrey and Sussex* 1829–31. Three plates and a title page vignette after Whittock were engraved for Allen's *New... history of the county of York* 1828–31. 'Sandgate ... with the new chapel...' after G. Shepherd appeared in S. W. H. Ireland's *England's topographer* (commenced publication 1828), and for J. Britton and E. W.

Brayley's *Devonshire and Cornwall illustrated* 1832, he engraved 'The subscription rooms and New London Inn, Exeter' and 'The baths, Southernhay, Exeter' after W. H. Bartlett.

Landseer, Thomas, A.R.A (c. 1795–1880) Landscape and figure engraver, although he was recognised as being good at all types of engraving. Eldest son and pupil of John Landseer, he was sent, with his brother Charles, to learn drawing from Benjamin Haydon. The majority of his important work (over

Thomas Landseer

125 plates) was done after pictures by his brother Edwin: it has been said that one depended upon the other for their popularity. His first plate, 'A Bull' (1811), was an etching after Edwin. In 1813 'Master T. Landseer' was awarded the Lesser Silver medal by the Society of Arts for an etching of animals and in the following year he gained the Silver Isis medal for an oil painting of a farmer's horse. Most of his work was done for the print publishers, and the first to achieve any notice was 'Dignity and impudence' (1841). His finest plate was said to be 'The Stag at bay' (1848). He seems to have done very few book plates on steel, one example being 'The falconer' after Edwin, engraved for *The Amulet* 1828, and for the *Art Journal* 1859, he did 'The marmozettes', also after Edwin. He was seventy-three when the Royal Academy elected him as an Associate in 1868. He died at 11 Grove Road, St John's Wood on 20 January 1880. Posthumous exhibitions of his work in Pall Mall showed the progress of English engraving over the previous sixty years from line to mixed style, and the resurgence of the mezzotint.   AJ; B; Br; SocA.

Law, G. (fl. 1830–1) Landscape engraver. 'The Coppice...' after Calvert was engraved for West's *Picturesque views ... in Staffordshire and Shropshire...* 1830–1.

Lawrie, Charles (fl. 1878) Historical engraver. Four plates of relics associated with famous people after J. L. Williams, 'Arrest of Alice Lisle' after E. M. Ward and 'The Battle of the Nile' after Arnald were published in Archer's *Pictures and royal portraits...* [c. 1878].

Layton, Charles and Edwin, of Fleet Street (fl. 1854) Engravers of landscapes. One of the firms engaged in the production of steel plates for minor publications. Three plates were done for F. Lankester's *Nineteen views of Bury St. Edmunds* 1854. Ho.

Lefrancq, F. (fl. 1878) Historical engraver. 'Sunday in the

backwoods of Canada' after T. Faed was published in Archer's *Pictures and royal portraits...* [c. 1878].

Le Conté, John (fl. 1870) Figure engraver. He engraved the title page vignette 'The expulsion' after David Scott, 'Jacob discovered by the bloody coat' after Guercino and 'The death of John the Baptist' after Rubens for an edition of John Brown's *Self-interpreting Bible...* published by William Mackenzie [c. 1870].

Le Keux, Henry (1787–1868) Landscape, architectural and figure engraver. He was born on 13 June 1787, the younger brother of John (q.v.), and baptised at St Dunstan's, Stepney. He was a pupil of James Basire in Quality Court, Chancery Lane, and at the end of his apprenticeship about 1808 he went to work on plates for some of John Britton's publications such as *The Beauties of England and Wales* and *Cathedrals*, as well as for J. P. Neale's *History and Antiquities of the Abbey Church of ... Westminster* 1818–23. Thirteen plates of monuments and effigies were engraved for Blore's *Monumental remains...* 1826. Among the earliest of his few steel book plates was a vignette of some buildings at night, probably in Florence after Turner in S. Rogers' *Italy* 1830, and for the same author's *Poems* 1834, he engraved 'St. Herbert's chapel' after Turner and 'A gateway' after T. Stothard, both being vignettes. Some similar plates appeared in *Forget me not* and other annuals, including 'The repentance of Ninevah' after Martin for *The Keepsake* 1832. 'Lake Coriskin' and 'Abbotsford' after Turner were done for Scott's *Poetical works* 1834, and seven plates were also done for Scott's *Provincial antiquities and picturesque scenery of Scotland* 1826. For the Associated Engravers he produced several plates, including 'The embarkation of St. Ursula' after Claude. He engraved plates for the *Oxford Almanack* from 1832 to 1839 inclusive, including 'Carfax Conduit in Newnham Park' after P. de Wint (1833) and 'Interior of Radclyffe Library' after F. Mackenzie (1836). In 1838 he was consulted by the Bank of England, together with Henry Corbould and William Wyon, on the production of a new design for bank notes, and the following year, 1839, at the age of fifty-two, he retired from engraving. He moved to Bocking in Essex and worked for Samuel Courtauld & Co., crape manufacturers, until a short time before his death, which occurred after a short illness on 11 October 1868 at the age of eighty-one. He was buried at Halstead, Essex. He had no pupils or assistants, and therefore engraved the whole of his plates himself. He joined the Artists' Annuity Fund in 1812.   AJ; Br; DNB; Ho; Ma; P.

Le Keux, John (1783–1846) Architectural engraver. He was born on 4 June 1783, at Sun Street, Bishopsgate, the eldest son of Peter Le Keux and Anne Dyer. He was baptised at St Botolph's, Bishopsgate, in September 1783. His father, to whom John was apprenticed, was descended from a Huguenot family, and was a wholesale pewter manufacturer. After engraving on pewter, John turned to copper in 1800, by reason of which he spent the remainder of his apprenticeship with James Basire. With Basire he became expert at architectural engraving, and did much of his best work for John Britton's publications, contributing thus to the Gothic revival in architecture. He married Sarah Sophia, daughter of John Lingard, on 27 September 1809 at St Mary's, Lambeth, and in 1812 was born his son John Henry (q.v.). His plates are also to be found in works by E. Blore, J. P. Neale and A. Pugin, and his steel plates are exemplified by 'Dryburgh Abbey' after D. Roberts for W. Scott's *Waverley novels*, 'St. Stephen's Chapel, looking east, Westminster' after R. W. Billings, dated 1 May 1835, for E. W. Brayley and J. Britton's *History of the ancient palace ... at Westminster* 1836, and for

The Keepsake 'Sala di Gran Senata' (1846) and 'Titian's studio, Venice' (1847) after Lake Price (these two were among his last plates). His longest series of book plates was the forty-two he engraved for J. Britton's *Dictionary of the architecture and archaeology of the Middle Ages* 1836–9. He joined the Artists' Annuity Fund in 1820, and was one of the signatories to the 1837 petition. He died on 2 April 1846, and was buried in Bunhill Fields cemetery.   AU; Br; DNB; R.

Le Keux, John Henry (1812–96) Architectural engraver. He was born on 23 March 1812, the son of John Le Keux (q.v.) and Sarah Sophia Lingard, at Argyll Street, Euston Road. He commenced engraving studies under James Basire, later becoming an assistant to his father. His earliest independent plate was 'City and bridge of Prague' after S. Prout, done for the *Continental annual* 1832, and in J. Carne's *Syria* 1836–8, he did the first of many engravings after W. H. Bartlett, i.e., 'Landing place in a small harbour at Rhodes' and 'Wall on the west side of the Antioch', both dated 1837, and 'Castle in Mount Amenus...' dated 1838. For R. Walsh's *Constantinople* 1838–40, he produced 'The mosque of Santa Sophia' after T. Allom (Plate 36), for J. Pardoe's *Beauties of the Bosphorus* 1840, he engraved 'The Mihrab of the mosque of Suleimanie' after Bartlett, and for Weale's *Studies and examples of English architecture* 1839, he also produced plates. His best-known series of plates were of scenes from Oxford and Cambridge, published by Charles Tilt. *Memorials of Oxford*, containing ninety-eight plates after F. Mackenzie, came out in three volumes in 1837, with a text by James Ingram. *Memorials of Cambridge*, published in two volumes in 1841, contained seventy-four plates after Mackenzie and J. A. Bell, with a text by Thomas Wright and H. L. Jones. The latter work was published in a new edition in 1860, and in 1981 Granta editions Ltd. reprinted the pictures in aid of a cancer appeal. Cambridge University Press reprinted this small volume in 1985. 'Temple Church' after Stanfield was done for Scott's *Waverley novels* and 'Cardiff', dated 1841, for Beattie's *Ports, harbours...* 1842. 'Interior of the cathedral Montreal' after Bartlett appeared in Willis's *Canadian scenery* 1842. 'Interior of the cathedral at Ulm' and 'St. Stephen's church, (Vienna)' after Bartlett were done for Beattie's *Danube* 1844 and 'The Waterloo Gallery' after Allom for Ritchie's *Windsor Castle* 1848. His association with Ruskin, some of the correspondence for which is in the National Art Library, resulted in a number of plates, among which were six for *The Stones of Venice* 1851–3, and sixteen for *Modern painters* 1856–60, most of them after the author's designs, such as 'Strength of old pine' and 'First mountain natural-ism', but with some after Turner, such as 'Nets in the rapid'. He did some plates for C. H. Hartshorne's *Illustrations of Alnwick, Prudhon and Warkworth* 1857 and Parker's *Medieval archaeology of Chester* 1858, and in B. Woodward's *General history of Hampshire* 1863 there appeared 'Interior of Winchester Cathedral. Beaufort's tomb' after W. H. Bartlett. 'Baalbeck (Baal-gad)' and 'Petra, (Selah) Edom' after Laborde and a family register designed by A. H. Warren were engraved for *The Self-interpreting Bible* 1864. He engraved plates for the *Oxford Almanack* after his own designs from 1855 to 1870, such as 'Oxford from the top of Bodley's library' (1866), but by 1864 he had moved to Durham to become manager to Messrs. Andrews, a firm of publishers with whom his wife had connections. The Norwegian Government commissioned a series of thirty-one plates representing views of Trondhjem cathedral, and from 1853 to 1865 he exhibited architectural drawings at the Royal Academy. Between 1850 and 1878 he designed four bookplates. He was also the inventor of a 'patent process', registered on 23 June 1841, for an improvement in line engraving, wherein two steel or copper plates were employed, one carrying the subject, the other a 'ground'. Colour could be used and more than two plates employed. (*Printing patents...* supplement, p. 322.) The process was used for three engravings that appeared in the quarto editions only of John Britton's *Autobiography* 1850 – two views of Kingston Church, Wiltshire, and a view at Charnbury. It was expensive, and therefore little used. He joined the Artists' Annuity Fund in 1838. He died at Durham on 4 February 1896, aged nearly eighty-four, and was buried in St Nicholas's Church there.   B; DNB; Fi; T.

Lemon, Henry (fl. 1847–80) Figure engraver. He worked mainly for the print publishers, but occasionally one of his prints was issued in a book. One such was 'Columbus at the convent of La Rabida' in *Wilkie gallery* [c. 1849]. Four historical plates appeared in Gaspey's edition of Hume and Smollett's *History of England...* [c. 1847] and 'Christ healing the sick in the Temple' after West in Fleetwood's *Life of Our Lord...* [c. 1855], the latter being reprinted, together with 'Revelations' after Howard, in *The New Testament* [c. 1860].

He also engraved for the *Art Journal* 'Empty chair: Abbotsford' after Sir William Allan (1855), 'Pet of the common' after J. C. Horsley (1863), 'Broken window' after W. H. Knight (1865) and 'Left in charge' after W. Hemsley (1870). One of his early prints, 'The reverie' after Absolon, was 'excellently engraved', according to the 1847 reviewer. He engraved 'Pity' afer H. Lejeune for the Art Union of London (1867), and after the same artist, 'Red riding hood' (1872). He held some strong views on Sunday working, since for that reason he refused to see the Count D'Orsay with regard to the touching up of his portrait of Queen Victoria on horseback. (W. P. Frith, *My autobiography*, 3rd edition, 1887, vol. 2, p. 340–3.) He exhibited at the Royal Academy between 1855 and 1866.   B; S; T.

Le Petit, A. (fl. 1832–43) Landscape engraver. There is a French engraver of this name who is known to have exhibited in the Paris Salon in 1837 and 1841, but no record exists of his having worked in England. The name is affixed to plates after T. Allom and G. Pickering which appeared in T. Rose's *Cumberland* and *Westmorland* 1832. These volumes also contained numerous plates engraved by William A. Le Petit (q.v.) and Thieme and Becker incline to the view that they are the same person, but there is insufficient evidence to support the idea. The engravings for *Cumberland* after Allom are 'Borrowdale, Cumberland', 'Sty Head Tarn...', 'Eskdale Mill, Wilton Beck...' and 'Carlisle castle...' (issued again in G. N. Wright's *Gallery of engravings* 1844–6), with 'Derwent and Bassenthwaite Lakes...' after Pickering. All the plates in *Westmorland* are after Pickering, viz., 'Rydal Hall from Fox How, Westmorland', 'Grassmere from Loughrigg Fell' and 'Windermere, Esthwaite and Coniston Lakes...'. He is probably the engraver of 'Goien' and 'Fragsburg' after Allom, which appeared in *Views in the Tyrol* [1836]; both are signed 'Le Petit'. 'Fortress of Bowrie in Rajpootana' after Westall appeared in Fisher's *Drawing room scrap book* 1836 and again in Roberts's *Hindostan...* 1847. 'The Delectable mountains' after Melville was done for Bunyan's *Pilgrim's progress* 1836. 'The Gardener' and 'Rocky landscape with figures' after Teniers were engraved for *The Royal Gallery of pictures...* 1839. 'Cotton plantations at Ning-po' and 'Amoy, from the outer anchorage' after Allom appeared in G. N. Wright's *China* 1843. He also engraved 'Newby Abbey, Dumfrieshire' and 'Kelso Abbey, Roxburghshire' (1 May 1834) after D. Roberts and 'Lauffenburg on the Rhine' after G. Balmer. B; T.

Le Petit, William A. (fl. 1829–46) Landscape engraver. Two views of Crickhowel, Brecknockshire, were engraved after the author's designs for Gastineau's *Wales illustrated...* 1830, and 'Childwall Abbey...' and 'Wavertree Hall...' after Austin were done for Pyne's *Lancashire illustrated...* 1831, together with two other plates after Harwood merely signed 'Le Petit'. At least ninety plates are known after T. Allom, thirty-nine of them (eight signed simply 'Le Petit') being engraved for J. Britton and E. W. Brayley's *Devonshire and Cornwall illustrated* 1832. Of the remaining three of the forty-two plates, two were after Bartlett. Examples of the engravings are 'Warlegh House, Devonshire', 'Plymouth Public Library' and 'East and West Looe, Cornwall'. Ten plates were engraved for T. Rose's *Cumberland* 1832 and included 'Keswick from Greta Bridge' after H. Gastineau, 'Wood Hall near Cockermouth' after T. Allom and 'Thirlmere, or Wythburn Water, Cumberland' after G. Pickering. For the same author's *Durham and Northumberland* seventeen plates were done after Allom, including 'Alnwick Castle, Northumberland', 'Hartlepool, Durham' and 'Cauldron Snout, Teesdale, Durham'. This last plate was reprinted, with two others engraved by Le Petit from *Devonshire and Cornwall illustrated*, in Fisher's *Drawing room scrap book* 1835. For Rose's *Westmorland* he did a further thirteen plates, which included 'Stock-Gill Force, Westmorland' after Allom, 'Lower fall at Rydal...' after G. Pickering and 'Lowther Castle and Park, Westmorland' after Allom, this last being used with two plates from different volumes in G. N. Wright's *Gallery of engravings* 1844–6. Thirteen engravings were done between 1831 and 1835 for E. Baines's *History of ... Lancaster* 1836 after Allom, Henderson, Pickering and Purser, of which 'Scaitcliffe', 'Preston', 'Vale of Lonsdale' and 'Rufford Hall' (very delicately engraved) were used again in G. N. Wright's *Lancashire* 1842. For Fearnside's *Tombleson's Thames* 1834, he engraved 'View from Maidenhead Bridge' and 'View from London Bridge' after W. Tombleson, and he was probably the engraver of 'Cloister near Isteiu' for Fearnside's *Picturesque beauties of the Rhine* [c. 1846] and 'Monument of Genl. Desaix' for Fearnside's *Tombleson's Upper Rhine* [c. 1835], both after Tombleson and signed 'Le Petit'. 'Tomb of Shere Shah' after Prout, 'The pass of Makundra' after Purser, 'Mah Chung-keow–Canton' after Boys and 'Perawa–Malwa' after Cotman were engraved for Elliot's *Views in India...* 1835. 'Scene on the Tessin...', dated 1 July 1834, and 'Freyburgh...', dated 1835, both after W. H. Bartlett, were published in W. Beattie's *Switzerland* 1836, and six plates after Allom (two signed 'Le Petit') were published in G. N. Wright's *China* 1843, including 'Coal mines at Ying-Tih' and 'Ancient tombs near Amoy', the latter sketched on the spot by Capt. Stoddart, R.N.

Leppard, W. (fl. 1837–45) Architectural engraver. 'Steine & Palace Brighton' appeared in *London and Brighton railroad* [c. 1842], and 'Overton, perfumer &c...' in Leppard's *Brighton and Hove directory* 1843. Other local views were published between 1837 and 1845.

Levy, G. (fl. 1855–78) Portrait and figure engraver. 'Prince Albert' after Williams was published in Archer's *Pictures and royal portraits...* [c. 1878]. For the *Art Journal* he engraved 'Silence' after Caracci (1855), ' "Noli me tangere" ' after Rembrandt (1857) and 'The bunch of grapes' after Metzu (1858).

Lewis, Charles George (1808–80) Landscape and figure engraver. He was born on 13 June 1808 at Enfield, the second son of Frederick Christian Lewis (q.v.), under whom he studied engraving. He worked mainly for the print publishers, making a name for engraving Edwin Landseer's pictures, e.g., 'To-ho' (an etching, 1830), 'Hafed' (1837), 'The falcons' (1843) and 'The otter hunt' (1847). 'View at Brighton' after Copley Fielding, published by Moon, Boys and Graves in July 1829, was engraved when he was twenty-one. He contributed twenty-four plates to the *Art Journal* between 1867 and 1882, eighteen of which were after Landseer, and from 1877, many of the plates were largely if not entirely etched in the Continental manner. He does not seem to have done many book illustrations and then not until the 1870s. He engraved designs after H. C. Selous for C. Kingsley's *Hereward the Wake*, published by the Art Union of London in 1870, and for *Picturesque Europe* 1876–9, he engraved 'Llyn Idwal' after E. M. Wimperis, after which he retired, in 1877. He joined the Artists' Annuity Fund in 1834. He died of apoplexy at Felpham, Bognor, Sussex, on 16 June 1880, aged seventy-two, and was buried in Felpham churchyard. AJ; B; Br; DNB; S.

Lewis, Frederick Christian (1779–1856) Landscape and portrait engraver of the old school who appeared to dislike steel and used it rarely. Born in London, he was apprenticed to J. C. Stadler, a German working in London, and was appointed engraver to Princess Charlotte, Leopold, King of the Belgians, George IV, William IV and Queen Victoria. He was also a painter, exhibiting regularly in London. He engraved chiefly after Sir Thomas Lawrence until the artist died in 1830, and drew, engraved and published three sets of views on Devonshire rivers beween 1821 and 1827, followed in 1843 by his *Scenery of the Devonshire rivers etched on 25 [copper] plates*, published by Longmans. His steel plate 'Giovanni and Garcia de Medici', an oval picture after Vasari, appeared in S. Rogers' *Italy* 1830, 'A portrait' after his own design was engraved for *Literary souvenir* 1834, and 'Spain' after W. Perring was published in Finden's *Tableaux* 1837. He joined the Artists' Annuity Fund 1825. He died of apoplexy at Enfield on 18 December 1856, aged seventy-seven. AJ; B; DNB; R; S; T.

Lewis, James (fl. 1813–37) Landscape and architectural engraver. He did some plates for J. P. Neale's *Views of the seats of noblemen...* 1818–24, 'Geneva', dated 28 October 1829, after S. Prout for T. Roscoe's *Tourist in Switzerland and Italy* 1830 and 'The Campanile, Venice', dated 28 October 1830, also after Prout, for Roscoe's *Tourist in Italy* 1831. 'Ghent' after C. Stanfield was engraved for L. Ritchie's *Travelling sketches on the Rhine* 1833 and 'Château of Dieppe' after Stanfield for Ritchie's *Travelling sketches on the sea coasts of France* 1834. 'Kelso Abbey (Roxburghshire)', dated 1837, after T. Allom appeared in W. Beattie's *Scotland illustrated* 1838, and 'The river Dora–Turin' after W. H. Bartlett was engraved for Beattie's *Waldenses* 1838. He joined the Artists' Annuity Fund in 1813. P.

Lewis, John (fl. 1828) Figure engraver. A design of a cherub inside a wreath was done, together with William Greatbach, after John Wood for the engraved title page of the *Literary souvenir* 1828.

Lightfoot, Peter (1805–85) Portrait, figure and historical engraver. 'Naiads' after Howard was engraved for the *Literary souvenir* 1833; for the 1834 volume, he did 'The contrast' after Wright and 'The fisher's wife' after Holmes; and for the 1835 volume, 'The key note' after Middleton and 'Fisher girl of Calais' after Rippingille. Six plates were engraved between 1 August 1833 and 1 July 1835 for E. Lodge's *Portraits...* 2nd edition 1835, including 'Edward Sackville...' and 'Francis Howard' after Van Dyke and 'William Pitt' after Hoppner. 'Rosolia' after Penley appeared in *Friendship's offering* 1837. Eight plates after Chisholm, Franklin, Hart and Melville were engraved for Wright's *Landscape-historical illustrations of Scotland* 1836–8. For R. Walsh's *Constantinople* 1838–40, he did 'The Aurut Bazaar...', 'The Barbyses, or Sweet waters of Europe' and 'Mosque of Shah-za-deh Djamese...', all after T. Allom, and after the same artist he engraved 'An itinerant doctor at Tien sing' for G. N. Wright's *China* 1843. Four plates, including 'The massacre of the innocents' after Rubens, appeared in Fisher's *Historic illustrations of the Bible* [1840–3], and 'The city of pestilence' after Mignard came out in Fisher's *Drawing room scrap book* 1842. For Maxwell's *Life of ... the Duke of Wellington* 1839–41, he engraved twelve plates, mainly portraits, notably, 'Arthur Wellesley' after Robert Home of Calcutta, 'Wellington' after Lawrence and 'Decisive charge at Waterloo' after A. Cooper. 'Death of the red deer', dated 28 November 1843, after Wilkie was engraved for Finden's *Royal Gallery of British Art* 1838–49, and 'Death of Chatham' after J. S. Copley, 'The flower maiden' after J. J. Jenkins (q.v.), 'There now, she hears it...' (a vignette) after T. Allom and 'The fair maid of Perth and Carthusian Monk' after A. Chisholm appeared in G. N. Wright's *Gallery of engravings* 1844–6. For T. Moore's *Poetical works* 1843, he engraved the frontispiece portrait 'Thomas Moore' after G. Richmond and a vignette on the engraved title page, 'Sloperton Cottage' after T. Creswick. 'The fête champêtre' after A. Watteau, 'The Spanish flower girl' after B. E. Murillo, 'The covenanter's marriage' after A. Johnston and 'The sisters' after C. Sohn were engraved for S. C. Hall's *Gems of European art* 1846, 'The gentle shepherd' for *Wilkie gallery* [c. 1849] and 'Field Marshal His Grace the Duke of Wellington' for Nolan's *Illustrated history of the British Empire in India* [1858–60]. 'The conversion of St. Paul...' after de Ferrara appeared in *The New Testament* [c. 1860]. From 1847 to 1880 he engraved a series of twenty-seven plates for the *Art Union* and the *Art Journal* after pictures by contemporary artists, which commenced with works by W. Hilton, i.e., 'Cupid armed' (1847), 'Cupid disarmed' (1848 and issued again in Mrs Hall's *Drawing room table book* 1849) and 'Stolen bow' (1852), followed by 'Disarming of Cupid' after W. E. Frost (1858 and used again in the *Works of Shakspere* [*sic*], *Imperial edition* 1872), 'Una' after W. E. Frost (1860), 'Les femmes savantes' after C. R. Leslie (1867), 'Mary Queen of Scots led to execution' after L. J. Pott (1875) and 'The professor's lecture' after Rossi (1880). In R. Southey's *Poetical works* 1880 was published the frontispiece portrait 'Robert Southey' by A. Lane after Lawrence, and the etched picture 'Mr. Southey's residence at Keswick' after Caroline Southey was done for the engraved title page. He engraved some plates for the Art Union of London: the first was 'Jephthah's daughter' after H. O'Neil, of which it was said that it was an improvement on the picture, and would add to the engraver's reputation. He had, moreover, delivered it on time, and the total cost of production was £2,530 8s. 0d. (*Art Union* 1846, pp. 142, 166). 'Sabrina' after W. E. Frost was completed for them in 1848. He was a signatory of the 1837 petition, and had T. Vernon (q.v.) as a pupil. He died at Blurton, Staffordshire, on 5 September 1885. AJ; B; M; P; S; T; YA 1886.

Linley, A. (fl. 1853) Landscape engraver. 'Brides of Venice' after W. Etty was issued in the *Art Journal* 1853.

Lizars, William Home (1788–1859) Portrait, figure and bank note engraver. He was born in Edinburgh, the son of Daniel Lizars, a well-known copperplate engraver and printer. He studied at the Trustees' Academy, where he met David Wilkie, and made good progress in his painting career. When his father died in 1812, he took over the engraving and printing business in order to support himself and his family. He did a number of book illustrations in the 1820s, notably, those for Audubon's *Birds of America* 1827–30. Two plates were engraved for Shepherd's *Modern Athens* 1829–31. In 1833 he did the engraved title pages and outline etchings for the hand-coloured illustrations to his brother-in-law's five volume *Naturalist's Library* 1833–7. Jane Home Lizars, William's sister, had married Sir William Jardine, 7th baronet, and up to 1845, fourteen volumes by him had appeared in the series. Eleven plates were engraved for Keith's *Evidence of the truth of the Christian religion*, 36th edition, 1848 and eight vignettes, mainly after W. Banks, and a map for Rutherfurd's *Border handbook* 1849. 'Tasso and Leonora' after Ducis appeared in *Casquet of literature* 1874. In 1826 he was elected Associate Engraver, thus becoming a founder member of the Royal Scottish Academy, and in 1834 was elected an Honorary member. He died on 30 March 1859, leaving a widow and family. AJ; B; Br; DNB; M; R; S.

Lizars, W. M. (fl. 1860–82) Portrait, figure and historical engraver. He was probably a son of William Home Lizars (q.v.). Some authorities have erroneously ascribed plates signed 'W. M. Lizars' to W. H. Lizars. It is probable that W. M. Lizars inherited his father's business in 1859. 'Saltaire' after H. Warren was published in Baines's *Yorkshire past and present* 1871–7, and 'The defence of Saragossa' after Wilkie, 'Waterloo...' after Clennel and three plates after J. L. Williams were done for Archer's *Pictures and royal portraits...* [c. 1878]. For the *Art Journal* he engraved 'The Ommeganck at Antwerp' after Wappers (1860), 'Puck and the fairies' after Dadd (1864 and used again in the *Works of Shakspere* [*sic*], *Imperial edition* 1872) (Plate 53), 'The scribes reading the chronicle to Ahasuerus' after O'Neil (1867) and 'Bohemian gipsies' after Portaels (1882).

Lloyd, B. F., & Co. (fl. 1846) Two plates are known in J. W. Ord's *History ... of Cleveland...* 1846. Ho.

Lonsdale, (fl. 1850) Architectural engraver. 'Brougham Castle, Penrith, Westmorland' after Lonsdale appeared in T. Dugdale's *England and Wales delineated* [1838–9].

Lowry, Joseph Wilson (1803–79) Landscape and scientific engraver. He was born on 7 October 1803, the only son of Wilson Lowry (q.v.) by his second wife, Rebecca Delvalle, and was trained in engraving by his father. Two Liverpool plates—'St. Paul's Church' and 'Church of the School for the Blind'—after Harwood were engraved for Pyne's *Lancashire illustrated...* 1831 and 'The Valley of the Rocks, near Linton, Devon' and 'Ilfracombe town and harbour' after Allom for Britton and Brayley's *Devonshire and Cornwall illustrated* 1832. Five more plates after Allom were done for works published in 1832 by T. Rose: *Cumberland* contained 'Interior of Carlisle cathedral...'; *Durham and Northumberland*, 'Lindisfarn Abbey...' and 'Durham cathedral' (used again in 1835 in Fisher's *Drawing room scrap book*); and *Westmorland*, 'Bley-water tarn...' (not very well done) and 'Long Sleddale slate quarry...'. For E. Baines's *History of ... Lancaster* 1836, he engraved after T. Allom 'Hulme Hall, near Manchester' (1833), 'Mule spinning' (1834) and 'Sefton Church, Lancashire' (1833) (the last of which was used again in two volumes by G. N. Wright, i.e. *Lancashire* 1842 and *Gallery of engravings* 1844–6). A plate of spinning machines, mule, jenny and throstle, 'lower loom' and 'Patent machines in the cotton manufacture' complete the set, which were also used in Baines's *History of the cotton manufacture in Great Britain* [1835]. Carne's *Syria* 1836–8 contained three plates after W. H. Bartlett, viz., 'The mouth of the Nahr-el-Kelb...' (1836) (used again in J. Kitto's *Gallery of scripture engravings* 1846–9), 'Ferry over the Orontes' (1837) and 'Mosque at Payass—the ancient Issus', (1838), and for R. Walsh's *Constantinople* 1838–40, he engraved two plates after T. Allom—'The great Bazaar, Constantinople' and 'The palace of Said Pasha'.

He also engraved scientific subjects, commencing with plates for the *Encyclopaedia Metropolitana* 1821, then for Phillips' *Geology of Yorkshire* 1835, and the Journals of the Institute of naval architects and the Royal Geographical Society. He was an engraver with the Geological Survey of Great Britain from its inception, and exhibited marine views at the Royal Academy and British Institution between 1829 and 1831. He died unmarried on 15 June 1879 at Robert Street, Hampstead Road, aged nearly seventy-six. B; DNB; M; T.

Lowry, Wilson (1762–1824) Architectural, landscape and figure engraver. Although he was born in Whitehaven, Cumberland, on 24 January 1762, the son of Strickland Lowry, the family soon afterwards moved to Worcester. His first experience of work was as a house painter on the outside of Warwick Castle and afterwards in London and Arundel. Returning to Worcester, he trained as an engraver with Mr Ross, where his first plate was a trade card for a Worcester fishmonger. In 1780 he went to London to work for John Boydell, but by some quirk of fate trained for four years as a surgeon. Returning to engraving, he etched for William Byrne, and forwarded plates for James Heath and others, and about 1790 invented the first ruling machine for engravers, by means of which areas of sea, sky, etc. were engraved with precision. He first used it in plate 9 (dated 3 April 1792) of volume 3 of J. Stuart and N. Revett's *Antiquities of Athens*. (Many steel engravers modified it in the early nineteenth century.) He substituted a diamond point for a steel one in 1798. He undertook a mammoth task at the end of 1800 when Benjamin Rees asked him to do the engraving for his *Cyclopaedia*, a job which occupied him until June 1820. Apart from engraving most of the plates, which he had to do in duplicate in order to obtain the 6,000 copies of each required, he or his daughters were responsible for drawing the illustrations where no artist is mentioned.

He took an interest in steel engraving from the very beginning, using Jacob Perkins's blocks in the main, and engraved one of the earliest bookplates, for the twelfth edition of the Revd David Blair's *Universal preceptor* 1820, the frontispiece of which was a diagram of the solar system printed from a hardened steel plate (Plate 2). In February 1821 he gave one of his Perkins blocks to Charles Turner, who produced a satisfactory mezzotint portrait on it. He sold the secret of his etching fluid for steel plates to Perkins and Charles Heath for £50, since it was considered to be the best in use at that time.

His first marriage had produced only daughters, but in 1796 he married Rebecca Delvalle (1761–1848), a lady of Spanish extraction, by whom he had his son, Joseph Wilson (q.v.). After a long and distressing illness, during which he was grateful for the support of the Artists' Annuity Fund, he died in London on 22 June 1824, aged sixty-two. A, 1825 p. 96–100; DNB; H; P, p. 387–8; R. Soc. Arts. Manuscript Minutes 1822: 1823 p. 99.

M

McClatchie, A. (fl. 1828–35) Architectural and landscape engraver. 'Asylum for female orphans' (signed 'A. McClatchy' and dated 7 June 1828), 'Egyptian Hall, Piccadilly', 'Gas works, near the Regent's Canal' (dated 14 December 1828) and 'Buildings, Highfield, Camden Road', all after T. H. Shepherd, were engraved for J. Elmes's *Metropolitan improvements* 1829, two plates for Shepherd's *Modern Athens* 1829–31, and 'The new baths, Margate' after G. Shepherd, dated 1829, was done for volumes 1 of S. W. H. Ireland's *England's topographer* (commenced publication 1828). Two more plates are known, both after W. Tombleson, namely, 'Maidstone, Kent' in Fearnside's *Tombleson's Thames* 1834 and 'Ruins of Haldenstein and Lichtenstein' for Fearnside's *Tombleson's Upper Rhine* [c. 1835].

McGahey, J. (fl. 1831–5) Architectural and landscape engraver. 'Cotton factories, Union Street, Manchester' after Austin and 'Twist factory, Oxford Street, Manchester' after Harwood appeared in Pyne's *Lancashire illustrated...* 1831, 'Vice-regal Lodge, Phoenix Park' and 'Tenerure, Co. Dublin' after G. Petrie were issued in G. N. Wright's *Ireland illustrated* 1831 and 'Melrose' after G. Barret, dated 1835, was published in Scott's *Lay of the last minstrel* 1839.

Macgregor, W. (fl. 1845) Figure engraver. 'Battle of Culloden' after Capt. W. McKenzie and five plates, each depicting six armorial bearings after U. or M. MacCoinich, were issued in volume 3 of J. Browne's *History of the Highlands* [c. 1845].

Mackenzie, E. (fl. 1861) Portrait engraver. 'Cervantes' after a print by D. F. Selma appeared in volume 1 of the *Imperial dictionary of universal biography* [c. 1861].

Mansell, F. (fl. 1828–35) Figure and architectural engraver. Four plates after Whittock and Gastineau were done for Allen's *New ... history of the county of York* 1828–31. A plate of the marriage festival of Isaac and Rebecca after C. Lorraine, dated 1 October 1832, 'Tobit and the angel' after Rembrandt, dated 1 August 1833 (a very poor plate), a landscape after Sir G. Beaumont, dated 1 December 1833, and 'Tobit and the angel' after Domenichino, dated 1 June 1834, were published in A. Cunningham's *Cabinet gallery of pictures by the first masters...* 1836. For E. W. Brayley and J. Britton's *History of the ancient palace ... at Westminster* 1836, he engraved three outline engravings after J. Hewitt of architectural details of St Stephen's chapel, two of them dated 1 October 1835.

Mansell, J. (fl. 1828–33) Figure and architectural engraver. 'Interior of the great tower of Richmond Castle' after Whittock was engraved for Allen's *New ... history of the county of York* 1828–31. 'Marriage à la mode—death of the countess' after Hogarth appeared in Hogarth's *Works* 1833.

Marchant, J. (fl. 1846) Ornamental engraver. He engraved all the borders to the portraits in *Beauties of Moore* 1846.

Marr, Charles W. (fl. 1821–36) Figure engraver. He was, perhaps, of German descent, since a number of artists of the same name are known to have been of that nationality. He was one of the first engravers to experiment with steel plates, using those prepared by Mr Hook in 1821, but soon afterwards working on those prepared by Charles Warren, which he found more suitable. He printed 8,000 copies from a soft steel plate engraved with delicate work, and then proceeded to take engraver's proofs, indicating that proof quality prints could be taken after a fair amount of wear. His book work included 'The village queen' after J. Boaden in *The Amulet* 1831, 'The vintage' after the same artist for *Friendship's offering* 1833 and a vignette, 'Demon of war', after J. M. Wright in S. C. Hall's *Book of Gems* 1836, and between October 1832 and April 1836 he engraved eight plates for A. Cunningham's *Cabinet gallery of pictures by the first masters...* 1836, i.e., 'Puck' and 'Cupid' after Reynolds, 'Cephabus and Aurora' after Poussin, 'The market girl' after Morland (first engraved for this book), 'Le chapeau de paille' after Rubens, 'Kemble as Hamlet' after Lawrence (in which some passages were engraved as black as a mezzotint) 'Vision of St. Augustine' after Garofalo and the frontispiece 'The blind fiddler' after Wilkie. He also engraved Wilkie's 'The village festival'.   Soc.Arts. MS minutes 1822/3 p. 97.

Martin, R. (fl. 1833) Map engraver. Resident at 124 High Holborn, he is known by two maps in Parry's *Historical account of the coast of Sussex* 1833. The first, of the coast of Sussex, carries two vignettes, one of Arundel Castle and the other of Battle Abbey, and the second is of Goodwood.

Matthews, C. (fl. 1828–43) Landscape engraver. He is known by three engravings after Jonas Moore, of Woolwich, Greenwich and Gravesend, for R. P. Cruden's *History of Gravesend...* 1843, and may also be the engraver of 'East view of the City of Westminster' in J. Britton's *Picturesque views of the English cities* 1828.   Ho.

Melville, H. (fl. 1826–77) Landscape and figure engraver. 'The gamester reformed' after H. Corbould was issued in *The Amulet* 1826, and 'Chester Terrace, Regent's Park' (signed 'H. Melvelle') after T. H. Shepherd, dated 26 April 1828, appeared in J. Elmes's *Metropolitan improvements* 1829. Two vignettes after his own designs – 'The King's cottage, Windsor Park' and 'Virginia Water' – were published in Huish's *Memoirs of George the fourth* 1830–2, and in Baines's *History of... Lancaster* 1836, there appeared 'Seals of... Lancaster', engraved in 1831. 'The throne investiture ... of a Knight of the Garter' and 'Tower of London. Great Horse armoury', both after Gilbert, were published in Tyrrell's *Royal history of England* 1877.

Merckel, C. F. (fl. 1878) Historical engraver. 'The Gunpowder Plot' after Ralston and 'Washington crossing the Delaware' after Leutze appeared in Archer's *Pictures and royal portraits...* [c. 1878].

Metzmacher, Pierre Guillaume (1815–?) Figure engraver. Born in Paris, and exhibiting there, he was self taught, and in 1843 published the *Portfeuille de l'Ornament*, containing thirty-two plates. 'The grape-gatherer of Capri' after R. Lehmann was published in the *Art Union* 1848, and was reissued in Mrs Hall's *Drawing room table book* 1849.

Meyer, Henry Hoppner (1782–1847) Portrait and stipple engraver. He was one of the engravers whose works appeared in books more by accident than design, and who was much more at home engraving on copper than on steel. He worked mainly for the print publishers, and engraved more than 250 portraits after the English masters. Thought to be the son of an engraver, he was the nephew of John Hoppner, from whom he acquired his second forename, and was a pupil of Bartolozzi. This training influenced his work in stipple and mezzotint, for which he was best known. His book work included 'Thomas Graham, Baron Lynedoch' after Lawrence in Wright's *Gallery of engravings* 1844–6, 'Henry Neele' after his own design in J. Britton's *Autobiography* 1850 and a self portrait of Correggio in the *Imperial dictionary of universal biography* [c. 1861]. A. W. Graham (q.v.) was one of his pupils.   B; Br; DNB; S; T.

Miller, J. (fl. 1833) Landscape engraver. 'Sidmouth, Devonshire' after W. Daniell, R.A., first appeared in *Watering places...* 1833, then in the *Fashionable guide...* [c. 1838] and in J. Tillotson's *Beauties of English scenery* 1860.

Miller, William (1796–1882) Landscape and figure engraver. He was born on 28 May 1796 at 2 Drummond Street, Edinburgh, the youngest son of George Miller, one of a Quaker family, and after day school in the city, he went, at the age of nine, with two elder brothers, to a Friends' boarding school in Leeds. In 1807 he returned home and had a private tutor. At fourteen he expressed a strong wish to become an engraver, an enthusiasm which his father did not share, planning instead his entry into his shawl manufacturing business. Warehouse work was so uncongenial to him that his father eventually gave way, and he was apprenticed in

William Miller

1811 to William Archibald, an Edinburgh engraver with Quaker connections. At the end of four years he set up on his own, one of his first commissions being plates to illustrate an encyclopaedia, possibly the 1817 edition of the *Encyclopaedia Britannica*. By this means, and with his father's help, he was able to go to London in 1819 to work for George Cooke, the landscape engraver at Hackney. During the next eighteen months his work improved enormously in the company of three fellow pupils, and he returned home in the autumn of 1821. He first used steel in December 1825, for an engraved title page to volume 2 of *Constable's Miscellany*, but his first book plate in this medium, 'On the Thames near Windsor' after W. Havall, was done in August 1828 for the 1829 volume of *The Winter's Wreath*. Thereafter he employed steel continuously for books, and at least 200 plates by him are known. They are listed in 'A Catalogue of engravings' appended to *Memorials of Hope Park...*, written by his son, William F. Miller, and privately printed in 1886 in a limited edition of fifty copies, forming one of the most complete records known of a steel engraver's output. The list which follows, therefore, is by no means complete, and is merely representative of his work. 'Lake of Como' after S. Prout was engraved for T. Roscoe's *Tourist in Switzerland and Italy* 1830. 'The Borghese Palace, Rome' after the same artist appeared in Roscoe's *Tourist in Italy* 1831 (used again in J. Evelyn's *Diary and correspondence* 1872). For *The Keepsake*, he engraved

'Seashore, Cornwall' after R. P. Bonnington (*sic*) (1831), 'Marly' after Turner (1832) and 'Palace of La Belle Gabrielle on the Seine' after Turner (1834); and for the *Literary souvenir*, 'The Tower of London' after Turner (1832) and 'Fairies on the sea-shore' after Danby (1833). Four plates after T. Allom appeared in books by T. Rose, i.e., 'Llanercost Priory Cumberland' in *Cumberland* 1832, 'Newcastle upon Tyne...' and 'North and South Shields...' in *Durham and Northumberland* 1832, 'Ullswater from Pooly Bridge' in *Westmorland* 1832, and four more after Allom ('Devon-port...', 'Saltram House...', 'Launceston Castle...' and 'Launceston church...') in J. Britton and E. W. Brayley's *Devonshire and Cornwall illustrated* 1832. 'Klumm...' and 'Trent' after C. Stanfield appeared in L. Ritchie's *Travelling sketches in the north of Italy* 1832 and 'Homeward bound. Distant view of the Brill' after Stanfield in Ritchie's *Travelling sketches on the Rhine* 1833. Four vignettes after J. M. W. Turner were done for S. Rogers' *Poems* 1834 (of a garden, the old manor house, the Rialto and Loch Lomond), and 'Dieppe' and 'Mont St. Michel within the walls' after Stanfield appeared in Ritchie's *Travelling sketches on the sea coasts of France* 1834. 'The coquette' (a ship in distress) after S. Williamson was published in Fisher's *Drawing room scrap book* 1835 and five plates after Austin, Prout and Purser in Elliot's *Views in India...* 1835, which also included 'The British Residency at Hyderabad' after Grindlay. 'St. Michael's Mount, shipwreck of Lycidas', a vignette after Turner, appeared in Milton's *Poetical works* 1835 (Plate 21), 'Pont Neuf, Paris' and 'Melun' after J. M. W. Turner in L. Ritchie's *Wandering by the Seine* 1835, 'Botallack Mine, Cornwall', 'Hastings from the sea' and 'Havre de Grace' after C. Stanfield in *Stanfield's coast scenery* 1836 and 'Hornby Castle' after G. Pickering in E. Baines's *History of ... Lancaster* 1836. 'The wreck' after J. Wilson and 'The storm' after S. Prout, both vignettes, appeared in S. C. Hall's *Book of gems* 1836, and in the 1838 volume were published 'Sunrise' (a vignette) after Turner, 'Venice' after R. P. Bonington and 'St. Michael's Mount', a vignette after J. C. Bentley (q.v.). A vignette, 'The dead eagle', after Turner was issued in T. Campbell's *Poetical works* 1837, a plate of the Island of Nexos after Copley Fielding in C. Wordsworth's *Greece* 1839 and 'Battle of Trafalgar' after C. Stanfield, dated 1 November 1839, and 'Sunset at sea after storm' after F. Danby, dated 1849, in Finden's *Royal Gallery of British Art* 1838–49. Eight plates after D. O. Hill were done for Wilson and Chambers's *Land of Burns* 1840 and 'Landscape, Roman edifices in ruins' after Claude Lorraine for Ackerman's *Engravings after the best pictures...* 1841–3 (engraved entirely by Scottish artists). Twelve views, mostly after daguerrotypes taken by the author, were engraved for Keith's *Evidence of the truth of the Christian religion...*, 36th edition, 1848.

A number of engravings were done for Scott's works after C. Stanfield, J. M. W. Turner, J. and A. Nasmyth, J. Thomson, W. Collins, W. L. Leitch, P. Paton, E. Terry, R. K. Penson, H. McCulloch, J. W. Archer, T. Creswick and T. Allom. Examples include 'Loch Katrine' (Turner), 'York Minster (moonlight)' (Stanfield), 'Peel Castle, Isle of Man' (Leitch), 'Worcester' (Creswick) and 'Ruins of Laodicia' (Allom). 'Entrance to Loch Scavaig' after J. Thomson, dated 1 August 1846, and 'Loch Katrine' after D. Mackenzie appeared in *Black's picturesque tourist of Scotland* 1849, 'Bolton Abbey' after Henry Warren in T. Baines's *Yorkshire past and present* 1871–7 and a vignette—'Giving of the law'—and 'The deluge' after J. Martin in the *Imperial Family Bible* 1844. 'Bethlehem' after W. L. Leitch, 'Jerusalem from the Mount of Olives' and 'Antioch in Syria' after H. Warren and

'Town and isthmus of Corinth' after S. Bough were done for the *Imperial Dictionary* 1866, and the six plates from the *Bible* and *Dictionary* were used again in the *Imperial Family Bible* of 1873. Thirteen plates were engraved for publication in the *Art Journal*, 'Dryburgh Abbey...' after J. A. Bell (1847) and 'Pool of the Thames' after A. W. Callcott (1848) appearing in its predecessor, the *Art Union*. Seven were after J. M. W. Turner, and included 'Prince of Orange landing at Torbay' (1852), 'Spithead' (a lifeless engraving) (1862) and 'Wreck off Hastings' (1866), his last plate for the periodical. Some of these were used again in R. W. Wornum's *Turner Gallery* [c. 1878]. His last work was a series of vignettes after Birket Foster for Hood's *Poems* 1872. 112 works are known to contain Miller's steel engraved plates. He had two assistants and six pupils at different times, none of whom, however, attained their master's eminence.

The family returned to their old home, Hope Park, in the 1820s, and it was here that he set up his workshop in 1831, and in which most of his important work was done. Twice married, his first wife, by whom he had several children, died after only a few years of marriage, and his second wife, Jane, survived him, together with a son and three married daughters. Very active in Quaker and social affairs he continued to work with undiminished skill until he was seventy-five. In 1826 he had been elected Associate Engraver and thus became a founder member of the Royal Scottish Academy, where he occasionally exhibited watercolours, but was one of the nine who were alarmed at the magnitude of the undertaking and withdrew after the first meeting. It was only in 1862 that he was elected an Honorary Member, and in 1866 he made an unsuccessful bid to be elected to the Royal Academy in London. Hope Park was renamed Millerfield in 1863 and was known as such until its demolition a year or so after William's death. This occurred at Sheffield, where he was visiting his daughter, on 20 January 1882 aged nearly eighty-six. He was buried in the cemetery of the Friends' Meeting House at Pleasance, Edinburgh.

In J. H. Slater's *Engravings and their value*, 5th edition, 1921, there was a reference indicating that the original metal plates engraved by Miller were still in existence (he probably refers to those after Turner in particular) and were printed from occasionally; their subsequent history is unknown. Miller is also credited with a pictorial bookplate for Hugh Bransby after A. Nasmyth (1820), which is not in the 'Catalogue of engravings'. AJ; Br; DNB; Fi; H; S. W. F. Miller, *Memorials of Hope Park...* priv. print. 1886. Some of his letters exist in the National Library of Scotland and documents relating to legal matters in the Scottish Record Office.

Mills, G. (fl. 1839) Landscape engraver. 'Harper's Ferry (from the Blue Ridge)' after W. H. Bartlett was engraved for volume 2 of N. P. Willis's *American scenery* 1840.

Mills, John (fl. 1830–3) Landscape and figure engraver. 'Roman remains on Lancing Down', a vignette signed 'I. Mills', appeared in Cartwright's *Parochial topography of the Rape of Bramber* 1830, and 'The bruiser, Charles Churchill' after W. Hogarth appeared in the 1833 edition of that artist's *Works*, published by Jones and Co. He was also a painter, working from 1801 to 1837. B; T.

Mitan, Samuel (1786–1843) Landscape engraver. He was the brother and pupil of James Mitan (1776–1822), and seems to have been one of the engravers employed by Charles Heath who was rarely allowed to put his name to a plate. For *The Keepsake* he engraved the presentation plate after

Stothard (1830), that after Chenevant (1831), and that after Corbould, together with the engraved title page after Stothard (1834). In the 1833 volume of the same annual, the half-title page is signed by C. Heath and the engraved title page by Lacey (probably Samuel Lacey (q.v.)). In the list of plates, however, the former is ascribed to S. Mitan, and his name is added as co-engraver to the latter. This clearly indicates that there are probably many of his engravings extant under other names. He was also employed by R. Ackermann on his publications, and did the plates for Captain (later Lt. Col.) Robert Batty's *French scenery* 1822. He engraved a bookplate for the London Mechanics' Institution, which was founded about 1823. He joined the Artists' Annuity Fund as a founder member in 1810, and died at The Polygon, Somers Town, on 3 June 1843. B; DNB; F.

Mitchell, James (1791–1852) Figure engraver. Although he is said to have practised in Edinburgh, it is difficult to see how he obtained the varied commissions in the early days of the annuals without being on the spot in London. His earliest work on steel was the engraved title page for the *Literary souvenir* 1825, and for *The Amulet* 1826, he did 'The dying babe' after J. M. Wright. For the *Literary souvenir* he also engraved 'The Contadina' after Eastlake (1827), 'Robert Burns and his Highland Mary' after Edmondstone (1831) and 'Lady Jane Grey' after Northcote (1832). *The Gem* carried 'The farewell' after Cooper (1829), 'The dorty bairn' and 'Saturday night' after Wilkie (1830) and 'Corsair' after Briggs (1832), and for *The Keepsake* he engraved 'George Aspen and Isabella' after Stephanoff and 'The Castle Hall' after Leslie (1830), 'The secret' after Smirke (1831) and 'Scandal' after Smirke (1832). For the 1829–33 Cadell edition of Scott's works, he engraved 'Edie Ochiltree' after Landseer and five other illustrations, after Fraser, Kidd, Stanfield and Wright. He seems to have taken a rest for a year or two, since in 1839 a review of Bunyan's *Pilgrim's progress* in the *Art Union* (p. 186) after noting him as an engraver for the volume adds 'Where has he been for years?' In the 1854 edition of the same work, he engraved 'Christian talking to his family', an oval design after Stothard. The frontispiece to Young's *Night thoughts* 1845 was after H. Corbould. 'The errand boy' after Wilkie appeared in S. C. Hall's *Gems of European art* 1846 and in *Wilkie gallery* [c. 1849], which latter volume also contained 'The dorty bairn'. Two of his best engravings were also after Wilkie, i.e., 'Alfred in the neatherd's cottage' (1829) and 'The ratcatchers' (1830). He joined the Artists' Annuity Fund in 1822, and was a signatory of the 1837 petition. He died in London on 29 November 1852, aged sixty-one, leaving a son, Robert (1820–73), also an engraver, and noted for his work after Landseer. AJ; DNB; R.

Mollison, James (fl. 1833–61) Portrait and figure engraver. 'Times of the day—morning' after W. Hogarth appeared in the 1833 edition of the artist's *Works*, published by Jones and Co. 'Gulliver in Brobdingnag' after Redgrave was issued in volume 2 of S. C. Hall's *Gems of European art* 1846, and a self portrait of Hogarth and 'Voltaire' after Largilhiere came out in the *Imperial dictionary* of universal biography [c. 1861].

Morgan, H. (fl. 1870) Figure engraver. 'The High Priest with his ephod and breastplate entering the holy place' after W. B. Scott was published in Murdoch's edition of the *Holy Bible* [c. 1870]. The plate was largely etched and machine ruled.

Morrison, James (fl. 1833–46) Portrait engraver. 'Samuel Crompton' after Allingham, dated 1833, appeared in Baines's

History of ... Lancaster 1836 and 'Sir Francis Burdett' after Lawrence in Wright's *Gallery of engravings* 1844–6.

Moses, Henry (1781–1870) Figure, landscape and historical engraver. He is best known for his work done in outline, which was peculiarly appropriate for architectural plans, sculpture, antiquities, heraldic representations, etc. The *Dictionary of National Biography* lists a number of books containing his plates from 1811, most of which were done on copper. Some of his later works, however, were almost certainly done on steel, among which were the twenty plates after the author's designs engraved for Gell's *Pompeiana...* 1832, dated between April 1830 and February 1832. The best of these was 'Pompeii, Achilles and Briseus'. In 1843 he engraved a series of twenty-two illustrations after H. C. Selous for Bunyan's *Pilgrim's progress* (which won a competition sponsored by the Art Union of London), the prints from which were issued to subscribers for 1844. Moses died on 28 February 1870 at Cowley in Middlesex. DNB.

Mossman, W. (fl. 1840–4) Landscape engraver. All his known plates are after W. H. Bartlett and appeared in a comparatively short space of time. This encourages the belief that he also followed some other branch of art, and can be identified with William Mossman the elder, who was a sculptor working in London and who died in April 1884. 'Palace of the Sweet Waters' was engraved for Pardoe's *Beauties of the Bosphorus* 1840, and 'Glengariff' appeared in volume 1 and 'Glenariff (County Antrim)' in volume 2 of Coyne's *Scenery and antiquities of Ireland* [c. 1840]. Seven plates, dated between 1840 and 1842, were done for Beattie's *Ports, harbours...* 1842, and included 'St. Bee's Head', 'Gloucester', 'Oystermouth (Swansea Bay)', 'The Mumbles rocks and lighthouse' and 'Hurst Castle'. This last engraving appeared in vignette form in Woodward's *General history of Hampshire* 1863. 'Village of Lorette' and four other plates were engraved for Willis's *Canadian scenery* 1842, and six engravings were done for Beattie's *Danube* 1844, namely, 'The Devil's-wall, St John's', 'Junction of the River Inn with the Danube (at Passau)', 'Castle of Spielberg', 'View from the Leopoldsberg...', 'The Nun's tower—Castle of Theben' and 'A wedding at Orsova'. B.

Mote, William Henry (fl. 1830–58) Portrait, figure and sculpture engraver. He was a prolific steel engraver, concentrating almost entirely on portraits, and the first dated plate by him is of Sir Thomas Bodley (1 January 1830), and appeared with thirty-five other engravings by him in Lodge's *Portraits ...* 2nd edition, 1835. The majority of the plates were signed 'W. T. Mote' (and one 'T. W.'): a few were correctly signed. Four plates were produced in 1830, four in 1831, six in each of the years 1832 and 1833, and eight in each of the years 1834 and 1835, some indication of the increased dexterity of his work. Plates were executed after artists such as Holbein, Lely, Kneller and Hoppner, and included portraits of Sir Christopher Hatton, William Warham, Archbishop of Canterbury, William Cavendish and Robert Harley, Earl of Oxford. *Finden's illustrations of the life and works of Lord Byron* 1833–4 contained 'Rt. Hon. Anne-Isabella, Lady Noel Byron' after W. J. Newton and 'Ada from the original miniature' after Stone, which is a good example of his work. Four portraits of eminent French ladies, including Marie Antoinette, all after F. J. Collignon were engraved for *Health's Versailles* [c. 1836], and were used again in *Keepsake français* 1840. One of his few excursions into landscape engraving appeared in R. Walsh's *Constantinople* 1838–40, with 'Interior of a Harem, Constantinople' and 'Halt of Caravaniers at a Serai,

Bulgaria', both after T. Allom. A total of forty-three plates were engraved for *The Keepsake*, commencing in 1835. The volumes for 1838–40, 1843–6 and 1848–57 all contained his work, much of it after R. Buckner. That for 1849 contained five plates, including 'Lady Constance Gower' and 'Lady Elizabeth Lascelles', both after Buckner, and that for 1850, four plates, including 'Isabel' after Wright and 'Elfrida' after E. Corbould. 'The late Duchess of Gordon' after Reynolds, 'Edith' after Louisa Sharpe and two other plates were done for *Heath's Book of beauty* 1835, seven plates after Chalon and Ross appeared in the 1839 volume, and for that of 1841 he engraved eight plates, all dated 1 October 1840, after Hayter, Chalon, Grant, Fisher and Mrs Hawkins, among which were 'The Lady Seymour as the Queen of love and beauty', 'Miss Isabella Montgomery' and 'Mrs. B. D'Israeli'. The 1847 edition of the same annual had 'Thou art not false, but thou art fickle' after Egg, 'Aurora Raby' after Frith, 'Medora' after J. W. Wright and 'Laura' after Hayter. This last engraving has a rather peculiar appearance: the figure, bed and draperies have the characteristics of a lithograph. For Finden's *Tableaux* 1840, he engraved 'The pilgrim' after J. Browne, and for Finden's *Gallery of beauty* 1841, 'Countess of Lovelace (daughter of ... Byron)' and 'Lady Louisa Cavendish', both after Chalon. From May 1845 to May 1846 he was engaged upon five plates for *Beauties of Moore* 1846, with 'The wreath' after Wood, 'Rich and rare' after Fisher, 'Sleeping beauty' (an exquisite plate) after Frith, 'The coming step' after Ward and 'Lea' after de Valentini. *Forget me not* 1846 contained 'The choicest flask' after Smyth and 'Sketch from nature' after Hering. Twelve plates after a variety of artists were done for Fisher's *Historic illustrations of the Bible* [1840–3], some of which appeared again in Kitto's *Gallery of scripture engravings* 1846–9. Twelve 'portraits' of Shakespeare's female characters were engraved after J. W. Wright, K. Meadows and Frith for *Heroines of Shakespeare* 1848, and among them were 'Jessica', 'Anne Page', 'Olivia' and 'Lady Macbeth'. 'The Marys at the sepulchre' after Veit and 'Supper at Emmaus' after Guercino were engraved for the *Book of Common Prayer* 1854. What was probably his longest series of plates appeared in *The Court album* 1852–7, where over sixty engravings, many after Hayter, were done in what for him was a new form, i.e., vignette or an oval shape. Examples are 'The Marchioness of Stafford', 'The princess of Saxe Weimar', 'Mrs. Jones of Pantglas', 'The Duchess dowager of Manchester and daughter' and 'Miss Fazakerley'. His portrait after a photograph by Annan of David Livingstone appeared in Chambers's *Biographical dictionary of eminent Scotsmen*, 2nd edition, 1875. He engraved eleven plates for the *Art Journal*, ten of which were of sculptures. Three plates, the first of a picture, appeared in the 1849 volume, two in that for 1851 and three each in those for 1852 and 1858. He is also known to have engraved portraits of Americans, and his plates were used in American publications. He joined the Artists' Annuity Fund in 1831 and signed the 1837 edition. S; St.

Mottram, Charles (1807–76) Landscape engraver. He was twenty-one and probably just out of his indentures when he engraved 'Allington Castle...' after Burford, dated 1828, with 'Pegwell Bay...' after G. Shepherd and 'Stone Castle, near Gravesend...' and 'North view of Belvidere...' after Fussell, for S. W. H. Ireland's *England's topographer* (commenced publication 1828), and about the same time he did three plates after T. H. Shepherd for Shepherd's *London and its environs* 1829–31, two of which were signed 'C. Motram' (the writing engraver was not yet familiar with his name).

'Birkenhead & the Cheshire shore from Liverpool' after Harwood was done for Pyne's *Lancashire illustrated...* 1831 and four plates after the author's designs for Gastineau's *Wales illustrated...* 1830. Then followed 'Kitley House...' and 'Mount Edgecumbe...' after T. Allom and 'Interior of the Athenaeum, Plymouth' after G. Wightwick for Britton and Brayleys' *Devonshire and Cornwall illustrated* 1832, and 'Grassmere Lake and village, Westmorland' after Pickering for T. Rose's *Westmorland* 1832. Three plates, including 'Hudibras; first adventure' and 'Marriage à la mode...' (Plate 17) were done for Hogarth's *Works* 1833, eight plates after Bartlett for Wright's *Picturesque beauties of Great Britain ...: Essex* 1831–4, 'Cawnpore' after Prout for Elliot's *Views in India...* 1835, 'Bold Hall' after Pickering for Baines's *History of ... Lancaster* 1836 and 'Lugano (Canton Tessin)' and 'The Lake of Lucerne...', both dated 1834 and after W. H. Bartlett, for Beattie's *Switzerland* 1836. The last-named plate was used again in D. Costello's *Piedmont and Italy* [c. 1855], together with 'Town of Lugano...', also after Bartlett. 'Gallery of mirrors, Versailles' (a well-engraved plate, full of detail) after F. Mackenzie was used in both *Heath's Versailles* [c. 1836] and *Keepsake français* 1840. 'Inverness' after W. Purser and 'The pass of Awe (Argyleshire)' after T. Allom, both dated 1836, were engraved for Beattie's *Scotland illustrated* 1838, 'Conference at the Isle of Wight' after G. Cattermole for R. Cattermole's *Great Civil War* 1846 and 'St. George's Chapel with part of the ceremony of an Installation of Knights of the Garter' after Mackenzie (another detailed and intricate plate) for L. Ritchie's *Windsor Castle* 1848. 'Grand entrance of the Chamber of Peers, Palace of the Luxembourg', 'Diana Gallery, Fonainbleau' and 'The Bourse, Paris', all after Allom, were done for *The Keepsake* 1848.

It was perhaps because of his close work that John Sellers of Sheffield asked him to engrave a plate three feet long for the Great Exhibition of 1851, in which the machine-ruled sky was 'perhaps the most severe test to which a steel plate can be subjected' (Great Exhibition Catalogue, 1851, vol. 2, p. 606). Two plates after C. Marshall and 'Leatherhead Church, Surrey' after J. W. Allen appeared in Fearnside and Harral's *History of London* [c. 1850], and *The Royal Shakespeare* 1883–4 contained 'Oberon and Titania' and 'Lear and Cordelia' after V. W. Bromley and 'Florizel and Perdita' and 'Ferdinand and Miranda' after J. D. Watson. A view of New York engraved by him was published in that city in 1855. He also worked occasionally in mezzotint and in a mixed style in which some plates, e.g. 'Last Judgment', were done after Martin. In his later years he worked for the print publishers, obtaining a reputation for engraving after Landseer, e.g. 'Marmozettes' and 'Lorie', published by H. Graves in 1876. He exhibited at the Royal Academy from 1861, notably, in 1876 exhibiting a proof impression of 'Shadow of the Cross' after Morris, published in 1873. He was born on 9 April 1807, and died after a short illness at 92 High Street, Camden Town, on 30 August 1876, aged sixty-nine. His contemporaries considered him to be one of their best engravers, a judgement based largely on the good quality of his work. AJ; DNB; St.

Mucklow, J. (fl. 1832) Landscape engraver. 'The Logan Rock', a rather poor vignette after T. Allom, appeared on the engraved title page of volume 2 of Britton and Brayley's *Devonshire and Cornwall illustrated* 1832.

Murdock, J. S. (fl. 1830–8) Architectural engraver. 'Dunbarton Castle' after Stanfield was engraved for Scott's *Waverley novels*, and 'Bridge of Messis...' after W. H. Bartlett appeared in volume 3 of J. Carne's *Syria* 1836–8.

N

Nargeot, Adrien Jean (1837–c. 1900) Line engraver and etcher, and figure engraver. Born in Paris on 9 August 1837, he worked and exhibited in Paris. In 1875, the *Art Journal* published 'Apotheosis of the Virgin' after Murillo, and 'Falstaff and Mrs. Ford' after Ralston appeared in volume 2 of *The Royal Shakespeare* 1883–4. It is just possible that one or other of these plates, if not both, was done by his master (and probably father) Jean Denis Nargeot (1795–after 1865), who was known to have engraved book illustrations.   B.

Nargert, M. (fl. 1878) Historical engraver. 'Sir David Baird discovering the body of Tipoo Sultan...' after Wilkie appeared in Archer's *Pictures and royal portraits...* [c. 1878].

Newman, John, and Co. (fl. 1838–1880) Landscape and architectural engravers. Originally trading as 'J. Newman', their first address in London, in around 1838, was 30 Bridge Street, but soon afterwards they moved to 48 Watling Street, and in 1875 to 69 Southwark Bridge Road. This firm produced many items, such as boxes, miniature books, table mats, etc., decorated with engravings, in addition to a number of plates done for local publications such as town guides. Many prints were also sold locally, and have local publishers, but none of their plates identifies an individual engraver. An example of such work is the engraving 'The Pavilion, Brighton. Engraved by J. Newman, published by J. Smith, Pool Valley, Brighton' and two series of *Six Brighton views* after F. W. Woledge 1842–3.

Nicholson, T. E. (fl. 1831–4) Figure engraver. In 1832 he engraved 'Death of Chatham' after Copley, published in A. Cunningham's *Cabinet gallery of pictures by the first masters...* 1836, and for the *Works* of W. Hogarth, he did eight plates for the 1833 edition, published by Jones and Co. He had also done seven plates for *Hogarth moralized...*, published by Major in 1831. 'Hargreaves's spinning jenny' was engraved in 1834 for volume 2 of Baines's *History of ... Lancaster* 1836.   Br.

O

Ogg, H. A. (fl. 1831–46) Landscape engraver. 'Walker's monument, Londonderry' and 'Sligo', both after T. M. Baynes, were published in G. N. Wright's *Ireland illustrated* 1831. He was also a landscape and portrait painter, exhibiting at Suffolk Street between 1844 and 1846. His portraits of R. B. Dodgson and his wife are in Blackburn Art Gallery.   B; Ho.

Onwhyn, Thomas (c. 1820–1886) Landscape engraver. Youngest son of Joseph Onwhyn, publisher of guide books and writer, Thomas is best known for his illustrations to Dickens. He also drew for guide books, notepaper headings, etc., but abandoned artistic work about 1860. 'Portsmouth (Royal Dock Yard)' after G. F. Sargent was published in R. Mudie's *Hampshire* 1838.   B; DNB.

Onwyn, R. (or B.) (fl. 1838) Architectural engraver. 'Abbey Church, Christchurch' after G. Carter was published in R. Mudie's *Hampshire* 1838. There is a possibility that the writing engraver intended to ascribe it to Thomas Onwhyn (q.v.) but the inscription on the plate is clear, except for the initial.

Outhwaite, J. (fl. 1831–79) Landscape engraver. Probably born in the first or second decades of the nineteenth century, he first lived in London, but by 1836 he was working as an engraver in Paris, where he seems to have spent the rest of his life, becoming naturalised in 1855. He was pupil of Edward Goodall, (q.v.) probably in the 1820s, but from 1836 to 1877 he exhibited in Paris, one such exhibition being at the Louvre in 1846. According to a report in the *Art Union* (June 1846, p. 161), he exhibited several book plates after Girardot and others which were 'most exquisitely engraved by this Englishman, established for many years in Paris, where he is much esteemed'. It goes on to add: 'The exhibition of engravings this year is poor; very few large works; the principal ones are book plates'. He engraved three plates after the author's designs for Gastineau's *Wales illustrated...* 1830, including 'Caerleon, Monmouthshire', and the *Art Journal* published his 'Village fete' after Teniers in 1855 and 'Riverbank' (quite a good example of the engraver's art) after Vander Heyden in 1857. 'Warwick Castle' after P. Skelton and 'St. Goar' after T. L. Rowbotham were issued in *Picturesque Europe*, published by Cassell in 1876–9. About 1860 he took Alphonse Lamotte (1844–1914) as a pupil.   B; T.

Outhwaite, T. (fl. 1836–76) Landscape engraver. 'Planta' after Allom was engraved for *Views in the Tyrol* [1836] and 'Cockatoo Island' after Skinner Prout for Booth's *Australia* [1873–6].

Outrim, John (fl. 181834–54) Figure engraver. Among his early work is 'Fisher children' after Collins in the *Literary souvenir* 1834 and 'Storm in harvest' after R. Westall for the 1835 volume. 'Rustic hospitality' after W. Collins and 'Behold the Lamb of God' after T. Uwins were engraved in 1842 and 1847 respectively for Finden's *Royal Gallery of British Art* 1838–49, and for S. C. Hall's *Gems of European art* 1846. He did 'The Bandit's wife' after Leopold Robert and 'Napoleon in the prison of Nice, 1794' after E. M. Ward, which last engraving was later reissued in the *Art Journal* 1879 on the occasion of the recent death of the painter. 'So Abraham departed' after Zuccarelli appeared in Fisher's *Historic illustrations of the Bible* [1840–3] and again in J. Kitto's *Gallery of scripture engravings* 1846–9. The *Art Union* of 1848 carried 'Dancing lesson' after T. Uwins, the *Art Journal* 1850, 'Sir Thomas More' after J. R. Herbert, the volume for 1852, 'Cavalier's pets' after Landseer, and for that for 1854, a semi-circular picture, 'Christ lamenting over Jerusalem', after Eastlake and 'Vintage in the South of France' after T. Uwins. This last plate was the cause of a row between the engraver and the publishers, upsetting for the first (and only) time their publication schedules. A bitterly worded explanation in the 1854 volume (p. 356) sets out the facts, which, briefly, were that the engraver had been given the picture on 29 September 1851 with a contract to finish it by 31 July 1852. Nearly two and a half years later and after much recrimination it was still not finished, so in desperation it was sent to Lumb Stocks, and the plate was finally issued later in the year. Significantly, this seems to have been the end of the engraver's career. A separate print, 'Highland breakfast' after Landseer, was published in 1842; his contemporary reputation was based upon his interpretation of this artist's work. He was a signatory of the 1837 petition.   B; S.

Owen (fl. 1838–51) Landscape and architectural engraver. Three plates (merely signed 'Owen') are known, i.e., 'Andover' after G. S. Shepherd in Mudie's *Hampshire* 1838, 'The four law courts, Dublin' after Bartlett in Wright's

Gallery of engravings 1844–6 and 'The Crystal Palace, west end' after Read & Co. in *Remembrances of the Great Exhibition* [1851].

Owen, S. (fl. 1828) Architectural engraver. 'West side of Langham Place' after T. H. Shepherd, dated 29 September 1828, was issued in J. Elmes's *Metropolitan improvements* 1829.

Owen, T. (fl. 1829–31) Architectural engraver. 'Croydon Church' after Whittock appeared in T. Allen's *History ... of Surrey and Sussex* 1829–31, and 'Christ Church and Coal Staith, Leeds' after Whittock was done for the same author's *New ... history of the county of York* 1828–31.

Owen, W. (fl. 1838) Architectural engraver. 'House of Representatives, Brussels' after J. Fussell was published in *Continental tourist* [1838].

P

Page, R. (fl. 1833–40) Figure engraver. 'The House of Commons' after Hogarth (signed 'R. Page & Son') appeared in Hogarth's *Works* 1833. Other plates signed 'R. Page & Son' were done for Chambers's *Biographial dictionary of eminent Scotsmen* 1835 (three vignette portraits after Hoppner (including 'Adam Duncan' (Plate 23)) and Kneller) and four Biblical scenes after Stothard, Hamilton and Raphael for *A New family Bible* [c. 1840].

Page, W. T. (fl. 1844–6) Portrait engraver. 'Rt. Hon. John Charles Spencer...', a vignette portrait after R. Page (q.v.), was issued in G. N. Wright's *Gallery of engravings* 1844–6.

Palmer, J. F. (fl. 1846) Landscape engraver. 'The Moselle bridge at Coblentz' after W. Tombleson appeared in Fearnside's *Picturesque beauties of the Rhine* [c. 1846].

Parkin, J. (fl. 1877) Portrait engraver. 'Mary Stuart, Queen of Scotland, at the age of 16...' after P. Bordone was published in Tyrrell's *Royal history of England* 1877.

Parr, R. (fl. 1836–8) Figure engraver. 'Combat'—a vignette—after A. Cooper and 'The fighting dogs' after C. Hancock were published in S. C. Hall's *Book of gems* in the 1836 and 1838 editions respectively. 'Mündig' (a racehorse) after Hancock was done for *New Sporting Magazine* 1835. There is perhaps a connection with the eighteenth-century line engraver of book plates Remi Parr (see DNB).

Pass, J. (fl. 1831) Architectural engraver. 'St. Philip's Church, Salford' appeared in W. H. Pyne's *Lancashire illustrated...* 1831, Baines's *History of ... Lancaster* 1836 and Wright and Allen's *Lancashire...* [c. 1845].

Paterson, G. (fl. 1836–46) Figure engraver. 'The widow' after C. Hancock was published in S. C. Hall's *Book of gems* 1836, and five plates after T. Allom were done for G. N. Wright's *China* 1843, namely, 'Raree show at Lin-sin-choo' and 'Dinner party at a Mandarin's house' in volume 1, 'Punishment of the Tcha or Cangue, Ting-hai' in volume 2 and 'Dyeing and winding silk' and 'China opium smokers' in volume 3. A further plate after Allom was a vignette, 'Love's early dream', which appeared in Wright's *Gallery of engravings* 1844–6. 'Adoration' after Murillo was engraved for S. C. Hall's *Gems of European art* 1846. There may be a connection with a G. or J. Paterson listed by Slater (in *Engravings and their value*, 6th edition, 1929) who seems to have worked in Glasgow and perhaps London, with plates after Herring and Ansdell.

Patten, E. (fl. 1836) Landscape engraver. 'Southwell, Nottinghamshire' and 'Monument to Lord Byron, Hucknall Church, Nottinghamshire', both after T. Allom, were published in T. Noble and T. Rose's *Counties of Chester...* 1836. He may be connected with a family of miniature and portrait painters working in the first half of the nineteenth century. Br; T.

Payne, Albert Henry (1812–1902) Landscape, architectural and figure engraver. Born in London on 14 December 1812, one of his early connections was with William Tombleson (q.v.), after whom he engraved a number of plates. 'Park Place, Henley...' Hungerford, new market', 'Wouldham Church, Kent' and 'Chatham, Kent' all appeared in Fearnside's *Tombleson's Thames* 1834, in which year he joined the Artists' Annuity Fund. 'Laufenberg', 'Lindau, Lake Constance', 'The first stone bridge over the fore Rhine' and 'Union of the three sources of the fore Rhine' were published in Fearnside's *Picturesque beauties of the Rhine* [c. 1846], and for Fearnside's *Tombleson's Upper Rhine* [c. 1835] he engraved a vignette on the engraved title page, comprising a view of a castle, framed in vine branches, and 'Mon^t of Marshal Saxe'. With one exception, all these plates were signed simply 'Payne'. 'The village of Zgarti' after W. H. Bartlett, dated 1836, was done for J. Carne's *Syria* 1836–8. Fifteen plates after Allom were engraved for *Views in the Tyrol* [1836], including 'Zenoberg', 'Escheloch', 'Maienberg' and 'Leonberg'. 'Cardinal Wolsey entering the Abbey of Leicester' after R. Westall was published in Tyrrell's *Royal history of England* 1877. In 1845 he issued *Payne's Universum; or pictorial world...*, edited by C. Edwards, containing nearly one hundred engravings on all kinds of subjects, of which a specimen plate, 'Whalers attacked by bears', engraved by Payne, was published in the *Art Union* 1845 (p. 241). Other works include *Payne's Royal Dresden Gallery* 1845, *Payne's Illustrations of London* 1846, *Payne's Orbitus pictus* 1851 and *Payne's Panorama of science and industry* 1859. He had become a partner in the firm of Brain and Payne of 12 Paternoster Row, which had published his *Universum*, and it was perhaps Tombleson's influence which turned Payne's attention towards Germany, where the former had publishing interests. In 1838, when he was twenty-six, Payne moved to Leipzig and founded a publishing house called 'Englische Kunstantelt', from which some, if not all, of his later works were issued. From publication lines on some of his prints it is clear that he also had an office in Dresden. His son Albert was born in Leipzig on 3 June 1842, became an engraver, and joined his father in the business. Albert died on 1 April 1921, and his father died in Leipzig on 7 May 1902, aged eighty-nine. Thomas Heawood (q.v.) also worked for Payne in Leipzig. B; T.

Penny, W. (fl. 1838) Line engraver. He engraved 'Silver sugar basin...' after T. M. Richardson and 'Seals of Cardinal Beaton and St. Andrews' for T. F. Dibdin's *Bibliographical ... tour in the northern counties of England* 1838. He can perhaps be identified with the line engraver William Penny at Midcalder near Edinburgh in about 1800 noted by Benezit. B; Ho; T.

Penstone, John Jewel(l) (fl. 1835–95) Portrait engraver. Two vignettes after J. Hayter appeared in *The Court album* 1852–7—'Miss Caroline Cholmeley' and 'Mrs. Phillipson'. He was also a portrait painter and exhibited at the Royal Academy from 1835 to 1848, and again in 1895. B; T.

Periam, G. A. (fl. 1835–52) Figure engraver. 'Prawn fishers' after Collins was engraved for the *Literary souvenir* 1835 and

'The secret' after Corbaux for *Friendship's offering* 1837. The title page vignette 'Death of Hinda (the fire-worshippers)' after Edward Corbould, published in T. Moore's *Lalla Rookh* 1838, is one of his best book plates. 'The raising of Jairus's daughter' after von Holst, 'Jesus and the Samaritan' after Guido and 'Alfred dividing the loaf' after B. West were engraved for S. C. Hall's *Gems of European art* 1846, and 'Alfred in the neatherd's cottage', 'The Highlander's return' and 'The Guerilla taking leave of his confessor', all after Wilkie, appeared in *Wilkie gallery* [c. 1849]. Then began his work for the *Art Journal*, with 'Clarissa Harlowe' after C. Landseer (1850), 'The fair sleeper' after H. Wyatt and 'Pride of the village' after J. C. Horsley (1851) and 'Florimel and the witch' after F. R. Pickersgill (1852). 'To arms! to arms!' after Pickersgill was engraved for *The Keepsake* 1852 and for the 1853 volume he did 'Scandal', an eighteenth-century period piece. This came to an end when he went to Mexico in 1853, whence there is no evidence that he returned; certainly no engravings after that date have been found.   AJ.

Peters, J. (fl. 1846) Landscape engraver. 'Linz' after W. Tombleson was engraved for H. G. Fearnside's *Picturesque beauties of the Rhine* [c. 1846].

Phelps, J. (fl. 1832) Landscape engraver. 'Keswick, Derwent, &c from the road to Kendal' and 'Bassenthwaite Lake, looking south, Cumberland', both after T. Allom, were engraved for T. Rose's *Cumberland* 1832. He is probably Joseph Phelps, pupil of Charles Warren (q.v.).

Phillibrown (fl. 1860–72) Portrait engraver. Two sets of portrait plates, simply signed 'Phillibrown', cannot firmly be assigned to any of the following engravers by that name. The Cabinet edition of E. Lodge's *Portraits...*, published by William Smith about 1860, contains 240 poorly executed stipple portraits, most of them in octagonal frames, of which 162 are unsigned and the remaining seventy-eight signed 'Phillibrown'. Plates of a similar style, eight signed by him, and twenty more unsigned, were used in Evelyn's *Diary* and published by Bell and Daldy in four volumes in 1872, and included portraits of Sir Walter Raleigh after Zucchero, John Seldon after Mytens and Elizabeth Queen of Bohemia after Honthorst.

Phillibrown, A. (fl. 1846) Figure engraver. 'The burial of Atala' after A. L. Girodet-Trioson was engraved for S. C. Hall's *Gems of European art* 1846.

Phillibrown, J. (fl. 1845) Figure engraver. Eighteen plates after Robert Smirke appeared in Cervantes' *Don Quixote*, published about 1845. One of the best plates is 'The funeral of Chrysostom'; others include 'The shepherdesses of the wood', 'Camilla's artifice', 'Sancho as governor of Barataria' and 'Death of Don Quixote'.

Phillibrown, Thomas (fl. 1833–49) Figure engraver. For W. Hogarth's *Works*, published by Jones and Co. in 1833, he engraved six plates, including 'The rake's progress, 5—marries an old maid' and 'Taste in high life'. For the *Art Journal* 1849 he did 'The Truant' after T. Webster. According to Stauffer he was a pupil of the Findens, and went to the United States before 1851, although Benezit puts it later at 1860. It is also said that he was an eccentric character, peculiar in appearance, and that he was a personal friend of Hablot K. Browne, who used him as a model for Mr Pickwick. B; St.

Portbury, Edward James (1795–1885) Figure engraver. Among his early book work is 'Epitaph in a country church yard' after R. Westall, dated 1 December 1820, which appeared in J. Sharpe's edition of Gray's *Poetical works* 1821. The earliest reference to his use of steel comes in an entry in Longman's Miscellaneous publications expenditure ledger A2 (p.43), where, under 'Moore's Lalla Rookh', there follows: '1826. Septr 22. To Portbury for steel plates £94-10'. Engravings for *The Amulet* include 'The dead fawn' (1828) and 'Sweet Anne Page' (1831), both after R. Smirke, for *The Keepsake* 'The false one' after H. Corbould, 'The ghost laid' after F. P. Stephanoff and 'The Persian lovers' after H. Corbould (1828), 'Fancy descending upon the muses' after H. Howard and 'The magic mirror' after J. M. Wright (1829), 'The portrait' after R. Smirke (1830) and 'The intercepted letter' after Mrs. Seyfforth (1837). For the *Literary souvenir* he did 'Minny O'Donnell's toilet' after Farrier (1829), 'Childe Harold and Ianthe' after Westall (1830), 'The sea-side toilet' after Holmes (1831), 'Going to mass' after Johannot (1832), 'The pledge: a Dutch family group' after Wattier (1833) and 'Peasants of the kingdom of Naples' after Howard (1835). 'Garrick' after Hogarth was engraved for the artist's *Works* 1833. 'The domestic scene', a vignette after Stephanoff, appeared on the engraved title page of *Wreath of friendship*. 'The Hindoo mother', an engraved title page vignette after Melville, appeared in Fisher's *Drawing room scrap book* 1836, which also contained 'The widow's mite' after Chisholm. 'MacMurrough's chant' after McClise and 'Murder of the Bishop of Liège' after Franklin appeared in Wright's *Landscape-historical illustrations of Scotland* 1836–8. 'Love teaching innocence' after Uwins and 'The Italian cottage' after P. Williams were done for S. C. Hall's *Book of gems* 1838. 'The deliverance of St. Peter from prison' after W. Hilton, dated 28 November 1843, was published in Finden's *Royal Gallery of British Art* 1838–49. 'The Hall of Glennaquick—a highland feast' after D. Maclise was issued in G. N. Wright's *Gallery of engravings* 1844–6 and 'The gipsey mother' after D. Wilkie appeared in *Wilkie gallery* [c. 1849]. Two round pictures after W. Etty were done for the *Art Journal*, viz., 'Bathers surprised by a swan' (1849) and 'Dangerous playmate' (1852). He is also known to have engraved some portraits. He died on 14 March 1885, aged ninety.   AJ 1885; T; Longman Archive, University of Reading.

Posselwhite, James (1798–1884) Portrait engraver. Sixteen portraits appeared in the *Imperial dictionary of universal biography* [c. 1861], and included Sir Richard Arkwright after Wright, Canova after Lawrence, Goethe after G. Dawe, Locke after Kneller, and self portraits of Rubens and Reynolds. He was born on 23 January 1798 and died in London on 12 December 1884. B; T.

Posselwhite, T. (fl. 1844) Figure engraver. 'The baron's daughter' after J. Hollins appeared in G. N. Wright's *Gallery of engravings* 1844–6. It is just possible that the initial 'T' was mistaken for 'J' by the writing engraver.

Pound, D. J. (fl. 1842–77) Portrait engraver. He was one of the later group of engravers, and did most of his portraits after photographs by Mayall, becoming in the process a most efficient reproductive engraver. What appears to be some of his early work is found in J. B. Burke's *Heraldic illustrations* 1845, where plates 3 and 8, depicting coats of arms, are signed 'D. Pound' and dated 1842 and 1843 respectively. For Ball's *History of the Indian Mutiny* [c. 1858], he engraved the frontispiece 'Lord Viscount Canning, Governor General of India', for *The Self-interpreting Bible* 1864, 'David and Abishai in Saul's tent' after Strahuber and for Tyrrell's *Royal history of England* 1877, he did the engraved title page to volume 1 'The late Prince Consort', the frontispiece to volume

2 'The late David Livingstone', and portraits of Robert Stephenson, Earl of Beaconsfield and William Ewart Gladstone for the same volume. T.

Presbury, George (fl. 1820–49) Landscape and figure engraver. A Mr G. Presbury, living at Upper John Street, Fitzroy Square, was in 1820 awarded the Silver Palette by the Society of Arts for a chalk drawing from 'Hercules' in the British Museum, and in 1824, a person of the same name living at 12 Denzell Street was awarded the Large Silver medal for a finished historical engraving. He engraved seven plates for W. Hogarth's *Works* 1833, published by Jones and Co., including 'The distressed poet'. 'The pilgrims' after Melville was done for Bunyan's *Pilgrim's progress* 1836, 'A Turkish divan—Damascus' after Bartlett for Carne's *Syria* 1836–8, 'Runjeet Singh and his Suwarree...' after Harvey for White's *Views in India...* 1838, twelve plates after Melville, Topham, etc. for Wright's *Landscape-historical illustrations of Scotland* 1836–8 and 'Eyoub Sultan—Fountain and Street of the Tombs', 'Caravansary at Guzel-Lissar...' 'Metropolitan church at Magnesia, Asia Minor. Installation of the Bishop' and 'Mausoleum of Sultan Mahomed Brusa', all after T. Allom, for R. Walsh's *Constantinople* 1838–40. Thirteen plates appeared in Fisher's *Historic illustrations of the Bible* [1840–3], some of which were reprinted in Kitto's *Gallery of scripture engravings* 1846–9. 'Evenings at home' after Allom was issued in Ellis's *Daughters of England* 1842, and at about the same time he engraved 'Address to the toothache' (a rather poor engraving) and 'The rigs o' barley', both after J.M. Wright, for various editions of R. Burns's *Complete works*. 'Aeneas and Dido' after P. Guerin was done for S.C. Hall's *Gems of European art* 1846 and five plates appeared in G.N. Wright's *Gallery of engravings* 1844–6, including 'The lady's sorrow' after F.W. Topham (q.v.). He joined the Artists' Annuity Fund in 1839. SocA.

Price (fl. 1846) Landscape engraver. 'Ehrenbreitstein' after Tombleson appeared in H.G. Fearnside's *Picturesque beauties of the Rhine* [c. 1846]. He can probably be identified with George Price (b. 1826), who was a pupil of the Findens, and who from 1853 to 1864 worked in the United States, returning to England in the latter year. Fi.

Prior, Thomas Abiel (1809–1886) Landscape and figure engraver. Born on 5 November 1809, his early work was done after Allom and Bartlett for the publishers Fisher and Virtue. He was twenty-three when 'Axwell Park, County of Durham' and 'Gibside, County of Durham' were engraved after T. Allom for T. Rose's *Durham and Northumberland* 1832, and, after that same artist, he did 'Radford Folly, near Nottingham' and 'Wollaton Hall, Nottinghamshire' for T. Noble and T. Rose's *Counties of Chester...* 1836. 'Ber-el-Kamar, and the palaces of Beteddein' after W.H. Bartlett, dated 1836, appeared in J. Carne's *Syria* 1836–8, 'The mock battle' after Allom in Wright's *Landscape-historical illustrations of Scotland* 1836–8, 'Abbotsford...', 'Edinburgh from Craigmillar Castle...' and 'Dunkeld (Perthshire)' after Allom in W. Beattie's *Scotland illustrated* 1838 and 'Outer cooling room of the baths' and 'Greek Church of St. Theodore, Pergamus' after Allom in R. Walsh's *Constantinople* 1838–40. 'Views of the ruins of Fort Ticonderoga' and 'Faneuil Hall, from the water' after Bartlett were engraved for N.P. Willis's *American scenery* 1840, 'Bazaar of the fig tree, Algiers...' after Allom for Wright's *Shores and islands of the Mediterranean* 1840, fourteen plates, eleven after Allom, for Brayley's *Topographical history of Surrey* 1841–8, five plates after Bartlett, Irton and Leitch for Wright's *Rhine, Italy and Greece* 1842, four

Thomas Abiel Prior

animal plates for Carleton's *sporting sketch-book* 1842, 'Bologna' after W. Brockedon for the latter's *Italy...* 1842–3, the frontispiece 'Black Gang Chine, Isle of Wight', dated 20 May 1842, for T. Roscoe's *Summer tour in the Isle of Wight* 1843, six plates after T. Allom for G.N. Wright's *China* 1843, among which was 'Transplanting Rice', 'Eton from Windsor Castle terrace' after J.D. Harding for L. Ritchie's *Windsor Castle* 1848 and 'The source of the fore Rhine at Mount Badus' after Tombleson for Fearnside's *Tombleson's Upper Rhine* [c. 1835]. 'The judgement of Solomon' after Steinle appeared in *The Self-interpreting Bible* 1864 and 'Whitby' (Plate 60) and 'Kingstown harbour [Dublin]' after Duncan in Anderson's *English landscapes and views* 1883. In 1846 he began his association with Turner and the print publishers by purchasing the drawing 'Heidelberg Castle' from the former, engraving it on copper, and publishing it himself from his address at 3 Elizabeth Place, Putney. A review of the print in the *Art Union* 1846 (p. 242) comments that the engraver was 'hitherto comparatively unknown, but, who, by this engraving, at once establishes indisputable claim to the highest professional rank'. This must have pleased the shy and retiring engraver, and the picture was subsequently re-engraved by him on steel for the *Art Journal* 1864 (issued again in R.W. Wornum's *Turner Gallery* [c. 1878]). His first plate for the *Art Journal* (for which he did fourteen from 1850 to 1871) was 'Venice—Grand canal' after Turner, and subsequent plates after this artist for that journal were 'The golden bough' (1851) and 'Goddess of discord' (1871). Independent plates after Turner were 'Zurich' (1852)—his first plate engraved for Graves—, 'Dido building Carthage' (1863), 'Apollo and the sybil' (1873), and 'The Fighting Temeraire', completed in September 1886, just over a month before his death. These are said to have been his best plates. His only mezzotint plate, done for Lloyd Bros., was 'More frightened than hurt' after J. Bateman (1847). It was also in 1847 that he did what is probably his best-known plate—' "Come unto these yellow sands!" ' after R. Huskisson, which appeared in the *Art Union* 1847, Mrs Hall's *Drawing room table book* 1849, and the *Works of Shakspere [sic], Imperial edition* 1872. In 1849 he engraved a plate for the Art Union of Glasgow, 'Whittington...' after F. Newenham, for presentation to all members. It was about 1860 that he moved to Calais to be near his son, who had settled there. Most of his time was then taken up with teaching drawing in the public schools of the town, and it was not unusual for him to take up to eight, nine or ten years to complete any plates he had on hand. When a plate was ready to be proved he made his annual visit to England, on the last of which, in 1886, he broke his usual custom and signed about twenty-five proofs of various plates in a very shaky hand. (He was also very lame.) He died on 8 November 1886 in Calais, aged seventy-seven. One of his watercolours of the Red fort and beach is in the museum at Calais. B; *Printseller & Collector*, 2, 1904, pp. 131–2.

Proctor, E. K. (fl. 1831) Architectural engraver. 'Thormond-gate Bridge, Limerick' and 'Custom House, Limerick' after W. H. Bartlett appeared in G. N. Wright's *Ireland illustrated* 1831. Ho.

Pye, John (1782–1874) Landscape engraver. Born on 7 November 1782, the second son of Charles Pye, author, of Birmingham, he was the cousin of William Radclyffe the engraver (q.v.). His father having taught him the rudiments of engraving, he was apprenticed to William Tolley the writing engraver, and attended Barber's classes. In 1801, he and William Radclyffe went to London, where John became the paid assistant to James Heath (to whom John's elder brother Charles was articled) and began work on various book illustrations. Like his brother, he preferred copper and among his important plates on this metal were 'Hardraw Fall'

John Pye

(said to be a plate upon which Pye prided himself), 'Junction of the Greta and Tees at Rokeby' and another good plate, 'Wycliffe near Rokeby', all done after J. M. W. Turner for Whitaker's *History of Richmondshire* 1823. The etching for the second plate was done by his father-in-law, Samuel Middiman (q.v.), whose daughter, Mary, John had married in 1808, and by whom he had a daughter Mary. The third plate was reissued in the *Art Journal* 1875, and they all appeared again in *Turner's Richmondshire* 1891. In 1828, Turner painted 'Ehrenbreitstein', inspired by Byron's *Childe Harold's pilgrimage*, expressly for Pye to engrave, which he did immediately on steel, the prints appearing in the *Literary souvenir* for 1829. Pye then kept the picture for another ten years to make a larger plate, provoking Turner to protest at this delay. (See Hunnisett, *Steel-engraved book illustration in England*, pp. 39–40.) Two vignettes after Turner–'The firefly' and 'Paestium'—were engraved for S. Rogers' *Italy* 1830, and in 1830 he engraved 'Sunset' after G. Barret, which was eventually published in *The Amulet* for 1831. It was originally destined for *The Anniversary*, but its publication in that annual was abandoned, and 3,400 prints were taken off for

use in Sharpe's *London Magazine*. The painter and engraver wrote a letter jointly to the *Athenaeum* complaining about S. C. Hall's publication in *The Amulet*; it was published on 25 December 1830, p. 811 (see Hunnisett *Steel-engraved book illustration in England*, p. 142). The plate is thought to be one of Pye's best line illustrations. 'Baalbec (ruins of the temple of the sun)' after D. Roberts, dated 4 April 1849, was engraved for Finden's *Royal Gallery of British art* 1838–49. He spent much time in France, and was able to compare conditions for engravers in Europe with those for engravers in the United Kingdom for the various bodies to which he presented the British engravers' case for better recognition. He wrote *The Patronage of British Art* 1845, and undertook the key role in engraving twenty-nine plates after pictures in the National Gallery, an undertaking originally suggested by the collector John Sheepshanks in 1830. In 1842 he finished 'Dover' after Callcott (published by F. G. Moon), which had been left in the etching stage by George Cooke at his death. He retired as an engraver in 1858, and thereafter advised fellow engravers on their work, and acted as an authority on Turner's work to the extent of judging, with Edward Goodall, the authenticity of a painting in an 1864 lawsuit. He was one of the founder members in 1810 of the Artists' Annuity Fund, which, for services rendered, presented him with an address and silver vase in 1830. A scrapbook on him exists at the offices of the Fund, and a collection of Pye manuscripts is in the Victoria and Albert Museum. He died at 17 Gloucester Terrace, Regent's Park, on 6 February 1874, in his ninety-second year. B; DNB; H; *Illus. London News*, 1874, p. 185; R (note: his date of birth is given in this source as 22 April 1782).

Pyne, W. J. (or W. H.) (fl. 1834) Figure engraver. 'A Dutch ale-house' after F. Mieris and 'Domestic harmony' after P. Van Dyke, dated 1 April and 1 July 1834 respectively, were published in volume 2 of A. Cunningham's *Cabinet gallery of pictures by the first masters . . .* 1836. He can perhaps be identified with William Henry Pyne (1769–1843), painter and writer.

R

Radclyffe, Edward (c. 1810–63) Landscape and figure engraver. Born in 1809 or 1810 in Birmingham, son of William Radclyffe (q.v.), he was his father's pupil in engraving, and attended the drawing school of J. V. Barber. In 1824, at the age of fourteen or fifteen, the Society of Arts awarded him the Silver Isis medal for an etching of animals, and in 1826, at the age of sixteen or seventeen, he won their Silver Palette for an engraving of cattle. At the end of his apprenticeship he went to London, in about 1830, and instead of seeking employment with a studio, set up on his own. Among his earliest book plates were 'Louis XIVth at the Chace, Versailles', 'The canal of Trianon', 'The orangery of Versailles from the water of the Swiss', all after W. Callow, and 'Second gallery of busts . . . Versailles' after F. Mackenzie, done for *Heath's Versailles* [c. 1836] and reissued in *Keepsake français* 1840. 'Burgstall' and 'Braunsperg' after Allom were done for *Views in the Tyrol* [1836], and a vignette, 'Villa Reale Naples', appeared on the engraved title page of *The Keepsake* 1836. Similar plates were done for other volumes of the annual (1837, and 1839 to 1846 inclusive) after Cattermole, Cox, Creswick, C. Radclyffe and Uwins. Vignettes after E. Corbould and Cox were done for the engraved title pages of *Heath's Book of beauty* 1839, 1841 and 1847. 'Falls of the

Machno' after D. Cox was engraved for T. Roscoe's *Wanderings and excursions in North Wales* 1836, 'The house of John Knox' and 'Fall of Foyers' after T. Allom, dated 1837 and 1836 respectively, for Beattie's *Scotland illustrated* 1838, 'Glendalough, County Wicklow' and 'Cove near Cork', vignettes after T. Creswick, for L. Ritchie's *Ireland...* 1837, 'Absalom's tomb, near Jerusalem' after Allom, dated 1838, for J. Carne's *Syria* 1836–8, 'The sands', a vignette after D. Cox, for S. C. Hall's *Book of gems* 1838 and seven engravings for C. Wordsworth's *Greece* 1839 after Creswick, Cox, Capt. Irton and his brother Charles William Radclyffe (1817–1903?). Ten plates after Allom were done for Brayley's *Topographical history of Surrey* 1841–8, including 'Windlesham Church', 'Richmond Hill' and 'Interior of Gatton church'. He engraved 'The landing place' after Danby for *Friendship's offering* 1844, plates after Bartlett for *Barber's picturesque illustrations of the Isle of Wight* [c. 1835], Willis's *American scenery* 1840 and the same author's *Canadian scenery* 1842, nineteen out of twenty-three plates for J. D'Alton's *History of Drogheda* 1844, two plates after G. Cattermole for R. Cattermole's *Great Civil War* 1846, 'Carisbrooke Castle, Isle of Wight' after G. F. Sargent for Beattie's *Castles and abbeys of England* 1845–51, the engraved title page vignette 'The Eagle Tower from Eton Bridge' after J. D. Harding for L. Ritchie's *Windsor Castle* 1848 and 'Nanking from the Porcelain Tower' after Allom for G. N. Wright's *China* 1843, and for *The Keepsake* 1847 he engraved the title page vignette of castle, moat and trees after his brother Charles William and 'The Baptistery, St. Mark's Church, Venice' after Lake Price. 'Villa Reale', a vignette, was engraved for the title page of Fearnside's *Picturesque beauties of the Rhine* [c. 1846] after T. Uwins. 'Battle of Vittoria' appeared in Hume and Smollett's *History of England...* 1854–5, 'Calcutta. The Esplanade', a vignette after Allom, in Nolan's *Illustrated history of the British Empire in India* [1858–60] and five plates after Warren and Houston in *The Self-interpreting Bible* 1864. A portrait of Milton was the frontispiece to Masson's *Life of Milton* 1870. 'Arch of Trajan, on the Mole, Ancona' after C. Vacher appeared in Costello's *Piedmont and Italy* [c. 1855] and 'The Lion Brewery, Lambeth' after Allom in Timbs's *Curiosities of London* 1867. He engraved seven plates which were published in the *Art Journal* between 1848 and 1866, including two after F. R. Lee, namely, 'The homeward bound' (1848) and 'Morning on the sea coast' (1851), and 'Hay-time' after D. Cox (1866). He also engraved views on Admiralty charts, of which 'The Persian Gulf' was exhibited at the 1862 Paris International Exhibition. From 1859 he turned to etching, which he used to prepare eleven designs after Cox, 300 sets of which were used as Art Union of London prizes in 1862, and commenced a *Liber studiorum* of Cox's work, of which he had only done three when he died in November 1863 at his home in Camden Town. He joined the Artists' Annuity Fund in 1835, and married Maria, daughter of Major Revell of Round Oak, Englefield Green, Surrey, in 1838. He exhibited at the Royal Academy from 1859 to 1863, and also dabbled a little in mezzotint, a medium used by his brother William (1812–1846), who also painted Edward's portrait. The name is variously spelt: Radclyffe, Radcliffe, Ratclyffe, Ratcliffe. AJ; B; DNB; H; SocA.

Radclyffe, J. (fl. 1835) Landscape engraver. 'Bridges of St. Cloud and Sevres' after J. M. W. Turner was published in L. Ritchie's *Wanderings by the Seine* 1835. 'Salzburg' and 'Schwatz on the River Inn' after Allom were engraved for *Views in the Tyrol* [1836]. He was probably a member of the same Birmingham family as Edward and William.

Radclyffe, Thomas (fl. 1810–30) Landscape engraver. For William West's *Picturesque views ... in Staffordshire and Shropshire...* 1830–1 he engraved thirty plates after F. Calvert for the Staffordshire volume and seventeen after Bissell, Calvert, Davis and Page for that on Shropshire. The engraved title page vignette to the Staffordshire volume 'Lichfield cathedral', 'Soho from the Ninevah Road', 'English Bridge, Shrewsbury' and 'Haughmond Abbey' are representative of his work. Two bookplates were engraved in 1810, and his name appears as joint printer (with William Radclyffe) on 'Plan of Kenilworth Castle' after Jeayes in Blair's *Graphic illustrations of Warwickshire* 1829. He was a member of the Birmingham family of engravers.

Radclyffe, William (1783–1855) Landscape engraver. Born in Birmingham on 20 October 1783, he was the grandson of John Radclyffe, whose daughter was the mother of John Pye (q.v.). The two engravers were thus cousins, and both attended J. V. Barber's school and were apprenticed to William Tolley the writing engraver. They helped each other to improve their engraving expertise, and at the end of their indentures in 1801 set off for London, where John's brother Charles was already apprenticed to James Heath. William returned to Birmingham, however, to become the leader of the city's group of engravers. He married before 1809 and his sons Edward, William and Charles William were also artists. He helped to establish the Academy of Arts in Birmingham, later to become the Royal Birmingham Society of Artists. In 1814 or 1815 J. T. Willmore (q.v.) became one of his many pupils, together with Thomas Garner (q.v.), and he was employed on engravings for topographical works, notably of Norwich and Warwick. Other pupils were Samuel Fisher, Griffiths and John Wrightson, and Joseph Goodyear and Thomas Jeavons also assisted him. (It was perhaps his daughter, a Miss M. Radclyffe, who obtained the Silver Palette from the Society of Arts for an etching of a landscape in 1822.) He engraved thirty-two plates for Blair's *Graphic illustrations of Warwickshire* 1829 between 1823 and 1829 after Barber, Cox, Harding, William Westall and P. de Wint. They include 'Warwick Castle' after Westall, 'Charlecote' after Harding and 'Kenilworth Castle' after Barber. He was engaged on nearly forty plates for *Jones's Views of the seats...* between 1829 and 1831. Four plates after Shepherd's drawings were done in T. H. Shepherd's *London and its environs* 1829–31, four in J. Elmes's *Metropolitan improvements* 1829 and six in Shepherd's *Modern Athens* 1829–31. Ten views after the author's designs were done for Gastineau's *Wales illustrated...* 1830 and ninety-seven plates for T. Roscoe's *Wanderings and excursions in North Wales* 1836 and *... in South Wales* 1836, including 'Pass of Llanberis' after Cox, 'Flint Castle' after J. Wrightson, 'Bettws-y-coed' after Creswick, a general view of 'Tintern Abbey' after Copley Fielding and 'The Mumbles light house' after E. Watson. 'The Roman Catholic Church at Surbiton' and 'View from Norbury' after Allom were done for Brayley's *Topographical history of Surrey* 1841–8. He contributed a single plate to a number of volumes in the 1830s and 1840s, such as Allen's *History of the county of Lincoln* [1830–1], Fisher's *Historic illustrations of the Bible* [1840–3], *The Keepsake* 1844 and *Wreath of friendship*. Of his others, four after Harding appeared between 1832 and 1833 in two volumes of T. Roscoe's *Tourist...* series, and after Bartlett, one was issued in Beattie's *Switzerland* 1836, two in J. Pardoe's *Beauties of the Bosphorus* 1840 and three in N. P. Willis's *American scenery* 1840. After J. M. W. Turner he engraved 'Mantes' and 'Marché aux fleurs and the Pont au Change' for L. Ritchie's *Wanderings by the Seine* 1835. Among his last works were 'Prayer in the desert' after W. Muller and 'Crossing the sands' after W. Collins, published in the *Art Union* for 1847 and 1848 respectively and republished in Mrs Hall's *Drawing room table book* 1849. He engraved the plates for the *Oxford Almanack* from 1840 to 1855, examples of which are 'Village of Iffley...' after de Wint (1841) and 'Old approach to Magdalen College' after F. Mackenzie (1847). He joined the Artists' Annuity Fund in 1813. He died in Birmingham on 29 December 1855.   AJ; B; DNB; H; SocA.

Raddon, William (fl. 1817–33) Portrait and figure engraver. Among his earliest works on steel was a series of five plates for H. Walpole's *Anecdotes of painting* 1827. These were portraits of Daniel Mytens after Van Dyck, a self-portrait of Sir Peter Lely, Samuel Cooper, Enoch Zeeman after Seipse and Luke Vosterman after Van Dyck. 'The game of tric trac' after Teniers, dated 1 August 1833, appeared in A. Cunningham's *Cabinet gallery of portraits by the first masters...* 1836. In 1831 he tried out new graver handles for the Society of Arts. He probably gave up engraving for entomology, which absorbed his energies up to about 1862 (his work in this field is represented in the British Museum by an album of water insects).   B.

Rawle, G. (fl. 1841–4) Architectural engraver. Four tiny outline views (well engraved on one plate), dated 1844, and 'Exterior view of Slyfield House...' after Allom appeared in Brayley's *Topographical history of Surrey* 1841–8. It is possible that he was one of Samuel Rawle's six children.

Rawle, Samuel (1771–1860) Landscape engraver. He came from Dunster in Somerset, the son of George Rawle, and was apprenticed to Thomas Bonnors, an engraver in Gloucester. By January 1796 he had moved to the London branch of the Bonnorses' business, and, turning to painting, he exhibited landscapes at the Royal Academy in 1801 and 1806. By 1798 he was engraving plates for the *European Magazine* and the *Gentleman's Magazine*, and he contributed to a number of well-known topographical books between 1816 and 1823. Between May 1828 and November 1829 he produced 'The Ortler-Spitz', 'Scene on the descent from the Splugen', 'Scene over Prinoland' (a vignette), 'Scene in the Valley of the Uraye' and 'Defile of the Dovedro', all after William Brockedon, for the latter's *Illustrations of the passes of the Alps* 1828–9. From notebooks in the St. Bride Printing Library he is known to have worked for the Findens, and he did plates for Britton's works and editions of Pinnock's *Geography*, etc. His son, possibly the G. Rawle above, was apprenticed to him and was engaged upon drawing outlines, etching, etc. Samuel Rawle had six children, born between 1801 and 1815.   H.

Read, W. (fl. 1824–55) Portrait, historical and landscape engraver. He did the engraved title page to Thomas Kelly's edition of the Revd John Brown's *Self-interpreting Bible* 1824 (Plate 6). 'The Saumarez River which never freezes' after the author's design was done for Ross's *Narrative of a second voyage...* 1835, and five plates after de Loutherbourg, Raphael, West, Smirke and Westall were done for *A New family Bible...* [c. 1840]. Six plates after Vertue, Tresham, Mortimer, Opie and Stothard appeared in Hume and Smollett's *History of England...* 1854–5, of which the vignette 'Departure of Richard 1st from Cyprus' after Tresham was the best. He can perhaps be identified with a portrait engraver working in London between 1824 and 1837 or a Scottish engraver from Elgin who did the illustrations to Shaw's *History of Moray* 1827 and portraits of Grant and Hay.   B; Print Coll. Q. 18 (1931) 269; T.

Redaway, James C. (fl. 1818–57) Landscape and architectural engraver. Some of his early work, which was on copper, appeared in J. P. Neale's *Views of the seats of noblemen...* 1818–24 and in Voltaire's *La Henriade...* 1825. 'East side of Park Crescent' after T. H. Shepherd was engraved for J. Elmes's *Metropolitan improvements* 1829, (Plate 8), 'The Castle from the Vennel' for Shepherd's *Modern Athens* 1829–31 and for T. Roscoe's *Tourist in Switzerland and Italy* 1830, he did 'Lausanne' after S. Prout. For the same author and after the same artist he engraved 'Bridge of Augustus, at Narni' for *Tourist in Italy* 1831, and after W. Brockedon he engraved 'Obelisk' (a vignette), 'Ascent on the Grand Croix' and 'Lake on the summit of the Bernadin', dated May 1827, August 1827 and February 1829 respectively, for the artist's *Illustrations of the passes of the Alps* 1828–9. 'The grotto in Castle Eden Dean', 'The Galilee, west end of Durham cathedral', 'The rushbearing at Ambleside, Westmorland' and 'Bowness from Belle Isle, Windermere', all after T. Allom, were first published in 1832 in T. Rose's *Durham and Northumberland* and *Westmorland*, and 'Whalley Abbey' after G. Pickering, dated 1831, appeared in Baines's *History of... Lancaster* 1836 and again in Wright's *Lancashire* 1842. Caunter's *Lives of the Moghul emperors* 1837 contained three of his plates after W. Daniell, dated 1 October 1836, and J. Carne's *Syria* 1836–8 had one plate after Allom, one after J. Salmon and five after W. H. Bartlett, after whom more plates are to be found in Beattie's *Waldenses* 1838 (one plate), Pardoe's *Beauties of the Bosphorus* 1840 (two plates), Beattie's *Ports, harbours...* 1842 (one plate), Beattie's *Danube* 1844 (one plate) and Bartlett's *Walks about ... Jerusalem* [1844] (one plate). 'Taj Bowlee, Bejapore' after Prout was engraved for Elliot's *Views in India...* 1835 and 'View near Deobun' after Stanfield was done for White's *Views in India...* 1838. Other plates by T. Allom are to be found in R. Walsh's *Constantinople* 1838–40 (two plates), Beattie's *Scotland illustrated* 1838 (one plate) and G. N. Wright's *China* 1843 (three plates). Seven of his plates appeared in Wright's *Gallery of engravings* 1844–6, including 'Mayence cathedral, Rhine' after W. L. Leitch, and 'Eton from the Locks' after W. Evans appeared in the *Art Journal* for 1857. He joined the Artists' Annuity Fund in 1826 and signed the 1837 petition.

Revel, Alfred (?–1865) Figure engraver. Known in Paris (where he was born) as an engraver of vignettes for book illustration, he engraved 'The studio of Paul Potter' after E. le Poittevin exclusively for the *Art Union* 1847; it was reissued in Mrs Hall's *Drawing room table book* 1849.

Richards, J (fl. 1832) Landscape engraver. 'Bacharach and St. Werner's Chapel' after Tombleson was engraved for *Tombleson's views of the Rhine* 1832.

Richardson, Charles (fl. 1835–42) Landscape and architectural engraver, working exclusively after W. H. Bartlett. 'Lugano (Canton Tessin)', dated 1835, with 'the effect by H. Gastineau', was published in Beattie's *Switzerland* 1836, 'Cemetery mosque of Ayub' in Pardoe's *Beauties of the Bosphorus* 1840 and 'Kenbane Castle' in J. S. Coyne's *Scenery and antiquities of Ireland* [c. 1840]. N. P. Willis's *American scenery* 1840 contained 'Brock's Monument (from the American side)' and Beattie's *Ports, harbours...* 1842 had 'Dundee, from the opposite side of the Tay'. He can perhaps be identified with a landscape painter of the same name from Newcastle (a son of Thomas Miles Richardson) who exhibited at the Royal Academy from 1855 to 1901. This is consistent with an engraver deserting his profession for painting later in life.   B; T.

Richardson, George K. (fl. 1833–1891) Landscape engraver. Among his earliest works were a landscape with figures after Waterloo, dated 1 November 1833, published in Cunningham's *Cabinet gallery of pictures by the first masters...* 1836, and 'Corfu' after Purser in *Friendship's offering* 1833. With very few exceptions, his other work was after W. H. Bartlett, such as 'The devil's bridge', 'Baths of Pfeffers', 'St. Peter's Island', 'The Valley of Lauterbrun' and 'Monte Rosa, and the Cervin', dated between 1834 and 1836 and published in W. Beattie's *Switzerland* 1836. Also after Bartlett, 'Susa', 'Prali—Val St. Martin' and 'The Balsille (during the attack)' were engraved for Beattie's *Waldenses* 1838, 'Straits of the Bosphorus', 'The Atheidan...' and 'Fort Constantinople' appeared in J. Pardoe's *Beauties of the Bosphorus* 1840, five plates, dated 1838–9, came out in N. P. Willis's *American scenery* 1840, 'Old weir bridge, Killarney', 'Salmon leap at Leaxlip' and 'Powerscourt from the Dargle' were published in J. S. Coyne's *Scenery and antiquities of Ireland* [c. 1840] and three plates came out in Willis's *Canadian scenery* 1842. One of his best plates was 'Bridge of Doune' after Bartlett (Plate 32) in W. Beattie's *Scotland illustrated* 1838, which also included three plates after Allom and one after H. McCulloch. Among his last steel plates were 'Buda and Pesth (from the Blocksberg)', 'Hildegardsberg' and 'Castle Wildenstein', all after Bartlett, in Beattie's *Danube* 1844 and 'The baggage waggon' after L. Clennell, engraved for S. C. Hall's *Gems of European art* 1846. He can perhaps be identified with George Richardson, eldest son of Thomas Miles Richardson, engraver of Newcastle. If so, he was brother to Charles (if Charles was indeed the son of Thomas Miles Richardson—see above). He exhibited at the British Institution and New Water Colour Society from 1828 to 1833, and was secretary of the Newcastle Water Colour Society. He died about 1891. B; T.

Richardson, William (fl. 1840–77) Landscape and figure engraver. He appears to be one of the Edinburgh group of engravers, and did some of his earliest steel plates for Wilson and Chambers's *Land of Burns* 1840. Each of the two volumes contained nine plates engraved by him after D. O. Hill, including 'Glen Afton', 'Auchtertyre'—the engraved title page vignette to volume 2—, 'Nithsdale', 'Kircudbright' and 'Jedburgh'. For W. Brockedon's *Italy...* 1842–3, he engraved 'Turin' and 'Modena' after S. Bough, 'Carrara' after Brockedon and 'Pozzuoli, the ancient Puleoli' after W. L. Leitch, and he did seven plates for the *Imperial Family Bible* 1844, three after J. Martin and one each after E. Walton, A. Penley, W. L. Leitch and E. Faulkner. Fifteen plates were done for editions of Scott's *Waverley novels*, and included 'Battlefield of Preston Pans' after Stanfield, 'View on Loch Long' after A. Nasmyth, 'The Tweed, Site of old drawbridge' after Hill, 'Oxford' after Creswick and 'The Bosphorus with the castles of Europe and Asia' after T. Allom. The engraved title page to volume 3 of Chambers's *Biographical dictionary of eminent Scotsmen*, 2nd edition, 1875 carried a vignette, 'King's College, old Aberdeen', after S. Bough, and 'Landscape—Aeneas landing in Italy' after Claude Lorraine was done for *Engravings after the best pictures of the Great Masters* 1841–3. 'Jamieson's Valley' and 'The Dandenong Ranges, Victoria' after Skinner Prout and 'The Basin Bank, Victoria' and 'Oven's River, Victoria' after N. Chevalier were engraved for Booth's *Australia* [1873–6]. Three plates were engraved for the *Art Journal*: 'Lake in Cumberland' after J. C. Loutherbourg (in which the sky is engraved using very fine lines) came out in the 1851 volume, 'Crossing the brook' after Turner (which was used again in Wornum's *Turner Gallery* [c. 1878]) in that for 1862 and 'Borrowdale' after S. Bough in

that for 1871. Of his independent prints, 'Windsor Castle, summer evening' after D. O. Hill and 'Tribute to the memory of... Wren' after C. R. Cockerell, both issued in 1843 by Alex Hill, may be mentioned. He was also a painter, exhibiting in London between 1842 and 1877. B.

Ridgway, William (fl. 1840–85) Figure and historical engraver. 'The angel warning Joseph in a dream' after Westall appeared in *A New family Bible* [c. 1840], and seven plates were done for Archer's *Pictures and royal portraits...* [c. 1878], and included 'The Battle of La Hogue [sic]' after B. West. 'Geraint and Enid ride away' after Gustave Doré was engraved for *The Story of Enid and Geraint* [1869] (Plate 55). For the *Art Journal* he engraved 'Ministering angels' after A. Muller, which appeared in the 1857 volume. Sixteen more plates followed up to 1885, among which were 'Going to school' after T. Webster (1861), 'Arming the knight' after J. C. Hook (1867), 'On the way to school' after E. Davis (1870), 'Back from Marston Moor' after H. Wallis (1875), 'A visit to Aesculapius' after E. J. Poynter (1885) and 'Lear and Cordelia' after M. Stone (1874). This last had been used in the *Works of Shakspere [sic]*, Imperial edition 1872, and 'Hotspur and Lady Percy' after Chalon and 'Benedick and Beatrice' after J. D. Watson were published in *The Royal Shakespeare* 1883–4. 'Light and darkness' after G. Smith was engraved for the Art Union of London (1871), and a scene from Goldsmith's *Good Natured Man* after W. P. Frith was being engraved for Pilgeram and Lefevre in 1872. He also published a pamphlet, *Art past and present. A few words to English artists on the state of art in this country* 1871. He exhibited at the Royal Academy from 1863 to 1885. He can perhaps be identified with an engraver of the same name engraving historical subjects in line for publishers in New York from about 1854 and much later, associated at one time with William Wellstood. AJ; St; T.

Roberts, Edward John (1797–1865) Landscape and architectural engraver. He seems to have been regarded primarily as an etcher for other engravers' plates, but he put his name to enough engravings to ensure that his work can be judged to have been quite as good in the line manner as that of any of his contemporaries. He trained under Charles Heath, probably about 1811, and by the end of his apprenticeship he was engraving such plates as 'Ford House', dated 1 November 1818, for J. P. Neale's *Views of the seats of noblemen...* 1818–24 and one for *Excursions through Sussex* 1818–22. He resided with Heath for many years, assisting in the multitudinous publications of that entrepreneur. His earliest steel plate seems to have been 'Sadak in search of the waters of oblivion' after J. Martin for *The Keepsake* 1828. Two engravings were done for T. H. Shepherd's *London and its environs* 1829–31 (signed 'J. E. Roberts'), 'Curious rocks, near Edinburgh ...' for Shepherd's *Modern Athens* 1829–31 and he did 'St. Mark's Place, Venice' after S. Prout for *Friendship's offering* 1831 and 'Christ entering Jerusalem' after Martin for the 1833 volume. Also after Prout, he did 'Hotel de Ville at Brussels', 'View in Nuremberg', 'The Porta Nigra, or Roman ruin at Treves' and 'Place of St. Antonio, Padua' for the *Continental annual* 1832. A long connection with W. H. Bartlett commenced in 1836 with 'Statue of Arnold von Winkelried...', which was done for W. Beattie's *Switzerland* 1836. It continued with a vignette, 'The Tuileries', after J. Salmon, which appeared in S. C. Hall's *Book of gems* 1838, two plates after G. F. Sargent and Capt. Irton, which appeared in C. Wordsworth's *Greece* 1839, four views, including the 'Interior of Cashel Abbey', which were done for J. S. Coyne's *Scenery and antiquities of Ireland* [c. 1840],

'Toronto' and 'Nelson's pillar, Montreal', which were done for Willis's *Canadian scenery* 1842, four vignettes, signed in the design, which were done for T. Roscoe's *Summer tour in the Isle of Wight* 1843 (one of which, 'The Bar-gate, Southampton', was used again in B. Woodward's *General history of Hampshire* 1863) and 'General view of London' and 'The light house, Aberdeen', which appeared in W. Beattie's *Ports, harbours...* 1842. 'Church of St. Pierre at Caen, Normandy' after Roberts was done for *The Keepsake* 1842. 'Porch of the cathedral at Ulm', 'Straubing' and 'Funeral vault of the Imperial Family...' after Bartlett were published in W. Beattie's *Danube* 1844 and 'The deluge' after Poussin on the engraved title page of M. Henry's *Exposition of the Old and New Testaments...* 1844. 'Basilica at Bethlehem' and 'Convent of Santa Saba' after Bartlett were done for Stebbing's *Christian in Palestine* [1847] and the artist's *Walks about ... Jerusalem* [1844] respectively, 'Wiesbaden' appeared on the engraved title page of *Continental tourist* [1838] after Radclyffe, and vignettes of Tintern Abbey and Raglan Castle after Bartlett were done for W. Beattie's *Castles and abbeys of England* 1845–51. 'Genoa' (quite a good example of his work) after Vacher was published in D. Costello's *Piedmont and Italy* [c. 1855], 'Staircase, Grand Master's House', a vignette after Bartlett, appeared in *Gleanings ... on the overland route* 1851, and a vignette, 'Walls of Lahore', after Carpenter appeared in Nolan's *Illustrated history of the British Empire in India* [1858–60]. Apart from the engraving already mentioned, 'Lyndhurst...' and 'Gateway to Basing House' after J. C. Armytage (q.v.) were issued in B. Woodward's *General history of Hampshire* 1863, together with 'Hall of St. Cross' after Bartlett, which was also used in the same author's *History and description of Winchester* 1860. His last important work, done after Birket Foster, was ten plates, including 'Heidelberg' and 'The Council-hall at Constanz', for H. Mayhew's *Upper Rhine* 1860. His earlier work on the Rhine appeared in Bulwer-Lytton's *Pilgrims of the Rhine* 1834 with designs after D. Roberts, who was no relation. He etched many of the plates published in the *Art Journal*, e.g. 'Lake of Lucerne' after Turner, engraved by Robert Wallis (q.v.) for the 1865 volume. He died on 22 March 1865, aged sixty-eight, and the series of plates engraved for the *Continental annual* and *Pilgrims of the Rhine* were sold with his works of art for the support of his family. AJ.

Roberts, F. Angelo (fl. 1832–75) Portrait and figure engraver. He worked for thirty years, from about 1832, in the studio of William Holl, acting as his assistant in company with Charles Holl (q.v.). This accounts for the few plates with his name attached to them, but among those so signed are 'Joseph made known to his brethren' after G. Jager, issued in the *Imperial Family Bible* 1873 and first published in 1844, and 'Thomas Campbell' after J. Lonsdale, 'James Montgomery' after T. H. Illidge and 'Rev. David Welsh' after G. Harvey, in R. Chambers's *Biographical dictionary of eminent Scotsmen*, 2nd edition, 1875.

Roberts, J. (fl. 1833–48) Landscape and portrait engraver. 'Margate pier and harbour' after W. H. Bartlett was issued in *Watering places...* 1833, and 'Latest portrait of Napoleon' after C. L. Eastlake appeared in the *Art Union* 1848.

Roberts, R. (fl. 1831–6) Landscape engraver. 'Pont y Prydd' after Gastineau was done for Gastineau's *Wales illustrated...* 1830, and 'Newly Bridge, Lancashire' after G. Pickering, dated 1835, was engraved for Baines's *History of ... Lancaster* 1836.

Robinson, Henry (fl. 1827–75) Portrait engraver. One of the most prolific of portrait engravers, he began his work on

steel with vignettes after H. Corbould on the title pages of the 1827 and 1828 volumes of *The Amulet*, followed by 'The snuff box', dated 1 October 1828, after F. P. Stephanoff and 'The young cottagers' after T. Gainsborough for *The Anniversary* 1829. He had done five portraits for H. Walpole's *Anecdotes of painting* 1827, and did sixty-two engravings from 1829 to 1835 for Lodge's *Portraits...*, 2nd edition, 1835. Five plates were done for Baines's *History of ... Lancaster* 1836, two of which were reissued in G. N. Wright's *Lancashire* 1842. 'The market cart' after T. Gainsborough, dated 1 September 1832, and 'The appearance of Christ to Peter' after A. Caracci, dated 1 April 1833, came out in A. Cunningham's *Cabinet gallery of paintings by the first masters...* 1836. 'The Irish hood' was used as a frontispiece to L. Ritchie's *Ireland...* 1837. One plate was used in the *Literary souvenir* 1835 and five portraits in Wilson and Chambers's *Land of Burns* 1840. Three plates were done for Fisher's *Drawing room scrap book* 1836 and two for the 1842 volume. 'Sir Walter Scott, Bart.' after Gordon was engraved for Wright's *Landscape-historical illustrations of Scotland* 1836–8 and fifteen plates for Fisher's *Historic illustrations of the Bible* [1840–3]. The engraved title page and four other plates were done for *Heath's Book of beauty* 1835, two portraits after Chalon and Landseer were done for the 1839 volume, and four appeared in the 1841 volume. Three portraits after Hayter came out in Finden's *Gallery of beauty* 1841. 'The Lady Helen' was done as the frontispiece to the 1837 volume of *The Keepsake*, and four plates after Stephanoff and Herbert came out in that for 1838. Other plates appeared in the volumes for 1839, 1840, 1842, 1843 and 1844. 'Florence' after J. W. Wright was engraved for the 1847 volume. Seven Scriptural plates appeared in the *Imperial Family Bible* 1844 (republished in 1873). Twelve of his engravings were issued in G. N. Wright's *Gallery of engravings* 1844–6, among them 'The secret discovered' after Miss Louisa Sharpe and 'Mountain solitude' after E. Corbould. 'The marriage of the Virgin' after C. Vanloo, 'The snake in the grass' after J. Reynolds, 'St. Martin dividing his cloak' after Rubens and 'The sanctuary' after E. M. Ward were engraved for S. C. Hall's *Gems of European art* 1846, and 'Victoria R' after R. Thorburn was the frontispiece to the *Art Union* 1847 and to Mrs Hall's *Drawing room table book* 1849. The engraved title page vignette and three other plates were engraved for the *Book of Common Prayer* 1854 and the frontispiece 'John Dryden' after Kneller for Dryden's *Poetical works* 1859. Seven portraits were done for Chambers's *Biographical dictionary of eminent Scotsmen*, 2nd edition, 1875, and 'Queen Elizabeth and the Duke of York' after E. M. Ward appeared in the *Works of Shakspere* [*sic*], *Imperial edition* 1872. 'A Persian prince...' and 'A Circassian lady' after D. Wilkie were published in *Wilkie gallery* [c. 1849], and in the *Art Journal*, 'Elaine' after G. Doré and 'Snake in the grass' after Reynolds were issued in the 1867 and 1872 volumes respectively. He joined the Artists' Annuity Fund in 1828, and tried out improved graver handles for the Society of Arts in 1831. He also engraved some plates for the print publishers, among them 'Bon jour messieurs' after F. Stone (1863). Some authorities identify him with John Henry Robinson (q.v.), but since several books contain plates signed 'H. and J. H.', there seems no reason to suppose that they were not different people. This view is supported also by the quality and quantity of the book work executed by this engraver, when compared with those of his near namesake.

Robinson, John Henry (1796–1871) Portrait and figure engraver. Born at Bolton in Lancashire in 1796, he spent his boyhood in Staffordshire, and in 1814 went to London to

John Henry Robinson

learn engraving as a pupil of James Heath, with whom he remained for just over two years. Setting up on his own, he engraved for the booksellers and after designs by Stothard and Westall. An example of work from this time is a vignette, 'Ode on the spring' (dated 1 February 1821), after R. Westall, issued in J. Sharpe's edition of Gray's *Poetical works* 1821. He seems to have left this kind of work soon after the arrival of steel since his work on this metal is rare after 1830. The self portrait of Rubens, 'Sir Godfrey Kneller' after Seipse and the self portrait of William Faithorne were done for H. Walpole's *Anecdotes of painting* 1827 and 'Psyche' after T. Lawrence was the frontispiece to *The Anniversary* 1829. 'A Spanish lady' after G. S. Newton was issued in the *Literary souvenir* 1827, and in the 1829 volume was issued 'The sisters' after Stephanoff, republished as 'Doretta and Isabel' in *Casquet of literature* 1874. 'Minstrel of Chamonix' after H. W. Pickersgill was issued in *The Amulet* 1830, 'Flower girl' after P. A. Gaugain was done for *Forget me not* 1830, and two vignettes (one of a dancer with tambourine and the other of a mother and five children on the seashore) after T. Stothard were engraved for S. Rogers' *Italy* 1830. The *Art Union* 1846 published 'Spanish flower girl' after Murillo, taken from an electrotype without conspicuous success, and a round picture, 'The young mother' after C. W. Cope, done in stipple and rather coarsely engraved, was issued in the *Art Journal* of 1877. Electrotypes were also used for 'The Lattice' and 'The Mask' after E. Landseer, engraved for the National Art Union (1843). He had Benjamin Phelps Gibbon as a pupil (q.v.). In 1856 he was elected as Associate Engraver of the Royal Academy against the opposition of G. T. Doo and J. T. Willmore, and in 1867 became a fellow of the Royal Academy when Doo retired. Although he became quite wealthy from his engraving (e.g. he earned £840 for engraving W. Mulready's 'Wolf and the lamb' for the Artists' Annuity Fund (1824–8)), he married a lady of property late in life, which made him financially independent and enabled him to retire to Petworth in Sussex, where he lived for a long time, and where he became a Justice of the Peace. He was a signatory to the 1837 petition. He first exhibited at the Society of British Artists, in 1824, exhibiting on that occasion six engravings, and continued to exhibit until 1864, at the Royal Academy and elsewhere. He gained a first-class medal in gold at the 1855 Paris International Exhibition, and worked intermittently at Petworth on one of his best plates, a portrait of Anne, countess of Bedford, after Van Dyck, which was exhibited at the Royal Academy in 1861 and 1864. He was also an honorary member of the Imperial Academy of Fine Arts at St Petersburg. He died at New Grove, Petworth, on 21 October 1871, aged seventy-five. Between 1850 and 1855 he engraved the vignette of Britannia which appeared on Bank of England notes from that time for at least a hundred years after a design by D. Maclise, and for the engraving of which Robinson was paid £100. AJ; B; *Illus. Lond. News*, 3 Aug. 1867, p. 116; Ma.

Rock & Co, of 11 Walbrook, London (fl. 1835–1873) The firm was founded in 1835 by William Frederick Rock and produced a series of topographical plates covering much of the country. Fifteen plates are known in F. Lankester's *Nineteen views of Bury St. Edmunds* 1854. Ad; Ho.

Roe (fl. 1838) Landscape engraver. 'View near Liege' after Fussell appeared in *Continental tourist* [1838].

Roffe, A. (fl. 1830–55) Portrait engraver. 'Edmund Burke' and 'Richard Sheridan' after J. Reynolds, 'Mrs. Fitzherbert' after R. Cosnay and 'Charlotte' were engraved for R. Huish's *Memoirs of George the fourth* 1830–2, and a plate of a medallion, 'The rescue' after W. Wyon, appeared in the *Art Journal* 1855 (Plate 46). He is almost certainly one of the family Roffe who were artists and engravers in the nineteenth century.

Roffe, Edwin (fl. 1852–77) Sculpture engraver. All his known work (nineteen plates) was executed for, or appeared in, the *Art Journal*: beginning with four plates that appeared in the volume for 1852, one appeared in that for 1853, two in that for 1855 and three in that for 1856; 'Fruit-gatherer' after E. Woolf and 'Huntress' after R. Wyatt were done for the 1857 volume; and in 1864, 1865 and 1875 one plate appeared in each volume, and in 1873 and 1877 two in each. From the 1865 volume, the originals were mainly high or low reliefs.

Roffe, John (1769–1850) Architectural engraver. He was the son of Joseph Roffe, schoolmaster, elder brother to Richard Roffe (q.v.) and was apprenticed to James Basire I on 1 February 1785. Most of his important work was done before the coming of steel, and was, therefore, on copper. He was in his late fifties when the new metal was introduced, and two of his plates probably on steel were 'Micklegate Bar, York' and 'New Bailey Bridge, Manchester' after W. Westall, published in T. Moule's *Great Britain illustrated . . .* 1830. He died at Upper Holloway on 14 December 1850, aged eighty-one. R.

Roffe, Richard (c. 1780–?) Landscape and portrait engraver. He was the son of Joseph Roffe, schoolmaster, younger brother of John Roffe (q.v.) and was apprenticed to James Basire I on 6 October 1795. 'Rt. Hon. George Canning MP' was engraved as the frontispiece to volume 4 of *Mirror of literature . . .* 1824. 'Chatham Dockyard from Fort Pitt' and 'Frognal, Kent' after G. Shepherd, dated 1 November 1828 and 1835 respectively, were published in S. W. H. Ireland's *England's topographer* (commenced publication 1828).

Roffe, William (fl. 1848–84) Sculpture and portrait engraver. His book illustrations included a vignette, 'Right Hon. Viscount Canning', after a photograph by Mayall, engraved as the frontispiece to volume 2 of Nolan's *Illustrated history of the British Empire in India* [1858–60], and two frontispieces, engraved in conjunction with J. J. Crew (q.v.), which are portraits from photographs of Dickens, Longfellow and Bulwer in the one, and Tennyson, Carlyle and Hawthorne in the other, to the 1874 and 1880 editions of *Casquet of literature*. A portrait, 'Bishop Milner', appeared in B.

Woodward's *History and description of Winchester* 1860 and again in the same author's *General history of Hampshire* 1863. His most important series of plates was the seventy-six he engraved for, or which appeared in, the *Art Journal* of sculpture beween 1848 and 1884. The series commenced in the 1848 volume, with 'Psyche' after Westmacott (drawn by H. Corbould), a stipple engraving, which was the main form used throughout, followed in the same year by four plates of various members of the Royal Family representing the four seasons, e.g. 'Winter—Prince of Wales', all after M. Thorneycroft and drawn by E. Corbould. 'Cupid and Psyche' after J. Gibson, 'Sunshine' after J. Durham and 'First cradle' after A. H. Debay appeared in the 1856 volume. He also engraved four pictures for the *Art Journal*, namely, 'The Surprise' after E. Dubufe (1854), 'Hagar and Ishmael' after C. Bauerle (1881), 'The mouse' after J. Reynolds (1883) and 'Song of the Nubian slave' after F. Goodall (1884).

Rogers, John (c. 1808–c. 1888) Landscape, portrait and figure engraver. A prolific and versatile engraver, most of his work was done in this country before 1850. His busiest time was between about 1829 and 1831, when he engraved twenty-three plates for S. W. H. Ireland's *England's topographer* (commenced publication 1828) (including 'St. Clement's Church, Sandwich', after H. Gastineau, 'Feversham, Kent' after Bartlett and 'Greenwich Hospital, Kent' after Campion), twenty-seven engravings after N. Whittock, J. Fletcher and H. Gastineau for T. Allen's *History … of Surrey and Sussex* 1829–31 (including 'Box Hill, Surrey', 'Arundel Castle' and 'Beachy Head') and three plates after T. H. Shepherd for the artist's *London and its environs* 1829–31. Fourteen plates after Allom, Bartlett, Rhodes and Salmon were done for Allen's *History of the county of Lincoln* [1830–1], and seventy-three, mostly after Whittock, for the same author's *New … history of the county of York* 1828–31. Six plates after Allom and Harwood were engraved for Pyne's *Lancashire illustrated…* 1831 and two of Swansea after the author's designs for Gastineau's *Wales illustrated…* 1830. He then engraved frontispieces for a series of literary and classical texts, e.g. of Julius Caesar for Caesar's *Commentaries* 1832, and in 1833 engraved thirteen plates after W. H. Bartlett, W. Daniell, D. Cox, M. Kavanagh, H. Gastineau and T. S. Robins for *Watering places…*, most of which were republished in *Fashionable guide…* [c. 1838], and included 'Rottingdean, Sussex' (after a picture also engraved by J. C. Allen (q.v.)), 'West Cowes, Isle of Wight' and 'Swanage, Dorsetshire'. Seventeen plates after Bartlett and Campion were engraved for Wright's *Picturesque beauties of Great Britain…: Essex* 1834, and 'The cloisters, Fountains Abbey' after Whittock appeared in Fisher's *Drawing room scrap book* 1835. 'Winter scene on the Catterskills' was engraved after Bartlett for N. P. willis's *American scenery* 1840 and after the same artist, 'The Menai Bridge…' for W. Beattie's *Ports, harbours…* 1842. A portrait of the author after Henry Room was engraved for William Beattie's *Waldenses* 1838, and appeared also in Beattie's *Danube* 1844 and in his *Castles and abbeys of England* 1845–51. Twenty-nine engravings after J. M. Wright, with one each contributed by A. Cooper and H. Melville, appeared in various editions of the *Complete works of Robert Burns*, notably, that of c. 1842. They are scenes from the poetry in the main, e.g., 'The cotter's Saturday night', 'Tam O Shanter', 'Highland Mary', 'The country lassie' and 'Duncan Gray', but also include portraits of two members of the Burns family. His engravings of Scriptural subjects abound in the Bibles of the time, one such series being decorated with frames in line around each central picture.

'Christ in the garden of Gethsemane' after Dolci and 'Christ and the woman of Samaria' after Hamilton appeared in *A New family Bible* [c. 1840]. Fifteen historical plates after well-known artists were done for Hume and Smollett's *History of England…* [c. 1847], edited by Gaspey. Portraits after Vertue and historical scenes after West (seventeen in all) were engraved for another edition of their *History of England…* 1854–5, and forty-three plates, mainly after the Old Masters, appeared in Fleetwood's *Life of Our Lord…* [c. 1855]. 'The Nativity' after Rubens, like the other engravings in this volume, was probably not engraved for it, but the addition of a frame engraved in outline, depicting supporting events, is characteristic of work of the second half of the nineteenth century, especially by the publisher John Tallis (Plate 51). Some of these were among the sixteen plates in *The New Testament* [c. 1860]. 'The fair Venetian', a vignette, appeared on the engraved title page of volume 1 of *Casquet of literature* 1874. A series of six portraits was engraved for Chambers's *Biographical dictionary of eminent Scotsmen*, 2nd edition, 1875, including 'William Drummond' after Jansen, which had also appeared in the first edition (1835).

He emigrated to the United States in 1851, accompanied by Charles Westwood (q.v.), and engraved portrait and subject plates for the book publishers in New York, where he was considered to be a good engraver. He died in New York about 1888, aged about eighty.   St.

Rolls, Charles (c. 1800–57) Figure engraver. In 1818, the Society of Arts awarded its Silver medal to C. Rolls of Bayham Street, Camden Town, for an outline drawing of the Farnese Hercules. In addition to being an engraver for book illustrations, he was also a painter of still life. Among his earliest steel plates was 'Lover's quarrel' after G. S. Newton, the frontispiece to the *Literary souvenir* 1826, and he engraved further plates for the 1828, 1829, 1830, 1832 and 1833 volumes. For *The Keepsake* he engraved 'Hebrew melody' after R. Westall (1828), 'Anne Page and Slender' after H. Richter (1829), 'The widow of Ems' after De Veria (1830), 'The use of tears' after R. P. Bonington (1831) and 'Alice' after H. Corbould, 'Pepita' after G. Cattermole and 'Jeanie in the outlaw's hut' after H. Richter (1833), and other plates were done for the 1832, 1834–7, 1840–2 and 1844 volumes. 'The accepted' after Sharp was engraved for *Friendship's offering* 1831 and 'Trysting time' after Hill for the 1837 volume. For *The Amulet* he engraved 'Blachavas' after R. Westall (1827), 'The morning walk' after T. Lawrence and 'The shepherd boy' after H. W. Pickersgill (1828), 'The orphans' after J. Wood (1831) etc., and for *The Anniversary* 1829, he did 'The lute' after R. P. Bonington, 'The (lost) ear rings' after M. A. Shee and 'Picapack' after R. Westall. A vignette of the Brides of Venice after T. Stothard was his contribution to Rogers' *Italy* 1830. An oval engraving, 'La belle Pucell', after J. Inskipp and 'Prayer to the Virgin' after Penry Williams were done for S. C. Hall's *Book of gems* 1836, and for the 1838 volume of the same work, he did a vignette, 'Allegorical', after F. W. Topham (q.v.), 'The poet Wordsworth' after H. W. Pickersgill, 'Scott in Melrose Abbey' after S. Hart, 'The fisherman's return' after C. Stanfield and 'Maternal affection' after R. Edmonstone. 'The pirate' after J. Inskipp, 'Fortunes of Nigel' after A. Cooper and 'The talisman' after Watson Gordon were done for Scott's *Waverley novels*, and 'The Peri's second pilgrimage' after E. Corbould and 'Nourmahal asleep' after F. P. Stephanoff were engraved for Moore's *Lalla Rookh* 1838. 'Taming the shrew', dated 1 January 1838, and 'Sir Roger de Coverley and the gipsies', dated 2 March 1830, both after C. R. Leslie, were

78

published in Finden's *Royal Gallery of British Art* 1838–49, and 'La belle Hamilton' after P. Lely and 'The poison cup' after J. R. Herbert were done for S. C. Hall's *Gems of European art* 1846. Six plates were engraved after G. Cattermole: 'Arrest of Strafford' and 'Seizure of the King at Holdenby' for R. Cattermole's *Great Civil War* 1846; and 'The sleeping captive' and three vignettes—'The tournament', 'The poet's bride' and 'Zoe at her balcony'—for Calabrella's *Evenings at Haddon Hall* 1845. 'The love letter' after H. Richter was issued in G. N. Wright's *Gallery of engravings* 1844–6. The *Art Journal* carried 'Rebekah at the well' after W. Hilton and 'Wayside in Italy' after P. Williams (1851), 'Tambourine', also after Williams, (1852) and 'The play-scene—Hamlet' after D. Maclise (1854), which was later issued again in the *Works of Shakspere* [sic], *Imperial edition* 1872. 'The Brigand's cave' after Uwins and 'The shrine' after Williams were published in *Casquet of literature* 1874.

He turned to work for the print publishers and Art Unions in the 1840s. 'Calabrian minstrels' after Wilkie was published by Ackermann in 1844 and 'Moment of victory' after A. Fraser was engraved for the Association for the promotion of the Fine Arts in Scotland (1841). He did twenty-one designs after H. C. Selous in outline to Bunyan's *Pilgrim's progress* (originally engraved by Henry Moses for the Art Union of London in 1844), and for the same body he engraved 'The last embrace' after T. Uwins, which appeared in 1847, and by some is considered to be one of his best works. Some fruit and flower pictures were exhibited at the British Institution between 1855 and 1857. He joined the Artists' Annuity Fund in 1822, and had as pupils Lumb Stocks (q.v.), from 1827 to 1833, and William Turner Davey (1818–?).   AU; S; SocA.

Rolls, Henry (fl. 1831–45) Figure engraver. Most of the works in which his engravings appear are those with which Charles Rolls was associated, and it is reasonable to assume that he was a younger brother of, and perhaps pupil and assistant to, Charles. 'Wetherby Bridge' after Gastineau was engraved for Allen's *New ... history of the county of York* 1828–31 and 'Je Suissesse' after Colin for *Keepsake français* 1831. This latter was issued again as 'The Swiss peasant' in *Wreath of friendship*. For *Friendship's offering* 1831 he engraved 'Auld Robin Gray' after Wood, for the 1837 volume 'The bridal morn' after Jenkins, and for the 1839 volume 'The maid of Padua' after Jenkins. 'Medora' after Pickersgill was engraved for the *Literary souvenir* 1828, and for further volumes were done 'The agreeable surprise' after Green (1829), 'The sisters of Scio' after Philipson (1830) and 'The canzonet' after Howard (1831). 'The corsair's bride' after J. Hollis appeared in *The Amulet* 1831, 'The gipsies' tent' after T. S. Cooper in S. C. Hall's *Book of gems* 1838 and 'Azim and Zelica' after E. Corbould in Moore's *Lalla Rookh* 1838. 'Death of the Earl of Lindsey' after G. Cattermole was done for R. Cattermole's *Great Civil War* 1846, ' "Lay not thine hand..." ' after Copley for Fisher's *Historic illustrations of the Bible* [1840–3], a vignette, 'The astrologer', after G. Cattermole for Calabrella's *Evenings at Haddon Hall* 1845 and 'A legend of Montrose' after R. Lauder for Scott's *Waverley novels*. 'The Greek mother' after H. Corbould appeared in *Casquet of literature* 1874. He joined the Artists' Annuity Fund in 1828.

Rolls, Joseph (fl. 1832–8) Figure engraver. He engraved 'The Holy Family with the adoration of the shepherds' after Titian for *The National Gallery* 1832 (Plate 16). 'Charles I taking leave of his family' after F. P. Stephanoff, was published in S. C. Hall's *Book of gems* 1838.

Rolph, John (fl. 1828–38) Landscape and architectural engraver. He may perhaps be identified with J. A. Rolph, who

engraved plates for J. P. Neale's *Views of the seats of noblemen* ... 1818–24, and for *Excursions through Sussex* 1818–22, who emigrated to the United States and was thought to be working in New York between 1834 and 1846 (and probably later), and who was connected with James Smillie and others. He is identified as having been born in England in 1799 and as having died in Brooklyn, New York, in 1862. All the steel plates seen in English books, however, are merely signed 'J. Rolph' or 'John Rolph', indicating that there is some doubt in identifying the engraver of these with J. A. Rolph. 'Canterbury cathedral...' and 'Rocks at Tunbridge Wells...' after G. Shepherd, dated 1 November 1828, appeared in S. W. H. Ireland's *England's topographer* (commenced publication 1828), and 'Haberdasher's alms houses, Hoxton' and 'Theatre Royal, Covent Garden' after T. H. Shepherd, dated 1828, came out in J. Elmes's *Metropolitan improvements* 1829. 'Part of the New Town, from Ramsay Gardens' was engraved for Shepherd's *Modern Athens* 1829–31. 'Pentillie Castle, Cornwall' and 'Cotele House, Cornwall' were engraved after Allom for J. Britton and E. W. Brayley's *Devonshire and Cornwall illustrated* 1832. Two plates after W. Tombleson (q.v.) were 'Cookham, Berks' for Fearnside's *Tombleson's Thames* 1834 and 'Breisach' for Fearnside's *Picturesque beauties of the Rhine* [c. 1846]. 'Akbar's Tomb—Secundra' after W. Purser was issued in Elliot's *Views in India* ... 1835. 'Thaxted...' and 'Saffron Walden church...' after Bartlett were engraved for Wright's *Picturesque beauties of Great Britain ...: Essex* 1834.   Fi; M.

Romney, John (1786–1863) Figure engraver. Associated with many of the important works of his day, his earliest excursion into steel was probably 'The school boy' after J. Farrier for *The Amulet* 1827, and for the 1828 volume of the same annual, he did 'The mouse-trap' after J. Ward. 'Auld Robin Gray' after Farrier was engraved for the *Literary souvenir* 1827, and for the 1828 volume he did 'The declaration' after Farrier and 'The stolen kiss' after Allan. 'Hudibras and Ralpho in the stocks', 'Hudibras leading Crowdero in triumph', 'Hudibras; the burning of the rumps', 'Four stages in cruelty; cruelty in perfection' and '...; reward of cruelty' after W. Hogarth were done for the artist's *Works* 1833, and for Scott's *Waverley novels* he engraved 'The antiquary' after F. P. Stephanoff. 'The orphan ballad singers' after W. Gill, probably his best-known work, appeared in Fisher's *Drawing room scrap book* 1835 and was reissued later in G. N. Wright's *Gallery of engravings* 1844–6. He published *Views of ancient buildings in Chester* 1851. He joined the Artists' Annuity Fund in 1813, and signed the 1837 petition. He died in Chester on 1 February 1863, aged seventy-seven.   DNB; R.

Rowe, H. (fl. 1846) Landscape engraver. 'Rodolphsyell' after Tombleson was published in Fearnside's *Picturesque beauties of the Rhine* [c. 1846].

Ruskin, John (1819–1900) Author, etc. Although he employed a number of engravers (notably, J. C. Armytage (q.v.)) to illustrate his *Modern painters* 1856–60, Ruskin etched nine plates for it himself, six after his own designs and three after J. M. W. Turner. Perhaps his most striking contribution was to volume 3 with 'Shores of Wharfe' after Turner, an outline etching divided diagonally top right to bottom left, the upper half printed in black and the lower in violet.

Russell, S. (fl. 1840) Landscape engraver. 'A Winter night' after J. M. Wright was published in the *Complete works of Robert Burns* [c. 1840]. 'Elijah raising the widow's son' after

Rembrandt and 'Christ bearing his cross' were published in *A New family Bible* [c. 1840].

Ryall, Henry Thomas (1811–67) Portrait and figure engraver. Born at Frome in Somerset in August 1811, he became a pupil of Samuel W. Reynolds, the mezzotint engraver. Although Ryall worked in mezzotint, much of his work was done in either line or stipple or a mixed style, adding mezzotint as well. He is said to have been the leading exponent in this field of his day. He worked largely for the print publishers, and became a very fashionable engraver, obtaining by his plates of members of the Royal Family the honorary title of Portrait and Historical engraver to the Queen. In January 1842 he was advertising a vacancy 'for a gentlemanly and well educated Youth' from his address at 1 Robert Street, Adelphi, and it can be speculated that H. B. Hall (q.v.) was appointed, since he assisted Ryall with engraving the portraits for the massive engraving of Sir John Hayter's 'Coronation of . . . Victoria', published in December 1842. For this plate he received a gold box from the French king, Louis-Philippe. He began his career with book illustrations, however, and those done on steel and in line for E. Lodge's *Portraits. . .*, 2nd edition, 1835 were engraved between April 1830 and December 1835. There were thirty-one altogether, after Old and Modern Masters, including 'Sir Thomas More' after Holbein, 'Lucy Harington' after Honthorst, 'Princess Charlotte of Wales' after Chalon and 'William Fielding' after Van Dyck, which last is an interesting example of a sky produced in stipple as opposed to the more familiar ruled parallel lines. 'Margarita Cogni' after G. Harlowe, 'Countess Guiccioli' after W. Brockedon and 'Rt. Hon. Sarah Sophia Fane, Countess of Jersey' after E. T. Parris were executed for *Finden's illustrations of the life and works of Lord Byron* 1833–4, four portraits after Bostock, Hayter, Landseer and Parris for *Heath's Book of beauty* 1835 and 'Fashion's idol' after Bostock for *The Keepsake* 1836. 'Robert Burns' after Naismith and 'Lucy Johnstone' after Sir Henry Raeburn appeared in Wilson and Chambers's *Land of Burns* 1840, and 'Selim and Zuleika' after H. Andrews and 'Marguerite, Countess of Blessington' after A. E. Chalon were issued in G. N. Wright's *Gallery of engravings* 1844–6. He also contributed to H. T. Ryall's *Eminent Conservative statesmen* 1836–8. He engraved the first print published by the Royal Irish Art Union, 'The blind girl at the Holy Well' after F. W. Burton (1841), and 'Spring in the Valley' after A. Penley for the West of England Art Union (1843). He occasionally painted in oils, particularly as the engraved book market dried up, and exhibited at the Society of British Artists in 1846 and at the Royal Academy in 1852 and 1859. He died at his residence at Cookham in Berkshire on 14 September 1867, aged fifty-six.   AJ; B; Br; DNB; T.

S

S., J., and Co. (fl. 1850–70) Trade engravers. A number of small vignettes of Brighton are known engraved by J. S. and Co. with stock numbers attached, issued between about 1850 and 1870.

Saddler, John (1813–1892) Landscape and architectural engraver. Born on 14 August 1813, he became a pupil of George Cooke, thus coming into contact with Turner's work. In one of its rare flashes of humour the *Dictionary of National Biography* relates an anecdote of Saddler taking a proof of a plate in which he had had a considerable hand for Turner's approval. In answer to an enquiry as to who had engraved the plate, Saddler credited his master with it, but the artist's eagle eye discerned otherwise, and he admonished the young man saying 'Go and tell your master he is bringing you on very nicely, especially in lying'. His earliest independent work on steel for books appeared in T. Noble and T. Rose's *Counties of Chester. . .* 1836 and comprised six plates after T. Allom, namely, 'Chatsworth, Derbyshire', 'Rooter or Root-Tor Rock, Derbyshire', 'Welbeck Abbey, Nottinghamshire', 'Nottingham Park' (a good example of his work), 'Rufford Hall, Nottinghamshire' and 'Newark Castle, Nottinghamshire'. For *Health's Versailles* [c. 1836], he engraved 'Versailles from the heights of Satory' after W. Callow, which was reissued in *Keepsake français* 1840. 'Plains of Payass—or Issus' after W. H. Bartlett, dated 1838, appeared in J. Carne's *Syria* 1836–8, and in 1840 he did at least eight plates for R. W. Billings's *Architectural illustrations of Carlisle cathedral* and two plates of the screen of St Catherine's Chapel in Carlisle Cathedral for the same author's *Illustrations of geometric tracery. . .* 1842. 'Padua' after Deroy (another good example of his work) and 'Bologna' (which was etched very sparingly) appeared in D. Costello's *Piedmont and Italy* [c. 1855]. Then followed a period when he worked with Thomas Landseer doing plates after Edwin Landseer. But he took a new lease of life in the 1860s, engraving 'Winchester cathedral (the nave looking east)' and a vignette, 'Winchester College (from the Warden's Garden)', after J. C. Armytage (q.v.) for B. Woodward's *History and description of Winchester* 1860. These two plates were used again, together with 'Winchester cathedral from N.W.' and 'Abbey Church, Romsey' after J. C. Armytage and 'Beaulieu Abbey' after W. H. Bartlett (all vignettes) and 'The oratory, Christchurch' after Nash, in Woodward's *General history of Hampshire* 1863. 'Rivaulx Abbey' and 'Hull' after H. Warren appeared in T. Baines's *Yorkshire past and present* 1871–7, 'Yniol shows Prince Geraint his ruined castle' after Gustave Doré was engraved for *The Story of Enid and Geraint* [1869], and eight plates after Skinner Prout and J. C. Armytage were done for Booth's *Australia* [1873–6]. 'The Thames from Richmond Hill', 'St. Michael's Mount, Cornwall' (also published in the *Art Journal* 1876), 'Old houses, Strasburg' and 'Hospenthal' after Birket Foster and 'Temple of Minerva, Sunium' after W. Simpson were issued in *Picturesque Europe* 1876–9. He retained his skill well in his sixties as shown by his work for the *Art Journal*. This began in 1868 with 'Sunset—St. Helliers, Jersey' after A. Clint, and continued with 'Christening party' after A. Bellows ('Crisp and brilliant') (1872), 'Homeless' after G. Doré (1875), 'Sunset—Sussex' after G. Cole (a good example) and 'Alms giving' after G. Doré (largely etched) (1877), 'Kentish hop gardens' after C. G. Lawson (1880) and another good engraving, 'Waning of the year' after the American artist Ernest Parton (1883). He exhibited engravings regularly at the Royal Academy and elsewhere between 1862 and 1883. When he died, he left unfinished an engraving of John Walter of *The Times* which had been started by F. Holl (q.v.) and was eventually completed by Hubert Herkomer. He was treasurer of the Artists' Annuity Fund for some years. In 1882 he left London to live at Wokingham in Berkshire, where he committed suicide by hanging, while the balance of his mind was disturbed, on 29 March 1892, aged seventy-eight   AJ; Br; DNB.

Salmon, S. (fl. 1834) Architectural engraver. 'The church of St. Ouen' after R. P. Bonington, dated November 1834, was published in the *Literary souvenir* 1835.

Sandon, J. (fl. 1828–31) Architectural engraver. 'Middleham Castle' after Gastineau was engraved for Allen's *New ... history of the county of York* 1828–31.

Sands Landscape engraver. There are a number of plates simply signed 'Sands', mostly connected with Tombleson's publications, which are probably but not certainly ascribable to Robert. They include 'Henley, Oxon' and 'Dorney Church, Bucks' from Fearnside's *Tombleson's Thames* 1834, 'Neuberg' and 'Katzenstein' after Allom from *Views in the Tyrol* [1836], 'Bregenz, Lake Constance' from Fearnside's *Picturesque beauties of the Rhine* [c. 1846] and 'Origin of the fore Rhine from Lake Toma' from Fearnside's *Tombleson's Upper Rhine* [c. 1835]. 'Netley Abbey from the Southampton Waters', dated 9 July 1841, was published in T. Roscoe's *Summer tour in the Isle of Wight* 1843.

Sands, E. (fl. 1840) Landscape engraver. 'Mossgiel' after D. O. Hill was published in Wilson and Chambers's *Land of Burns* 1840.

Sands, H. (fl. 1834) Architectural engraver. 'Garrick's villa at Hampton' after W. Tombleson (q.v.) was published in Fearnside's *Tombleson's Thames* 1834.

Sands, James (fl. 1832–44) Landscape engraver. His earliest work of importance was done after Thomas Allom, after whom he did a total of twenty-eight plates for the volumes on *Cumberland, Durham and Northumberland* and *Westmorland* by Thomas Rose first published in 1832. Of the seven plates in the first, 'Carlisle Cathedral...' and 'Gilsland Spa...' are examples, and in the second 'Darlington, from the road to Yarm', 'Royal Arcade, Newcastle', 'Morpeth, market place' and 'Lumley Castle, Durham' represent his work, out of the sixteen plates he did. The five plates from the third book include 'Mardale Green, Westmorland', and 'Patterdale Bridge...'. *Watering places...* 1833 contained 'Brunswick Sq. and Terrace, Brighton' after W. H. Bartlett, republished in *Fashionable guide...* [c. 1838]. Six plates, dated between 1832 and 1834, were published in E. Baines's *History of ... Lancaster* 1836 and comprised two plates of Roman antiquities, two of panel sculpture and 'Winwick Church' (all after T. Allom and the last being issued again in Wright's *Lancashire* 1842) and 'Liverpool from Toxteth Park' after G. Pickering. 'Belvoir Castle from the dairy', 'Haddon Hall, Derbyshire' and 'Belvoir Castle, Leicestershire' were published in T. Noble and T. Rose's *Counties of Chester...* 1836 (the last was reissued in Wright's *Gallery of engravings* 1844–6). 'Destruction of Doubting Castle' after Melville appeared in Bunyan's *Pilgrim's progress* 1836, 'Braes of Balquhidder' after Melville and 'Ordeal of touching the body' after Franklin in Wright's *Landscape-historical illustrations of Scotland* 1836–8, 'Val Angrogna' after Brockedon in Beattie's *Waldenses* 1838 and 'Jangheera, or the Fakeer's Rock, on the Ganges' after Stanfield and 'Entrance to the Keree Pass' after Bentley in White's *Views in India...* 1838. 'Six detached pillars of the great temple at Balbec', 'Cave of the school of the prophets' (almost entirely etched) and 'Scene and Khan on the Liettani River...' after W. H. Bartlett were engraved for J. Carne's *Syria* 1836–8. Ten plates after Allom and W. L. Leitch appeared in R. Walsh's *Constantinople* 1838–40, and included 'New palace of Sultan Mahmoud the 2nd' and 'The princes islands...', both good examples after Allom. 'The cathedral' after D. Roberts was published in S. C. Hall's *Book of gems* 1838. 'Yale College (Newhaven)', 'Ballston Springs' and 'View of the Passaic Falls' after W. H. Bartlett were done for N. P. Willis's *American scenery* 1840, 'Timber slide & bridge on the Ottawa' after Bartlett for the same author's *Canadian scenery* 1842 and 'Hagar in the desert' after Mola

for Fisher's *Historic illustrations of the Bible* [1840–3]. 'The quay, Yarmouth' after Bartlett was issued in Beattie's *Ports, harbours...* 1842. Eight plates after Allom appeared in G. N. Wright's *China* 1843, and included 'The Great Wall of China', 'The Tungting Shan' and 'Mouth of the river Chin-kiang'. Two plates after Bartlett and Allom respectively appeared in J. Kitto's *Gallery of scripture engravings* 1846–9. 'Death of Bishop Heber' after Melville and 'Basle on the Rhine, Switzerland' after S. Prout were issued in Wright's *Gallery of engravings* 1844–6. Sands joined the Artists' Annuity Fund in 1835. According to Benezit, he was also an architect, which accounts perhaps for the predominance of engravings after Allom, also an architect. B; T.

Sands, John (fl. 1855) Landscape engraver. 'View of the Chigi Palace, Lariccia', which was published in Costello's *Piedmont and Italy* [c. 1855], is clearly signed 'John Sands', and is after W. Westall from a sketch by Col. Cockburn. No other engraving has been found with this name, and it may be that the forename is a writing engraver's mistake for 'James'.

Sands, Robert (1782–1855) Landscape engraver. He was the son of James Sands, tailor, and was apprenticed to James Basire II on 2 April 1799. He is believed to have been an older brother of James Sands (q.v.), with whom he probably collaborated, since they appear to have worked upon the same books in many cases. His name first appears on some plates in J. P. Neale's *Views of the seats of noblemen...* 1818–24, but his work on steel began with six plates after T. Allom for T. Rose's *Cumberland* 1832, including 'Carlisle', 'Cockermouth' and 'Buttermere...', followed by 'Hexham from the west...' and 'Bywell on the Tyne' after Allom for Rose's *Durham and Northumberland* 1832. Three plates after Bartlett were engraved for Wright's *Picturesque beauties of Great Britain...: Essex* 1834, 'Island near Henley, Berks' after W. Tombleson was engraved for Fearnside's *Tombleson's Thames* 1834, 'Nottingham Castle' and 'Mortimer's Hole, Nottingham Castle' after Allom appeared in T. Noble and T. Rose's *Counties of Chester...* 1836 and eight plates, each dated between 1832–5, were done for E. Baines's *History of ... Lancaster* 1836. One plate, 'Chapter House, Furness Abbey' after Allom, was issued again in Fisher's *Drawing room scrap book* 1835, in G. N. Wright's *Lancashire* 1842 and in the same author's *Gallery of engravings* 1844–6. Four plates after Purser and Prout were engraved for Elliot's *Views in India...* 1835 and 'Loch Lomond' after Melville for Wright's *Landscape-historical illustrations of Scotland* 1836–8. 'Ruins of Balbec', 'The river Barrada...' and 'Exterior of the Great temple Balbec' after Bartlett were done for J. Carne's *Syria* 1836–8 and seven plates, six after Allom and one after Bartlett, appeared in W. Beattie's *Scotland illustrated* 1838, including 'Hawthornden...' and 'Corsregal Abbey near Maybole...'. 'Tophana—entrance to Pera' after Allom appeared in R. Walsh's *Constantinople* 1838–40, 'Fountain and Mosque of Chahzade' after Bartlett in J. Pardoe's *Beauties of the Bosphorus* 1840 and 'Sanquhar with Crichton Peel' after D. O. Hill in Wilson and Chambers's *Land of Burns* 1840. 'View from Fort Putnam', 'Rail-road scene, Little Falls...', 'Pulpit Rock...' and 'Northampton (Massachusetts)' after Bartlett were engraved for N. P. Willis's *American scenery* 1840, and, after the same artist, 'The port of London' was done for W. Beattie's *Ports, harbours...* 1842. Three plates after Bartlett were done for Willis's *Canadian scenery* 1842 and five plates after Allom for Wright's *China* 1843. He joined the Artists' Annuity Fund in 1812. There is also a Robert Sands junior, an engraver, who joined the Fund in 1835. Robert senior seems to have also engraved portraits. B; T.

Sangar (fl. 1860) Figure engraver. 'Going to market' after Ames appeared in *The Cottage girl...* [c. 1860].

Sangster, Samuel (1804–72) Figure engraver. He was a pupil of William Finden, and probably much of his early engraving is hidden in the work of the studio. His earliest independent steel plate, dated 1 October 1828, was 'Beatrice' after H. Howard, published in *The Anniversary* 1829, and a good example of his work. 'Don Quichotte' after Bonnington (*sic*) and an engraved title page vignette after Colin appeared in *Keepsake français* 1831. For *The Amulet* he did 'Death of Eucles' after B. R. Haydon, 'The lute' after H. Liverseege, 'The fiesta of Madonna dei Fiori' after T. Uwins and 'No song, no supper' after Kenny Meadows for the 1832 and subsequent volumes. For the *Literary souvenir* he engraved 'The Deveria family' after Deveria (1832), 'Children in prayer' after Uwins (1833), 'Innocence' after Greuze (1834) and 'The billet-doux' after Newton (1835). 'Sleeping beauty' (an octagonal picture) after W. Meadows and 'Child and flowers' after R. Rothwell were published in S. C. Hall's *Book of gems* 1838, and 'Neapolitan peasants' after T. Uwins, dated 1 November 1838, was engraved for Finden's *Royal Gallery of British Art* 1838–49. This latter plate was regarded as one of his best. Two oval pictures were engraved after T. Stothard for editions of Bunyan's *Pilgrim's progress*, i.e., 'The pilgrims overtaken by Evangelist' and 'The pilgrims passing through the Valley of the shadow of Death', and 'Thankful children' after T. Uwins appeared in *Casquet of literature* 1874. Seven plates were engraved for the *Art Journal* between 1847 and 1857, commencing with 'The fair student' after G. S. Newton (1847), printed from electrotypes of the original plate, which had been published some time before; there followed 'Syrian maid' after H. W. Pickersgill (1850), 'The victim' after A. L. Egg (1851), 'Juliet and the nurse' after H. Briggs (1852) (also used in the *Works of Shakspere* [*sic*], *Imperial edition* 1872), 'The sepulchre' after W. Etty (coarsely engraved and etched) (1853), 'First love' after J. J. Jenkins (q.v.) (with a curved top) (1855) and 'Scene from "Midas"' after D. Maclise (1857). He engraved R. Rothwell's 'The noviciate mendicants' and Martin Shee's 'Belisarius' for the Royal Irish Art Union in 1842 and 1844 respectively. He also painted in oils. He probably retired from engraving in the 1860s and died at 83 New Kent Road on 24 June 1872, aged sixty-eight. AJ; Br; DNB.

Saunders, J. (fl. 1832–38) Landscape and architectural engraver. 'Valley of Engeholle and ruins of Schonberg' after W. Tombleson appeared in Fearnside's *Tombleson's views of the Rhine* 1832 and in *Continental tourist* [1838], and 'Ruins at Burkheim', also after Tombleson, was published in Fearnside's *Tombleson's Upper Rhine* [c. 1835].

Schmollinger, W. (fl. 1832) Map engraver. He did five plans after the author's designs for Gell's *Pompeiana...* 1832.

Scott, P. (fl. 1849) Architectural engraver probably of Scottish origin. 'The Scott monument', a vignette after G. M. Kemp, was published in *Black's picturesque tourist of Scotland* 1849.

Scott, R. (fl. 1845–74) Figure and heraldic engraver of Edinburgh. Four plates of armorial bearings after Mac-Coinich appeared in volume 4 of Browne's *History of the Highlands* [c. 1845]. 'Altars &c. of the Temple...' (signed 'R. Scott Edin.') was issued in *The Self-interpreting Bible* 1864 and 'The sailor's children' after Beaume in *Casquet of literature* 1874. There is a possible connection with the Edinburgh engraver Robert Scott (1771–1841), father of William Bell Scott (q.v.).

Scott, William Bell (1811–90) Landscape and figure engraver. Born at Edinburgh on 12 September 1811, he was the son of Robert Scott, by whom he was taught engraving. Although he became proficient at it, he rebelled at the drudgery and routine and, in 1837, went to London where he painted, etched and engraved until, in 1843, he was made master of the Newcastle School of Design, a post he held until 1858. His steel engraved work is represented by 'Glen Ericht', 'Huntly Castle' and 'Abruthven', all after W. Brown, and 'Spout of Pitlochry' after A. Donaldson, all four done for Hooker's *Perthshire illustrated* 1843, the frontispiece to volume 2 of J. Browne's *History of the Highlands* [c. 1845], 'Falls of Acharn' after D. M. Mackenzie, and 'David playing before Saul' after his own design for an edition of the *Bible* [c. 1870]. He also published *Murillo and the Spanish school of painting* 1873, with fifteen engravings on steel. He was known primarily as a poet and writer of books on art. He died on 22 November 1890 at Penkill Castle, Argyllshire, in his eightieth year. B; Br; DNB; *Illus. London News*, 97, 1890, p. 710.

William Bell Scott

Scriven, Edward (1775–1841) Portrait and figure engraver. According to his own account, he was born at Alcester, eight miles from Stratford-upon-Avon, but the *Dictionary of National Biography* states that his name does not appear on the parish register there. There may be several reasons for this. He also records a friendship with William Courand of Evesham, who, together with his parents, encouraged him to become a pupil of Robert Thew (1758–1802), then residing (c. 1789) at Northall in Hertfordshire, with whom he stayed for seven or eight years, until about 1797. During this time they were both employed by Boydell on his Shakespeare Gallery, working largely in stipple, and this laid the foundation for Scriven's later style, which he strengthened with line in due course. Thew was engraver to the Prince of Wales, and when he died, in 1802, his former pupil succeeded him (for reasons that it is not hard to see), becoming in due course Historical engraver to George IV. In 1813 he was living in Clarendon Square, Somers Town, and by then the Society of Arts had given him the Lesser Gold medal for his engraving of a self-portrait of Gerhard Douw. In 1815 he gained the Gold Isis medal for five engravings from B. West's picture of Christ

Edward Scriven

rejected. He engraved for a number of well-known works and was developing a relationship with the publisher John Murray; a letter of 21 September 1826 refers to a commission to engrave a portrait of Byron. In another letter of 8 April 1829, he explains to Murray why steel engravings cost more than those on copper (see B. Hunnisett, *Steel-engraved book illustrations in England* 1980, p. 167). Among his earliest works on steel was 'Sir Christopher Wren' after Kneller for H. Walpole's *Anecdotes of painting* 1827, followed by 'Thomas Howard, Duke of Norfolk' after Holbein, dated 1 May 1830, for E. Lodge's *Portraits...*, 2nd edition, 1835. 'Francis Egerton' after Craig, dated 1831, and 'N. Grimshaw' after Lonsdale appeared in E. Baines's *History of ... Lancaster* 1836, 'Louis the fourteenth' after Rigaud in *Heath's Versailles* [c. 1836] (reissued in *Keepsake français* 1840), 'Namouna' after K. Meadows in Moore's *Lalla Rookh* 1838, 'Edward Gibbon' after J. Reynolds in Milman's *Life of Gibbon* 1839 and 'The maid's trial' after J. Browne in Finden's *Tableaux* 1840. 'The Countess Mahon' was engraved for *Heath's Book of beauty* 1839, and 'The repose in Egypt' after Guido appeared in Fisher's *Historic illustrations of the Bible* [1840–3]. 'Second epistle to Davie, a brother poet', 'Halloween' and 'The twa dogs' after J. M. Wright were engraved for the *Complete works of Robert Burns* [c. 1842], and 'Wm. Alexander, Keeper of Prints, British Museum' after H. Eldridge was issued in J. Britton's *Autobiography* 1850. 'Edward, Duke of Kent' after Sir William Beechey was issued in G. N. Wright's *Gallery of engravings* 1844–6, and ten portraits of famous people were published in the *Imperial dictionary of universal biography* [c. 1861], including 'Captain Cook' after Dance, 'Edward Jenner' after J. R. Smith and 'William Wilberforce' after G. Richmond. He was a founder member and first secretary of the Artists' Annuity Fund when it was set up in 1810 (see Hunnisett, op. cit. p. 58). He had as his pupil Benjamin Phelps Gibbon (q.v.) from about 1816, together with Robert William Sievier, who gave up engraving in about 1823 to become a sculptor and manufacturer. He died on 23 August 1841 leaving a widow and five children. He was buried in Kensal Green cemetery, and the members of the Artists' Annuity Fund provided a monument to his memory. Br; DNB; P; R; S; SocA; T.

Sears, R. (fl. 1832–3) Landscape and architectural engraver. 'Lathom House' after G. Pickering, dated 1832, appeared in E. Baines's *History of ... Lancaster* 1836 and 'Deal from Upper Deal Mall' after G. Hayward and 'Rye' and 'Clifton Baths, Margate' after W. H. Bartlett in *Watering places...* 1833 (the last two were used again in *Fashionable guide...* [c. 1838]). He may be connected with Fenner, Sears & Co. (q.v.).

Setchell, H. (fl. 1833) Figure engraver. 'The foundlings' was published in W. Hogarth's *Works* 1833.

Sharpe, Charles William (1818–99) Figure engraver. He was a grandson of William Sharpe, probably the book and print seller of Steelhouse Lane, Birmingham, from 1807 to 1814. A Charles Sharpe, engraver, copperplate printer and bookseller of 7 Ann Street, from 1820 to 1821, may have been his father. Charles William Sharpe's ties with the city were such that he was included as a Birmingham engraver in the 1877 exhibition. His aunts Louisa (later Mrs W. Seyffarth) and Eliza Sharpe were well known as illustrators, especially in the annuals. About 1816, William took the family to London, where he is believed to have established himself in Regent Street (where he remained until his death in 1842). Among Charles William Sharpe's earliest works were 'Cup-tossing' after N. J. Crowley 'The death of Queen Elizabeth' after P. Delaroche, 'The misers' after D. Teniers and 'The blind fiddler' and 'The village politicians' after D. Wilkie. These were engraved for S. C. Hall's *Gems of European art* 1846, but it is unlikely that an untried engraver would have been asked to contribute, and there must be work earlier than this. The two Wilkie engravings were used again in *Wilkie gallery* [c. 1849], together with 'The peep o'day boy's cabin', which was used again in the *Art Journal* 1850. He engraved thirty-three plates altogether for the *Art Journal*, beginning with 'Pilgrims in sight of Rome' after C. L. Eastlake in the *Art Union* 1848 (used again in Mrs Hall's *Drawing room table book* 1849), and continuing with 'Undine' after D. Maclise (1855), 'A country blacksmith' after J. M. W. Turner (1860) (used again in Wornum's *Turner Gallery* [c. 1878]), 'The Post office' after F. Goodall (1862), 'The Zouave's story' after F. W. Topham (q.v.) (1865), 'Macbeth' after A. Johnston (1877) and 'Old noblesse in the Conciergerie' after W. H. Fisk (1879), his last in the series. 'The farewell' after McIntosh appeared in *The Cottage girl...* [c. 1860]. 'Dr. Johnson at Lord Chesterfield's' after E. M. Ward was published in Timbs's *Curiosities of London* 1867, and the *Works of Shakspere* [sic], *Imperial edition* 1872 contained 'Christopher Sly' and 'Talbot and the Countess of Auvergne' after W. Q. Orchardson, 'Orlando' after D. Maclise, 'The lady's tailor' after H. S. Marks, 'Queen Katherine' after C. R. Leslie and 'Ariel' after H. J. Townsend (Plate 47). (All of these had been issued in the *Art Journal* between 1855 and 1873), 'Cranmer at the Traitor's Gate' after Goodall was engraved for Archer's *Pictures and royal portraits...* [c. 1878]. *Picturesque Europe* 1876–9 carried 'Meyringen' after G. G. Kilburne, and *The Royal Shakespeare* 1883–4 had 'Speed and Launce' after C. Green, 'Portia and Shylock' after J. D. Watson, 'Bertram and Helena' after F. Dicksee and 'Falstaff and the Chief Justice' after F. Barnard. His work for the Art Union of London included 'Raising the maypole' after F. Goodall (1862), 'Hamlet' after Maclise (1868) and 'The death of Nelson' after Maclise (1876), begun about 1867. According to W. P. Frith in his autobiography, it was said that the Art Union of London paid £3,000 for Sharpe's plate 'Ramsgate sands', possibly about 1854. In 1874 his name was put forward for election to the Royal Academy, but he was not successful, although he exhibited there from 1858 to 1883. He appears to have worked in Brixton, but moved to Burnham Beeches,

Maidenhead, where his aunt Eliza died in 1873 or 1874. His son Edward was a painter, gained a silver medal at the Royal Academy Schools for a pastel drawing of a nude negro in 1867, and in 1869 emigrated to Montreal, Canada, where he died soon afterwards. His artist daughter Margaret married Frank Willis, also an artist. AJ; B; C; Ro; S; T; Mr. A. Wilson, Liverpool; *The Working papers for an historical directory of the West Midlands book trade to 1850*, 1977–83.

Shaw, George B. (fl. 1835–75) Portrait and figure engraver. For Scott's *Waverley novels* he engraved 'Colonel Gardiner' and 'Graham of Claverhouse...' after P. Lely, 'James Douglas, Earl of Morton', 'Robert Dudley, Earl of Leicester', 'James I' and 'George Villiers, Duke of Buckingham', this last after S. Austin. A vignette self portrait of Sir Henry Raeburn was engraved for Chambers's *Biographical dictionary of eminent Scotsmen* 1835. 'Coeur de Lion at the bier of his father' after Chisholm and 'The Laird of Macnab' after Fraser appeared in *Casquet of literature* 1874. In the *Art Union* 1848 there was 'The fisherman's wife' after P. F. Poole, which also appeared in Mrs Hall's *Drawing room table book* 1849. 'Cottage children' after T. Gainsborough (largely etched in line and stipple) was published in the *Art Journal* 1850. 'James Beattie' after Reynolds, 'Maj. Gen. David Stewart' after Gordon and 'James Douglas' appeared in Chambers's *Biographical dictionary of eminent Scotsmen*, 2nd edition, 1875.

Shaw, T. W. (fl. 1833) Figure engraver. 'Sigismonda' after W. Hogarth was published in Hogarth's *Works* 1833.

Shenfield. (fl. 1832) Architectural engraver. 'Castle of Johannesberg' after Tombleson appeared in *Tombleson's views of the Rhine* 1832.

Shenton, Henry Chawner (1803–66) Figure engraver. He was born at Winchester, and came to London about 1817 to become a pupil of Charles Warren (q.v.), whose daughter he married some time before 1824. The death of his master in 1823 saw him almost at the end of his indentures, and as a comparatively young man with family responsibilities (Henry Chawner junior was born in 1825) he needed work urgently. This he found with the annuals, e.g., 'Children of Ravendale' after T. Stothard for *The Amulet* 1827, and between 1825 and 1832 he exhibited at the Society of British Artists. He also joined the Artists' Annuity Fund, in 1825. 'The miniature' after Wood was engraved for *Friendship's offering* 1833 and 'The departure for Waterloo' after Edmondstone for the *Literary souvenir* 1834. He engraved 'The merry fiddler' after J. Berkheyden, dated 1 June 1833, 'A Jew merchant' after Rembrandt, dated 1 October 1833, and 'Christ reasoning with the Pharisees' after da Vinci, dated 1 April 1834, all of which appeared in A. Cunningham's *Cabinet gallery of pictures by the first masters...* 1836. 'Queen Elizabeth at Greenwich Hospital' after Melville was done for Wright's *Landscape-historical illustrations of Scotland* 1836–8. 'Day's sport in the Highlands' after A. Cooper, dated December 1840, and 'Loan of a bite' after W. Mulready, dated 1849, were engraved for Finden's *Royal Gallery of British Art* 1838–49, and 'Olden hospitality' after J. R. Herbert was done for S. C. Hall's *Gems of European art* 1846. For the *Art Journal* he engraved 'Country cousins' after R. Redgrave (1854) and 'Death of Cleopatra' after Guido (1861), but this last had to be finished by H. Bourne (q.v.) since Shenton's eyesight was failing, and this marked the virtual end of his engraving career. He engraved a few plates for the print publishers, e.g., 'Smoking the cobbler' after W. Kidd, published by Ackermann in 1840, and also for the Art Union of London, for which he engraved 'Tired huntsman' after C. Landseer

(1841), 'The clemency of Coeur de lion' after J. Cross (1857) and 'The labour of love' after F. Dicksee (1863), which was his last plate and had to be finished by C. H. Jeens (q.v.). Other plates by him were 'The stray kitten' after W. Collins and 'The hermit' after A. Fraser. He died on 15 September 1866 at his home in Camden Town. His eldest son Henry Chawner, a sculptor, had died in 1846 at the age of twenty-one, and he is believed to have had a second son, William Kernot Shenton (1836–78), who was also a sculptor, and who was related to J. H. Kernot, the engraver (q.v.). AJ; B; DNB; S.

Shepherd, Thomas Hosmer (1793–1864) He was primarily a draughtsman and watercolour painter, but engraved a few plates as well. Believed to be the son of George Shepherd and brother of George Sidney Shepherd, both of whom contributed designs to many books of the 1830s, he was employed by Frederick Crace to make watercolour drawings of buildings all over London, many of which were soon afterwards destroyed, leaving his pictures as the sole record in some cases. These were used in the several books with which he was associated, among which were *London and its environs* 1829–31, for which he engraved 'Merchant Tailor's School', 'St. Mary at Hill', 'New Church, Saffron Hill' and 'New church... Holborn', all after his own designs. Thirteen plates were engraved after the author's designs for Gastineau's *Wales illustrated...* 1830, among which was 'The Sugar Loaf and Skyrrid mountains, Monmouthshire', which was used again in Woodward's *History of Wales* 1853. 'Scout Scar, near Kendal...' and 'Skelwith Bridge' after T. Allom appeared in T. Rose's *Westmorland* 1832 and 'Wasserstely' after Tombleson (a good example) in Fearnside's *Picturesque beauties of the Rhine* [c. 1846]. B; Br; T. J. F. C. Phillips. *Shepherd's London* 1976.

Sherratt, Thomas (fl. 1836–84) Figure engraver. 'The court of Haddon Hall' after T. Allom was engraved for T. Noble and T. Rose's *Counties of Chester...* 1836, for the *Works of shakspere* [*sic*], *Imperial edition* 1872 he did 'Queen Isabella and her ladies' after G. H. Boughton (reissued in the *Art Journal* 1874), and 'The two roses' after J. D. Watson appeared in *The Royal Shakespeare* 1883–4. He did a total of ten plates for the *Art Journal*, commencing with 'Preparing for the chase' after J. Mourenhout (1857) (a rather poor engraving), and further including 'Woman of Samaria' after H. Tidey (1872), 'Lorenzo and Jessica' after P. F. Poole (1881) and 'Henry III of France and the Dutch envoys' after C. J. Staniland (1884)—his last. 'The Gipsy' after J. Phillip was an oval engraving signed 'T. Sherratt junior', which gives rise to the speculation that he might have been the Thomas Sherratt who was working for the publishers in Detroit, USA, about 1870, and who was a portrait engraver. St.

Shury, George Salisbury (fl. 1838–61) Landscape engraver. He is probably the son of John Shury (q.v.), with whom he also collaborated (some plates are signed 'John Shury and Son'). This probably accounts for the paucity of plates signed by him and the multitude signed by John. 'Bishop's Waltham' after F. N. Shepherd was published in R. Mudie's *Hampshire* 1838 and 'Dinant' after J. Salmon in *Continental tourist* [1838]. He also did 'Traviata' after F. Beard for the print publisher Moore, McQueen & Co. (1861). He is also known to have done some portraits and to have worked in stipple. AJ; B; S.

Shury, John (fl. 1818–48) Landscape and architectural engraver. Thirty-three plates after H. Gastineau and N. Whittock were engraved for Allen's *New ... history of the*

county of York 1828–31, of which 'The Museum and New Bridge, Scarborough' is a good example (Plate 7), four after the author for Allen's History of the county of Lincoln [1830–1] and five after Whittock and two after Gastineau for Allen's History ... of Surrey and Sussex 1829–31, including 'Guildford', 'Arundel Church, Sussex' and 'Sompting Church, Sussex'. Most carried the legend 'Engraved on steel by J. Shury'. 'James Stuart, Earl of Murray', a vignette, was engraved for Chambers's Biographical dictionary of eminent Scotsmen 1835. A total of seventy-three plates were engraved by him for R. Mudie's Hampshire 1838, after G. H. Shepherd, J. Salmon, J. Wrightson, D. H. McKewan, F. N. Shepherd, T. Shepherd and C. Radclyffe. Eleven plates were done for E. W. Brayley's Topographical history of Surrey 1841–8, after McEwan, Harding, Pyne, Shepherd and Thompson. Thirty-two engravings were done, mostly signed 'John Shury and Son', for Continental tourist [1838], after J. Fussell, J. Salmon and G. S. Shepherd, and included the frontispiece 'Town Hall, Brussels', 'Waterloo', 'Cathedral, Liege', 'Ems' and 'Sonnenberg'. 'Spa' was 'Drawn by Jno Shury, Jun.', who was probably yet another son. A 'Jno. Shury' of 16 Charterhouse Street is given as an engraver who tested some new graver handles in 1831 for the Society of Arts.   SocA.

Simmonds, W. (fl. 1846) Historical engraver. 'Defence of Wardour castle' after G. Cattermole was published in R. Cattermole's Great Civil War 1846. This could be by William Henry Simmons (q.v.).

Simmons, William Henry (1811–82) Figure and historical engraver. He was born in London on 11 June 1811, and about 1825 became a pupil of William Finden, by whom he was taught line engraving. This he abandoned sometime in the early 1840s for mezzotint, in which most of his later work was done, and of which he became a leading exponent. One of his earliest independent plates was 'Twin sisters' after T. Lawrence, dated November 1834 and published in the Literary souvenir 1835 (it was signed 'W. H. Simmonds'). 'Cupid and Psyche' (a charming oval picture) after W. Etty, 'The Shepherd's home' after W. Collins and a vignette, 'Cupid's assault', after J. Franklin were done for S. C. Hall's Book of gems 1836, and for the 1838 edition of the work, he supplied an engraved title page vignette of a palette and easel after E. T. Parris, 'The maid at prayer' after G. Jones and 'Little Red Riding Hood' after J. Inskipp. 'Jenny's first love letter' after Webster was engraved for Friendship's offering 1837, and 'The first family' after Wagner and 'The captivity' after Führich appeared in The Pictorial Bible 1855. One of the few line engravings from his later career was 'Mors Janua vitae' after J. N. Paton (1870). He died on 10 June 1882, and in his obituary in the Year's Art 1883 was described as an 'engraver on steel'. He joined the Artists' Annuity Fund in 1835.   AJ; B; DNB.

Sims, W. (fl. 1829) Architectural engraver. 'Court House, Leeds' after Whittock was engraved for Allen's New ... history of the county of York 1828–31.

Skelton, William (1763–1848) Portrait engraver. He was over sixty years of age when 'Wenceslaus Hollar', which is likely to have been his only plate on steel, was published in H. Walpole's Anecdotes of painting 1827. In 1833 he was living at 1 Stafford Place, Pimlico.   DNB.

Sluyter, Dirk Jurriaan (1811–86) Figure engraver. He was the son of an engraver in Amsterdam, where he was born, lived and died. He engraved on copper, steel and wood, as

well as being a painter. An oval picture, 'The dogs of the regiment', after B. T. Gempt appeared on the engraved title page of Casquet of literature 1874, which also included 'Dutch children' after Israels and 'The lady's page' after Hollander.

Smith (fl. 1830–50) Three vignettes of Great St Bernard and the Alps after J. M. W. Turner (which were drawn on his visit to the Alps in 1802 and first published here after 28 years (Plate 12)) and Petrarch's house at Arqua after S. Prout appeared in S. Rogers' Italy 1830, merely signed 'Smith'. 'Near Hampton, Middlesex' after Bartlett and 'Canonbury Tower, Islington' after Leach were published in T. Dugdale's England and Wales delineated [1838–9], also signed just 'Smith'.

Smith, A. (fl. 1860) Figure engraver. 'The angel freeing the Apostles' after Kirk appeared in Pearce's Altar at home ... [c. 1860].

Smith, Charles John (1803–38) Landscape engraver. Born in Chelsea, the son of James Smith, a surgeon, he was a pupil of Charles Pye (q.v.) from about 1817, and is said to have done some of the later plates for C. Stothard's Monumental effigies, which commenced publication in that year. In 1829 he published a series entitled Autographs of royal, noble and illustrious persons with memoirs by J. G. Nichols, and in 1830, twenty-five of his plates were issued in E. Cartwright's Parochial topography of the Rape of Bramber, including 'Selden's House' after his own design (and like about half of them, a vignette printed onto the text page), 'Sandgate Lodge' after E. G., 'Steyning Church' and 'Seal of the Borough of Horsham' after his own design. 'Brighton East', 'New entrance, Pavilion, Brighton', 'Brighton West', 'Hurstmonceaux Castle' and 'Fairlight Hill and Hastings', all after C. Scott, were published in J. D. Parry's Historical and descriptive account of the Coast of Sussex 1833. For M. A. Tierney's History of the Arundel 1834, he engraved the frontispiece to volume 2, 'North view of Arundel Church' after 'G. C[onstable?]', and 'Nave of Arundel Church' after 'Edw. Lear'. He certainly engraved seven, and possibly did two more, plates for Graphic illustrations of Samuel Johnson ... 1837, including 'Grammar School, Lichfield' after J. Buckler, a vignette—'Kettel Hall, Broad St. Oxford'—after the same artist 'The residence of George Stevens [sic], F.R.S. ...' (Plate 31) and 'Dr. S. Johnson's House, Bolt Court, Fleet Street' after his own design. Smith probably engraved the facsimile letters, for which kind of work he had gained a good reputation in 1829 through his Autographs ..., mentioned above. He also engraved some plates of illuminated manuscripts for T. F. Dibdin's Bibliographical ... tour in the northern counties of England 1838. He had completed six out of a projected eight numbers of Historical and literary curiosities when he died of paralysis in Albany St, London, on 23 November 1838. He had been elected Fellow of the Society of Antiquaries in 1837.   Br; DNB; T.

Smith, Edward (fl. 1824–49) Landscape and figure engraver. He was probably from Edinburgh, but appears to have worked mostly in London. Among his earliest plates were some done for Walker's Effigies Poeticae 1824, followed by 'The sleeping congregation' in Hogarth moralized 1831 and three plates in the 'Industry and idleness' series after W. Hogarth in Hogarth's Works 1833. 'Entrée dans l'église' after Johannot appeared in Keepsake français 1831. 'Scene in Kattiawar—travellers and escort' after C. Stanfield (sketched by Capt. Grindlay) and 'Cottage courtship' after T. Stothard appeared in Fisher's Drawing room scrap book 1835, and 'Dutch lady' after F. Bol, dated 1 December 1832, 'Mrs.

Siddons as the tragic muse' after J. Reynolds, dated 1 February 1833, and 'The Queen of Hearts' after Vangol, dated 1 July 1833, were published in A. Cunningham's *Cabinet gallery of pictures by the first masters* ... 1836. 'Wycoller Hall, Christmas 1650' after H. Melville was done in 1834 and published in E. Baines's *History of ... Lancaster* 1836 and in G. N. Wright's *Lancashire* 1842, and 'Bazaar at Jaffa' and 'Mr. Barker's villa at Suadeah' after W. H. Bartlett were issued in J. Carne's *Syria* 1836–8. 'Contadini family prisoners with banditti' after C. L. Eastlake, dated 2 March 1840, was engraved for Finden's *Royal Gallery of British Art* 1838–49, and 'The jew's harp' after D. Wilkie was done for S. C. Hall's *Gems of European art* 1846. This last plate was used again for *Wilkie gallery* [c. 1849], accompanied by another of his engravings–'The piper'. 'The Baron's Hall at Christmas' after H. Melville and 'Cemetery of the Smolensko Church' after A. G. Vickers appeared in G. N. Wright's *Gallery of engravings* 1844–6. Three plates, probably on copper, were done for *Engravings after the best pictures of the Great Masters* 1841–3 (in which only Scottish engravers were employed)– two were after Wilkie and one after Rubens. He tried out some improved graver handles in 1831 for the Society of Arts, and a number of his plates after Wilkie were issued by the print publishers between 1844 and 1846. He also seems to have engraved some portraits.   AJ; B; Br; SocA; T.

Smith, Frederick (fl. 1836–63) Architectural engraver. 'Interior of the Pantheon, Rome' after D. Roberts, 'View of the Church of St. Agnes' after G. B. Moore, 'Three columns of Jupiter Tonans, Rome' after T. H. Cromek, 'Ponte Salerno...', 'Columns of Phocas...' and 'St. Peter's from the Villa Pamfili-Doria' after W. L. Leitch and 'Temple of Vesta...' and 'View of the Temple of Antoninus and Faustine, Rome' after T. H. Cromek appeared in D. Costello's *Piedmont and Italy* [c. 1855], and a vignette, 'Insects', after J. O. Westwood was done for B. Woodward's *General history of Hampshire* 1863. He joined the Artists' Annuity Fund in 1836.

Smith, G. B. (fl. 1842–88) Architectural engraver. Twelve plates of 'Gothic panelling of Carlisle Cathedral' after R. W. Billings (q.v.) were issued in the artist's *Illustrations of geometric tracery* ... 1842, and similar plates, many after the same artist, appeared in R. W. Billings's *Baronial ... Antiquities of Scotland* 1852, the same author's *Illustrations ... of Durham* ... 1846, J. Raine's *Brief account of the Palace of Auckland* ... 1852 and T. Rickman's *Attempt to discriminate the styles of architecture* 1881. Twenty beautifully finished engravings of various English cathedrals after T. Evaston were done for Sharpe's *Seven periods of English architecture*, 3rd edition, 1888. Ho.

Smith, H. (fl. 1829) Architectural engraver. 'Ruins of Court Street Chapel' and 'Charing Church and the remains of the Archbishop's Palace' after G. Shepherd were published in S. W. H. Ireland's *England's topographer* (commenced publication 1828).

Smith, J. (fl. 1872) Portrait engraver. 'Oliver Cromwell' after R. Walker appeared in J. Evelyn's *Diary and correspondence* 1872.

Smith, J. C. (fl. 1845) Heraldic engraver. Plates of coats of arms (nos. 3 and 9) were published in J. Burke's *Heraldic illustrations* 1845.

Smith, John (c. 1798–?) Landscape and figure engraver. He is believed to have been born about 1798 and to have attended the Royal Academy Schools. Among his early works were 'Unitarian Chapel...' and 'Wesleyan Chapel...' Liver-pool after Pyne, for W. Pyne's *Lancashire illustrated* ... 1831, 'Powderham Castle, Devonshire' after W. H. Bartlett, issued in J. Britton and E. W. Brayley's *Devonshire and Cornwall illustrated* 1832, 'Ruins of Drachenfels' after Tombleson, for *Tombleson's views of the Rhine* 1832 and 'Gallery of Gondo' after C. Stanfield, for L. Ritchie's *Travelling sketches in the north of Italy* 1832. For L. Ritchie he also did 'Rheinstein' after Stanfield in *Travelling sketches on the Rhine* 1833 and 'Château Gaillard from the east' (a very poor engraving) after J. M. W. Turner in *Wanderings by the Seine* 1835. 'Chertsey Bridge' after W. Tombleson was done for Fearnside's *Tombleson's Thames* 1834, 'Castel Gondolpho' and 'Fort de Bard' after J. D. Harding for T. Roscoe's *Tourist in Italy* 1833, 'Bellinzona (Canton Tessin)' (the effect by T. Creswick) and 'Gallery in the "Trou Perdu"...' after W. H. Bartlett for W. Beattie's *Switzerland* 1836 and 'The Abbotsford family' after D. Wilkie for Scott's *Waverley novels*. 'Solway Firth. Embarkation of Queen Mary' after Melville was done for Wright's *Landscape-historical illustrations of Scotland* 1836–8, 'Nassuk on the Guadervery' after Dibdin for Bacon's *Oriental annual* 1840 and three plates after Bartlett for Willis's *Canadian scenery* 1842. 'Gleneagles' after W. Brown, 'Old church of Muthill' and 'The rumbling bridge on the Bran' after A. Donaldson, 'The upper falls of Moness' after J. A. Houston and 'The black castle of Moulin' and 'Scene in the Garry' after D. M. Mackenzie were engraved for Hooker's *Perthshire illustrated* 1843, and at least two of these plates appeared again in J. Browne's *History of the Highlands* [c. 1845], together with 'Dunkeld from Torrhill' and 'The Roman camp at Ardoch' after J. C. Brown, 'Burial place of the Macnabs' after D. M. Mackenzie and 'Garth Castle' after A. Donaldson. Three plates after Tombleson were done for two books by Fearnside: *Picturesque beauties of the Rhine* [c. 1846] contained 'Ilanz' and *Tombleson's Upper Rhine* [c. 1835] had 'Eglisau' and 'Tusis'. B; T.

Smith, O. (fl. 1846) Landscape engraver. 'Swing bridge, Bonn' after W. Tombleson was published in Fearnside's *Picturesque beauties of the Rhine* [c. 1846].

Smith, Samuel S. (1809–79) Figure engraver. 'Cafes in Damascus' after W. H. Bartlett, dated 1836 and published in J. Carne's *Syria* 1836–8, is one of his earliest plates, after which he seems to have turned to figure engraving. 'The witches dance in Tam O'Shanter' and 'John Anderson my Jo' after J. M. Wright appeared in the *Complete works of Robert Burns* [c. 1842], and 'Titian's model' and 'The empty cradle' after F. M'Ian were done for S. C. Hall's *Gems of European art* 1846. For volumes of the *Art Journal* from 1853 to 1880 he engraved sixteen plates, including four after Eastlake–'Visit to the nun' (1856), 'Carrara Family, 1406' (1853), 'Good Samaritan' (1858) and 'An Italian family' (1867)–'St. Agnes' after Domenichino (1859), 'The wife's portrait–Pepys's diary' after A. Elmore (1866), and his last, 'David playing before Saul' after D. W. Wynfield (1880). 'Hamlet and Ophelia' after J. D. Watson appeared in *The Royal Shakespeare* 1883–4. He married Emma, the artist daughter of engraver Peltro William Tomkins. He died in March 1879 at St John's Wood, aged seventy.   AJ; Br; DNB.

Smith, T. (fl. 1831) Figure engraver. Two plates from 'The rake's progress' (nos. 5 and 7) after W. Hogarth were published in *Hogarth moralized* 1831.

Smith, W. B. (fl. 1818–35) Landscape engraver. 'Loch Lomond and Ben Lomond from below Tarbet' after C. Stanfield was published in Scott's *Waverley novels*.

Smith, William Raymond (fl. 1818–48) Landscape and animal engraver. W. R. Smith of Seymour Crescent, Euston Square, was awarded the Silver Isis medal by the Society of Arts in 1819 for an engraving of a landscape. He contributed several plates to J. P. Neale's *Views of the seats of noblemen...* 1818–24, and began his work on steel, in 1828, with a vignette of Greek temple and buildings after C. Stanfield for the engraved title page of *The Anniversary* 1829. 'Royal York Baths, Regent's Park' and 'Sussex Place...' after T. H. Shepherd, both dated 5 April 1828, appeared in J. Elmes's *Metropolitan improvements* 1829, 'Lago Maggiore' after Turner was done for *The Keepsake* 1829, 'Fish market, Rome' after S. Prout, dated 28 October 1829, appeared in T. Roscoe's *Tourist in Italy* 1831, and in the 1833 volume (with the same title) appeared 'Garagliano' and 'Savona, coast of Genoa' after J. D. Harding. 'Dieppe' after Harding was engraved for *Keepsake français* 1831. 'Innsbruck, Principal street' after C. Stanfield was published in L. Ritchie's *Travelling sketches in the north of Italy* 1832, and 'The market waggon' after Gainsborough and a plate of a seaport in the Mediterranean after Claude Lorraine, dated 1832 and 1833 respectively, appeared in A. Cunningham's *Cabinet gallery of pictures by the first masters...* 1836. 'Roslin Castle' after Turner appeared in Scott's *Poetical works* 1834. 'Château and village of Polignac' and 'Lyons' after J. D. Harding, both dated 28 October 1833, were published in T. Roscoe's *Tourist in France* 1834. 'Castle and Valley of Misocco...' after W. H. Bartlett appeared in W. Beattie's *Switzerland* 1836, 'The Valley of the shadow of death' and 'The celestial city' after Martin in Bunyan's *Pilgrim's progress* 1836, 'Pont de la Crêt' and 'The Balsille...' after Brockedon in Beattie's *Waldenses* 1838, 'Dunbar Castle (Lothian)' after T. Allom in Beattie's *Scotland illustrated* 1838 and 'Roumeli Hissar, or the Castle of Europe' after Allom in R. Walsh's *Constantinople* 1838–40. A very well done plate, 'View on the River Stour' after J. Constable, dated 2 March 1840, was published in Finden's *Royal Gallery of British art* 1838–49, and 'Melrose from Turn Again' after Stanfield appeared in Scott's *Waverley novels*. His longest series of plates were fourteen engravings in T. C. Hofland's *British angler's manual* 1839, including 'Artificial flies', 'Hampton, Middlesex' and 'Snowdon, from the Inn at Capel Curig' after the author's designs, and seventeen vignettes in E. Jesse's *Anecdotes of dogs* 1846, including 'Spaniels', 'Newfoundland dog' and 'Bulldog', thirteen of them after designs by the engraver. 'Abinger Hall' after Thompson appeared in Brayleys' *Topographical history of Surrey* 1841–8, and 'Windsor Castle from the Home Park' after J. D. Harding was issued in L. Ritchie's *Windsor Castle* 1848. He joined the Artists' Annuity Fund in 1820, and signed the 1837 petition. An independent print, 'The dying camel' after Henry Warren, was published by Boys in 1845. SocA; T.

Smyth, John Talfourd (1819–51) Portrait, figure and landscape engraver. Born in Edinburgh, he trained at the Trustees' Academy under Sir William Allan, but in 1835, at about the age of sixteen, firmly decided to become an engraver and rarely painted again. He became a pupil to a local engraver, who died in his first year, so he was largely self-taught, and in 1838 moved to Glasgow, where he worked hard to support himself for the next seven years. About 1845 he returned to Edinburgh, and worked primarily for the print publishers. 'Drummond Castle' and 'Killiecrankie' after J. C. Brown, for J. Browne's *History of the Highlands* [c. 1845], are two of his rare book illustrations proper. He engraved 'The comforter' after Ary Scheffer and 'John Knox administering

the sacrament' after Wilkie for the *Art Union* of 1846 and 1848 respectively, both plates being reissued in Mrs Hall's *Drawing room table book* 1849. He engraved ten portraits of contemporary painters for the *Art Union* 1847, and for the *Art Journal* 1850 he did 'The last in' after W. Mulready and 'Arabs dividing the spoil' after Sir William Allan. He was engraving J. Faed's 'First step' when he died of overwork at the early age of thirty-two on 18 May 1851. Contemporaries estimated that he would have quickly reached the top of his profession had he lived. AJ; DNB.

Snowville, G. (fl. 1840) Figure engraver. He engraved the illustrations to Charles Daly's edition of Pope's *Poetical works* [c. 1840] after designs by Weigall.

Spencer. (fl. 1832) Landscape engraver. Five plates of Tutbury Castle and Church were published in Sir Oswald Mosley's *History of ... Tutbury* 1832. Ho.

Sprent, W. (fl. 1837–60) Landscape engraver. 'Egg-market, Antwerp' after Bartlett was engraved for van Kampen's *History and topography of Holland and Belgium* [1837]. A publication line on 'Newington Causeway, London' engraved for *Mighty London* [c. 1860] gives 'W. Sprent, 47, King Square E.C.'.

Staines, Robert (1805–49) Figure engraver. Born on 21 October 1805, he was taught engraving by J. C. Edwards (q.v.), but from about 1823 spent the second half of his apprenticeship with the Findens, accompanied by his fellow student Richard Hatfield (q.v.). Until about 1834 or 1835, he worked well for the studio, but it was not until that time that he put his own name to a plate. The first such was probably 'Henri IV and Gabrielle d'Etrées' after R. Westall, dated November 1834, and published in the *Literary souvenir* 1835. Twelve plates after Allom, Chisholm, Franklin, Harvey, Melville and Topham were engraved for Wright's *Landscape-historical illustrations of Scotland* 1836–8, 'Donna Elena' after Penley for *Friendship's offering* 1837, 'The somnambulist' after Miss Sharpe for *The Keepsake* 1840 and 'The Grisette' after Frith for the 1846 volume of the latter annual. Seven plates after various artists appeared in Fisher's *Historic illustrations of the Bible* [1840–3], three of which were used again in J. Kitto's *Gallery of scripture engravings* 1846–9. 'Rice sellers at the Military Station...' and 'Scene from the spectacle of "The Sun and Moon"' after T. Allom were engraved for G. N. Wright's *China* 1843, 'Death of the Virgin' after A. F. Caminade for S. C. Hall's *Gems of European art* 1846, and 'Goring carousing' and 'Cromwell conferring with the lawyers' after G. Cattermole for R. Cattermole's *Great Civil War* 1846. A finely engraved plate, 'The sisters', after E. Wattier and 'The lady of Liege' after J. W. Wright were done for *The Keepsake* 1847 and 'The Turkish letter writer' after Wilkie appeared in *Wilkie gallery* [c. 1849]. 'Joseph interpreting Pharaoh's dream' after Cornelius and 'Jeremiah amid the ruins of Jerusalem' after Bendemann appeared in *The Pictorial Bible* 1855. His last plates appeared in the *Art Journal* 1849, viz., 'Sancho and the duchess' after C. R. Leslie and 'Malvolio' after D. Maclise. This last plate was used again in the *Works of Shakspere* [sic], Imperial edition 1872. He joined the Artists' Annuity Fund in 1833. He was naturally delicate, so that when dysentery attacked him in August he gradually declined, and died on 3 October 1849, leaving three children as orphans. He married three times and when he died his third wife was already dead. AJ.

Staines, W. (fl. 1840) Figure engraver. 'Azim and Shireen' after Maclise and 'The sister's farewell' after E. Corbould were engraved for *The Keepsake* 1841.

Stalker, Ebenezer (fl. 1801–33) Figure and landscape engraver. He is known to have been engraving in London in 1801, and his name is found on some well-engraved vignettes of 1815 attached to publications from Philadelphia. Presumably he emigrated to the United States and then returned to England, where his name appeared again, in 1823. He engraved two plates for T. H. Shepherd's *Modern Athens* 1829–31, and 'The enraged musicians' after W. Hogarth was published in Hogarth's *Works* 1833. He joined the Artists' Annuity Fund in 1810 and was still a member in 1843.   Fi; P.

Stancliffe, J. (fl. 1864–67) Figure engraver. Three plates for the *Art Journal* were 'Temptation of Andrew Marvell' after C. Landseer (1864), 'Countess Isabella of Croye' after A. Elmore (1866) and 'The eft' after H. Lejeune (1867), this last being engraved in conjunction with Lumb Stocks.

Starling. There are several of this name working as engravers, presumably all of the same family. Two plates after the author's designs were done for Gell's *Pompeiana . . .* 1832 and 'Ludwigshafen, Lake Constance' after Tombleson was issued in Fearnside's *Picturesque beauties of the Rhine* [c. 1846]. All three were merely signed 'Starling', and there is insufficient evidence to decide which one was responsible.

Starling, J. (fl. 1831–36) Landscape engraver. Two Liverpool views—'Abercrombie Square' after Pyne and 'Statue of George III in London Road' after Allom—were engraved for Pyne's *Lancashire illustrated . . .* 1831. 'Falmouth, Cornwall' and 'Falmouth Harbour' after T. Allom were engraved in 1831 for J. Britton and E. W. Brayley's *Devonshire and Cornwall illustrated* 1832, and 'Ferry House regatta; Windermere Lake' (a good example of his work) and 'Storrs Hall, Windermere Lake . . .', also after Allom, appeared in T. Roses's *Westmorland* 1832. 'The Valais and Martigny from the Forclas . . .' after W. H. Bartlett, dated 1 September 1835, was published in W. Beattie's *Switzerland* 1836, and 'Fall on the hind Rhine in the Rofflen' after Tombleson was done for Fearnside's *Tombleson's Upper Rhine* [c. 1835].

Starling, M. J. (fl. 1829–67) Landscape engraver. 'Caergwle, Flintshire' and 'Pont-y-pair, Caernarvonshire' after H. Gastineau appeared in the artist's *Wales illustrated . . .* 1830. Three plates after T. H. Shepherd were done, in 1831, for Shepherd's *London and its environs* 1829–31, 'The Exchange, Manchester' after Harwood and 'Market-street, Cunliffe . . .' after Allom were engraved for Pyne's *Lancashire illustrated . . .* 1831, fourteen plates after Allom and Bartlett were done for Britton and Brayley's *Devonshire and Cornwall illustrated* 1832 and 'Mill Beck . . .' and 'Vale of St. John . . .' after G. Pickering were published in T. Rose's *Cumberland* 1832. For Rose's *Westmorland* 1832 he engraved 'Levins Hall . . .' and 'Appleby . . .' after Allom, the latter being one of his best plates. 'Newcastle from the Side' and 'Lilburn Tower' are also worth a mention, having appeared with three others, all after Allom, and 'Northwest view of Brenckburn priory . . .' after J. Dobson in Rose's *Durham and Northumberland* 1832. 'South front of Belvoir Castle, Leicestershire' and 'Monuments to the Earls of Rutland in Bottesford Church . . .' after Allom were engraved for T. Noble and T. Rose's *Counties of Chester . . .* 1836 (the second plate was signed 'J. M. Starling') and 'The Exchange, Manchester' after Harwood appeared in E. Baines's *History of . . . Lancaster* 1836. Plates after W. H. Bartlett were engraved for W. Beattie's *Switzerland* 1836 ('Val Vedro—Simplon' and 'Mount Pilatus . . .', the latter being another good example of his work), J. Carne's *Syria* 1836–8 ('Scene in Mount Lebanon', 'Rhodes . . .' and two others) and Beattie's *Waldenses* 1838 ('Church and school of

Felix Neff-Dormeilleuse'). Further work after T. Allom was published in W. Beattie's *Scotland illustrated* 1838 ('The Moray Firth . . .' and 'Oban . . .'), R. Walsh's *Constantinople* 1838–40 ('The Bath') and G. N. Wright's *China* 1843 ('Chapel in the great temple, Macao', showing an unusually delicate treatment of the sky, 'Fort Victoria, Kowloon' and 'West gate of Ching-Keang-Foo', the last signed 'J. M. Starling'). 'Village of Neree' after Bentley was engraved for White's *Views in India . . .* 1838, and thirty-one plates were done, mostly after Allom, for Brayley's *Topographical history of Surrey* 1841–8, the best of which was 'Losely Halls: interior of drawing room'. 'Falcon glass house, Blackfriars' after Allom appeared in J. Timbs's *Curiosities of London* 1867.

Starling, Thomas M. (fl. 1820–48) Map engraver of 1 Wilmington Square, Islington. He engraved folding maps of Switzerland for W. Beattie's *Switzerland* 1836, of Scotland for the same author's *Scotland illustrated* 1838, and another for Beattie's *Waldenses* 1838. A vignette, 'Mickleham Priory', after Allom was published in Brayley's *Topographical history of Surrey* 1841–8. He also engraved two bookplates, dated 1820 and 1840.   F.

Starling, William Francis (fl. 1833–45) Landscape and figure engraver. He contributed some plates to *Illustrations of Shakespeare* 1833, and went on to engrave 'Castle near Tripoli . . .' after W. H. Bartlett, dated 1837, for J. Carne's *Syria* 1836–8. 'Friedrichshafen' after Tombleson was issued in Fearnside's *Tombleson's Upper Rhine* [c. 1835]. He also did some work for an edition of Shakespeare's works in 1842. He joined the Artists' Annuity Fund in 1839.   T.

Steed, J. (fl. 1846) Landscape engraver. 'Conservatory at Wiesbaden' after Tombleson was published in Fearnside's *Picturesque beauties of the Rhine* [c. 1846].

Stephenson, James (1808–1886) Landscape and figure engraver. He was born on 26 November 1808 in Manchester, the son of Thomas Stephenson, boot and shoe maker. After some schooling he was apprenticed to an engraver, John Fothergill, but at the end of his indentures about 1829, he went to London to work for William Finden. In 1830 he was living at 111 Upper Seymour Street, Somers Town, and when there he was awarded the Large Silver medal by the Society of Arts for an engraving of an historical subject. It was during this first period of residence in London that the majority of his book illustrations were undertaken, starting with 'Fall of the Staurbach (Canton Bern)' after W. H. Bartlett, dated 1 July 1834, for W. Beattie's *Switzerland* 1836 (Plate 19). Then followed 'Court of the Alberca' after D. Roberts, dated 28 October 1834, for T. Roscoe's *Tourist in Spain. Granada* 1835, 'Haunts of the sea fowl' after W. Collins, dated November 1834, for the *Literary souvenir* 1835 and 'The love letter' after H. Liverseege for S. C. Hall's *Book of gems* 1836. It is thought that Liverseege was responsible for encouraging Stephenson's removal to London. By this time his ability must have been apparent, because he was asked to engrave three of the plates for *Stanfield's coast scenery* 1836: 'St. Michael's Mount, Cornwall', 'Dartmouth Castle' and 'East Cliffe, Hastings'. 'A Mogul trooper' and 'The hunting cheetah' after W. Daniell and dated 1 October 1836 were engraved for Caunter's *Lives of the Moghul emperors* 1837, and 'Remains of the port of Seleucia . . .' after W. H. Bartlett, dated 1837, appeared in J. Carne's *Syria* 1836–8. 'Dunbarton Castle' after Melville was done for Wright's *Landscape-historical illustrations of Scotland* 1836–8 and 'The Tower of the Clergy, Oporto' after Holland for Harrison's *Tourist in Portugal* 1839. He returned to Manchester in about 1838 and continued to work on books, e.g., *Manchester as it is* 1839 and C. Swain's *Mind and other poems*, but he also commenced his portrait work, which, with his large engravings for the print publishers, took up much of his mature life. He returned to London and settled there about 1847, and in 1852 produced his first plate for the *Art Journal*, 'The casement' after G. S. Newton, although the engraving carries no names. Thereafter, there appeared in that journal 'The ballad singer' after D. Maclise (1865) 'Kept in' after E. Nicol (1871), 'The wayfarers' after T. Graham (1873), 'A. Tennyson' after G. F. Watts (1874), 'Edward II and Piers Gaveston' after M. Stone (1875), 'The challenge' after W. Q. Orchardson (1884) and 'The favourites of Emperor Honorious' after J. W. Waterhouse (1886). Other book plates were 'Burlington Quay' (1837) after G. Balmer, which was issued in Balmer's *Views of ports and harbours ...* 1838, 'The siren' after J. G. Middleton and 'The Spanish peasant boys' after Murillo in S. C. Hall's *Gems of European art* 1846, the engraved title page vignettes after A. H. Wray for J. Timbs's *Curiosities of London* 1867 (he was considered to be a master of vignettes), 'Whitby', 'Leeds, from Holbeck' and 'Halifax, from the Beacon Hill', the last two being after H. Warren, in T. Baines's *Yorkshire past and present* 1871–7, portraits of Mary, wife of John Evelyn, and of Henry the Fourth (of France) in J. Evelyn's *Diary and correspondence* 1872 and 'The Bridge of Gondo' after Birket Foster in *Picturesque Europe* 1876–9. In 1874 his name was put forward for election to the Royal Academy, where he had exhibited from 1856, but he was unsuccessful. While in Manchester from 1838 to 1847 he lived first of all in King Street and then at 14 St Ann's Street. In 1845 he was the Honorary Secretary of the Manchester Academy of Arts. Thomas Oldham Barlow became his pupil at the age of twenty-two in 1846. Stephenson died at his house in Dartmouth Park Road, Kentish Town, on 28 May 1886. AJ; Br; DNB; SocA.

Stevenson, T. (fl. 1854) Figure engraver. 'The nymph' after T. Phillips appeared in the *Art Journal* 1854.

Stewart, James (1791–1863) Figure engraver. His plates are quite rare in books, one example being 'The legacy' after J. Inskipp for *The Amulet* 1831. He was born in Edinburgh about November 1791 and was a pupil of Robert Scott (q.v.), but seems to have worked mainly on large plates from the beginning. He moved with his family in 1830 to London, where he found it less easy to make a living and was possibly compelled to take book work in order to make ends meet. One or two disappointments led him to emigrate in 1833 to South Africa, from where he never returned, dying there in 1863. Apart from his large plates, which are well chronicled, any of his minor works come from the short period of three years, 1830–3. He joined the Artists' Annuity Fund in 1812 and was still a member in 1843. AJ (by far the best source); DNB; S; T.

Stocks, Lumb (1812–1892) Figure engraver. He was born at Lightcliffe, near Halifax, on 30 November 1812, the son of an eminent coal mine owner, and was educated at Horton, near Bradford, where his drawing instructor was C. Cope, the father of Charles West Cope, a famous contemporary painter. He was determined to become an engraver, however, and in 1827, at the age of fifteen, was apprenticed to Charles Rolls (q.v.) in London for six years, at the end of which, in 1833, he set up on his own. He exhibited miniature and crayon portraits between 1832 and 1836. 'La pensée' after Stone and 'Euphrosyne' after Stothard were engraved for the *Literary souvenir* 1835, and for *The Keepsake* he did 'The favorite [sic]

Lumb Stocks

flower' after Stothard and 'The reprieve' after Herbert (1836), 'Remembrance' after Wright and 'The Greek wife' after Parris (1837), 'The unearthly visitant' after Herbert and 'Speranza appearing to Vane among the mountains' after Meadows (1839), 'The invalid' after Montague and 'Beatrice and her mother' after Stephanoff (1840), 'The signal' and 'The Lady Ida' after Herbert and two other plates (1841), 'The ring' after E. Corbould (1842) and 'The haunted spring' after Poole and 'The soirée' after Lami (1843). S. C. Hall's *Book of gems* 1836 contained 'Lady Jane Beaufort' after J. R. Herbert, 'Summer flower' after H. Howard and 'Infant Bacchus' after M. A. Shee, and the 1838 volume had 'The dog' after E. Landseer, 'Saliator' after D. Maclise, and 'The country child' after W. Collins. 'Zelica discovering the veiled prophet' and 'The Peri's first pilgrimage' after E. Corbould were engraved for T. Moore's *Lalla Rookh* 1838, and 'Procession to the christening' after P. Williams (1 November 1839), 'Preparing Moses for the fair' after D. Maclise (July 1841) and 'Nell Gwynne' after C. Landseer were done for Finden's *Royal Gallery of British Art* 1838–49. 'Cromwell viewing the body of the King' after G. Cattermole appeared in R. Cattermole's *Great Civil War* 1846 and 'St. Cecilia' after Domenichino, 'The Infant St. John' after Murillo, 'Soldiers gambling' after S. Rosa and 'Robinet' after Reynolds in S. C. Hall's *Gems of European Art* 1846. 'The armourer's tale', 'Knight's departure for the tournament' (a vignette), and 'The aged minstrel' after G. Cattermole were published in Calabrella's *Evenings at Haddon Hall* 1845 and 'Prudence, piety and charity...' and 'Mr. Greatheart attacks Giant Grim', oval pictures after T. Stothard, in J. Bunyan's *Pilgrim's progress*. Twenty-three plates appeared in the *Art Journal* between 1849 and 1884, including 'Chapeau de Brigand' after T. Uwins (1849), 'Crossing the ford' after W. Mulready (1852), 'Apollo killing the python' after J. M. W. Turner (1860), 'Florizel and Perdita' and 'Autolycus' after C. R. Leslie (1867) (used again in the *Works of Shakspere*, [sic], *Imperial edition* 1872), 'The fight interrupted' after W. Mulready (1875) and 'Princes in the Tower' after J. E. Millais (1884). His book work virtually ceased in the 1840s. In 1842 he engraved A. W. Callcott's 'Raffaele and the Fornarina' for the Art Union of London, and several plates followed for the Association for the promotion of the Fine Arts in Scotland including 'The Death of the Gallant Grey' after Gourlay Steele from *Six engravings in illustration of the Lady of the Lake ... 1868* (Plate 54). The death of John Landseer in 1852 enabled Stocks to be elected to the Royal Academy as an associate in his stead, polling thirteen votes to Thomas Landseer's ten. He was exhibiting his engravings regularly at the Royal Academy and when John Henry Robinson (q.v.) died in 1871 Stocks was elected a fellow of the Royal Academy in December of that year. In 1873 he joined the Council of the Royal Academy, in 1875 became its Auditor, in the 1880s was twice on the Hanging Committee for Engravings, and in 1892 was one of the twelve member Fine Arts Committee for the Chicago Exhibition. Among his many plates from the later years several can be selected, e.g., 'Claude Duval' after W. P. Frith (1865), his most important work 'Meeting of Wellington and Blucher at the Battle of Waterloo' after D. Maclise (1867), 'Sister's kiss' after Sir Frederick Leighton (1884) and 'Spanish letterwriter' after Burgess, exhibited in 1888 when he was seventy-six. He died on 28 April 1892, leaving a widow, several sons and a daughter. His eldest son was Bernard O. Stocks, a mezzotint engraver, Walter Fryer Stocks was his second son, Arthur his third son (also an engraver) and Katherine his daughter. His widow, Ellen, died at Culmington Rectory, Shropshire, on 13 March 1898. In 1883 he was living at 9 Richmond Villas, Seven Sisters Road, London. A limited revised edition of *A Catalogue of line engravings by Lumb Stocks R.A., Engraver 1812–1892* by J. P. Stocks was published at Penticton, British Columbia, in 1978. AJ; B; Br; DNB; H; *Illus. Lond. News* 13 January 1872, p. 27; S; Sa; T; YA.

Stodart, Edward William (1841–1914) Engraver of sculpture. He was probably the son of George J. Stodart (q.v.). Most of his work was done for the *Art Journal*, where eighteen plates were issued between 1864 and 1884, the date of his father's death. It is likely, therefore, that from the age of twenty-three he assisted his father, by whom he is likely to have been trained. Plates included 'The hunter' after Mrs Thorneycroft and 'Go to sleep' after J. Durham (1864), 'Play' after J. T. Crittenden (1869) and 'Commerce' after T. Thorneycroft (1871). This last plate, which was of the Albert Memorial in Hyde Park, was used originally in J. Timbs's *Curiosities of London* 1867. His son Edward Jackson (1879–1934) was also an engraver. B; M; T.

Stodart, George J. (?–1884) Portrait and sculpture engraver. 'Miss Ellen Home Purves' after Bostock was engraved for *Heath's Book of beauty* 1839 and 'The siege of Gibraltar' after Copley for Hume and Smollett's *History of England ...* [c. 1845]. 'Francis Joseph I, Emperor of Austria' (a circular picture) appeared in Costello's *Piedmont and Italy* [c. 1855], ten portraits after pictures and photographs in Nolan's *Illustrated history of the British Empire in India* [1858–60] and 'Rt. Hon. W. E. Gladstone MP' after a photograph by Elliott and Fry in Taylor's *Family history of England* [c. 1860]. 'Charles Dibdin' after Philips appeared in Woodward's *General history of Hampshire* 1863, 'Sir Henry Edwards' and 'Charles Brook' after photographs in Baines's *Yorkshire past and present* 1871–7, and 'Thomas Graham' after Lawrence, 'James Hogg' after Gordon and 'Francis Jeffery' after Hayter in Chambers's *Biographical dictionary of eminent Scotsmen*, 2nd edition, 1875. 'The Songstress' (a portrait of the Countess of Essex) after Jackson and 'Sir Abraham Hume' after Reynolds appeared in the *Art Journal* for 1853 and 1854 respectively, and from 1860 to 1884 he engraved twenty-eight sculpture plates, including 'Medicine' after E. Hahnel (1860). He engraved a stipple portrait of David Stoner, published about 1835, and another of Washington,

which earned Stodart an entry in a dictionary of American artists. He died on 28 December 1884. AJ; Fi; T.

Stodart, T. (fl. 1838) Figure engraver. 'Zuleikha' after Jenkins and 'Walter and Ida' after E. Corbould were engraved for *The Keepsake* 1838.

Stokes, J. (fl. 1846) Landscape engraver. 'Castle of Argenfels' and 'Ruins of Sonnenberg' after Tombleson were published in Fearnside's *Picturesque beauties of the Rhine* [c. 1846].

Stone, J. (fl. 1832) Landscape engraver. 'Ruins of Rheinfels' after Tombleson was published in Fearnside's *Tombleson's views of the Rhine* 1832.

Storer, Henry Sargant (1795–1837) Architectural engraver. He was the son of James Sargant Storer (1771–1853), with whom he collaborated in a number of publications. He engraved several plates for J. P. Neale's *Views of the seats of noblemen ... 1818–24*, but on steel he is known to have done 'St. Asaph, Flintshire' and 'St. Asaph cathedral, Flintshire', both after H. Gastineau, in Gastineau's *Wales illustrated ... 1830*. Br; DNB.

Storm, G. F. (fl. 1834–51) Portrait and landscape engraver. Born in England, he emigrated to Philadelphia, USA, about 1834. Although he is thought to have stayed for only a short time, he engraved a considerable number of American portraits and became expert at stipple and etching. His book work dates from his return to England, and he was responsible for an outline engraving (possibly an etching), 'Modern Jerusalem', after W. H. Bartlett for Bartlett's *Walks about ... Jerusalem* [1844] (signed 'G. P. Storm'), and a folding plate, 'Panorama of Alexandria', was etched by him for Bartlett's *Nile boat* 1849. Two vignette portraits—'Rev. John Whitaker' after Henry Bone and 'Francis Baily' after T. Phillips, both dated 1849—were issued in J. Britton's *Autobiography* 1850. A mural tablet to L'Isle Adam was engraved for Bartlett's *Gleanings ... on the overland route* 1851, and he etched a large folded picture of 'Modern Alexandria' for the same volume. Fi.

Stow, Geo[rge?] (fl. 1830) Architectural engraver. 'Town Hall, Sheffield' and 'Skipton Castle' after Whittock were engraved for Allen's *New ... history of the county of York* 1828–31.

Stowe, J. (fl. 1829–31) Architectural engraver. 'Guildford Castle' after N. Whittock, dated August 1829, appeared in T. Allen's *History ... of Surrey and Sussex* 1829–31. 'The Manor-house, Sheffield', 'Entrance to Skipton Castle' and 'Aysgarth Force' after Whittock were engraved for Allen's *New ... history of the county of York* 1828–31.

Stubbs, J. (fl. 1830–3) Figure and landscape engraver. 'The harlot's progress, 6—The funeral' after W. Hogarth appeared in Hogarth's *Works* 1833, and 'The pier at Scarborough' after W. Westall was issued in T. Moule's *Great Britain illustrated ... 1830*. He can perhaps be identified with James Henry Phillipson Stubbs (1810–64), a pupil of the Findens (q.v.). Br.

Swan, Joseph (?–1872) Landscape engraver. Described as an engraver and publisher, he arrived in Glasgow about 1818, and began publishing his plates in the *Glasgow Mechanics' Magazine* 1824. He continued in works by J. M. Leighton, including *Select views of Glasgow and its environs ... 1828*, *Select views on the River Clyde ... 1830* (with forty-two plates), *Strath-clutha; or, the beauties of the Clyde* 1839 and *History of the County of Fife* 1840. Professor Wilson's *Views of the Lakes of Scotland* 1834 contained forty-nine plates, and two books after Charles Mackie came next, i.e., *Historical description of Paisley ... 1835* (six plates) and

Joseph Swan

Historical description of the town of Dundee... 1836 (twelve plates). A. Fullarton's *Topographical ... gazetteer of Scotland* 1844 also contained some of his plates. Fourteen engravings of his appeared in Sir William Hooker's *Perthshire illustrated* 1843 after James Stewart, William Brown, A. Donaldson and D. Mackenzie, including the engraved title page vignette 'Glen Tilt—huntsmen reposing', 'Scone Palace...', 'Kinfaun's Castle', 'Ballendean' and 'Grave of Bessie Bell and Mary Gray'. Nine engravings after J. Fleming appeared in J. Browne's *History of the Highlands* [c. 1845], including 'Loch Tay', 'Loch Achray' and, in volume 2, a vignette of Ardvraick Castle. His son joined him in the business in 1858 and stayed until 1861, and Swan appears to have retired in 1869. He engraved the maps for the Glasgow Post Office Directories from 1848 to 1858, and was responsible for thirty-one bookplates between 1820 and 1840. He died about 21 September 1872. F; H, p. 203.

Syms (or Symns) W. (fl. 1829–31) Architectural engraver. 'Lambeth Church and Palace' and 'The infirmary, Chichester' (signed 'W. Symns'), both dated 1829 and after N. Whittock, were published in T. Allen's *History ... of Surrey and Sussex* 1829–31, and 'Lyons Inn Hall' and 'Bernard's Inn Hall' (also signed 'W. Symns') after T. H. Shepherd were done for the artist's *London and its environs* 1829–31.

T

Taylor, William (fl. 1830–58) Landscape and architectural engraver. 'Exchequer Gate Lincoln' after the author's design was engraved for Allen's *History of the county of Lincoln* [1830–1], 'View near Rhaiadar, Radnorshire' after Gastineau for Gastineau's *Wales illustrated...* 1830 and 'Church of St. Helen, Sephton' after Harwood and 'St. Mary's Church, Prescot' after Austin for Pyne's *Lancashire illustrated...* 1831. 'Calder Abbey...' and 'Egremont, from the Ravenglass Road' after G. Pickering were engraved for T. Rose's *Cumberland* 1832, and six plates appeared in J. Britton and E. W. Brayley's *Devonshire and Cornwall illustrated* 1832 after T. Allom (including 'Lydford cascade' (a vignette) and 'Oakhampton Castle...') and 'Mount Radford College,

Exeter' after W. H. Bartlett. Other plates after Allom were issued in Rose's *Durham and Northumberland* 1832 (two of Chillingham Castle), Rose's *Westmorland* 1832 (four, including 'Windermere Lake...' and 'Patterdale...') and T. Noble and T. Rose's *Counties of Chester...* 1836 ('Dovedale...' and 'Chatsworth...'). Plates after W. Tombleson were done for Fearnside's *Tombleson's Thames* 1834 (five, including 'Hedsor...' and 'Nore lights'), Fearnside's *Picturesque beauties of the Rhine* [c. 1846] ('Heidelberg' and 'Chur') and *Tombleson's Upper Rhine* [c. 1835] ('Rheinwald glacier'). Four plates after Cattermole, Cox and Purser were engraved for Elliot's *Views in India...* 1835, including 'Grass rope-bridge at Teree-Curwall' after Cox. Other plates after W. H. Bartlett came out in W. Beattie's *Switzerland* 1836 ('Cathedral of Sion—Valais', 'The summit of the Jungfrau' and 'Wetterhorn, Rosenlaui' (in which the mountain effects are well done)) and J. Carne's *Syria* 1836–8 ('Kalendria—coast of Cilicia', 'Camp of Ibrahim Pasha, near Adana' and 'Scheich's house at Zebdane'). 'Knowsley Hall...' after G. Pickering was first used in E. Baines's *History of ... Lancaster* 1836, and later appeared in G. N. Wright's *Gallery of engravings* 1844–6. 'Stair case ... Painted Chamber, Westminster' and 'House of Commons as fitted up in 1835' after R. W. Billings were engraved for E. W. Brayley and J. Britton's *History of the ancient palace ... at Westminster* 1836. 'Source of the River Jumna' after Bentley was done for White's *Views in India...* 1838 and 'St. John & Luzern' after Bartlett for Beattie's *Waldenses* 1838. 'Reading the news' after D. Wilkie was published in *Wilkie gallery* [c. 1849], and again in the 1850 volume of the *Art Journal*, which magazine also included 'Red cap' after G. Lance (1851) and 'The installation' after B. West (1852). 'The garden isle', the frontispiece to Adams's *History ... of the Isle of Wight* 1858, was designed by T. Hellyer and drawn by Luke Limner. He is known to have engraved four bookplates in 1840. He also signed the 1837 petition. F.

Taylor, W. J. (fl. 1833–6) Landscape and figure engraver. A landscape after R. Wilson, dated 1 September 1833, and 'Hagar and the angel' after Claude, dated 1 February 1834, appeared in A. Cunningham's *Cabinet gallery of pictures by the first masters...* 1836. 'Auer' and 'Tarantisberg' after Allom and 'Zoebenberg—Stein' and 'St. Afra—Mortari' appeared in *Views in the Tyrol* [1836].

Templeton, J. (fl. 1864) Landscape engraver. 'Murano' after W. L. Leitch was published in W. Brockedon's *Italy...*, 2nd edition, 1864.

Thibault, Charles Eugène (1835–c. 1884) Figure engraver. For the *Art Journal* he engraved 'The broken thread' and 'La reverie' (1878) and 'At the fountain' (1884), all after J. E. Aubert.

Thom, Andrew (fl. 1845) Landscape engraver. 'Loch Rannoch' after J. Fleming was published in J. Browne's *History of the Highlands* [c. 1845]. He probably had connections in Edinburgh.

Thomas, John (fl. 1830–5) Landscape and architectural engraver. Among his earliest works were 'Llanwrst Bridge' and 'Llanwrst Church', and 'Beaumaris, Isle of Anglesey' after H. Gastineau, for Gastineau's *Wales illustrated...* 1830, and 'St. George's Church, Everton' after Pyne and '"More-Stret"' after Austin for Pyne's *Lancashire illustrated...* 1831. Most of his work was after T. Allom, commencing with eleven plates for J. Britton and E. W. Brayley's *Devonshire and Cornwall illustrated* 1832 (including 'The paths on the beach,

Dawlish', 'Dartmouth castle and harbour' and 'Dolcoath copper mine, Camborne, Cornwall', together with 'Berry Arbor, near Ilfracombe', a good plate after J. Harwood), two plates each for T. Rose's *Durham and Northumberland* 1832 ('Corbridge...' and 'Houghton Castle...') and the same author's *Westmorland* 1832 ('Underlay Hall' and 'South view of Lowther Castle') and 'St. Knighton's Kieve near Boscastle' in Fisher's *Drawing room scrap book* 1835. For the *Literary souvenir* he engraved 'A shipwreck off the Isle of Wight' (1833), 'St. Michael's Mount, Cornwall' (1834) and 'Venice. San Salute' (1835), all after C. Bentley. 'Hindoo Temple— Benares' after Boys was engraved for Elliot's *Views in India...* 1835.

Thompson, David (fl. 1832–58) Landscape engraver. 'Rheineck Castle' after Tombleson was published in *Tombleson's Views of the Rhine* 1832, and 'Village of Besherrai...' after W. H. Bartlett and 'Valley of Jehoshaphat and Brook Kedron' after J. Salmon, both dated 1838, appeared in J. Carne's *Syria* 1836–8. 'Pozzuolo, and the Mole of Caligula' after Leitch was engraved for Wright's *Shores and islands of the Mediterranean* 1840. 'The landslip at East End' after W. B. Cooke appeared in Adams's *History, ... of the Isle of Wight* 1858.

Thompson, D. G[eorge] (d. c. 1870) Historical engraver. Forty-two plates signed 'D. G. Thompson' appeared in the *Universal Family Bible...*, published in Southampton by E. A. Hancock some time between 1850 and 1870. Most of them were after A. Fraser, the most interesting being 'Destruction of Pharaoh's host' and 'Jael killing Sisera' (Plate 57). This may be the Thompson who spent some of his early life in India, where his brother held an official position, and who later emigrated to America about 1856 and died there about 1870. B; Fi.

Thomson, James (1788–1850) Portrait and figure engraver. Baptised on 5 May 1788 at Mitford in Northumberland, where his father was curate, he was the fourth son of the Revd James Thomson of Nunriding Hall, who afterwards became Rector of Ormesby in Yorkshire. At the suggestion of family friends (Lady Anna Hudson, daughter of the Marquis of Townsend, and Sir John Trevelyan) he was articled to an engraver, Mackenzie, of Margaret Street, Cavendish Square, in London about 1803 (his family had given him up for lost when he took nine weeks to reach London by boat from South Shields), with whom he passed seven years of slavery. So, in order to learn more, he joined Anthony Cardon about 1810 and stayed with him until about 1812. Much of his early work with the annuals and other popular books was after bas-reliefs and sculpture: for example, the *Literary souvenir* 1826 published 'Lady Louise Jane Russell' after the Chantrey statue, drawn by H. Corbould; the engraved title page of *The Keepsake* 1831 had a stipple engraving of a bas-relief of Hermes after Flaxman done as a vignette with borders by H. Corbould; the 1836 edition of S. C. Hall's *Book of gems* issued 'Fancy and desire' a vignette of a sculpture after R. Westmacott, 'The mother' a bas-relief after E. H. Baily and 'Muse instructing youth' a bas-relief after W. Wyon; and after W. Wyon, 'Flora' another bas-relief, drawn by H. Corbould, was done for the 1838 edition. Another sculpture, 'The Honourable Anne Seymour Damer', was engraved for H. Walpole's *Anecdotes of painting* 1827, together with five portraits after Seipse and 'Mrs. Anne Killigrew' after Lely. Between May 1829 and June 1831 he engraved five portraits for E. Lodge's *Portraits...*, 2nd edition, 1835 after Holbein and Van Dyck, and for *The Amulet* 1828 he did 'The lady of

Ilkdale' after J. Jackson, signed 'J. Thompson'. This mis-spelling of his name was a common occurrence, and resulted in similar entries appearing under both names in *Bryan's dictionary of painters and engravers*. 'Marie Amélie, reine de français' after Hersent and 'Miss Croker' after Lawrence appeared in *Keepsake français* 1831. *The Keepsake* contained 'The Brighton beauty' after Chalon and 'Camilla' after Bostock (1836), 'The Countess of Guiccioli' after Chalon (1839), 'Mary as the Improvisatatrice' after Leslie (1840) and 'Victoria, Princess Royal' after Lucas (1846). 'The Countess of Wilton' after Lawrence, 'The sisters' after Hayter (Plate 24) and 'Mary' after Leslie were engraved for Heath's *Book of beauty* 1835, 'Margaret' after Chalon for Scott's *Poetical works* 1835 and 'The raising of Lazarus' after Rembrandt for Fisher's *Historic illustrations of the Bible* [1840–3]. The frontispiece of the author after H. Room was engraved for J. Pardoe's *Beauties of the Bosphorus* 1840, and for the *Complete works of Robert Burns* [c. 1842] he did 'Allan Cunningham' also after Room. J. Kitto's *Gallery of scripture engravings* 1846–9 contained ' "He cried with a loud voice" ' after Rembrandt, and for *Beauties of Moore* 1846 he did 'High born Ladye' after S. Hart. 'Household treasures', 'The arrival' and 'The bridal eve' after E. T. Parris, 'LEL' (Laetitia Elizabeth Landon) after D. Maclise, ' "Kate is craz'd" ' after J. Jenkins and 'The Peris of the north' after J. Hayter appeared in G. N. Wright's *Gallery of engravings* 1844–6, and 'Mrs. Young, wife of H. M.'s late consul in Palestine' and 'Hebrew women reading the scriptures at Jerusalem' after D. Wilkie came out in *Wilkie gallery* [c. 1849]. A stipple portrait, 'John Britton', was the frontispiece of Britton's *Autobiography* 1850 after R. W. Satchwell and T. Uwins, and portraits of Dr Cartwright, Cuvier, Franklin (after J. A. Duplessis), George F. Handel, Raffaele and John Sobieski appeared in the *Imperial dictionary of universal biography* [c. 1861]. He married Miss Lloyd of Rhayader, Radnorshire, and had two daughters— Anne, who married the artist Frederick Goodall, son of the engraver Edward Goodall (q.v.), and Eliza. He died of pulmonary consumption after a long illness, having been confined to bed for the last six weeks of his life, on 27 September 1850 at 97 Albany Street, Regent's Park, at the age of sixty-two. He joined the Artists' Annuity Fund in 1825 and signed the 1837 petition. He had R. A. Artlett (q.v.) as his pupil. AJ; B; DNB; R; S.

Thurgar, W. (fl. 1854) Architectural engraver. A plate of the remains of the Abbey church, Bury St Edmunds, after G. Thompson was published in F. Lankester's *Nineteen views of Bury St. Edmunds* 1854. Ho.

Tingle, James (fl. 1824–50) Landscape and architectural engraver. Between May 1827 and July 1829 he engraved eleven plates for J. Elmes's *Metropolitan improvements* 1829, and in the next two years did twenty more for T. H. Shepherd's *London and its environs* 1829–31, all after T. H. Shepherd. Six plates after Gastineau were engraved for Gastineau's *Wales illustrated...* 1830 (including two of Tintern), views of two Manchester churches after Harwood for Pyne's *Lancashire illustrated...* 1831 and 'Pompeii. Pedestal in the Forum' after Gell for Gell's *Pompeiana...* 1832. 'The two Foscari' after S. Prout was done for T. Roscoe's *Tourist in Switzerland and Italy* 1830. After T. Allom he engraved 'Royal Arcade, Newcastle-upon-Tyne' and 'Featherstone Castle...' for T. Rose's *Durham and Northumberland* 1832 and for the same author 'Milnthorpe Sands...' and 'Interior of Sizergh Hall...' for *Westmorland* 1832. Plates after W. Tombleson were published in *Tombleson's views of the Rhine* 1832 ('Church of the Virgin Mary at Oberwesel',

'Castle of Pfalz...' and 'Rudesheim'), Fearnside's *Tombleson's Thames* 1834 (eight plates, including 'Bray Bucks' (Plate 20) and 'Hammersmith Bridge', with 'St. Catherine's Docks' after Calvert) and Fearnside's *Picturesque beauties of the Rhine* [c. 1846] (four plates, including 'Remagen...' and 'Strasburg'). 'Interior of the chapter house, Lincoln Cathedral' and 'The high Bridge over the Witham, Lincoln' were published in T. Noble and T. Rose's *Counties of Chester...* 1836, 'Christian and Hopeful escaping from Doubting Castle' after H. Melville in Bunyan's *Pilgrim's progress* 1836, four plates after Allom, Harwood and G. Pickering (including 'Power loom weaving' and 'Blue coat school, Oldham') in E. Baines's *History of ... Lancaster* 1836, 'The Grass Market. Death of Porteous' after T. M. Richardson in Wright's *Landscape-historical illustrations of Scotland* 1836–8, 'Pra del Tor' after Bartlett in Beattie's *Waldenses* 1838, 'Crossing the Choor Mountain' after Stanfield in White's *Views in India...* 1838 and six plates after Allom, F. Herve and W. L. Leitch in R. Walsh's *Constantinople* 1838–40 (including 'Route through the Balkans', 'Mosque of Sultan Salim, Scutari' and 'Castle of Parga, Albania'). Engravings after the designs of W. H. Bartlett appeared in J. Carne's *Syria* 1836–8 (eight, including 'The pass of Beilan...' and 'Zarapha...'), three of which were reissued in J. Kitto's *Gallery of scripture engravings* 1846–9, in N. P. Willis's *American scenery* 1840 ('The United States Bank, Philadelphia') and in Willis's *Canadian scenery* 1842 ('Prescot Gate, Quebec'). The engraved title page of L. Townsend's *Alphabetical chronology of remarkable events...*, published as part of T. Dugdale's *England and Wales delineated* [1838–9] carried the engraving 'The new Gresham College, London'. Five plates after T. Allom were published in G. N. Wright's *China* 1843, and included 'Silk farms at Hoo-chen' and 'Loading tea junks at Tseen-tang'. He also worked in aquatint. He joined the Artists' Annuity Fund in 1835. T.

Tingle, Robert (fl. 1828) Architectural engraver. Probably a brother of James Tingle, unless the writing engraver made a mistake and this Tingle was James. 'Brewer's alms houses, Mile End' after T. H. Shepherd, dated 17 January 1828, was published in J. Elmes's *Metropolitan improvements* 1829.

Todd, R. (fl. 1830–1) Landscape engraver. 'Alton Towers, Staffordshire' after J. Fradgley and 'Tong Castle...' after Calvert were engraved for West's *Picturesque views ... in Staffordshire and Shropshire...* 1830–1.

Tombleson, William (c. 1795–?) Landscape engraver. He is thought to have been born about 1795. A man of many parts, he appears to have been an engraver who saw the publishing possibilities of his work, and issued plates and books on the Rhine and the Thames in the 1830s which were probably as well known on the Continent as in England. (See B. Hunnisett, *Steel-engraved book illustration in England* 1980, p. 161.) Some of his early plates were done for J. P. Neale's *Views of the seats of noblemen...* 1818–24, but his first considerable work in steel was done for J. Elmes's *Metropolitan improvements* 1829, for which between March 1827 and August 1828 he engraved thirteen plates, all after T. H. Shepherd, including 'Bank of England', 'Hanover Lodge, Regents Park' and 'Waterloo Place', and he did 'East India House, Leadenhall St.' dated 31 October 1829, for T. H. Shepherd's *London and its environs* 1829–31, again after T. H. Shepherd. Ten plates were done for Shepherd's *Modern Athens* 1829–31. 'Storrs, Windermere Lake...' and 'Furness Abbey...' after Harwood were engraved for Pyne's *Lancashire illustrated...* 1831. 'Monte Aventino' after S. Prout

was done for T. Roscoe's *Tourist in Italy* 1831, a vignette, 'Entrance to Bath...' after Shepherd for J. Britton's *Bath and Bristol* 1829, four plates after T. Allom for J. Britton and E. W. Brayley's *Devonshire and Cornwall illustrated* 1832, including two of Devonport and 'Clovelly...', and after the same artist 'Colwith Force...' and 'Dungeon Gill...' for T. Rose's *Cumberland* 1832. Four plates after Bartlett were done for Wright's *Picturesque beauties of Great Britain ... Essex* 1831–34. He seems to have done few for his own publications, one exception being 'Cologne' after his own design for Fearnside's *Picturesque beauties of the Rhine* [c. 1846]. 'Falkland Palace...' and 'Glammis Castle...' after Allom were engraved for W. Beattie's *Scotland illustrated* 1838, and 'Lockport, Erie Canal' after W. H. Bartlett was done for N. P. Willis's *American scenery* 1840. It would appear that he also worked for Fenner, Sears & Co. (q.v.) in the early 1830s, where he worked with T. Engleheart, F. W. Topham and H. Beckwith (qq.v.). He joined the Artists' Annuity Fund in 1827. B; H; Ro; T.

Topham, Francis William (1808–1877) Landscape and architectural engraver. Born in Leeds on 15 April 1808, he was apprenticed to an uncle who was a writing engraver, possibly Samuel Topham, who engraved some bookplates between 1800 and 1840 (Fincham). When he came to London in 1830 he was twenty-one and just out of his apprenticeship. His first work here consisted of engraving coats of arms. Soon afterwards he joined the firm of Fenner, Sears & Co. (q.v.) and was first put under T. Engleheart (q.v.) to engrave a South Seas view, but since this seemed to his employers to be too difficult a task for him, he was considerably helped by William Tombleson (q.v.), who finished the plate for him. Another fellow engraver was Henry Beckwith (q.v.), whose sister Topham married. Probably, his first published work as a book engraver under his own name was the provision of an ornamental frame to an engraving by Samuel Fisher, 'Roman column at Igel near Treves' after S. Prout, which appeared in the *Continental annual* 1832. A disagreement with Alaric Watts over the payment for an engraving led to Topham's introduction to S. C. Hall, for whose *Book of gems* 1836 he engraved two vignettes—'Poetry and painting' after E. T. Parris for the engraved title page and 'Wreath of flowers' after Miss Byrne. For the 1838 edition of the same work he designed and engraved a tailpiece of lyre, urn, flowers and books. He then gained more regular employment, with George Virtue and Henry Fisher the publishers, and for the latter engraved 'Christian church at Tortosa' after W. H.

Francis William Topham

Bartlett, dated 1837, for J. Carne's *Syria* 1836–8. Other commissions included: 'Holm Peel Castle...' 'Sir Kenneth and the Baron of Gilsland' and 'Bertha at the camp of the Crusaders' after his (Topham's) own designs for Wright's *Landscape-historical illustrations of Scotland* 1836–8; three plates after T. Allom for R. Walsh's *Constantinople* 1838–40, including 'The Valley of Unkiariskillesse...' (a very well engraved plate); J. Pardoe's *Beauties of the Bosphorus* 1840, with three plates after Bartlett, including 'Tomb in the cemetery of Scutari'; N. P. Willis's *American scenery* 1840, with 'The narrows, Lake George' and 'Bridge at Glens Hall (on the Hudson)' after Bartlett; and three plates after Bartlett for J. S. Coyne's *Scenery and antiquities of Ireland* [c. 1840]. '"And they went to Ophir..."' after Melville appeared in Fisher's *Historic illustrations of the Bible* [1840–3] and eight plates after Bartlett in Willis's *Canadian scenery* 1842. 'Ness sands lighthouses', 'Greenock' and 'Barmouth', also after Bartlett, were done for W. Beattie's *Ports, harbours...* 1842 and 'Scene near the Weltenberg' and 'Ruins of Golumbacz', again after Bartlett, for W. Beattie's *Danube* 1844. 'Skirmish on the retreat to Busaco' after J. Gilbert appeared in W. H. Maxwell's *Life of ... the Duke of Wellington* 1839–41 and 'Scotch drink' after J. M. Wright was done for the *Complete works of Robert Burns* [c. 1842]. 'Sortie from Lathom House' after G. Cattermole appeared in R. Cattermole's *Great Civil War* 1846 and 'Greenwich Park and Palace...' in Scott's *Waverley novels*. 'City and Lake of Constance...', 'Festival of Al-Mohurram' after H. Melville and 'The robber's death bed' appeared in G. N. Wright's *Gallery of engravings* 1844–6, and for the same author's *China* 1843 he engraved 'Imperial Palace at Tseaou-shan'. His last important book work was probably for S. C. Hall's *Gems of European art* 1846, for which he engraved his own 'The wayfarers', indicating perhaps how far his painting studies had advanced, 'Arabs of the Bishareen Desert' after H. Warren, 'The opium seller' after W. Muller, 'Travellers at the well' after J. Zeitter and 'The benevolent cottagers' after Sir Augustus Callcott. 'Jacob's well at Sychar' after Bartlett was published in Stebbing's *Christian in Palestine* [1847]. Having since his childhood been more interested in painting, but owing to his father's opposition having been unable to pursue it until he went to London, as soon as he was able he gave up engraving. The break came at about the time he was elected to the Old Water Colour Society in 1848. He joined the Artists' Annuity Fund in 1837. He died while on a visit to Spain at Cordova on 31 March 1877, and was buried in the Protestant cemetery there. AJ; Br; DNB; F; H; Ro.

Treacher, E. G. (fl. 1838) Architectural engraver. 'Ruins at the head of the Knight's Street, Rhodes' after W. H. Bartlett was published in J. Carne's *Syria* 1836–8.

Turnbull, J. (fl. 1850) Architectural engraver. 'Hall of mirrors, Colosseum, Regents Park' after C. Marshall was issued in W. G. Fearnside and T. Harral's *History of London* [c. 1850].

Turnbull, Thomas (fl. 1836–43) Landscape and architectural engraver. 'Beauvais Cathedral, the aisle of the transept looking north' after R. Garland, dated 1 July 1836, was published in B. Winkles's *French cathedrals* 1837, and 'Salisbury cathedral; the lady chapel' after H. Winkles and 'Wells cathedral, chapter house' after R. Garland appeared in *Winkles's ... Cathedral churches of England...* 1836–42. 'Seleucia' after W. H. Bartlett was engraved for J. Carne's *Syria* 1836–8, 'Greek Church of Baloukli...' after T. Allom for R. Walsh's *Constantinople* 1838–40, 'Rock of Casel' after

Bartlett for J. S. Coyne's *Scenery and antiquities of Ireland* [c. 1840] and 'The gothic church (New Haven)', also after Bartlett, for N. P. Willis's *American scenery* 1840. 'Pavilion of the Star of Hope, Tong-chow' after Allom was done for G. N. Wright's *China* 1843, and for the same author's *Rhine, Italy and Greece* [1841], he did 'The Giant's stairs, Ducal Palace, Venice' after W. L. Leitch (Plate 40).

Tye, J. (fl. 1830–1) Architectural engraver. 'Etruria Hall, seat of Josiah Wedgwood...' after Calvert and 'Davenport House, Shropshire' after H. Harris were engraved for West's *Picturesque views ... in Staffordshire and Shropshire...* 1830–1.

Tyson, (fl. 1860) Figure engraver. 'A French glee maiden' after Fairly was published in *The Cottage girl...* [c. 1860].

V

Varrall, John Charles (fl. 1818–58) Landscape and architectural engraver. His earliest works on steel were probably the twenty-seven plates after Gastineau engraved for Gastineau's *Wales illustrated...* 1830, four of which were used again in Woodward's *History of Wales* 1853. 'The Sands at Llanstephen' and 'Llanstephen Castle' are good examples of his work (Plate 13). Between February 1827 and November 1828 he produced 'Colonne de Joux', 'Scene in the Val Romanche', 'Ponte Tremola' and 'Fall of the Toccia' after W. Brockedon for the artist's *Illustrations of the passes of the Alps* 1828–9. 'Eskdale...' after G. Pickering was done for T. Rose's *Cumberland* 1832, two plates after Gell for Gell's *Pompeiana...* 1832, 'Nonnewert' after C. Stanfield for L. Ritchie's *Travelling sketches on the Rhine* 1833, 'Eu, looking towards Triport' after Stanfield for Ritchie's *Travelling sketches on the sea coasts of France* 1834 and 'Approach to Royat' and 'Thiers' after J. D. Harding, both dated 28 October 1833, for T. Roscoe's *Tourist in France* 1834. 'Convent of Il Santo Cosimato, near Tivoli' after J. D. Harding, dated 28 October 1832, was published in T. Roscoe's *Tourist in Italy* 1833, and for Roscoe's *Tourist in Spain. Granada* 1835 he did 'Gaucin...' after D. Roberts, dated 28 October 1834. 'Nuneham Courtenay, Oxon' and 'Greenhithe, Kent' after W. Tombleson were done for Fearnside's *Tombleson's Thames* 1834, 'Stockport' after Pickering for E. Baines's *History of ... Lancaster* 1836, 'Swingenberg' after Allom for *Views in the Tyrol* [1836], 'Tripoli' after W. H. Bartlett for J. Carne's *Syria* 1836–8 and 'Dryburgh Abbey...', 'Bracklin Bridge' and 'Loch Katrine...', all after Allom, and 'Dunrobin Castle...' after W. H. Bartlett for W. Beattie's *Scotland illustrated* 1838. 'The Abbey and hills from near Mussooree' after Dibdin was engraved for White's *Views in India...* 1838, 'Scene in the Pass of the Guill...' after Bartlett for Beattie's *Waldenses* 1838 and 'The Subas House, Boorhanpur' after Taylor for Bacon's *Oriental annual* 1840. 'Yeni Djami...' and 'The City walls (descending to the port)' after Bartlett were engraved for J. Pardoe's *Beauties of the Bosphorus* 1840, 'Matlock Bath' and 'Dunottar Castle...' after Bartlett for W. Beattie's *Ports, harbours...* 1842, 'Storming of Bristol' and 'The Scots pursued after the Battle of Preston' after G. Cattermole for R. Cattermole's *Great Civil War* 1846 and 'Windsor Castle from the Long Walk' after J. D. harding for L. Ritchie's *Windsor Castle* 1848. 'Ruins of Sponeck' after Tombleson appeared in Fearnside's *Picturesque beauties of the Rhine* [c. 1846], 'Ruins of Bodmin, with the Frauenberg', also after Tombleson, in Fearnside's *Tombleson's*

Upper Rhine [c. 1835], and 'Boulevard du Temple' after Callow and 'Steamer entering Folkstone [*sic*] harbour in a heavy gale' after Clint in *The Keepsake* 1849. Three plates after Marshall appeared in Fearnside and Harral's *History of London* [c. 1850], and two vignettes after Walton were published in Adams's *History ... of the Isle of Wight* 1858. He joined the Artists' Annuity Fund in 1820 and signed the 1837 petition.

Vernon, Thomas (c. 1824–72) Figure engraver. He was born in Staffordshire about 1824. He studied in Paris and was a pupil of P. Lightfoot (q.v.). For volume 3 of *The Works of John Bunyan* 1852–3 he engraved 'Christiana & her family ...' after Stothard. For the *Art Journal* he engraved 'Infant Bacchus' after Sir Martin Shee, issued in the 1852 volume, and in the next year he emigrated to New York. Here he worked chiefly for the banknote companies, but is said to have returned to England in 1856 or 1857. The *Art Journal* 1855 published his plate 'Virgin Mother' after W. Dyce, described by a later critic as 'an exquisitely beautiful plate' (AJ. 1872, p. 75). There followed for that journal 'The Amazon' after F. Winterhalter (1857), 'Abundance' after J. van Eycken (1859), 'The Lady Constance' after F. Winterhalter (1860), 'The novice' after A. Elmore (1865), 'Olivia' after C. R. Leslie (1863) and 'Othello relating his adventures' after C. W. Cope (1872). These last two plates were used again in the *Works of Shakspere* [*sic*], *Imperial edition* 1872. His last plate was 'Christ healing the paralytic' after Murillo. This picture was the property of Col. Tomline, MP, who presented the plate (and, presumably its proceeds) to the Newspaper Press Fund. Other plates were 'Madonna and Child' after Raphael and 'First born' after C. W. Cope. He seems never to have made much money, and died poor on 23 January 1872, aged about forty-eight. He was elected a member of the Graphic Society in 1867.   AJ; B; Br; DNB; Fi; S.

W

Wagner, F. R. (fl. 1851) Figure engraver. 'Flower girl' after H. Howard was engraved for the 1851 volume of the *Art Journal*.

Wagstaff, Charles Eden (1808–50). Portrait and figure engraver. He appears to have worked mainly for the print publishers, especially in the 1840s. 'Tyrol' after J. Browne was published in Finden's *Tableaux* 1837, and 'The lily of the valley' after Frank Stone in Fisher's *Drawing room scrap book* 1836. Eight portraits after various artists were published in the *Imperial dictionary of universal biography* [c. 1861] including 'Sir J. Banks', 'Dryden', 'Luther' and 'James Watt'. He joined the Artists' Annuity Fund in 1832, when he was twenty-four, became its Treasurer in 1843, and was President from 1840 to 1842. He has been identified with an engraver with the same initials who is said to have been working in Boston, Massachusetts, about 1840–5. This identification seems to be unlikely to be true, since our engraver was heavily committed to work for the print publishers at that time (seven plates were published between 1843 and 1845), and in February 1843 he was Secretary of the 'Amicable Society' (Junior Artists' Annuity Fund). In 1846 he was the Secretary of the Institute of Fine Arts, with Frank Howard as Chairman. These two signed a document accusing the governing body of mismanagement, and a separate action of the Treasurer was reported in the *Art Union* 1846 to have caused a rift in the Institute. In 1847 Wagstaff was the Treasurer, and Howard the Secretary, of a Society, originally of thirty-two, but later of forty, members, each of whom subscribed £5 to hire the Great Room in the Egyptian Hall for a season for a 'Free Exhibition. All artists, including engravers on copper, steel or wood are invited to take places'. (AU 1847, p. 142).   AU; S; St.

Wagstaff, J. E. (fl. 1838–42) Portrait and figure engraver. 'The merry imp' after J. Boaden, a very charming outline vignette in stipple, was published in S. C. Hall's *Book of gems* 1838. 'Duke of Wellington' after H. W. Pickersgill was issued independently in 1842.

Wagstaff, W. (fl. 1833) Portrait engraver. 'S. T. Coleridge' afer A. Wivell was published in *Finden's illustrations of the life and works of Lord Byron* 1833–4.

Walker, Frederick F. (1805–?) Figure engraver. Six plates were engraved for W. Hogarth's *Works* 1833, including 'The harlot's progress, 1. Ensnared by a procuress', 'Times of day—Evening' and 'Industry and idleness—12.'. 'The parting of Hinda and Iran' after F. P. Stephanoff was published in T. Moore's *Lalla Rookh* 1838, 'Show room of a Canton merchant at Peking' after T. Allom in G. N. Wright's *China* 1843 and 'The shepherds of Arcadia' after N. Poussin in S. C. Hall's *Gems of European art* 1846. 'Last effort and fall of Tipoo Sahib' after Singleton was published in Nolan's *Illustrated history of the British Empire in India* [1858–60] and 'Christ and his disciples in the cornfields' after Warren in *The Self-interpreting Bible* 1864. He joined the Artists' Annuity Fund in 1836.   B; T.

Walker, John and Charles (fl. 1827–95) Map engravers. They drew and engraved two maps for E. Baines's *History of ... Lancaster* 1836, and one of Devonshire for J. Britton and E. W. Brayley's *Devonshire and Cornwall illustrated* 1832.

Wallis, C. (fl. 1833–8) Landscape engraver. 'Lewes, Sussex' after W. Purser was published in *Watering places ...* 1833, and was used again in *Fashionable guide ...* [c. 1838], together with 'Woolwich from Sandy Hill' and 'Blackwall' after E. Pritchett. It has not been possible to connect him with the three Wallis brothers who follow, or to identify him with the Charles Wallis said to be working in 1823.   B; T.

Wallis, Henry (c. 1805–90). Landscape engraver. He was the youngest of the three brothers, sons of Thomas Wallis (d. 1839), figure engraver, who worked as assistant to Charles Heath until Heath's death. He was probably taught engraving by his father or brothers, and could only just have been out of his apprenticeship when he engraved 'Irish holy well' after Penry Williams for *The Amulet* 1827; he was twenty-one or twenty-two. In 1828 (April 21) he did 'The Coliseum, Regents Park' and 'York Gate, Regents Park' after T. H. Shepherd for J. Elmes's *Metropolitan improvements* 1829, and 'Hale Place ...' and 'Licensed Victualler's Asylum, Kent Road, near London' after T. M. Baynes, both dated October 1830, for S. W. H. Ireland's *England's topographer* (commenced publication 1828). Two Liverpool views after Austin and Harwood were engraved for Pyne's *Lancashire illustrated ...* 1831. He was possibly the engraver for 'Kellerton Park ...' and 'St. Andrews Church, Plymouth' after Bartlett and Allom respectively in J. Britton and E. W. Brayley's *Devonshire and Cornwall illustrated* 1832 and 'Northfleet, Kent' after W. Tombleson in Fearnside's *Tombleson's Thames* 1834, each of which is merely signed 'Wallis'. Thirteen plates after Bartlett were done for Wright's *Picturesque beauties of Great Britain ... Essex* 1831–4 and 'Singham Mahal, Torway—Bejapore' after Cox for Elliot's *Views in India ...*

1835. Seven plates were published in *Watering places...* 1833 after T. Allom, C. Bentley, W. Purser, G. Sharpe and J. Salmon, including 'Sheerness, Kent' and 'Beulah Spa, Norwood'. All seven were used again in *Fashionable guide...* [c. 1838], together with twenty-two other engravings, after E. Pritchett, J. B. Pyne, A. Vickers, J. Phillips and T. H. Shepherd. They included 'Pavilion, Brighton' (a vignette on the engraved title page), 'Windsor from the meadows', 'The Parade, Tunbridge Wells' and 'View in Regent Street'. Two plates after T. Allom appeared in J. Britton and E. W. Brayleys' *Devonshire and Cornwall illustrated* 1832, i.e., 'Plymouth breakwater...' and 'The Barbican, Pool &c, Plymouth', two more in T. Rose's *Cumberland* 1832 and two more in the same author's *Westmorland* 1832. 'The wreck', a vignette after W. Chambers, was done for S. C. Hall's *Book of gems* 1836, and in 1834 and 1835 he was engaged upon five plates after W. H. Bartlett for W. Beattie's *Switzerland* 1836, including 'View of Thun...' and 'Lake of Lungern...'. 'Washington, from the President's House' and 'View from Mount Ida' after W. H. Bartlett were engraved for N. P. Willis's *American scenery* 1840. Plates after T. Creswick were done for L. Ritchie's *Ireland...* 1837 ('Sackville Street, Dublin' and 'Lighthouse at Howth'), and these were used again in S. C. and A. M. Hall's *Ireland* 1841–3, together with 'St. Patrick's Bridge, Cork' and 'Killaloe on the Shannon, Clare'; all four were vignettes. 'Pignerol, from the east...' after Bartlett was engraved for Beattie's *Waldenses* 1838. For W. Beattie's *Scotland illustrated* 1838 he engraved three plates after T. Allom and one after W. Purser, including 'Town and Castle of Stirling...' and 'Bridge of Don...', and seven engravings after T. H. Shepherd and A. W. Wray appeared in T. Dugdale's *England and Wales delineated* [1838–9]. In the 1840s when he was between thirty-five and forty-five he had two successive attacks of paralysis, forcing him to abandon engraving, so he took up picture dealing instead. He ran into a bad patch in the late 1850s and in 1861 was offered the managership of the French Gallery in Pall Mall by the owner Gambart, whom he bought out in 1867 for £1,000. In 1871 he retired in favour of his son Thomas and died a wealthy man on 15 October 1890. B; Br; DNB; J; Maas, *Gambart*, 1975, pp. 45, 98, 129–31, 151–2, 200, 270.

Wallis, Robert (1794–1878) Landscape engraver. Born in London on 7 November 1794, he was the eldest son of Thomas Wallis (d. 1839), a figure engraver who worked for Charles Heath. Robert seems to have spent his youth in the country, only returning to London about 1818, although he had been taught engraving by his father. He was twenty-four when he returned to London, and immediately found work in J. P. Neale's *Views of the seats of noblemen...* 1818–24, and in *Picturesque views on the southern coast of England* 1826, to which he contributed 'Ramsgate' and 'Folkestone' (both after Turner, of the engraving of whose works Robert became a leading exponent). 'Cascades of Gavarnie' after J. Hardy, published in *Forget me not* 1825, is one of the early examples of an engraver making the best use of steel as a design medium instead of treating it merely as a means of obtaining more prints from a plate. An inscription plate designed by Mrs Pope and 'The last man' after G. Jones appeared in *The Amulet* 1828, 'Buckfastleigh Abbey, Devonshire' after Turner appeared in the *Literary souvenir* 1827 and 'A fête champêtre' after Danby was done for the 1828 volume. 'Haddon Hall' after R. R. Reinagle appeared in *The Bijou* 1828, 'York House, St. James's Park' and 'Regent Street from the Circus Piccadilly' after T. H. Shepherd, both dated 9 February 1828, in J. Elmes's *Metropolitan improvements* 1829 and 'Castle of

Chillon' after C. Stanfield and 'Newstead' after F. Danby, both dated 1 October 1828, in *The Anniversary* 1829. What are probably his most famous engravings are those for S. Rogers' *Italy* 1830. These were six vignettes after J. M. W. Turner, including those of Meillerie, St. Maurice, The Roman pontiffs, an adventure, a ship under sail and a farewell (garden, lake and hills), with an engraving of a tomb at Arqua after S. Prout. A vignette of a ruined abbey, Wharfedale, also after Turner, appeared in S. Rogers' *Poems* 1834, and three more vignettes after Turner were issued in T. Campbell's *Poetical works* 1837. In all three books the plates are signed simply 'Wallis'. He was also probably the engraver of 'Château St. Germain' after W. Brockedon, dated March 1828, in the artist's *Illustrations of the passes of the Alps* 1828–9 (again it is signed 'Wallis'). 'Bridge of sighs' after S. Prout, dated 28 October 1829, was done for T. Roscoe's *Tourist in Switzerland and Italy* 1830. Seven plates of Liverpool scenes after Allom, Austin and the Pynes were engraved for Pyne's *Lancashire illustrated...* 1831 and 'Lac de Como' after Stanfield for *Keepsake français* 1831. For *The Keepsake* he engraved 'Lake Albano' (1829), two views of Virginia Water (1830), 'Saumur' (1831), 'St. Germain-en-Laye' (1832), 'Ehrenbreitstein' (1833) and 'Havre' (1834), all after Turner, and 'Exterior gallery round the Ducal Palace, Venice' (1837) and 'Cortele Salviati' (1846), both after Lake Price. 'Resurrection' after Martin was done for *The Amulet* 1831, four plates after Prout for Roscoe's *Tourist in Italy* 1831 (including 'The Rialto, Venice' and 'Rimini') and 'Remains of a Moorish bridge on the Darro' after Roberts for Roscoe's *Tourist in Spain. Granada* 1835. 'Lago Maggiore', 'St. Pietro de Castello, Venice', 'Murano' and 'Strasburg' after C. Stanfield were published in L. Ritchie's *Travelling sketches in the north of Italy* 1832 and five similar engravings were done after Stanfield for Ritchie's *Travelling sketches on the Rhine* 1833, with a further six in *Travelling sketches on the sea coasts of France* 1834, including 'Abbeville', 'Water mills at Eu' and 'Distant view of Mont St. Michel', which is a good example of his work. 'Ruins' after D. Roberts appeared in the *Literary souvenir* 1835, and a vignette of headland, sun and sea after Turner was done for S. Rogers' *Poems* 1834. 'Hermitage Castle' and 'Kelso' after Turner were done for Scott's *Poetical works* 1833–4 and 'Taj Mahal–Agra' after Prout for Elliot's *Views in India...* 1835. 'Liverpool from the Mersey' after S. Austin, dated 1831, appeared in E. Baines's *History of... Lancaster* 1836, seventeen plates after W. H. Bartlett in W. Beattie's *Switzerland* 1836 (including 'Mont Blanc from the Jura', two plates entitled 'Tell's Chapel...' and 'Thun with the Bernese Alps', a vignette, 'Kilkeeny Castle...', after T. Creswick in L. Ritchie's *Ireland...* 1837 and six engravings after Bartlett, Allom, McCulloch and Campion in Beattie's *Scotland illustrated* 1838. Twelve plates after Bartlett and Brockedon were engraved for Beattie's *Waldenses* 1838. Ten plates after Bartlett were done for J. S. Coyne's *Scenery and antiquities of Ireland* [c. 1840] (including 'Clondalkin', 'Larne' and 'Clew Bay from West Port'), and what was considered to be his best plate by some, 'Lake of Nemi' after Turner, dated June 1842, was published in Finden's *Royal Gallery of British Art* 1838–49. Fourteen engravings after Bartlett were issued in N. P. Willis's *American scenery* 1840, eight after the same artist in J. Pardoe's *Beauties of the Bosphorus* 1840, eight more after T. Creswick in S. C. and A. M. Hall's *Ireland* 1841–3, ten after Bartlett in W. Beattie's *Ports, harbours...* 1842 and fifteen after Bartlett in Willis's *Canadian scenery* 1842. 'Olevano' and 'Bergamo' after W. Brockedon and W. Cowen respectively were done for Brockedon's *Italy...* 1842–3. 'Two engravings after W. H. Bartlett appeared in the artist's *Walks *about ... Jerusalem* [1844] and eleven after the same artist in W. Beattie's *Danube* 1844, including 'Ratisbon or Regensberg', 'Monastery of Melk' and 'Nicopoli'. 'Polesden' after Allom was published in Brayley's *Topographical history of Surrey* 1841–8. 'The Queen at Burlington' and 'Destruction of the property of Royalists' after G. Cattermole appeared in R. Cattermole's *Great Civil War* 1846 and 'The hawking party at rest' after P. Wouvermans, 'The writing master' after F. Mieris, 'The hermit' after G. Douw and 'The brothers' after Vogel in S.C. Hall's *Gems of European art* 1846. Eight plates after Bartlett, including 'Solomon's Pools (near Bethlehem)', were published in Stebbing's *Christian in Palestine* [1847]. 'Windsor Castle from the Great Park' and 'Fishing Temple, Virginia Water' after J.D. Harding were done for L. Ritchie's *Windsor Castle* 1848 and 'Tarsus with Mount Taurus' and 'Arches in Alexandria Troas' after Bartlett for Conybeare and Howson's *Life and epistles of St. Paul* 1854. Fourteen of his engravings were published in the *Art Journal* between 1849 and 1880, including three after Turner, viz., 'On the Thames' (1854), 'Brighton Chain pier' (1862) and 'Lake of Lucerne' (1865), which last had been etched by E.J. Roberts (q.v.), 'Passing cloud' after J.C. Hook (1865) and a reissue of 'The writing master' in 1880. The second and third of the Turner plates, together with 'Orange merchantmen going to pieces', were used again in Wornum's *Turner Gallery* [c. 1878]. 'The approach to Venice' after Turner was his last important work, and a proof was exhibited at the Royal Academy in 1859. Shortly afterwards he gave up engraving and retired to Brighton, where he enjoyed good health until a year or two before his death, on 23 November 1878, aged eighty-four. He joined the Artists' Annuity Fund in 1823, and had J.B. Allen (q.v.) to work for him. AJ; DNB; H.

Wallis, William (1796–?) Landscape and architectural engraver. He was the second of the three brothers, sons of Thomas Wallis (d. 1839). He engraved plates for J.P. Neale's *Views of the seats of noblemen...* 1818–24, and for *Excursions through Sussex* 1818–22. Between March 1827 and April 1829 he engraved nineteen plates for J. Elmes's *Metropolitan improvements* 1829, and 'Sondrio' and 'Bordighera' after W. Brockedon for the artist's *Illustrations of the passes of the Alps* 1828–9, and between November 1829 and April 1830 he did twelve engravings for T.H. Shepherd's *London and its environs* 1829–31. 'Literary Institution and cathedral ... Bath', and 'The King's Bath Pump Room ... Bath' after T.H. Shepherd were published in J. Britton's *Bath and Bristol* 1829, three views in T.H. Shepherd's *Modern Athens* 1829–31, 'Domo d'Ossola' and 'Milan cathedral' after S. Prout in T. Roscoe's *Tourist in Switzerland and Italy* 1830 (the last-named plate appearing again in *The Keepsake* 1831 and in D. Costello's *Piedmont and Italy* [c. 1855]), twenty-two plates after Gastineau in the artist's *Wales illustrated...* 1830, 'Rouen cathedral' after Prout in the *Continental annual* 1832 and 'St. Mark's Church, Venice' after the same artist in T. Roscoe's *Tourist in Italy* 1831, and 'Hall of the Abencerages' after D. Roberts was done for Roscoe's *Tourist in Spain. Granada* 1835. 'Interior of Zwinger Palace, Dresden' after Prout was engraved for *The Keepsake* 1832 and 'Caius Marius mourning over the ruins of Carthage' after Martin for the 1833 volume. 'Interior of Godshill Church' after T. Barber came out in *Barber's picturesque illustrations of the Isle of Wight* [c. 1835]. Plates after W.H. Bartlett came out in W. Beattie's *Switzerland* 1836, including 'Street in Sion-Valais' and 'Zurich' (one of his best examples) among six in all; 'Rhodes...' and 'Jaffa' (another good plate) in J. Carne's *Syria* 1836–8; 'Church of St. Francisco, Oporto' and

'Monument of Don John, Batalha' after Holland in Harrison's *Tourist in Portugal* 1839; and 'Mosque of the Sultana Valide (from the port)' in J. Pardoe's *Beauties of the Bosphorus* 1840. 'Stirling Castle' (another good plate) appeared in W. Beattie's *Scotland illustrated* 1838 after T. Allom, who was also the artist for 'St. George's Hall' in L. Ritchie's *Windsor Castle* 1848, and 'Hammond discovering the King's attempt to escape from Carisbrook' after G. Cattermole was done for R. Cattermole's *Great Civil War* 1846. 'The cathedral at Worms' after S. Prout appeared in G.N. Wright's *Gallery of engravings* 1844–6, and for Woodward's *General history of Hampshire* 1863 four vignettes were included—'Market cross, Winchester' and 'Walls of Southampton' after Bartlett and 'Winchester cathedral, east end' and 'Holy Ghost Chapel' after J.C. Armytage. 'Ruins of Laodicia' after S. Bough was used in the *Imperial Family Bible* 1873, (originally published in 1844). He joined the Artists' Annuity Fund in 1820. DNB.

Wands, Charles (fl. 1844–73) Figure engraver. Five plates were engraved for *The Works of John Bunyan* 1852–3, and 'The paralytic healed' after 'Vandycke' (*sic*) was done for the *Book of Common Prayer* 1854. 'Abraham offering up Isaac' after J.S. Copley (surrounded by an ornamental border by Luke Limner) appeared in *The Self-interpreting Bible* 1864 and 'Angel with a book' after J. Martin in the *Imperial Family Bible* 1873 (originally published in 1844). For *Casquet of literature* 1874, he did the engraved title pages to volumes 2 and 4—'Ailsa Craig' after J.F. Williams and 'Robin Hood' after D. McNee respectively. He may have been connected with a Glasgow engraver, Charles Wands, who flourished there between 1800 and 1844. T.

Ward (fl. 1832) Landscape engraver. 'St. Goarhaven and ruins of the Katz' after Tombleson was engraved for *Tombleson's views of the Rhine* 1832.

Warren, A.W. (1781?–1856) Figure, historical and technical engraver. He was thought to be Ambrose William a brother of Charles Warren (q.v.) and worked mainly for the book publishers in his early days. He did one plate, dated 1 February 1815, for Ottley's *Engravings of the ... Marquis of Stafford's ... pictures* 1818, and during the same decade engraved some of the plates for the *Transactions of the Society of Arts*, e.g., those of coal mines after C. Varley in the 1816 volume. Among his early steel plates were 'George Jameson' and 'Peter Vanderbank' after Seipse and Kneller respectively for H. Walpole's *Anecdotes of painting* 1827, and 'The nativity' after P. Veronese and 'Striking a bargain' after D. Teniers, dated 1833 and 1834, were published in A. Cunningham's *Cabinet gallery of pictures by the first masters...* 1836. 'Death of Dhondiah' after A. Cooper and 'Retreat from Waterloo' after J. Gilbert came out in Maxwell's *Life of ... the Duke of Wellington* 1839–41, 'Rob Roy' after C.R. Leslie in Scott's *Waverley novels* and 'Stag hounds' after R.B. Davis in Carleton's *Sporting sketch-book* 1842. 'The Nativity' after Veronese appeared in *A New family Bible* [c. 1840], and seventeen plates after numerous artists were published in Hume and Smollett's *History of England...* 1854–5. He also engraved plates for *The Gem* 1830–1. His most important single plates were 'The beggar's petition' after Witherington (1827) and 'The new coat' after D. Wilkie (1832). Most of his plates were signed 'A.W. Warren'. He also did some work in mezzotint. He joined the Artists' Annuity Fund in 1810 as a founder member, and tried out some new graver handles for the Society of Arts in 1831. B; Br; DNB; H; R; S; T.

Warren, Charles (1766–1823) Portrait and figure engraver.

Charles Warren

He was born on 12 June 1766, and was possibly the son of James Warren, a shoemaker, and his wife, Eleanor, of Cox's Square, Spitalfields, Stepney. He was first employed in engraving copper cylinders for calico printers in London. He also engraved for the gunsmiths, which gave him an introduction to the mechanics of engraving on steel. He married at the age of eighteen, and the need to support a family made him turn to work for the booksellers, at which he made a name for himself. He was one of the twenty-four Governors of the Society of Engravers, from 1802, a founder member in 1810 of the Artists' Annuity Fund, and its President from 1812 to 1815. He was elected to the Society of Arts in 1804, and engraved frontispieces to its *Transactions* for nine years. He became interested in the problems associated with the forgery of banknotes, and was asked, because of his experience with the Plymouth Dock Bank, to contribute to the Society of Arts' investigations, which culminated in its *Report ... relative to the mode of preventing the forgery of banknotes* 1819; in the process, he produced in May 1818 the first successful engraving on steel in England. Previous attempts by Jacob Perkins and others involved the case-hardening of soft steel blocks, with the possible destruction of the engraver's work if the steel buckled, so for about four years, Warren worked on the problems of producing plates of the correct hardness to do away with the hardening process. By 1821 the problems were virtually solved, and the first book illustration known on steel *plate* (as opposed to the thick *blocks* used by Perkins) was the frontispiece and engraved title page after T. Uwins for Philip Doddridge's *Rise and progress of religion* (May 1822) (Plate 4), followed by the frontispiece and engraved title page after the same artist for Milton's *Poetical works* (September 1822).

Other engravers, e.g., William Holl the elder (q.v.), Charles Marr (q.v.) and W. T. Fry (q.v.), engraved on his plates, and the evidence of his work was published by the Society of Arts when they awarded him their Large Gold medal in 1823. He made steel plates acceptable to engravers in general, and contributed a solution to the problems of etching on steel. He had also engraved 'The broken china jar' after D. Wilkie for P. Coxe's *Social day* 1823, which for many years was considered (mistakenly) to be the first steel engraving. He died suddenly in the middle of a conversation at East Hill, Wandsworth, on 21 April 1823, aged fifty-six, and his pupil Joseph Phelps provided the information for the communication published in the Society of Arts' *Transactions*. Thomas Fairland, Samuel Davenport (q.v.) and H. C. Shenton (q.v.) (his son-in-law) were also his pupils. His brother A. W. Warren (q.v.) received his Gold medal from the hands of the Duke of Sussex in May 1823. DNB; H, chap. 3; Royal Society of Arts *Journal*, July and August 1977, pp. 488–91, 590–3.

Warwick, R. (fl. 1838) Landscape engraver. 'View near Selain' and 'View near Rouillon' after J. Fussell were published in *Continental tourist* [1838].

Wass, Charles W. (1818–1905) Figure engraver. He is said to have worked for the booksellers, but his book plates are rare. He worked for the print publishers in the mid-1840s, but combined his engraving with work as a picture dealer, although he was 'Engraver to H.R.H. the Duchess of Cambridge'. He lived at the Adelphi. Five of his plates were issued in the *Art Journal*, however, between 1846 and 1848, commencing with 'The sisters' after Sir William Ross (1846), and after the same artist, 'The blossoms', a picture of two girls (1847). In 1847 there was an outline engraving of the Judgment of Paris after W. Etty, an essay towards a full engraving in stipple and mezzotint. In 1848 'Coral finders' and 'Cupid and Psyche', also after W. Etty, were issued, the latter being an oval picture. In the following year Wass wrote a letter, dated 21 November 1849, to the Royal Society of Arts on the death of Etty. AU; S.

Waters, J. (fl. 1832) Landscape engraver. 'Rudesheim' (wayside cross) after Tombleson was published in *Tombleson's views of the Rhine* 1832.

Watkins, H. (fl. 1840) Landscape engraver. 'Madessa Bidur' after Taylor appeared in Bacon's *Oriental annual* 1840. He may have been the same person as H. G. Watkins (q.v.).

Watkins, H. G. (fl. 1830–41) Landscape engraver. 'Llanberis Lake...' after Gastineau was engraved for Gastineau's *Wales illustrated...* 1830, and used again in B. Woodward's *History of Wales* 1853. The former volume also contained 'Criccieth Castle'. 'Rhayader' after T. Creswick was issued in L. Ritchie's *Wye and its associations* 1841. He was possibly a brother of W. G. Watkins (q.v.). Ho; T.

Watkins, W. G. (fl. 1828–48) Landscape engraver. Between June 1828 and June 1829 he engraved eight plates after T. H. Shepherd for J. Elmes's *Metropolitan improvements* 1829, including 'East side of Park Square, and Diorama...' (Plate 8) and twelve after the same artist for Shepherd's *London and its environs* 1829–31. Ten plates were done for Shepherd's *Modern Athens* 1829–31 and 'Eltham Place, Kent' and 'New church. Blackheath' after T. M. Baynes for S. W. H. Ireland's *England's topographer* (commenced publication 1828). Ten plates after Allom, Harwood and Pyne were engraved for Pyne's *Lancashire illustrated...* 1831 (including views of Bolton, Liverpool and Manchester), and six plates after Bartlett and Campion were done for Wright's *Picturesque beauties of Great Britain ... Essex* 1834. 'Donnington Hall, Cheshire', 'Castle of Ashby de la Zouch, Leicestershire', 'Clumber, Nottinghamshire' and 'Nottingham and its environs' after T. Allom were engraved for T. Noble and T. Rose's *Counties of Chester...* 1836, 'The basin of Neptune, Versailles' after W. Callow for *Heath's Versailles* [c. 1836] (used again in *Keepsake français* 1840) and 'Moreton Hall,

Lancashire' after G. Pickering, 'Town Hall, Liverpool' after 'G. & C. Pyne', and 'Cartmel Church, Lancashire', also after Pickering, for E. Baines's *History of . . . Lancaster* 1836. This last plate is a delightful one, and was used again in G. N. Wright's *Lancashire* 1842. 'Sardis' after Allom was engraved for R. Walsh's *Constantinople* 1838–40. 'Esther accusing Haman' after Hamilton and 'Christ walking on the sea' after de Loutherbourg appeared in *A New family Bible* [c. 1840] and 'Ruins, Virginia Water' after J. D. Harding in Ritchie's *Windsor Castle* 1848. He was possibly a brother of H. G. Watkins (q.v.).   B.

Watt, James Henry (1799–1867) Portrait and figure engraver. Born in London, he was educated at Mensall's Academy in Kentish Town, and at the age of sixteen was apprenticed to Charles Heath. From him he seems to have received a bare training, relying largely on his natural flair for drawing to achieve artistic competence. He was naturally employed on the book illustrations upon which his master was engaged, and some authorities assert, erroneously, that all his plates were on copper, but it is true that the majority of his work, especially for the print publishers, was on it. Examples of his work on steel are 'Lady Georgiana Agar Ellis' after Lawrence for the *Literary souvenir* 1831, 'Christ rejected' after B. West, dated 1 May 1834, for A. Cunningham's *Cabinet gallery of paintings by the first masters . . .* 1836 and 'A portrait' after A. E. Chalon, dated November 1834, for the *Literary souvenir* 1835, engraved in conjunction with W. H. Watt (q.v.), who was almost certainly his younger brother. A plate of Mrs Sheridan's lost voice: an allegory, after T. Stothard, and signed 'Watt', in S. Rogers' *Poems* 1834 can be ascribed to him. He engraved swiftly and accurately, as is shown by his plate of 'Ninon d'Enclos' after G. S. Newton for Alaric Watts, which his brother (probably W. H. Watt (q.v.)) saw James about to start as he went to bed, and by six o'clock the next morning the head was done and scarcely needed any retouching. He also worked for *The Amulet*. His separate plates began to be produced in the 1830s, and included 'Procession of the flitch of bacon' after T. Stothard (1832), 'May day in the time of Queen Elizabeth' after C. R. Leslie (1836), 'The Highland drovers' (1841) and 'Courtyard in the olden time' (1847), both after E. Landseer, and 'Christ blessing little children' after C. L. Eastlake (1859). He was afflicted with ill health and domestic problems for many years, making him somewhat of a recluse. He died in London on 18 May 1867, aged sixty-eight.   AJ; DNB; R.

Watt, Thomas (fl. 1843–50) Landscape engraver. 'Hermitage at Dunkeld' after D. McKenzie was published in Sir William Hooker's *Perthshire illustrated* 1843, and 'Scene on the Tummel . . .' after J. A. Houston and 'Comrie Castle' after J. C. Brown appeared in J. Browne's *History of the Highlands* [c. 1845]. 'The Saviour' after Decaisne appeared as the frontispiece to Fleetwood's *Life of Our Lord . . .* [c. 1855].

Watt, William Henry (1804–?) Portrait and figure engraver. Almost certainly the younger brother of James Henry Watt (q.v.), he engraved 'Richard Dahl' (after a self-portrait) and 'Isaac Becket' for H. Walpole's *Anecdotes of painting* 1827, and 'Heart of Midlothian' after J. Burnett and 'Peveril of the Peak' after R. P. Bonington for Scott's *Waverley novels*. Fifteen plates, including 'The march to Finchley', were issued in *Hogarth moralized* 1831. For the *Literary souvenir* 1831 he engraved 'A Magdalen' after Coreggio, and 'Vespers' after Boxall was done for the 1832 volume. Two rather poor engravings—'Henrietta Maria, Queen of Charles I' after Van Dyck and 'Spanish peasant boy' after Murillo—, together

with 'Portrait of himself' after J. H. Mortimer and 'A mother and child' after Parmegiano, were published in A. Cunningham's *Cabinet gallery of paintings by the first masters . . .* 1836, 'The cold beauty' after T. G. Hurlstone in S. C. Hall's *Book of gems* 1836 and 'Mercy raised by Goodwill at the wicket gate' after T. Stothard in J. Bunyan's *Pilgrim's Progress*. He joined the Artists' Annuity Fund in 1828 and signed the 1837 petition. He engraved 'Una entering the cottage' after W. Hilton for the Art Union of London (1843), and issued 'The manuscript' after C. R. Leslie (1839) and 'The pets' after E. Landseer (1844) through the print publishers. He exhibited genre paintings in London in 1854 and 1857.   T.

Watts, J. (fl. 1832–46) Landscape engraver. 'Braubach and the Marksburghe' after Tombleson was published in *Tombleson's views of the Rhine* 1832 and used again in *Continental tourist* [1838]. 'Tower near Andernach' and 'Neuwid & Mon^t of Genl La Hoches', also after Tombleson, appeared in Fearnside's *Picturesque beauties of the Rhine* [c. 1846].

Watts, W. (fl. 1846) Landscape engraver. 'Andernach' after Tombleson was published in Fearnside's *Picturesque beauties of the Rhine* [c. 1846].

Weatherhead, J. (fl. 1869) Figure engraver. A rather poor plate 'Theseus' of a sculpture was published in the *Art Journal* 1869.

Webb, Edward (fl. 1833) Landscape engraver. 'Bowes' Tower', a vignette after Turner, was engraved for Scott's *Poetical works* 1833–4.

Wedgwood, John Taylor (1783–1856) Figure, portrait and landscape engraver, working in London at 52 Portman Place, Paddington. His few steel plates were done for A. Cunningham's *Cabinet gallery of paintings by the first masters . . .* 1836, and were a landscape after Salvator Rosa, 'The watering place' after T. Gainsborough and 'Christ praying in the garden' after Correggio. He joined the Artists' Annuity Fund in 1813 and signed the 1837 petition. He died at Clapham on 6 March 1856, aged seventy-three.   Br; R; S; T.

Weeks, H. (fl. 1832) Landscape engraver. 'Bacharach' after Tombleson was engraved for *Tombleson's views of the Rhine* 1832.

Weeks, J. (fl. 1832) Landscape engraver. 'St. John's Church near Niederlahnstein' after Tombleson was engraved for *Tombleson's views of the Rhine* 1832.

Wehmeyer, W. P. (fl. 1874) Figure engraver. An oval picture, 'Childhood', after Pieneman was done for the engraved title page of *Casquet of literature* 1874.

Wells. (fl. 1846) Architectural engraver. 'Boppart Church' after Tombleson was published in Fearnside's *Picturesque beauties of the Rhine* [c. 1846].

Wesley, J. (fl. 1828–31) Architectural engraver. 'The New Museum, with part of the ruins of St. Mary's Abbey, York' was published in T. Allen's *New . . . history of the county of York* 1828–31.

West, W. (fl. 1840) Figure engraver. 'Samuel before Eli' after Copley appeared in *A New family Bible* [c. 1840], published by George Virtue, and 'Christ blessing the little children' after Overbeck, signed simply 'West', carried the imprint of Virtue and Co, but appeared in an edition of the *Bible* 1877, published by the Oxford University Press. He was probably William West, a London book plate engraver (fl. c. 1830–40).   B; T.

Westwood, Charles (?–1855) Landscape engraver. He was said to have been born in Birmingham. Among his earliest steel plates was 'Mont Blanc from the Baths', dated March 1827, together with 'Fort of Fenestrelles', dated May 1827, both after W. Brockedon, for the artist's *Illustrations of the passes of the Alps* 1828–9. 'New church, Regent Square, Sidmouth Street' after T. H. Shepherd, dated 12 April 1828, was published in J. Elmes's *Metropolitan improvements* 1829, 'Scene at Abbotsford' after E. Landseer, done for *The Keepsake* 1829, was a rare example of the artist's work to appear in books (Plate 11), 'Ducal Palace at Venice' after S. Prout was done for T. Roscoe's *Tourist in Switzerland and Italy* 1830 (issued again as 'Grand Canal and Doge's Palace, Venice' in G. N. Wright's *Gallery of engravings* 1844–6), and 'The Piazzetta, Venice' after Prout appeared in Roscoe's *Tourist in Italy* 1831. Two plates after Tombleson were done— one appeared in Fearnside's *Tombleson's Thames* 1834 ('Seat of—Drummond Esq., Twickenham') and one in Fearnside's *Picturesque beauties of the Rhine* [c. 1846] ('Mon^t of the battle of St. Jacob near Basle'). In 1851 he emigrated to the United States with John Rogers (q.v.), but although he was a good engraver, he had dissipated habits and committed suicide in 1855. This possibly explains his omission from the exhibition of engravings by Birmingham men held in that city in 1877. St; T.

Westwood, W. (fl. 1835) Landscape engraver. 'Blackgang chine' after W. H. Bartlett appeared in *Barber's picturesque illustrations of the Isle of Wight* [c. 1835]. He was possibly a brother of Charles Westwood (q.v.).

Wetherhead, W. (fl. 1843) Landscape and figure engraver. All his plates are after T. Allom and include 'Punishment of the Bastinado', 'Apartment in a Mandarin's House, near Nanking', 'Altar piece in the Yun-Stzoo-Stzee Temple, Tinghai' and 'Sowing rice at Soo-chow-foo' in G. N. Wright's *China* 1843, and a vignette, 'The father's pledge', in the same author's *Gallery of engravings* 1844–6.

White (fl. 1830–1) Architectural engraver. 'Beamhurst Hall' after Underwood and 'The Lodge, near Ludlow' after Page were engraved for West's *Picturesque views ... in Staffordshire and Shropshire...* 1830–1.

Whitfield, Edward Richard (1817–?) Figure engraver. He was a pupil of Augustus Fox. He engraved 'Calandrino, Bruno and Buffalmacco in search of the heliotrope' after P. Briggs, and 'Domenichino's mistress' after Domenichino (1840). His 'Cupid bound' after T. Stothard was published in the *Art Journal* 1852, and for the 1854 volume his 'Finding the body of Harold' after W. Hilton was done. He left England to live in Dresden in 1859. T.

Whittock, Nathaniel (fl. 1829–48) Draughtsman and lithographer. He is better known as an artist, his plates being engraved extensively for the topographical books published in the 1820s and 1830s, but he is known to have etched if not engraved six plates in E. W. Brayley's *Topographical history of Surrey* 1841–8. Four plates are after his own designs. A plan of Virginia Water was after W. A. Delamotte, and 'Course of the River Mole' was after J. R. Thompson. Br.

Wildblood, A. W. (fl. 1847) Figure engraver. 'The mother's welcome' after L. Pollack was issued in the *Art Union* 1847 and again in Mrs Hall's *Drawing room table book* 1849.

Wilkinson, W. S. (fl. 1829–36) Landscape and architectural engraver. 'Christchurch and part of Christ's Hospital' 'Bow church, Cheapside' and 'St. Mary Magdalen' all after T. H. Shepherd appeared in Shepherd's *London and its environs*

1829–31 and 'Launceston, Cornwall' and 'St. Austle [*sic*] Cornwall' after T. Allom in J. Britton and E. W. Brayley's *Devonshire and Cornwall illustrated* 1832. 'Somerset House...' after J. Ross was done for the artist's *Narrative of a second voyage...* 1835, and 'Croxteth Hall...' after Copley Fielding, dated 1831, appeared in E. Baines's *History of ... Lancaster* 1836.

Willis, J. (fl. 1846) Landscape engraver. 'Bath Ems' after W. Tombleson appeared in Fearnside's *Picturesque beauties of the Rhine* [c. 1846].

Willis, W. (fl. 1835) Architectural engraver. 'Sandrock Hotel' after T. Barber (q.v.) appeared in *Barber's picturesque illustrations of the Isle of Wight* [c. 1835]. It is just possible that the name was erroneously engraved for 'Wallis': W. Wallis (q.v.) engraved one other plate in the book.

Willmore, Arthur (1814–88) Landscape engraver. Born in Birmingham on 6 June 1814, he was the younger brother of James Tibbetts Willmore (q.v.), was probably his pupil and worked for him for a number of years. Among his earliest signed plates were 'Certaldo' and 'Chiusa' after W. Brockedon and 'Como' after G. Barnard for the former's *Italy... 1842–3*. Three views appeared in T. Roscoe's *Summer tour in the Isle of Wight* 1843, all of which were vignettes and of which 'Custom House, Portsmouth' was a good example of his work. Ten plates after T. Allom appeared in G. N. Wright's *China* 1843, including 'The pass of Wangchow' and 'Kite flying at Hae-hwan...' (Plate 41). Six plates after W. H. Bartlett were published in W. Beattie's *Castles and abbeys of England* 1845– 51, including 'Kenilworth Castle', 'The western window, Tintern' and 'Manorbeer Castle near the church'. 'Nain' after Bartlett was engraved for Stebbing's *Christian in Palestine* [1847]. More plates after Bartlett were done for Bartlett's own books: *Nile boat* 1849 (all vignettes), including 'The Pyramids' and 'The two Colossi'; *Footsteps of Our Lord* 1851 (all vignettes), including 'Arch of Titus' and 'Rhodes' (another good example); *Pictures from Sicily* 1853 (all vignettes), including one by Benoist; *The Pilgrim Fathers* 1853 (all vignettes), including 'Delfthaven' and 'Standish chapel and pew'; *Jerusalem revisited* 1854, including 'Pool of Bethesda' and 'Damascus gate'; and *Forty days in the desert*, [1848], including 'Castle of El-Kureiych'. He also engraved after Bartlett for Cony-beare and Howson's *Life and epistles of St. Paul* 1854, including 'Antioch', 'Corinth' and 'Miletus', the last-named being after Laborde. 'Wilkie in search of Murillo' after Wilkie appeared in *Wilkie gallery* [c. 1849], and 'Milan' and 'Verona', the last after W. Callow, were used in D. Costello's *Piedmont and Italy* [c. 1855]. Eight plates after E. W. Cooke, Leitch and Walton were done for Adams's *History ... of the Isle of Wight* 1858, 'Bombay' and 'Benares', vignettes after Allom, were done for Nolan's *Illustrated history of the British Empire in India* [1858–60], and 'The Pyramids' appeared in *Scripture sites and scenes...* [1849]. Another vignette after W. H. Bartlett, 'St. Cross from the River Itchen', appeared in B. Woodward's *History and description of Winchester* 1860 and his *General history of Hampshire* 1863. Plates after Birket Foster were published in Mayhew's *Upper Rhine* 1860 (i.e., 'Strasburg', 'Frieburg', 'Rhine falls, Schaffhausen' (Plate 52) and 'The Lake of Constanz...') and *Picturesque Europe* 1876–9 (i.e., 'Windsor Castle', 'At Burnham Beeches' 'Norham Castle', 'Melrose Abbey', 'Venice' and 'Moulin Huet Bay, Guernsey', with 'Dover Castle' after D. McKewan). 'Enid tends Geraint' and 'Geraint charges the bandits' after Gustave Doré were engraved for *The Story of Enid and Geraint* [1869]. 'Fountain's Abbey' was published in T. Baines's *Yorkshire past and present* 1871–7. Twelve plates after Brierly, Chevalier and Skinner Prout were done for Booth's *Australia* [1873–6]. 'Cologne from the river', 'Rome from the Vatican' and 'Ancient Rome', all after J. M. W. Turner, appeared in R. W. Wornum's *Turner Gallery* [c. 1878]. From 1852 to 1885 twenty of his plates appeared in the *Art Journal* (including the three of Turner's mentioned above in 1861, 1864 and 1865): 'Thyatira' after T. Allom (1863), 'Wreck of Dover' after C. Stanfield (1869), 'The eagle's nest' after E. Landseer and 'The evening hour' after B. W. Leader, a fitting end to the series in 1885. Plates for the Art Union of London included 'Landing fish at Egmont' after E. W. Cooke (1872), 'Return of the Life Boat' after E. Duncan (1877) and 'Attack of the Vanguard (1588)' after O. W. Brierly (1884). He also engraved 'Volunteer review, Edinburgh 1860' after S. Bough for the print publishers when his brother became ill and he finished the one or two of his brother's plates then outstanding. In 1874 his name was put forward for election to the Royal Academy, but it was not successful. He died on 3 November 1888, after a long illness brought on by lung disease, caused, it is said, by his stooping over his plates. AJ; Br; T.

Willmore, James Tibbetts (1800–63) Landscape engraver. Born on 15 September 1800 at Bristnald's End, Handsworth, near Birmingham, a son of James Willmore, a manufacturer of silver articles (which business he handed over to a younger brother, and moved to a farm at Maney, Sutton Coldfield, where James was brought up). At the age of fourteen James was apprenticed to William Radclyffe the engraver in Birmingham, and was also taught drawing by Joseph Vincent Barber and Samuel Lines. 1822 saw the end of his apprenticeship, his marriage, and in 1823 his removal to London, where he was employed by Charles Heath for three years, so his early plates are doubtless hidden under his master's name. Among his early signed steel plates were eight done between August 1827 and November 1829 for W. Brockedon's *Illustrations of the passes of the Alps* 1828–9 (including 'Baths of Bormio' and 'Saorgio'), all after the author's own designs. 'The tournament' after Martin was engraved for the *Literary souvenir* 1830 and 'Heidelberg Castle' after Roberts for the 1833 volume. Five engravings after S. Prout were published in T. Roscoe's *Tourist in Switzerland and Italy* 1830, and after the same artist and for the same author, he did three for *Tourist in Italy* 1831. 'City and Bridge of Dresden' after Prout was engraved for the *Continental annual* 1832. After C. Stanfield

James Tibbetts Willmore

he engraved five plates for L. Ritchie's *Travelling sketches in the north of Italy* 1832 (including 'Roveredo'), 'Transberg', 'Calais' and 'Triport' for his *Travelling sketches on the sea coasts of France* 1834, 'Castle of Heydelberg' and 'Cologne' in his *Travelling sketches on the Rhine* 1833 and 'View on the Solway...' and 'Cliffs near Arbroath...' for Scott's *Waverley novels*. 'Lochmaben Castle', a vignette after Turner, was done for Scott's *Poetical works* 1833–4. *Finden's illustrations of the life and works of Lord Byron* 1833–4 contained 'The Vale of Tempe' after W. Purser. 'Vico Varo near Tivoli' and 'Nice, coast of Genoa' after J. D. Harding appeared in T. Roscoe's *Tourist in France* 1834 and 'Windsor Castle...' and 'Eton from the playing fields', also after Harding, in L. Ritchie's *Windsor Castle* 1848. One of his earliest plates after J. M. W. Turner was 'Nantes', done for *The Keepsake* 1831, followed by 'Château Bernard' in *Keepsake français* 1831, 'Vernon', 'Pont de l'Arche', 'The Lanterne at St. Cloud' and 'Paris from the Barrière de Passy' in L. Ritchie's *Wanderings by the Seine* 1835 and 'Oberwesel on the Rhine', dated 10 April 1842, in Finden's *Royal Gallery of British Art* 1838–49. A series of plates for *The Keepsake* included 'Isola Bella, Lago Maggiore' after Stanfield and 'Byron's dream' after Harding (1832), 'A fire at sea' and 'Destruction of both Houses of Parliament' after Turner (1836), 'The Sea, The Sea!' (a vignette) after Turner (1837), an engraved title page vignette after Carmichel (1838), three plates after Bentley, Harding and Westall (1839), 'The Indian maid' after Harding and 'The tomb of the last heir of M–' after Catermole (*sic*) (1840), 'Morning' after Bentley (1841), 'View from West Point on the Hudson' after Creswick (1842), 'View on the Hudson' after Creswick (1843), 'Lord Byron's room in the Palazzo Moncenigo' after Lake Price and 'The glen of the grave' after Warren (1845), 'The opening of the Coal Exchange by His Royal Highness Prince Albert' after Carmichael (1851) and 'Scarborough' after Carmichael (1852). 'Copeland Islands ...' after J. Ross was published in the artist's *Narrative of a second voyage...* 1835, 'Loxa' and 'The Bridge of Ronda' after D. Roberts in T. Roscoe's *Tourist in Spain. Granada* 1835, 'Gallery of Battles, Versailles' (Plate 29) and 'Palace of Versailles...' after F. Mackenzie in *Heath's Versailles* [c. 1836] (reissued in *Keepsake français* 1840), both good examples of line engraving, five plates in W. Beattie's *Switzerland* 1836 after W. H. Bartlett, six engravings after T. Creswick, all vignettes, in L. Ritchie's *Ireland...* 1837, six after Bartlett, Allom and H. McCulloch in Beattie's *Scotland illustrated* 1838 and 'Angels appearing to the shepherds' after J. Martin and 'The Lane' after T. C. Hofland in S. C. Hall's *Book of gems* 1838. Seven plates after Bartlett, Brockedon and Harding were done for Beattie's *Waldenses* 1838. 'Ruins of Carthage' after Linton, dated 1 January 1838, 'Oberwesel on the Rhine' after Turner, dated 10 April 1842, and 'Battle of Waterloo' after Jones, dated 31 March 1849, were engraved for Finden's *Royal Gallery of British Art* 1838–49, 'Batalha' after Holland for Harrison's *Tourist in Portugal* 1839, six plates after G. B. Campion and A. Cooper for Maxwell's *Life of ... the Duke of Wellington* 1839–41, four engravings after Bartlett for J. S. Coyne's *Scenery and antiquities of Ireland* [c. 1840], four after Bartlett for J. Pardoe's *Beauties of the Bosphorus* 1840 (including 'Cemetery at Scutari'), 'Mauchlin, Gavin Hamilton's House' after D. O. Hill for Wilson and Chambers's *Land of Burns* 1840 and eleven plates for N. P. Willis's *American scenery* 1840 after Bartlett (including 'A forest on Lake Ontario' and 'Washington's House, Mount Vernon'). Six vignettes after T. Creswick appeared in S. C. and A. M. Hall's *Ireland* 1841–3 and thirteen after Leitch, Stanfield, and others were done for Brockedon's *Italy...*

1842–3. 'The Tower of London' after Bartlett appeared in W. Beattie's *Ports, harbours...* 1842 and five plates after Bartlett were done for Willis's *Canadian scenery* 1842. 'Castle of Persenberg' after Bartlett appeared in Beattie's *Danube* 1844, four plates after G. Cattermole in R. Cattermole's *Great Civil War* 1846 and 'Bringing home the deer' after A. Cooper in S. C. Hall's *Gems of European art* 1846.

During the late 1830s Willmore did work for the print publishers, and some of his most successful works after Turner were 'Alnwick Castle by moonlight' [c. 1838], 'Mercury and Argus' (1841) and 'Ancient Italy' (done for the National Art Union 1843). At least twenty engravings after Turner had been done by the time his engraving 'Venice' after Turner appeared in the *Art Journal* for 1849; 'Dido and Aeneas' (1863) – his last plate – 'The Fighting Temeraire' and 'Childe Harold's pilgrimage' (1864) and 'Mercury and Argus' (1865) were re-engravings on steel of his earlier works. Eight plates in all appeared in the *Art Journal*. 'Italy' after Turner was done for the Art Union of London (1861).

On 10 February 1843 he was elected to the Royal Academy as an Associate Engraver against F. Bacon, C. E. Wagstaff, D. Lucas and T. Lupton in the first ballot, and by twenty-five votes to four against F. Bacon in the second. He was unsuccessful (against Robinson and Doo) in achieving full honours in 1856. The 1843 election was to replace John Bromley, and followed the exhibition of Willmore's 'Ancient Italy' proof at the Academy in that year. He joined the Artists' Annuity Fund in 1828 and held most of the important posts in it, so that when he was unable to work from about 1860 he was awarded £40 a year, but as paralysis set in early in 1862, the Royal Academy acceded to a request from his brother in March of that year to place him on their pension fund. He died on 12 March 1863, aged sixty-two, and was buried in Highgate cemetery. His work was exhibited at Birmingham in 1877 and at the Fine Art Treasures Exhibition at Folkestone in 1886. A Joseph Willmore, perhaps an uncle, was said to be working as a goldsmith in Birmingham between 1810 and 1815, and in 1940 Charles Willmore Emlyn presented a portrait of the engraver (illustrated above) to Birmingham Art Gallery.   AJ; Br; DNB; H; R; Royal Acad. minutes; Sa; T.

Wilmshurst, J. (fl. 1836–42) Architectural engraver. 'Chichester Cathedral; view in the presbytery' after R. Garland appeared in volume 2 of *Winkles's ... Cathedral churches of England...* 1838.

Wilson, A. (fl. 1840) Figure engraver. 'Grandmother asleep' after Decaisne was published in *Casquet of literature* 1874. It may be possible to identify him with Andrew Wilson (1780–1848) of Edinburgh.   T.

Wilson, Daniel (fl. 1835–54) Landscape engraver. He was a pupil of the mezzotinter Charles Turner, but did most of his work in line. 'Arbroath Abbey from the west' after C. Stanfield appeared in Scott's *Waverley novels*, 'Kilmarnock, Market Cross' after D. O. Hill in Wilson and Chambers's *Land of Burns* 1840 and 'Apollyon defeated by Christian' and 'The escape from Doubting Castle', oval engravings after T. Stothard, in J. Bunyan's *Pilgrim's Progress*, 10th edition, 1854. He joined the Artists' Annuity Fund in 1841.   T.

Wilson, J. (fl. 1846) Architectural engraver. 'Castle of Rheinstein' after W. Tombleson was published in Fearnside's *Picturesque beauties of the Rhine* [c. 1846].

Wilson, R. (fl. 1832) Architectural engraver. 'Ruins at Andernach' after W. Tombleson appeared in *Tombleson's views of the Rhine* 1832.

Winkles, Benjamin (fl. 1828–42) Architectural engraver. 'The new church, Tunbridge Wells' and 'Aylesford church and bridge, Kent' after W. H. Bartlett and 'The Fryars at Aylesford' and 'The Bishop's Palace at Maidstone' after G. Shepherd were engraved for S. W. H. Ireland's *England's topographer* (commenced publication 1828), which work also contained 'Interior of Rochester Castle, Kent' after Bartlett, but this was merely signed 'Winkles'. 'Part of Lord Street, with St. George's Church in the distance...' and 'Part of Lord Street, and South John Street...' after Harwood were engraved for Pyne's *Lancashire illustrated...* 1831 and 'Pompeii. Tepidarium' and 'Pompeii. General view of the Pantheon' after the author's designs for Gell's *Pompeiana...* 1832. His *French cathedrals* 1837 contained thirty-nine plates engraved by him after designs by R. Garland, Hablot Browne, W. G. Colman and S. A. Hart of the cathedrals of Amiens, Notre Dame in Paris, Chartres, Beauvais, Evreaux and Rouen; all the plates are dated between January and December 1836. In 1836 he joined with his brother Henry (q.v.) to publish *Winkles's ... Cathedral churches of England...* in three volumes, published in 1836, 1838, and 1842 respectively. His name appears on 145 plates: thirty-four in volume 1, fifty-one in volume 2 and sixty in volume 3. These were after J. Archer, B. Baud, Hablot Browne, R. Garland, S. A. Hart, J. Salmon, T. H. Shepherd, C. Warren, W. Warren and H. Winkles of the cathedrals at Salisbury, Canterbury, York, St Paul's [London] (Plate 25), Wells, Rochester and Winchester in volume 1, Lincoln, Chichester, Ely, Peterborough, Norwich, Exeter, Bristol and Oxford in volume 2, and Lichfield, Gloucester, Hereford, Worcester, Durham, Carlisle, Chester, Ripon, Llandaff, (St David's), St Asaph and Bangor in volume 3. 'Bank of Ireland, Dublin (south portico)' after G. Petrie appeared in G. N. Wright's *Gallery of engravings* 1844–6 and 'Castle of Choquier' and 'Andernace' after Salmon and G. Shepherd in *Continental tourist* [1838]. He probably accompanied his brother Henry (q.v.) on his visits to Germany.

Winkles, Henry (fl. 1818–42) Landscape and architectural engraver. Since he was exhibiting in London between 1818 and 1823 and had contributed several plates to J. P. Neale's *Views of the seats of noblemen...* 1818–24, he was a mature artist by that time, so was born at the end of the eighteenth century and served his time, unless he was self-taught, in the first two decades of the nineteenth century. It is possible, too, that he was taught by the aquatint engravers, since he was also adept in that style. Between June and December 1824 two plates after Pugin were published. They were republished, together with some aquatints of his (Winkles'), in E. W. Brayley's *Illustrations of Her Majesty's Palace at Brighton* 1838. By 1824 also, the German engraver from Carlsruhe, Karl Ludwig Frommel (1789–1863), had visited England to investigate English methods of engraving, and, discovering the new art of steel engraving, had encouraged Winkles to return to Carlsruhe with him. He did, and together they set up a studio for steel engraving in that city. By 1824 therefore, Winkles, must have already become proficient in it and must have been one of the pioneers in the field. He was back in London in 1832, and his 'Ruins of Falkenberg' after Tombleson appeared in *Tombleson's views of the Rhine* 1832, followed by 'Cowes, Isle of Wight' after R. Winkles (probably his brother) in *Watering places...* 1833 (used later in *Fashionable guide...* [c. 1838]). Twenty-two plates were engraved after Tombleson for Fearnside's *Tombleson's Thames* 1834, including 'Bisham Abbey, Berks', 'Walton Bridge', 'Adelphi Terrace' and 'Teeston Bridge,

Kent', and for *Barber's picturesque illustrations of the Isle of Wight* [c. 1835] he did 'Cowes', 'Bonchurch', 'Ventnor Cove' and 'St. Boniface Down' after T. Barber and 'Watcombe Bay' and 'Shanklin Chine' after W. H. Bartlett. 'Castle of Reichenau' and 'Mill of the Rocks near Istein', together with 'Waterfalls in the Rofflen' (signed simply 'Winkles'), after Tombleson were published in Fearnside's *Tombleson's Upper Rhine* [c. 1835], and 'Bonn', 'Fall of the Rhine near Schaffhausen' and 'Convent of Disentis', also after Tombleson, in Fearnside's *Picturesque beauties of the Rhine* [c. 1846]. He joined with his brother Benjamin to publish *Winkles's ... Cathedral churches of England* ... and for volume 1, 1836, he engraved three plates of Salisbury cathedral after J. Archer and Hablot Browne, three plates of Canterbury cathedral after Browne and R. Garland, and one plate of York cathedral (Minster) after Garland. For volume 2, 1838, he did one engraving of Ely cathedral after R. Garland. He had returned to Germany by 1838 and was in partnership with Friedrich Abresch; he also set up the firm of Winkles and Lehmann in Leipzig. By 1842 he was on his own at 22 Dresdener Strasse, Leipzig, and he took on Alfred Krausse (1829–94) (q.v.) as his pupil. This could not have happened much before 1843, when Krausse was fourteen, the normal age for commencing an apprenticeship. Winkles joined the Artists' Annuity Fund in 1823. B; Sp; T.

Winkles, J. R. (fl. 1829–31) Architectural engraver. 'St. Anne's Church, Wandsworth' after N. Fletcher was published in T. Allen's *History ... of Surrey and Sussex* 1829–31, and 'Bolton Abbey' after Whittock was done for Allen's *New ... history of the county of York* 1828–31. He may have been a brother of Benjamin, Henry and Richard (qqv.).

Winkles, Richard (fl. 1829–36) Architectural engraver. 'Trinity Church, Southwark', 'St. James, Bermondsey' and 'Portland Place, Brighton' after N. Whittock, the last two dated 1829, 'Barnes, Surrey' after G. T. Philips, dated July 1830, 'Norbiton House, Surrey' after J. Fletcher and 'Kew Gardens, Surrey' after G. S. Phillips appeared in T. Allen's *History ... of Surrey and Sussex*, 1829–31 'The Court house Beverly' and 'Byland Abbey' after Whittock and 'Whitby Abbey' after Gastineau in Allen's *New ... history of the county of York* 1828–31, 'Town Hall, Borough High Street' after T. H. Shepherd in Shepherd's *London and its environs* 1829–31, ten plates after Allom, Harwood and Pyne in Pyne's *Lancashire illustrated* ... 1831 and 'The drawbridge at Sandwich' after G. Shepherd, dated April 1832, in S. W. H. Ireland's *England's topographer* (commenced publication 1828). 'Interior of the Bismah Kurm, Caves of Ellora' after Cattermole was engraved for Elliot's *Views in India* ... 1835. For E. Baines's *History of ... Lancaster* 1836 he engraved 'Interior of the Exchange news-room' after Harwood and 'The Town Hall, Manchester' after T. Allom, which was used again in G. N. Wright's *Lancashire* 1842. He may have been the brother of Benjamin and Henry Winkles (qq.v.).

Winter, George (fl. 1842–52) Architectural engraver. He was possibly of German origin since artists of this name were known in Munich and Nuremberg in the eighteenth century. He lived at 5 Frederick Place, Gray's Inn Road, London. He engraved three architectural plans in outline of Carlisle Cathedral with some fine-line work, 'Etched by G. Winter', for R. W. Billings's *Illustrations of geometric tracery* ... 1842, and in the same author's *Architectural illustrations and description of Kettering Church* 1843 he engraved six views— the west doorway, west front, north-east view, view across the chancel looking south, east end from the churchyard and the

north porch. In addition, he did thirteen plates of outline architectural detail, all after the author's designs. He did thirty-one engravings for Billings's *Illustrations ... of Durham* 1846, and six for the same author's *Baronial ... Antiquities of Scotland* 1852. Br.

Wix, J. (fl. 1846) Landscape engraver. 'Oberlanstein' after Tombleson was published in Fearnside's *Picturesque beauties of the Rhine* [c. 1846].

Woodman, Richard (1784–1859) Portrait engraver. Born in London on 1 July 1784, he was the only son of an historical engraver, and he was educated at the Philological School, Marylebone Road. In 1799, at the age of fifteen, he was apprenticed to Robert Mitchell Meadows, stipple engraver and author of *Lectures on engraving*, who died some time before 1812. He was taught colouring by James Holmes, a fellow pupil, and at the end of his apprenticeship he left Meadows and was employed in working up engravings of William Westall's designs. In 1806 or 1808 he went to Etruria to superintend the engraving department of the Wedgwood potteries, but did not like the work and returned to London, where he made watercolour copies for engravers and worked as a painter of miniatures. There are not many of his engravings on steel, but they included 'Mark Akenside' after Pond, and 'Jan Tzatzoe ...' after H. Room, both of which appeared in G. N. Wright's *Gallery of engravings* 1844–6, a frontispiece of John Bunyan after T. Stothard for various editions of the *Pilgrim's progress*, and 'Giovanni Boccaccio', 'Bossuet', 'Erskine', 'Rembrandt' and 'Cardinal Richelieu' after various artists, which were published in the *Imperial dictionary of universal biography*, [c. 1861]. He was a founder member of the Artists' Annuity Fund in 1810, and its President in 1838–9. In his latter days he gave up engraving and worked exclusively in watercolour. He exhibited occasionally at the Royal Academy between 1820 and 1850. In 1809 he married the daughter of the sculptor, Charles Horwell, and four children of the marriage survived him, two of the boys taking after their father as copyists. In May 1857 he fell down some steps in the National Gallery, banging his head, and for two years his condition deteriorated until in September 1859 he became very much worse and died on 15 September 1859. AJ; Br; DNB.

Woods, John (fl. 1835–50) Architectural engraver. He lived at Woodland Cottage, Pond Lane, Clapton, Stamford Hill, London. Four plates, done between July and October 1835, were published in E. W. Brayley and J. Britton's *History of the ancient palace ... at Westminster* 1836, and included 'Interior of the Star Chamber, Westminster' and 'Cloister NW Angle, St. Stephen's Chapel' after R. W. Billings; the other two were after J. R. Thompson and W. Capon. Three engravings of Rochester and Winchester cathedrals after R. Garland and Hablot Browne were issued in 1836 in volume 1 of *Winkles's ... Cathedral churches of England* ..., 'Notre Dame cathedral; the nave looking east' after Hablot Browne in B. Winkles's *French cathedrals* 1837 and thirty-two plates after G. F. Sargent in the three volumes of R. Mudie's *Hampshire* 1838, including 'Alresford', 'Mitcheldever', 'Hurst Castle ...', and 'Freshwater Bay'. A plate of the Island of Santa Maura after W. Purser appeared in C. Wordsworth's *Greece* 1839, 'Manheim' after Tombleson in Fearnside's *Picturesque beauties of the Rhine* [c. 1846], and 'Worms cathedral' after Tombleson in Fearnside's *Tombleson's Upper Rhine* [c. 1835]. Thirty-four plates, with probably ten more by him, were engraved for W. G. Fearnside and T. Harral's *History of London* [c. 1850], in which a statement on the title page ascribes all the engravings to John Woods, even though they are unsigned. Many have no artist given either, but those which can be identified include J. H. Shepherd, Hablot Browne, R. Garland and J. Salmon. Engravings include the engraved title page vignette 'Monument and St. Magnus Church', 'Quadrant, Recent Street', 'Horse Guards', 'Somerset House, Strand' and 'Billingsgate'. Most of these engravings were first published in 1838. Ad; p. 439–41.

Woolnoth, Thomas (1785–c. 1841) Portrait and figure engraver. He was known for his theatrical portraits in stipple and line, as well as larger plates after Correggio and Van Dyck. About 1816–7 he took William Walker (1791–1867) as a pupil. His work on steel included 'Crypt under St. Stephen's Chapel...' after R. W. Billings, dated 1 October 1835, which appeared in E. W. Brayley and J. Britton's *History of the ancient palace ... at Westminster* 1836, 'France' after F. P. Stephanoff in Finden's *Tableaux* 1837, a vignette, 'Rev. John Skinner', in Wilson and Chambers's *Land of Burns* 1840, 'The Spanish page' (a stipple plate) after Murillo, together with 'Little Kate of Kensington', which was signed merely 'Woolnoth', in G. N. Wright's *Gallery of engravings* 1844–6 and 'La Perouse', and 'Calvin' and 'Corneille' (these last two signed 'Woolnoth'), in the *'Imperial dictionary of universal biography'* [c. 1861]. He wrote, illustrated and published *Flowers of infancy* 1839 and illustrated Sarah Bowdich's *Juvenile album* 1841. 'Maria, nun of Santa Clara', a vignette after Grevedon, appeared in *Casquet of literature* 1874.

He joined the Artists' Annuity Fund in 1824, and became Engraver in Ordinary to Her Majesty (presumably Victoria). AU; B; Br; D; R; S; T.

Woolnoth, William (c. 1770–?) Landscape and architectural engraver. Believed to have been born about 1770, he was possibly an older brother of Thomas Woolnoth (q.v.). He engraved the illustrations after T. Hastings to *A graphical illustration of the metropolitan cathedral churches of Canterbury...* 1816 (republished in 1836), some of those in J. P. Neale's *Views of the seats of noblemen...* 1811–24 and ninety-six plates in E. W. Brayley's *Ancient castles of England and Wales* 1825. 'Broad Street, Bloomsbury' and 'Holborn Bridge' after T. H. Shepherd were engraved for Shepherd's *London and its environs* 1829–31, and 'Temple of Mars Ultor, Rome' after S. Prout (signed 'Woolnorth') for T. Roscoe's *Tourist in Italy* 1831. 'Triad figure, interior of Elephanta', 'Aurungzebe's tomb, Rozah' and 'A Chinese junk—Canton river' after Prout and 'Dus Awtar—Caves of Ellora' (Plate 18), 'Rameswur—Caves of Ellora' and 'Interior of Dher Warra, Caves of Ellora' after Cattermole were engraved for Elliot's *Views in India...* 1835. Three plates after R. W. Billings, dated 1835, were done for E. W. Brayley and J. Britton's *History of the ancient palace ... at Westminster* 1836 and four plates after W. H. Bartlett for W. Beattie's *Switzerland* 1836. Plates of York, St Paul's and Wells cathedrals after Hablot Browne and R. Garland were done for volume 1 of *Winkles's ... Cathedral churches of England...* 1836 and six engravings of the cathedrals of Amiens, Beauvais and Notre Dame, Paris, after R. Garland for B. Winkles's *French cathedrals* 1837. 'Heriot's Hospital...' and 'The pass of Inverfarrakaig...' after T. Allom were engraved for W. Beattie's *Scotland illustrated* 1838, 'Approach to Mount Briançon, from Mount Dauphin...' after Bartlett for Beattie's *Waldenses* 1838 and 'Aberystwyth Castle...' after Gastineau for Dugdale's *England and Wales delineated* [1838–9]. British Museum Catalogue; T.

Worms, H. (fl. 1837) Landscape and architectural engraver.

'Botanic garden, Brussels' and 'West front, Antwerp cathedral' after Bartlett were engraved for van Kampen's *History and topography of Holland and Belgium* [1837].

Worthington, William Henry (c. 1795–c. 1839) Portrait and figure engraver. He is said to have exhibited portraits and other subjects from 1819 at the Royal Academy and British Institution. Plates appeared in *Physiognomical portraits* 1821 and Walker's *Effigies Poeticae* 1824. Thirty-six plates were done for *Portraits of the sovereigns of England* 1824, and engravings after T. Stothard appeared in Pickering's *History of England* 1826. His plates on steel included nineteen engravings of portraits for H. Walpole's *Anecdotes of painting* 1827 after Seipse, Kneller, Van Dyck, etc., including 'Mabuse', 'Thomas, Earl of Arundel' and 'Sir John Vanbrugh'. 'Sir Walter Scott and family', dated 1 September 1827, after D. Wilkie and 'Portrait of a lady' after Sir Thomas Lawrence were done for *The Bijou* 1828, nine engravings were done for *Hogarth moralized* 1831 and three for Hogarth's *Works* 1833. Twelve plates, dated between September 1832 and August 1834, were done for A. Cunningham's *Cabinet gallery of pictures by the first masters...* 1836, and included 'Bacchus and Ariadne' after Titian, 'St. John in the wilderness' after A. Caracci, 'The last supper' after Murillo, 'The adoration of the magi' after Rembrandt and 'Death of Cleopatra' after Guido Reni. B; Br; S; T.

Wrankmore, J. (fl. 1838) Figure engraver. 'Pleasure-tired' after Cattermole was published in S. C. Hall's *Book of gems* 1838.

Wrankmore, T. (fl. 1838) Figure engraver. 'Romans instructing ancient Britons' after Briggs was published in S. C. Hall's *Book of gems* 1838.

Wrankmore, W. C. (fl. 1836–9) Figure engraver. 'The young destructive' after C. Wrankmore was published in Fisher's *Drawing room scrap book* 1836 and 'The wicket gate' after Melville in Bunyan's *Pilgrim's progress* 1836. 'The maiden's vow' after J. W. Wright appeared in *Friendship's offering* 1837 and 'Who's there?' after J. M. Wright was done for the 1839 volume of the annual.

Wright, A. (fl. 1828–33) Figure engraver. 'Suitors rejected' after W. H. Worthington was done for *The Bijou* 1828, and one plate was engraved for Hogarth's *Works* 1833.

Wright, J. A. (fl. 1847–84) Figure engraver. In the *Art Union* of 1847, 'The gentle shepherd' after D. Wilkie was used as a replacement for another plate which was not delivered on time, and in the *Art Journal* 1853, 'The dead robin' after H. Thompson appeared. 'Richard and Lady Anne' after J. D. Watson was published in volume 1 of *The Royal Shakespeare* 1883–4.

Wright, Richard Lewis (fl. 1829–40) Architectural engraver. 'Percy's shrine and restored altar screen' after O. Jewitt was issued in volume 2 of G. Poulson's *Beverlac...* 1829, and 'Stamford Street' after his own design, dated April 1830, was published in T. Allen's *History ... of Surrey and Sussex* 1829–31. He also engraved three bookplates in 1840. Fi; Ho.

Wright, Thomas (1792–1849) Portrait engraver. He was born in Birmingham on 2 March 1792, but was brought to London as a child. Before he was fourteen he was apprenticed to Henry Meyer (1782–1847) (q.v.), and at the end of his apprenticeship he joined his fellow pupil William Thomas Fry (q.v.) in completing engravings etched by Fry and to which Fry's name was attached. In this period, 1813 to 1817, he engraved a popular plate of Princess Charlotte and Prince Leopold in a box at the Covent Garden Theatre after George Dawe, and from this a firm friendship developed with the artist. Wright left Fry in 1817 to concentrate on portrait engraving, for which he had a good talent, and did the portraits for *Essex, Suffolk and Norfolk characters* 1820 after Dawe and Wivell. Dawe went to Russia about this time, and Wright followed him in 1822 to St Petersburg, and for four years engraved there some portraits of the Royal Family (for which he was given diamond rings), and 'The Military Gallery' after Dawe. He returned to England in 1826 and married Dawe's sister. He engraved ten portraits for E. Lodge's *Portraits...*, 2nd edition, 1835, dated between May 1829 and February 1831, after Holbein, Walker and Van Dyck (including 'Thomas Sackville, Earl of Dorset', 'Sir Kenelm Digby' and 'Dorothy Sidney...'), and for Huish's *Memoirs of George the Fourth* 1830–2 he engraved 'Caroline' and 'H. Brougham, Esq., M.P.' after A. Wivell. During this period he also engraved the portraits published in Mrs A. Jamieson's *Beauties of the Court of Charles II* 1833. In 1830 he returned to Russia to arrange his brother-in-law's testamentary affairs, was induced to say another fifteen years and brought out there 'Les contemporains Russes', a series of portraits engraved and drawn by himself, published in St Petersburg. He returned to England finally in 1845 and began the plate 'Infant Hercules' after Reynolds, but he did not live to complete it, owing to a prolonged illness from which he died on 30 March 1849 at George Street, Hanover Square. He was a member of the Academies of St Petersburg, Florence and Stockholm. He presented a complete collection of about 300 prints to the Hermitage Gallery. AJ; Br; DNB; R; T.

Wrighton, T. (fl. 1830–1) Architectural and landscape engraver. Eight plates, including 'Tixhall Hall...' after Calvert and 'Pitchford Hall, Shropshire', were engraved for West's *Picturesque views ... in Staffordshire and Shropshire...* 1830–1.

Wrightson, John (?–1865) Landscape engraver. An engraving of the Plains of Marathon after his own design (in which the sky was very well engraved) and one of the Ruins of the Temple of Minerva at Aegina after F. Arundell were published in C. Wordsworth's *Greece* 1839. He emigrated to the United States about 1854, and worked in Boston and New York. He returned to England soon after 1860 and died in 1865. He must have had connections with Birmingham, because some illustrations to Milton, an etched 'Study of the Lake' and four other engravings were exhibited at the Exhibition of engravings by Birmingham men in 1877. All were after his own designs. He could have been connected with the publishing firm of the name of Wrightson in Birmingham. St.

Wrightson, R. (fl. 1850) Architectural engraver. 'Town Hall, Bruges' after J. Monthelier appeared in a publication by John Tallis [c. 1850].

Wyld, James (1812–87) Map engraver. He was well known as a geographer, but from his establishment at Charing Cross East he was responsible for engraving maps, two of which appeared in T. Roscoe's *Wanderings and excursions in North Wales* 1836 – one of the River Wye and adjacent country from Monmouth to Ross and another of the country from Chepstow to Monmouth. DNB.

Y

Young (fl. 1835) Architectural engraver. 'Ruins of Limbirg' after Tombleson appeared in Fearnside's *Tombleson's Upper Rhine* [c. 1835]. There is insufficient evidence to assign it to either of the following.

Young, E. (fl. 1834) Architectural engraver. 'Interior of Durham Cathedral from the nine altars' (quite a good engraving) after T. Allom was engraved for T. Rose's *Durham and Northumberland* 1832 and 'Hare Hall...' and 'Leigh Priory...' after Bartlett for Wright's *Picturesque beauties of Great Britain ... Essex* 1834.

Young, R. (fl. 1836–8) Landscape engraver. 'Alexandria' after W. H. Bartlett was published in J. Carne's *Syria* 1836–8, and was used again in J. Kitto's *Gallery of scripture engravings* 1846–9. 'Lebanon' and 'Jerusalem' after Leitch appeared in *The Self-interpreting Bible* 1864.

THE
PLEASURES OF HOPE,
WITH
OTHER POEMS
BY
THOMAS CAMPBELL.

Drawn by R.Westall,R.A.   Engraved on Steel by C.Heath.

Or lisps with holy look his evening prayer.
p. 21.

LONDON;
PRINTED FOR LONGMAN, HURST, REES, ORME, AND
BROWN; AND FOR
STIRLING AND SLADE, EDINBURGH.
1820.

Perkins, Fairman & Heath.

1   1820   Thomas Campbell. *The pleasures of hope.* Engraved title page engraved by Charles Heath. 2¾ × 2¼ in.

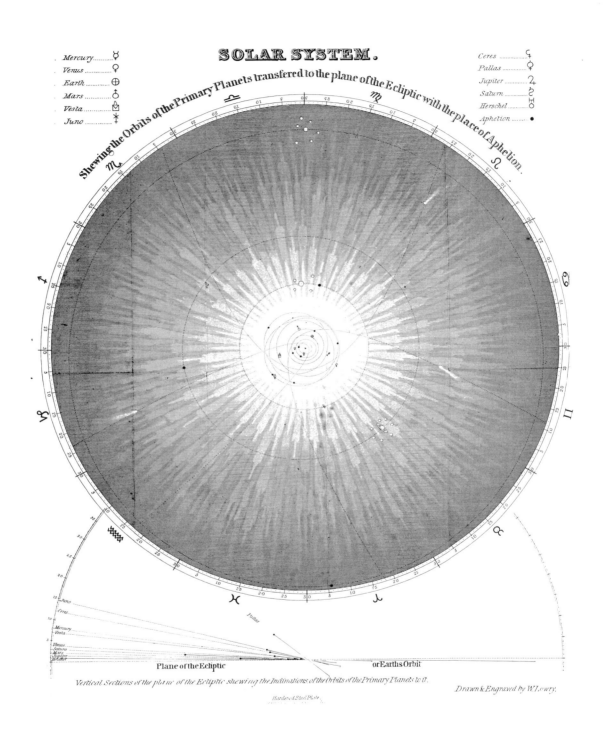

SOLAR SYSTEM.

Shewing the Orbits of the Primary Planets transferred to the plane of the Ecliptic with the place of Aphelion.

Mercury........☿
Venus..........♀
Earth..........⊕
Mars...........♂
Vesta..........⚶
Juno...........⚵

Ceres..........⚳
Pallas.........⚴
Jupiter........♃
Saturn.........♄
Herschel.......♅
Aphelion.......●

Plane of the Ecliptic   or Earths Orbit

Vertical Sections of the plane of the Ecliptic shewing the Inclinations of the Orbits of the Primary Planets to it.

Drawn & Engraved by W.Lowry.

Hardened Steel Plate.

2   1820   Revd. David Blair. *The universal preceptor*. 12th edition. Frontispiece engraved by Wilson Lowry. 7¼ × 7¼ in.

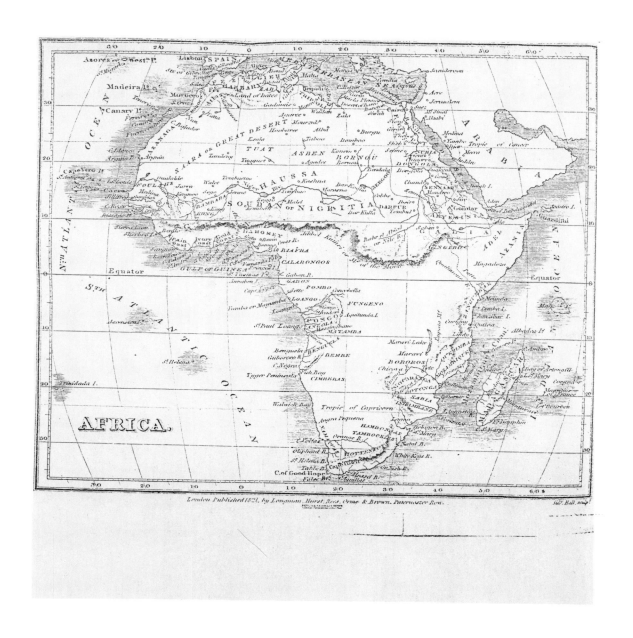

3   1821   Revd. J. Goldsmith. *Geography; illustrated on a popular plan* ... New edition. 1824. Page 669 engraved by Sidney
Hall. 6¼ × 7⅜ in.

The
RISE & PROGRESS of
RELIGION IN THE SOUL.
By
P. DODDRIDGE D.D.

T. Uwins del.   Engraved C. Warren sculp.

What is your life? Is it not even as a vapour that Appeareth
for a little time and then Vanisheth away.   Vide Chap. 3

LONDON:

Printed for F.C.&J.Rivington & the other Proprietors.
1822.

T. Uwins del.   on Steel C. Warren sculp.

Printed for F.C.&J.Rivington & the other Proprietors.
1822.

4   1822   Philip Doddridge. *The rise and progress of religion* ... Frontispiece and engraved title page engraved by Charles
Warren. 4½ × 6¼ in.

Engraved on Steel by T.A.Dean.

WILLIAM SHAKSPEARE.

From the Chandos Portrait in the possession of the Marquis of Buckingham.

Published by C and J Rivington and Partners, July, 1823.

5   1823   William Shakespeare. *The Plays of* . . . Frontispiece engraved by T.A. Dean. 4½ × 3⅜ in.

The
SELF INTERPRETING
BIBLE
with an Evangelical Commentary
By the Late
REV.D JOHN BROWN,
Minister of the Gospel
AT
Haddington.

Containing Marginal

Embellished with

References & Reflections

Elegant Engravings

London
Published by THO.S KELLY, 17 Paternoster Row.
1824

6   1824   Revd. John Brown. *The Self-interpreting Bible*. Engraved title page engraved by W. Read. 13 × 8⅛ in.

Drawn by N.Whittock. Engraved on Steel by J.Shury.

THE MUSEUM AND NEW BRIDGE, SCARBOROUGH.

London, Published by J.T.Hinton, No 4, Warwick Sqr December, 15, 1828.

7   1828   Thomas Allen. *A new ... history of the county of York*. Volume 3, page 446 engraved by John Shury. 3½ × 5¾ in.

Drawn by Tho. H. Shepherd.   Engraved by J. Redaway.

EAST SIDE OF PARK CRESCENT.

Drawn by Tho. H. Shepherd.   Engraved by W. Watkins.

EAST SIDE OF PARK SQUARE, AND DIORAMA,
REGENT'S PARK.

8   1829   James Elmes. *Metropolitan improvements*. Page 88, upper engraving by James Redaway and lower by W.G. Watkins. 8¾ × 5⅝ in.

Drawn by C. & G. Pyne.

Engraved by John Davies.

ENTRANCE TO THE TUNNEL OF THE LIVERPOOL & MANCHESTER RAIL-WAY, EDGE-HILL.

RESPECTFULLY INSCRIBED TO THE MARQUESS OF STAFFORD AND OTHER SHAREHOLDERS.

BY THE PUBLISHERS.

Drawn by C. & G. Pyne.

Engraved by John Davies.

BIRKENHEAD FERRY, OPPOSITE LIVERPOOL.

9   1829   W.H. Pyne. *Lancashire illustrated* ... Page 20 engraved by John Davies. 9⅜ × 8 in.

Painted by Sir Thos. Lawrence, P.R.A.   Engraved by Charles Heath.

M^{RS} PEEL.

Printed by E.Brain.

10   1829   *The Keepsake* 1829. Frontispiece engraved by Charles Heath. 4⅜ × 5¼ in.

Painted by Edwin Landseer A.R.A.   Engraved by C.Westwood.

SCENE AT ABBOTSFORD.

Printed by Mc Queen.

Pub^d for the Proprietor by Hurst Chance, & Co St Paul's Churchyard & R Jennings, 2, Poultry.

11   1829   *The Keepsake* 1829. Page 258 engraved by Charles Westwood. 3½ × 4¾ in.

THE GREAT ST. BERNARD.

NIGHT was again descending, when my mule,
That all day long had climbed among the clouds,
Higher and higher still, as by a stair
Let down from Heaven itself, transporting me,
Stopped, to the joy of both, at that low door,
That door, which ever, as self-opened, moves
To them that knock, and nightly sends abroad
Ministering Spirits.   Lying on the watch,

THE SANDS AT LLANSTEPHAN,
CAERMARTHENSHIRE

13   1830   Henry Gastineau. *Wales illustrated* ... Volume 2, engraved by John Charles Varrall. 8⅝ × 5¾ in.

POMPEII.

FACSIMILE OF THE HEAD OF ACHILLES

14   1830   Sir William Gell. *Pompeiana* ... Volume 1, page 157, engraved by Fenner, Sears & Co. 6½ × 4¾ in.

Painted by J.E.Clark R.A.   Engraved by Charles Heath.

15   1830   *The Keepsake* 1830. Page 332, engraved by Charles Heath. 4⅜ × 3¼ in.

Engraved by Joseph Rolls.

THE HOLY FAMILY WITH THE ADORATION OF THE SHEPHERDS.

From the Original Picture by Titian in
The National Gallery.

N° 30.

Jones & C.º Temple of the Muses, Finsbury Square, London.

16   1832   *The National Gallery.* Number 30, engraved by Joseph Rolls. 4 × 5 in.

Engraved by C. Mottram.

MARRIAGE A LA MODE.

SCENE WITH THE QUACK.

From the Original Picture by Hogarth.

Jones & C.º Temple of the Muses, Finsbury Square London.

17   1833   William Hogarth. *Works* ... Trusler's edition. Engraved by Charles Mottram. 4⅞ × 6⅛ in.

18   1833   Robert Elliot. *Views in India* . . . Page 24 engraved by William Woolnoth. 4½ × 6¾ in.

19   1834   William Beattie. *Switzerland*. Volume 2, page 93, engraved by James Stephenson. 7¼ × 4⅝ in.

20   1834   W.G. Fearnside. *Tombleson's Thames* ... Page 62, engraved by James Tingle. 4¼ × 5⅞ in.

St Michaels Mount. Shipwreck of Lycidas.

21   1835   John Milton. *Poetical works*. Volume 6, engraved title page, engraved by William Miller. 4¾ × 3¼ in.

J. Ross.

J. Cousen.

VICTORY,

Dismasted in a Gale, June 14, 1829.

Printed by J. Yates.

London, Published 1834, by Captain J. Ross, R. N.

22   1835   Sir John Ross. *Narrative of a second voyage* ... Page 32, engraved by John Cousen. 4 × 6¼ in.

ADAM DUNCAN

VISCOUNT CAMPERDOWN, ADMIRAL OF THE BLUE &c.&c.

Published by Blackie & Son, Glasgow

23   1835   Robert Chambers. *Biographical dictionary of eminent Scotsmen* Volume 2, page 156, engraved by R. Page & Son.
5 × 3¾ in.

Drawn by J. Hayter.   Engraved by J. Thomson.

The Sisters.

London Published for the Proprietor by Longman & Cº Paternoster Row.- Rittner & Cº Paris. Asher, Berlin.

24   1835   *Heath's Book of beauty 1835. Edited by the Countess of Blessington.* Page 76 engraved by James Thomson. 5¼ × 3¾ in.

ST PAUL'S CATHEDRAL.

NORTH EASTERN VIEW

25   1836   Thomas Moule. *Winkles's ... Cathedral churches of England ...* Volume 1, page 74 engraved by Benjamin
Winkles. 4⅜ × 5⅜ in.

C. Stanfield. R.A.   W. Chevalier. sc

ARCHED ROCK.
ISLE OF WIGHT.

26   1836   William Clarkson Stanfield. *Stanfield's coast scenery* ... Page 49, engraved by William Chevalier. 3¾ × 5½ in.

Drawn by G. Balmer.   Engraved by W. Finden.

ENTRANCE TO THE PORT OF BERWICK.

27   1836   George Balmer. *Views of ports and harbours* ... Page 28 engraved by William Finden. 5¾ × 5¾ in.

Painted by T Creswick   Engraved by E Finden

BRIGHTON.

SUSSEX.

28   1836   George Balmer. *Views of ports and harbours* ... Frontispiece engraved by Edward Finden. 7 × 5 in.

Gallery of Battles.
VERSAILLES.

29   1836   Charles Heath. *Heath's Versailles*. Page 90 engraved by James Tibbetts Willmore. 4⅞ × 6⅞ in.

Drawn by T. Uwins, R.A.   Engraved by H. Egleton.

Georgia

30 1837 *Finden's Tableaux . . . of national character . . . Edited by Mrs. S.C. Hall.* First series. Page 22, engraved by [W.] H. Egleton. 9½ × 7¾ in.

Hampstead March 6 1774

My dear Sir

Many thanks both for your suffrage and your congratulations, for they are equally honourable to me. I shall not fail to join the club on Friday evening. Dr Johnson desires I will call on him, & he will introduce me. — Pray what is the usual time of meeting? I am, Dear Sir, your most obliged & faithful

G Steevens

THE RESIDENCE OF

GEORGE STEEVENS, F.R.S.

HAMPSTEAD HEATH.

31   1837   *Graphic illustrations of Samuel Johnson.* Page 23, engraved by Charles John Smith. 2¾ × 3½ in.

32   1837   William Beattie. *Scotland illustrated.* Volume 1, page 182, engraved by George K. Richardson. 4¾ × 6⅞ in.

One morn a Peri at the gate
Of Eden stood, disconsolate;

Paradise & the Peri. p.154.

33   1838   Thomas Moore. *Lalla Rookh*. Page 153, engraved by Charles Heath 5 × 3¾ in.

T. Allom.   H. Adlard.

DRAWN FROM NATURE BY G. F. WHITE, ESQ.

THE VILLAGE OF MEANCOO, HIMALAYA MOUNTAINS.

34   1838   George Francis White. *Views in India* . . . Page 70, engraved by Henry Adlard. 5¼ × 7¾ in.

INTERIOR OF St SOPHIA'S.

INTERIEUR DE SAINTE SOPHIE.   *DAS INNERE DER St SOPHIENKIRCHE.*

35.   1838   Julia Pardoe. *Beauties of the Bosphorus.* Page 63, engraved by James Carter. 6¾ × 4⅞ in.

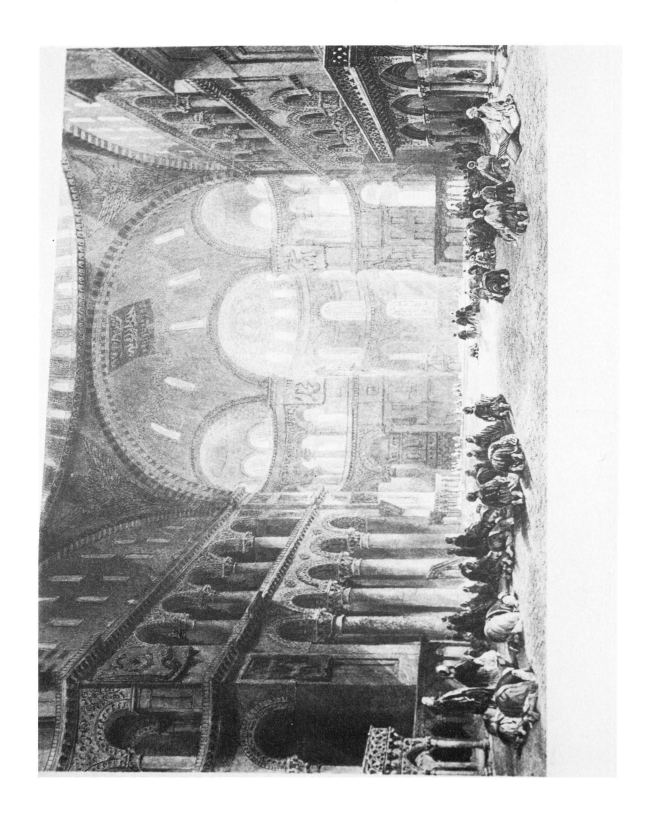

36   1838   Robert Walsh. *Constantinople*. Volume 1, page 45, engraved by John Henry Le Keux. 4⅞ × 7½ in.

COLONNADE OF CONGRESS-HALL.

(Saratoga Springs)

COLONNADE DE L'HÔTEL DU CONGRÈS.   DIE SAULENREIHE DES CONVERSATIONS HAUS.

37   1839   Nathaniel Parker Willis. *American scenery*. Volume 1, page 21, engraved by Henry Griffiths. 6⅞ × 4⅝ in.

The Custom House, Dublin.

38   1840   James Stirling Coyne. *The scenery and antiquities of Ireland.* Volume 1, page 103, engraved by Thomas Higham.
4¾ × 7 in.

39   c.1840   John Wilson and Robert Chambers. *The land of Burns*. Volume 2, page 7, engraved by Thomas Jeavons. 3⅝ × 5½ in.

Drawn by W.L. Leitch.   Engraved by T. Turnbull

The Giants Stairs, Ducal Palace, Venice.

L'Escalier du Géant, Venise.   *Der Riesen Stiege, Venedig.*

FISHER, SON & Cº LONDON & PARIS.

40   1841   George Newnham Wright. *The Rhine, Italy and Greece.* Volume 1, page 18, engraved by Thomas Turnbull.
      6⅞ × 5⅛ in.

Kite flying at Kue-hwa, or the Ninth Day of Ninth Moon.

Drawn by T. Allom.

Engraved by A. Willmore

41   1843   George Newnham Wright. *China*. Volume 4, page 6, engraved by Arthur Willmore. 4⅞ × 7½ in.

42   1847   *Heath's Book of beauty, 1847. Edited by the Countess of Blessington.* **Page 79, engraved by H. Austin.** 6⅞ × 4⅞ in.

43   1847   Henry Stebbing. *The Christian in Palestine.* Pages 126–7, engraved by James Charles Armytage. 9¼ × 15½ in.

HINDOO AND MAHOMEDAN BUILDINGS.

44   1848   Emma Roberts. *Hindostan* ... Frontispiece, engraved by Ebenezer Challis. 7⅜ × 5⅜ in.

THE LION IN LOVE.

45 1855 *Art Journal.* Page 64, engraved by James H. Baker. 7⅝ × 8¾ in.

THE RESCUE.

FROM THE MEDAL EXECUTED BY W. WYON, R.A.

FOR THE LIVERPOOL "SHIPWRECK AND HUMANE SOCIETY."

H. J. TOWNSEND. PINXT

C W SHARPE SCULPT

A R I E L .

(THE TEMPEST)

47   1855   *Art Journal*. Page 188, engraved by Charles William Sharpe. 5¾ × 10½ in.

Drawn by Frederick Barry.   Engraved by Saml Bradshaw

48   1856   W.H.D. Adams. *The history ... of the Isle of Wight*. Page 16, engraved by Samuel Bradshaw. 6 × 5½ in.

THE RENT DAY.

PAINTED BY SIR DAVID WILKIE, R.A.   ENGRAVED BY W. GREATBACH.

49   c.1856   Samuel Carter Hall. *Gems of European art*. Series 2, page 29, engraved by William Greatbach. 6 × 8¾ in.

The Dryad's Crown.

53   The Dryad's Crown.

50   1860   John Ruskin. *Modern painters* ... Volume 5, page 37, engraved by James Charles Armytage. 6½ × 9¼ in.

THE NATIVITY

LUKE, Ch.2.v.7.

Painted by Ribera.

Engraved by J.Rogers.

51   c.1860   Rev. John Fleetwood. *The life of Our Lord and Saviour Jesus Christ*. Page 13, engraved by John Rogers. 5¾ × 4⅜ in.

B. Foster   A Willmore

Rhine Falls. Schaffhausen.

52   1860   Henry Mayhew. *The Upper Rhine*. Page 307, engraved by Arthur Willmore. 4⅜ × 6⅜ in.

R. LADD, PINXT   W. M. LIZARS, SCULPT

PUCK AND THE FAIRIES.
(MIDSUMMER NIGHTS DREAM)

53   1864   *Art Journal*. Page 130, engraved by W.M. Lizars. 8¼ × 8¼ in.

The Death of the Gallant Grey

Canto I Stanza IX LADY OF THE LAKE

54   1868   Royal Association for the Promotion of the Fine Arts in Scotland. *Six engravings in illustration of the Lady of the Lake for the members of* ... Page [1], engraved by Lumb Stocks. 8 × 8¾ in.

Drawn by Gustave Doré.   Engraved by W.Ridgway.

55   [1868] *The Story of Enid and Geraint.* Plate IX, engraved by William Ridgway. 9¼ × 7 in.

TOWN HALL, LEEDS.

56   1871   Thomas Baines. *Yorkshire, past and present* ... Volume 1 engraved by C. Fenn. 6⅜ × 7¾ in.

Jael Killing Sisera

Judges 4th Ch. 21 v.

57   1876   *The Universal Family Bible* . . . Page 281, engraved by D.G. Thompson. 10 × 6¾ in.

58   [1878]   Thomas Archer. *Pictures and royal portraits* ... Volume 2, page 96, engraved by John J. Crew. 5 × 6⅞ in.

M. Retzsch   J. Brain

59   1879 Johann von Goethe. *Faust*. Page 108, engraved by John Brain. 3¾ × 4½ in.

60　1883　J.C. Anderson. *English landscapes and views* ... Plate 5, engraved by T.A. Prior. 8½ × 15¾ in.

LORD JOHN RUSSELL.

61   c.1885   James Taylor. *The age we live in* ... Engraved by Holl (probably Francis Holl). 5 × 4 in.

62   1890   *Art Journal*. Page 257, engraved by James Charles Armytage. 6¼ × 9¾ in.

Select List of Nineteenth Century Books Quoted

Place of publication is London unless otherwise stated.

H. D. Acland. *Illustrations of the Vaudois in a series of views...* C. Tilt. 1831.

E. Acton. *Modern cookery...* 5th ed. Longman. 1856. (First published 1845).

W. H. D. Adams. *The history, topography & antiquities of the Isle of Wight.* Smith, Elder. 1858.

T. Allen. *The history and antiquities of London, Westminster...* Cowie & Strange. 1827–37. 5 vols.

T. Allen. *History of the counties of Surrey and Sussex...* I. T. Hinton. 1829 [–31] 2 vols.

T. Allen. *The history of the county of Lincoln...* Leeds. John Saunders. 1830–1.

T. Allen. *The history of the county of Lincoln...* John Saunders Junior. 1834. 2 vols.

T. Allen. *A new and complete history of the county of York...* I. T. Hinton. 1828–31. 3 vols.

[T. Allen]. *Picturesque beauties of the counties of Surrey and Sussex...* G. Virtue. [1839].

The Amulet; or Christian and literary remembrancer. 1826, 1827, 1828. W. Baynes & Son.

The Amulet. A Christian and literary remembrancer. 1831. F. Westley and A. H. Davis.

The Amethyst or Christian's Annual... 1832, 1833, 1834. Edinburgh. W. Oliphant & Son.

J. C. Anderson. *English landscapes and views...* Roberts & Leete. 1883.

The Anniversary; or poetry and prose for MDCCCXXIX. John Sharpe. 1828.

T. Archer. *Pictures and Royal portraits illustrative of English and Scottish history from the introduction of Christianity to the present time...* Blackie & Son. [1878]. 2 vols.

F. Bacon. *The Works...* new ed. Longman 1889–90. 7 vols.

T. Bacon. *The Oriental annual containing a series of tales, legends and historical romances.* C. Tilt. 1840.

E. Baines, *junior. History of the cotton manufacture in Great Britain...* H. Fisher. [1835].

E. Baines. *History of the County Palatine and Duchy of Lancaster...* Fisher, Son & Co. 1836. 4 vols.

T. Baines. *Yorkshire, past and present...* William Mackenzie. [1871–7] 4 vols in 2.

C. Ball. *The history of the Indian Mutiny...* London Printing and Publishing Company. [c. 1858] 2 vols.

[G. Balmer] *Views of ports and harbours, watering places...* C. Tilt. 1838.

T. Barber. *Barber's picturesque illustrations of the Isle of Wight...* Simpkin Marshall. [1835].

W. H. Bartlett. *Footsteps of Our Lord and his apostles in Syria, Greece and Italy...* 4th ed. A. Hall, Virtue & Co. 1859. [First published 1851].

W. H. Bartlett. *Forty days in the desert, on the track of the Israelites...* 4th ed. A. Hall & Co. [c. 1853]. (First published 1848).

[W. H. Bartlett] *Gleanings, pictorial and antiquarian, on the overland route.* Hall, Virtue & Co. 1851.

W. H. Bartlett. *Jerusalem revisited.* T. Nelson and Sons. 1864. (First published A. Hall. 1854).

W. H. Bartlett. *The Nile boat; or, glimpses of the land of Egypt.* 3rd ed. A. Hall, Virtue & Co. 1852 (First published 1849).

[W. H. Bartlett] *Pictures from Sicily...* A. Hall, Virtue & Co. 1853.

W. H. Bartlett. *The Pilgrim Fathers; or, the founders of New England in the reign of James the First.* A. Hall, Virtue & Co. 1853.

[W. H. Bartlett] *Scripture sites and scenes.* A. Hall & Co. [1849].

W. H. Bartlett. *Walks about the city and environs of Jerusalem.* 3rd ed. G. Virtue. [1849]. (First published 1844).

R. Batty. *Welsh scenery.* R. Jennings. 1825.

W. Beattie. *The castles and abbeys of England...* J. S. Virtue. [c. 1845–51] 2 vols.

W. Beattie. *The Danube...* Virtue & Co. [1844].

W. Beattie. *Scotland illustrated...* G. Virtue. 1838. 2 vols.

W. Beattie. *The ports, harbours, watering places and coast scenery of Great Britain.* G. Virtue. 1842. 2 vols.

W. Beattie. *Switzerland.* G. Virtue. 1836. 2 vols.

W. Beattie. *The Waldenses; or Protestant valleys of Piedmont...* G. Virtue. 1838.

[Bible] *The Holy Bible... notes... by... Haydock.* J. G. Murdoch. [c. 1870].

[Bible] *The Imperial family Bible...* Blackie & Son. 1873. (First published 1844).

[Bible] *The pictorial Bible... notes... by John Kitto.* W. & R. Chambers. 1855. 5 vols.

[Bible] *The practical and devotional family Bible...* condensed by... John M'Farlane. Glasgow. W. Collins. 1860.

[Bible] *A new family Bible... notes... by E. Blomfield.* G. Virtue. [c. 1840] 2 vols.

[Bible] *The self-interpreting Bible... elucidated by... Henry Cooke.* Glasgow. Blackie and Son. 1864.

[Bible] *The self-interpreting Bible ... by... John Brown.* Glasgow. W. Mackenzie. [c. 1870].

[Bible] *The Universal family Bible...* Southampton. E. A. Hancock. [c. 1860].

[Bible] *The New Testament by the Revd. Matthew Henry.* J. Tallis & Co. [c. 1860].

The Bijou; or annual of literature and the arts. W. Pickering. 1828.

R. W. Billings. *Architectural illustrations of Carlisle cathedral.* T. & W. Boone. 1840.

R. W. Billings. *Illustrations of geometric tracery from the paneling [sic] belonging to Carlisle cathedral.* T. & W. Boone. 1842.

R. W. Billings. *Architectural illustrations and description of Kettering church.* T. & W. Boone. 1843.

A. & C. Black. *Black's picturesque guide through North and South Wales & Monmouthshire.* 8th ed. A. & C. Black. 1858.

A. & C. Black. *Black's picturesque tourist of Scotland.* 7th ed. A. & C. Black. 1849.

[A. Blair] *Graphic illustrations of Warwickshire.* Birmingham. Beilby, Knott ... 1829.

E. Blore. *The monumental remains of noble and eminent persons...* Harding, Lepard & Co. 1826.

The Book of Common Prayer... Blackie & Son. 1854.

E. C. Booth. *Australia.* Virtue & Co. Ltd. [1873–6].

J. Boswell. *The life of Samuel Johnson...* G. Bell & Sons. 1884. 2 vols.

A. Brannon. *Brannon's graphic delineations of the most prominent objects in the Isle of Wight...* Wootton, Isle of Wight. A. Brannon. [c. 1860].

E. W. Brayley *and* E. Walford. *A topographical history of Surrey.* 2nd ed. J. S. Virtue & Co. Ltd. 1878–81. 5 vols.

E. W. Brayley *and* J. Britton. *The history of the ancient palace and late Houses of Parliament at Westminster.* J. Weale. 1836.

J. Britton. *The Auto-biography of...* Printed for the author. 1850.

J. Britton. *Bath and Bristol...* Jones and Co. 1829.

J. Britton *and* E. W. Brayley. *Devonshire and Cornwall illustrated...* H. Fisher. 1832.

W. Brockedon. *Illustrations of the passes of the Alps...* Printed for the author. 1828–9. 2 vols. in 1.

W. Brockedon. *Italy, classical, historical and picturesque...* Duncan & Malcolm. [1842–3].

[W. Brockedon] *Italy, illustrated and described...* Blackie and Son. 1864. [New edition of *Italy, classical...*].

J. Browne. *A history of the Highlands and of the Highland clans...* New ed. Edinburgh. A. Fullarton & Co. [c. 1845] 4 vols.

J. Bunyan. *The Pilgrim's progress.* J. Murray. 1830.

J. Bunyan. *The Pilgrim's progress.* Fisher, Son & Co. [1836].

J. Bunyan. *The Pilgrim's progress.* H. G. Bohn. 1854.

J. Bunyan. *The works of... Edited by George Offor...* Glasgow. Blackie and Son. 1852–3 3 vols.

J. Burke. *Heraldic illustrations* . . . E. Churton. 1845.

R. Burns. *The complete works of* . . . G. Virtue. [c. 1842].

G. G. N. Byron. *Finden's illustrations of the life and works of Lord Byron.* J. Murray. 1833–4. 3 vols.

G. G. N. Byron, *Childe Harold's pilgrimage* . . . J. Murray. 1845.

G. G. N. Byron, *The poetical works of* . . . J. Murray. 1844 (First published 1837).

Baroness de Calabrella. *Evenings at Haddon Hall.* H. G. Bohn. 1850 (First published 1845).

T. Campbell. *The pleasures of hope* . . . Longman, Hurst . . . 1821.

T. Campbell. *The poetical works of* . . . E. Moxon. 1837.

J. W. Carleton. *The sporting sketch-book* . . . How & Parsons. 1842.

J. Carne. *Syria, the Holy Land, Asia Minor &c. illustrated* . . . Fisher, Son & Co. [1836–8] 3 vols.

E. Cartwright. *The parochial topography of the Rape of Bramber* . . . Vol. 1 Part 2 J. B. Nichols & Son. 1830.

The Casquet of literature; being a selection of poetry and prose . . . *Edited* . . . *by Charles Gibbon* . . . Blackie & Son Ltd. 1874–5. 6 vols.

R. Cattermole. *The Great Civil War of the times of Charles I and Cromwell.* Fisher, Son & Co. [1846] (Originally published in 1841).

J. H. Caunter. *Lives of the Moghul emperors.* C. Tilt. 1837.

B. Cellini. *Memoirs* . . . Tr. Thomas Roscoe. H. G. Bohn. 1847.

M. Cervantes. *Don Quixote de la Mancha* . . . C. Daly. [c. 1845].

R. Chambers. *A biographical dictionary of eminent Scotsmen* . . . Glasgow. Blackie & Son. 1835, 4 vols.

R. Chambers. *A biographical dictionary of eminent Scotsmen* . . . [4th ed.] revised . . . Blackie & Son. 1875. 3 vols.

W. Clarke. *Pompeii* . . . M. A. Nattali. 1849. 2 vols.

Continental annual and romantic cabinet for 1832 . . . *edited by William Kennedy* . . . Smith, Elder & Co. [1832].

Continental tourist, and pictorial companion. Black & Armstrong. [1838] [Republished c. 1849 by Parry & Co. with cover title and engraved title page *Belgium and Nassau*].

W. J. Conybeare *and* J. S. Howson. *The life and epistles of St. Paul.* Longman. 1854. 2 vols.

E. Cook. *The poetical works of* . . . F. Warne. [1869].

D. Costello. *Piedmont and Italy from the Alps to the Tiber.* [James S. Virtue] [c. 1855] (a work made up of plates from earlier volumes, e.g. Beattie's *Switzerland*, and is dated variously up to 1861).

The cottage girl; or, the marriage-day. By the author of 'The Gipsey bride' . . . London Printing and Publishing Co. [c. 1860].

The Court album; a series of portraits of the female aristocracy . . . D. Bogue. 1852–7. 6 vols.

W. Cowper. *The life and works of* . . . Saunders and Otley. 1835. 8 vols.

W Cowper. *Private correspondence* . . . H. Colburn. 1824. 2 vols.

J. S. Coyne. *The scenery and antiquities of Ireland* . . . G. Virtue. [c.1840].

G. Crabbe. *The poetical works of* . . . New edition. J. Murray. 1847. 8 vols.

G. Cruikshank. *Eighty-two illustrations on steel, stone and wood* . . . W. Tegg. [1870].

A. Cunningham. *The cabinet gallery of pictures by the first masters* . . . G. and W. Nicol. 1836. 2 vols.

W. C. Devereux. *Lives & letters of the Devereux, Earls of Essex.* J. Murray. 1853. 2 vols.

P. Doddridge. *The rise and progress of religion in the soul* . . . Longman. 1822.

J. Dryden. *The poetical works of* . . . *notes by* . . . *Joseph Warton.* Routledge, Warne. 1859.

T. Dugdale. *England and Wales delineated* . . . J. & F. Tallis. [1838–9].

E. Edwards. *Life of Sir Walter Raleigh.* Macmillan. 1868. 2 vols.

R. Elliot. *Views in India, China and on the shores of the Red Sea* . . . *descriptions by Emma Roberts.* H. Fisher . . . 1835. 2 vols.

S. Ellis. *The daughters of England* . . . Fisher, Son & Co. [1842].

J. Elmes. *Metropolitan improvements; or, London in the nineteenth century* . . . Jones & Co. 1829.

Engravings after the best pictures of the Great Masters . . . Ackermann & Co. [1843].

J. Evelyn. *Diary and correspondence of* . . . *Edited* . . . *by William Bray* . . . New ed. Bell & Daldy. 1872. 4 vols.

The Fashionable guide and directory to the public places of resort... T. Fry. [c. 1838].

H. G. Fearnside. *Picturesque beauties of the Rhine*... Black and Armstrong. [c. 1846].

W. G. Fearnside. *Tombleson's Upper Rhine.* Black and Armstrong. [c. 1835].

W. G. Fearnside. *Tombleson's Views of the Rhine*... W. Tombleson & Co. 1832.

W. G. Fearnside. *[Tombleson's Thames] Eighty picturesque views on the Thames and Medway*... Tombleson & Co. [1834].

W. G. Fearnside *and* T. Harral. *The history of London*... Orr and Co. [c. 1850] (Originally published 1838).

Finden's Gallery of beauty... edited by *P. G. Patmore.* Tilt and Bogue. [1841].

W. & E. Finden. *Royal gallery of British art.* J. Hogarth. 1838–49.

Finden's Tableaux. A series of... *scenes of national character, beauty and costume*... Edited by *Mrs. S. C. Hall.* C. Tilt. 1837.

Finden's tableaux: the iris of prose, poetry and art for MDCCCXL... Edited by *Mary Russell Mitford.* C. Tilt. [1839].

H. Fisher. *Fisher's drawing room scrap book*... H. Fisher. The volumes for 1835, 1836 and 1842.

Fisher, Son & Co. *Historic illustrations of the Bible. Principally after the Old Masters.* Fisher, Son & Co. [1840–3] 4 series in 2 vols.

P. Fisher, *pseud.* (i.e. William Andrew Chatto). *The angler's souvenir.* Tilt. 1835.

J. Fleetwood. *The Life of Our Lord and Saviour Jesus Christ*... *illuminated*... Glasgow. J. Lumsden. [?1870].

J. Fleetwood. *The Life of Our Lord and Saviour Jesus Christ;*... *To which is added, evidences of the truth of Christianity; by Beilby Porteus*... London Printing and Publishing Company. [?1860].

Forget-me-not, a Christmas and New Year's present... R. Ackermann. Volumes for 1823, 1825, 1846.

J. Forster. *Life and times of Oliver Goldsmith.* 5th ed. Chapman & Hall 1871. 2 vols.

Friendship's offering, a literary album and Christmas and New Year's present... Smith, Elder & Co. Volumes for 1831, 1833 [which incorporated *Winter's wreath*], 1837, 1839, 1844.

H. Gastineau. *Wales illustrated*... *comprising the picturesque scenery, towns, castles, seats of the nobility and gentry, antiquities &c*... Jones & Co. [1830]. 2 vols.

W. Gell. *Pompeiana; the topography, edifices, and ornaments of Pompeii, the result of excavations since 1819*... Jennings & Chaplin. 1832. 2 vols.

J. W. von Goethe. *Goethe's Faust in two parts. Translated by Anna Swanwick*... G. Bell and Sons. 1879.

O. Goldsmith. *The miscellaneous works of*... J. Murray. 1837. 4 vols.

Graphic illustrations of the life and times of Samuel Johnson, LLD. J. Murray. 1837.

C. C. F. Greville. *The Greville memoirs*... Longmans, Green... 1896. 8 vols.

G. Grote. *A history of Greece*... New ed. Murray. 1887–8. 10 vols.

A. M. Hall. *The drawing room table-book.* G. Virtue. (1849).

A. M. Hall. *Sketches of Irish character*... M. A. Nattali. 1844.

S. C. Hall, *editor. The books of gems. The poets and artists of Great Britain*... Saunders and Otley. 1836.

S. C. Hall, *editor. The book of gems. The modern poets and artists of Great Britain*... Whittaker & Co. 1838.

S. C. Hall. *editor. Gems of European art: the best pictures of the best schools.* G. Virtue. 1846. 2 vols. Vol. 2 undated.

S. C. *and* A. M. Hall. *Ireland: its scenery, character &c.* How and Parsons. 1841–3. 3 vols.

S. C. *and* A. M. Hall. *A week at Killarney*... J. How. 1843. 8 plates. Later editions, (e.g. 1850, 1858) published by Virtue, contained varying numbers of plates.

W. H. Harrison. *The tourist in Portugal.* R. Jennings. 1839. (Jenning's Landscape annual for 1839).

P. Hawker. *Instructions to young sportsmen in all that relates to guns and shooting.* 4th ed. Longman, Hurst... 1825. Also 9th ed. 1844.

Heath's Versailles. Longman & Co. [c. 1836].

Heath's book of beauty... Edited by *the Countess of Blessington.* Longman, Rees... Volumes for 1835, 1839, 1841, 1847.

R. Heber. *Narrative of a journey through the upper provinces of India, from Calcutta to Bombay, 1824–5*... J. Murray. 1828. 2 vols.

M. Henry. *An exposition of the Old and New Testament*... Fisher, Son & Co. 1844. 3 vols.

Heroines of Shakespeare; comprising the principal female characters in the plays of the great poet. D. Bogue. 1848.

J. H. Hinton, *the elder. The history and topography of the United States*... I. T. Hinton & Simpkin Marshall. 1830–2. 2 vols.

J. H. Hinton, *the elder. History of the United States of America from the earliest period to the present time*... J. & F. Tallis. [c. 1849]. 6 vols. in 2.

T. C. Hofland. *The British anglers' manual*... Whitehead & Co. 1839.

W. J. Hooker. *Perth-shire illustrated*... Glasgow. J. Swan. [1843].

T. H. Horne. *The Biblical keepsake*... J. Murray. 1837.

R. Huish. *Memoirs of George the fourth*... T. Kelly... 1830. 2 vols.

D. Hume *and* T. Smollett. *History of England... with a continuation by the Rev. T.S. Hughes.* A.J. Valpy. 1834–6. 21 vols.

D. Hume *and* T. Smollett. *The history of England... to the reign of George the third; and thence continued to the present time. By Thomas Gaspey*... J. & F. Tallis. [c. 1847]. 5 vols.

D. Hume and T. Smollett. *The history of England*... New ed. G. Bell. 1854–5. 15 vols. (Continuation by T. S. Hughes).

Imperial dictionary of universal biography, comprising a series of original memoirs of distinguished men, of all ages and all nations... John Francis Waller, editor. W. Mackenzie. [c. 1861]. 3 vols. in 4.

R. Inglis. *Gleanings from the English poets*... Edinburgh. Gall & Inglis. [c. 1865].

S. W. H. Ireland. *England's topographer, or a new and complete history of the county of Kent*... G. Virtue. Vol. 1 1828, Vols 2 & 3 1829, Vol. 4 undated.

E. Jesse. *Anecdotes of dogs*... R. Bentley. 1846.

J. H. Jesse. *Memoirs of the court of England during the reign of the Stuarts, including the protectorate.* R. Bentley. 1840. 4 vols.

H. M. Jones. *The gipsy mother; or, the miseries of enforced marriage; a tale of mystery*... Virtue, Tallis & Co. [1833].

The Keepsake. Hurst, Chance & Co. 1828–32. Longmans 1833–47. D. Bogue 1848–56. Edited successively by F. M. Reynolds, Hon. Mrs. Norton, Lady E. S. Wortley, Countess of Blessington and Miss Power.

Keepsake français, ou Souvenir de littérature contemporaine. Paris. Giraldon-Bovinet. London. Whittaker, Treacher & Co. Volumes for 1831, 1840.

A. Keith. *Evidence of the truth of the Christian religion*... 36th ed. Edinburgh. W. Whyte & Co. 1848.

J. Kitto. *The gallery of scripture engravings, historical and landscape*... Fisher, Son & Co. [1846–9] 3 vols.

[C. Knight]. *Paris and its historical scenes.* C. Knight. 1831. 2 vols.

E. Landseer. *The works of*... Virtue & Co. [c. 1877]. (Most are plates previously published in the *Art Journal*).

The Literary souvenir; or, cabinet of poetry and romance... Hurst Robinson & Co. 1825–6. Longman 1827–34. Whittaker & Co. 1835–7 Edited by A. A. Watts.

Livy. *The history of Rome.* Jones. 1830.

E. Lodge. *Portraits of illustrious personages of Great Britain*... Harding and Lepard. 1835. 12 vols.

T. McCrie. *The life of John Knox*... 2nd ed. Edinburgh. J. Clarke. 1840.

N. Machiavelli. *The history of Florence*... G. Bell & Sons. 1891.

R. M. Martin. *The Indian Empire: its history, topography... With a full account of the Mutiny*... London Printing and Publishing Company. [1858–61] 3 vols.

P. Massinger *and* J. Ford. *Dramatic works*... E. Moxon. 1840.

D. Masson. *The life of John Milton.* Macmillan. [c. 1870] 7 vols.

W. H. Maxwell. *Life of Field Marshal His Grace the Duke of Wellington*... A. H. Baily. 1839–41. 3 vols.

H. Mayhew. *The Upper Rhine; the scenery of its banks and the manners of its people... Mayence to the Lake of Constance.* Routledge... 1860.

H. H. Milman. *The life of Edward Gibbon.* Murray, 1839.

J. Milton. *The poetical works of...* T. Tegg. 1841.

The Mirror of literature, amusement, and instruction... J. Limbird. 1824. Vols. 3 and 4.

The Modern traveller. A popular description... of the various countries of the globe. Spain and Portugal. J. Duncan. 1826. 2 vols.

T. Moore. *Finden's beauties of Moore.* Chapman & Hall. 1846. (Reprinted by Tallis [1853]).

T. Moore. *Lalla Rookh; an Oriental romance.* 19th edition. Longman... 1838.

T. Moore. *The Life of Lord Byron... with his letters and journals... complete in one volume.* J. Murray. 1844.

T. Moore. *The poetical works...* Longman. 1843.

R. Mudie. *Hampshire...* Winchester. Robbins; London. Orr & Co. 1838. 3 vols.

T. Noble *and* T. Rose. *The counties of Chester, Derby, Leicester, Lincoln and Rutland, illustrated...* Fisher & Son. 1836.

E. H. Nolan. *The illustrated history of the British Empire in India and the East, from the earliest times to the suppression of the Sepoy Mutiny in 1859...* J. S. Virtue. [1858–60] 2 vols.

S. Ockley. *The history of the Saracens...* 4th ed. H. G. Bohn. 1847.

J. Ogilvie, *editor. The Imperial dictionary, English, technological, and scientific...* Glasgow. Blackie and Son. 1850. 2 vols.

J. M. Pardoe. *The Beauties of the Bosphorus...* G. Virtue. 1840.

J. D. Parry. *An historical and descriptive account of the Coast of Sussex...* Brighton, Wright and Son. London. Longman. 1833.

F. L. Pearce. *The Altar at home; or, family communion for every day throughout the year.* Husk & Co. [c. 1860].

Picturesque Europe. Cassell, Petter & Galpin. [1876–9] 5 vols.

A. Pope. *The works...* Murray. 1870. 10 vols.

J. Prior. *Life of Oliver Goldsmith.* Murray. 1837. 2 vols.

W. H. Pyne *and others. Lancashire illustrated in a series of views, towns, public buildings* ... H. Fisher, Son & Peter Jackson. 1831.

L. N. R. *The Book and its story; a narrative for the young...* S. Bagster. 1854.

Remembrances of the Great Exhibition... Ackermann & Co. [1851].

L. Ritchie. *Ireland picturesque and romantic...* Longman... 1837. (Heath's Picturesque annual for 1837).

L. Ritchie. *Travelling sketches in the north of Italy, the Tyrol and on the Rhine...* Longman. 1832 (Heath's Picturesque annual for 1832).

L. Ritchie. *Travelling sketches on the Rhine, and in Belgium and Holland...* Longman... 1833 (Heath's Picturesque annual for 1833).

L. Ritchie. *Travelling sketches on the sea-coasts of France.* Longman... 1834. (Heath's Picturesque annual for 1834).

L. Ritchie. *Wanderings by the Seine, from Rouen to the source...* Longman... 1835 (Turner's annual tour 1835).

L. Ritchie. *Windsor Castle and its environs; including Eton College.* 2nd ed. *with additions by Edwd. Jesse...* H. G. Bohn. 1848. (Originally published as Heath's Picturesque annual for 1840).

E. Roberts. *Hindostan its landscapes, palaces, temples, tombs; the shores of the Red Sea; and the sublime and romantic scenery of the Himalaya mountains...* Fisher, Son & Co. [1848]. (Most of the plates were first published in Elliot's *Views in India* and White's *Views in India*).

S. Rogers. *Italy; a poem.* T. Cadell. 1830.

S. Rogers. *Poems.* T. Cadell. 1834.

T. Roscoe. *Summer tour to the Isle of Wight; including Portsmouth, Southampton, Winchester, the South Western railway...* J. & F. Harwood. 1843.

T. Roscoe. *The tourist in France.* Jennings & Chaplin. 1834. (Landscape annual for 1834).

T. Roscoe. *The tourist in Italy.* R. Jennings & W. Chaplin. 1831. (Landscape annual for 1831).

T. Roscoe. *The tourist in Italy.* Jennings & Chaplin. 1833. (Landscape annual for 1833).

T. Roscoe. *The tourist in Spain. Granada.* R. Jennings and Co. 1835. (Jennings' Landscape annual for 1835).

T. Roscoe. *The tourist in Switzerland and Italy.* R. Jennings. 1830. (Landscape annual for 1830).

T. Roscoe. *Wanderings and excursions in North Wales* . . . Tilt. 1836.

T. Roscoe. *Wanderings and excursions in South Wales; including the scenery of the River Wye* . . . Tilt. [1836].

T. Rose. *Cumberland: its lake and mountain scenery* . . . Peter Jackson, late Fisher, Son & Co. [1847].

T. Rose. *Durham and Northumberland; their lake and mountain scenery* . . . Peter Jackson, late Fisher, Son & Co. [1847].

T. Rose. *Westmorland; its lake and mountain scenery* . . . Peter Jackson, late Fisher, Son & Co. [1847] (These three volumes were originally published together as *Westmorland, Cumberland, Durham and Northumberland, illustrated.* H. Fisher. 1832. 3 vols.)

J. Ross. *Narrative of a second voyage in search of a North-west passage and of a residence in the Arctic regions during the years 1829[–33]* . . . A. W. Webster. 1835.

Royal Association for the promotion of the Fine Arts in Scotland. *Six engravings in illustration of the Lady of the Lake* [by Scott] *for the members* . . . Royal Association . . . 1868.

J. Ruskin. *Modern painters* . . . Smith, Elder & Co. 1843–60. 5 vols.

J. Ruskin. *The Stones of Venice.* 4th ed. Orpington. G. Allen. 1886. 3 vols. (First published 1851–3).

J. Rutherfurd. *Rutherfurd's Border hand-book* . . . Kelso. J. Rutherfurd. 1849.

W. Scott. *The lay of the last minstrel* . . . Tilt. 1839.

W. Scott. *The poetical works* . . . Edinburgh. A. and C. Black. 1853.

W. Scott. *The poetical works* . . . Edinburgh. A. and C. Black. 1869.

W. Scott. *Poetical works* . . . *edited by Wm. Minto.* Edinburgh. A. and C. Black. 1888.

W. Scott. *Provincial antiquities and picturesque scenery of Scotland* . . . J. and A. Arch. 1826. 2 vols.

W. Scott. *Waverley novels.* Centenary edition. Edinburgh. A. and C. Black. 1871. 25 vols. (This is representative of many editions of the novels, which contains most of the engravings done for the work. For this reason, the title is not dated in the text).

W. Shakespeare. *The plays of* . . . C. & J. Rivington. 1823.

W. Shakespeare. *The Royal Shakspere* . . . *text of Professor Delius* . . . Cassell & Company. 1883–4. 3 vols.

W. Shakespeare. *The Works of Shakspere, Imperial edition, edited by Charles Knight* . . . Virtue & Co. Ltd. [1872]. 2 vols.

E. Sharpe. *The seven periods of English architecture* . . . 3rd ed. E. & F. N. Spon. 1888.

T. H. Shepherd. *London and its environs in the nineteenth century* . . . Jones & Co. 1829–31.

T. H. Shepherd. *Modern Athens, . . . or Edinburgh in the nineteenth century* . . . Jones & Co. 1829–31.

R. B. Sheridan. *The dramatic works* . . . G. Bell. 1881.

R. Southey. *The poetical works* . . . Longmans . . . 1880.

W. C. Stanfield. *Stanfield's coast scenery. A series of views in the British Channel* . . . Smith, Elder & Co. 1836.

A. P. Stanley. *The life and correspondence of Thomas Arnold.* B. Fellowes. 1846.

H. Stebbing. *The Christian in Palestine; or, Scenes of sacred history* . . . G. Virtue. [1847].

Tacitus. *The works* . . . Jones. 1831.

J. Taylor. *The age we live in* . . . *a history of the nineteenth century, from the Peace of 1815 to the present time* . . . W. Mackenzie. [c. 1885] 2 vols.

J. Taylor. *The family history of England* . . . W. Mackenzie. [c. 1870]. 6 vols.

[A. Tennyson] *The story of Enid and Geraint, re-told from ancient Welsh, Norman, German and Scandinavian legends, and modern poetic versions* . . . E. Moxon. [1869].

A. Tennyson. *The Works* . . . C. Kegan Paul & Co. 1880.

C. Thirlwall. *A history of Greece.* Longman . . . 1837. 3 vols. (The cabinet cyclopaedia . . . ed. Lardner).

M. A. Tierney. *The history and antiquities of the castle and town of Arundel*... G. & W. Nicol. 1834. 2 vols.

J. Timbs. *Curiosities of London*... New ed. Virtue & Co. [1867] (Originally published 1855).

J. M. W. Turner. *Richmondshire ... introduction by Marcus B. Huish*... J. S. Virtue. 1891.

H. Tyrrell *and others*. *The Royal history of England from the earliest period to the present time*... J.G. Murdoch. 1877. 2 vols.

N. G. Van Kampen. *The history and topography of Holland and Belgium*. Tr. by W.G. Fearnside. Virtue. [1837].

Views in the Tyrol from drawings by T. Allom... C. Tilt. [1836].

H. Walpole. *Anecdotes of painting in England*... *With additions by the Rev, James Dallaway*... *A new edition*... *by Ralph N. Wornum*. Swan Sonnenschein. 1888. 3 vols. (Dallaway's edition published 1827).

R. Walsh. *Constantinople and the scenery of the seven churches of Asia Minor illustrated*... Fisher, Son & Co. [1838–40] 2 vols.

The Watering places of Great Britain and fashionable directory... J. Robbins. 1833.

W. West. *Picturesque views*... *in Staffordshire and Shropshire*... Birmingham. W. Emans. 1830. 2 vols.

G. F. White. *Views in India chiefly among the Himalaya Mountains*... Edited by Emma Roberts... Fisher, Son & Co. 1838.

D. Wilkie. *The Wilkie gallery; a selection of the best pictures*... G. Virtue. [c. 1849].

N. P. Willis. *American scenery; or, land, lake and river illustrations of Transatlantic nature*... G. Virtue. 1840. 2 vols.

N. P. Willis. *Canadian scenery illustrated*... G. Virtue. 1842. 2 vols.

N. P. Willis. *Pencillings by the way*... A new edition, with additions. H. G. Bohn. 1845.

J. Wilson *and* R. Chambers. *The land of Burns, a series of landscapes and portraits, illustrative of the life and writings of the Scottish poet*... Glasgow. Blackie and Son. 1840. 2 vols.

B. Winkles. *French catherals*... C. Tilt. 1837.

H. and B. Winkles. *Winkles's architectural and picturesque illustrations of the cathedral churches of England and Wales*... E. Wilson and C. Tilt. 1836–42. 3 vols.

B. B. Woodward *and others*. *A general history of Hampshire, or the county of Southampton, including the Isle of Wight*. Virtue & Co. [1863] 3 vols.

B. B. Woodward. *A history and description of Winchester*. Winchester. J. Wells. 1860.

B. B. Woodward. *The history of Wales, from the earliest times, to its final incorporation with the kingdom of England*... Virtue & Co. 1853.

C. Wordsworth. *Greece; pictorial, descriptive and historical*... W. S. Orr & Co. 1839.

World of fashion and Continental Feuilletons... Bell. Vol. 14 1837, (Commenced publication 1825).

R. W. Wornum, *editor*. *The Turner gallery; a series of sixty engravings from the principal works of Joseph Mallord William Turner*... J. S. Virtue. [1878].

The Wreath of friendship: a token of regard... E. Lacey. [c. 1832].

G. N. Wright. *China*... Fisher, Son & Co. [1843]. 4 vols.

G. N. Wright. *The gallery of engravings*... Fisher, Son & Co. [1844–6] 3 vols.

G. N. Wright. *An historical guide to the city of Dublin*... 2nd edition. Baldwin & Cradock. 1834.

G. N. Wright. *Lancashire; its history, legends and manufactures*. Fisher, Son & Co. [1842].

G. N. Wright. *Landscape-historical illustrations of Scotland and the Waverley novels*... Fisher, Son & Co. [1836–8] 2 vols.

G. N. Wright. *The Rhine, Italy and Greece*... Fisher, Son & Co. [1841–2] 2 vols.

G. N. Wright. *The shores and islands of the Mediterranean*... Fisher, Son & Co. [1840].

T. Wright. *Caricature history of the Georges*... Chatto & Windus. 1876. (First published 1848).

T. Wright. *The picturesque beauties of Great Britain*... *Essex*. G. Virtue... 1834.

W. Wycherley *[and others]* *The Dramatic works*... E. Moxon. 1840.

Xenephon. *The whole works of*... Jones. 1831.

E. Young. *Night thoughts, on life, death, and immortality*. Manchester. S. Johnson and Son. 1845.

The Youth's magazine or evangelical miscellany for the year 1838. Hamilton, Adams & Co. 1838. (Vol. 1 fourth series).